The Opening of Japan

A DIARY OF DISCOVERY IN
THE FAR EAST, 1853–1856

The Opening of Japan

A DIARY OF DISCOVERY IN THE FAR EAST, 1853-1856

FROM THE ORIGINAL MANUSCRIPT IN THE MASSACHUSETTS HISTORICAL SOCIETY

By Rear Admiral George Henry Preble, U.S.N.

EDITED BY BOLESLAW SZCZESNIAK

University of Oklahoma Press : Norman

LIBRARY OF CONGRESS CATALOG CARD NUMBER: 62–16484

 Composed and printed at Norman, Oklahoma, U.S.A., by the University of Oklahoma Press. First edition.

For My Sons, Andrew and Jacek, Who Belong to the New American Generation

Preface

In the manuscript collection of the Massachusetts Historical Society in Boston there is preserved a bound volume of 565 pages of fine blue paper filled with a distinctive handwriting. It is the diary of George Henry Preble, written while he served on the U.S.S. *Macedonian,* one of the ships engaged in the East Indies Expedition to Japan, China, and the Ryukyu Islands (Okinawa Archipelago) under the command of Commodore Matthew Calbraith Perry. Spanning the years 1853–56, the diary contains valuable observations made by Preble during the historic mission which opened Japan.

The text of the original manuscript is here faithfully reproduced, replete with its original spellings and peculiarities of style; the names of ships, however, are printed in italics instead of Preble's quotation marks. A special difficulty in regard to the preservation of the text was Preble's strange and constant use of dashes, short and long, instead of conventional punctuation, which sometimes made it difficult for me to understand what he meant. I have therefore substituted, wherever I felt it necessary, appropriate punctuation marks to make clear the meaning of the text. This is the only liberty I have taken in editing the diary.

The identification of U.S. Navy personnel and vessels of war mentioned in the diary was made from Lewis R. Hamersly's *List of Officers of the Navy of the United States and of the Marine Corps from 1775–1900 . . . Compiled from the Official Records of the Navy Department,* to which volume is appended "A List of the Vessels of

War of the United States Navy, 1797–1900." Other sources of information explored are indicated in footnotes or included in the bibliography, which also contains works quoted or referred to in the diary. Little-known geographical names and unfamiliar factual, historical, and literary references have been briefly explained, but a few obscure friends of Preble, or other persons, could not be identified with certainty. The appendix lists the old spellings of Asian geographical names, along with their modern equivalents in Chinese or Japanese. In compiling these, I followed the spellings in L. Richard's *Comprehensive Geography of the Chinese Empire*, E. J. Dingle's *The New Atlas and Commercial Gazetteer of China*, and *Teikoku kan-man chiho-meikan (Japanese, Korean and Manchurian Geographic Names)*.

My thanks are due several persons, but especially to Stephen T. Riley of the Massachusetts Historical Society for aid in securing the Society's permission to publish the diary; to my friends Marshall T. Smelser and L. Leon Bernard for suggestions in connection with the reading of my manuscript; to Miss Eileen A. Conley of the University of Notre Dame for her assistance in searching for library materials; to the librarians who gave me such friendly service during my work at the Harvard Library; and to Professor Stanley J. Parry, C.S.C., for encouragement in the present laborious but also gratifying work.

Boleslaw Szczesniak

Notre Dame, Indiana
September, 1962

Contents

Illustrations

George Henry Preble

George Henry Preble was born on February 25, 1816, in Portland, Maine, of an old American family noted for its naval officers, educators, and writers. His father, Enoch Preble (1763–1842), was a sea captain, and his mother, Sally Cross, came from an old New England family. Commodore Edward Preble (1761–1807) was his uncle, and Brigadier General Jedidiah Preble (1707–1784), who distinguished himself in the American Revolution, was his grandfather. George Henry's ancestor, Abraham Preble (d. 1663), emigrated from Kent, England, and settled in Scituate, Plymouth Colony, about 1636. In 1642, Abraham married Judith Tilden, the third daughter of Nathaniel Tilden, an English immigrant from Tenterden, Kent. Ancestor Abraham, as is well evidenced, was the first magistrate, or mayor, of the city of York, Maine.[1]

The Prebles established a fine home in Falmouth (now Portland), Maine, and distinguished themselves by contributing to American national progress. They were quite conscious of this fact and expressed their satisfaction therewith in various publications, but especially in collections of family records and papers, most of which now

[1] For brief biographical data concerning George Henry Preble and his family, see *Dictionary of American Biography* (cited hereafter as *DAB)*, XV, 183–84; L. R. Hamersley (ed.), *A Naval Encyclopaedia*, 661–63; *Lamb's Biographical Dictionary of the United States* (cited hereafter as *LBD)*, VI, 338–41; and G. H. Preble, *Genealogical Sketch of the First Three Generations of Prebles in America* (cited hereafter as *Sketch)*.

repose in the Library of Congress, the Maine Historical Society, and the Massachusetts Historical Society.

To the same family belongs William Pitt Preble (1783–1857) of York, Maine, jurist, diplomat, railwayman, and contemporary of George Henry Preble. He made his home in Portland after 1818 and there compiled a genealogical record of the entire Preble family. He ably expressed their pride in the family's accomplishments, which from the "Puritan fathers . . . from generation to generation, have occupied a respectable position in private life, and civil, judicial, and military lines."[2]

These diversified professional achievements did not detract from the Prebles' interest in historical writings, or even in creative poetry. General Jedidiah Preble composed patriotic verses;[3] William P. Preble showed some poetic talent; and just before his death, our George H. Preble published *Grog: A Mixture of Prose and Verse, Brewed by G. H. Preble*,[4] a testimony of his literary tastes. George was also a self-made historian, having to his credit several important research works relating to American naval history and to the genealogy of his family.[5] His life, however, following his father's example, constitutes a fine record in the service of the United States Navy.

Finishing his Portland schooling and home tutoring, George was appointed midshipman from the state of Maine on October 10, 1835, and served on the frigate *United States* in the Mediterranean and Caribbean from May, 1836, to November, 1838. He was then ordered to the Naval School at Philadelphia from January to June, 1841, where he became a warranted passed midshipman, standing seventh in a class of twenty-four. He was acting lieutenant of the schooner *Madison* and the brigantine *Jefferson* in the Florida Expedition from August, 1841, to August, 1842. He returned sick and was attached to the *Ohio* at Boston from October, 1842, to May, 1843. Next he served as acting master and acting lieutenant on the

[2] Cf. W. P. Preble, *A Genealogical Sketch of the Preble Families*, 4.

[3] *Sketch*, 112–15.

[4] See also his verses in the diary.

[5] The Harvard University Library has practically all published works by G. H. Preble, some with his autographs and marginal notes. See also the bibliography in this volume.

sloop *St. Louis,* during its circumnavigation of the globe and in the East Indies, from May 23, 1843, to September, 1845. This led him to South China for a new assignment which was to have a connection with his visit ten years later. The *St. Louis,* as a part of a squadron, witnessed the diplomatic negotiations of Caleb Cushing (1800–1879), who was sent in 1844 to establish commerce and friendly relations with China. While the talks were in progress, Preble received a new duty at Canton, where he was made commandant of the first[6] American military force landing in China (June–July, 1844), a move designed to protect the U.S. consulate and American citizens and to support, by display of power, Cushing's negotiations with the unfriendly Chinese authorities. Preble concisely described the situation in his *Genealogical Sketch*:

> The *St. Louis* (U.S. Sloop-of-War) sailed for the East Indies, May 23rd, 1843, in company with the frigate *Brandywine,* Commodore F. A. Parker, by whom Acting Master Preble was appointed Acting Lieutenant, August 9, 1843. The squadron, of which the *St. Louis* formed one, was intended to support and aid by the exhibition of physical force, if necessary, the negotiations of the Hon. Caleb Cushing, which resulted in our first treaty with China.[7]

Upon his return home, Lieutenant Preble was married to Susan Zabiah Cox, daughter of John Cox and Thankful Harris (Gore); the ceremony was performed in Portland on November 18, 1845, by Dr. Ichabod Nichols of the Unitarian Church. Four children blessed this union: Henry Oxnard, born at Portland on January 4, 1847; Susie Zabiah, born at Portland on September 1, 1850; Mildred, born and died on April 23, 1859, at Portland; and George Henry Rittenhouse, born July 10, 1860, at Charlestown Navy Yard, Massachusetts.

Preble's life now was divided between duty near his family and foreign assignments. In 1846–47, on board the schooner *Petrel* dur-

[6] *Sketch,* 202–205. For the Caleb Cushing mission, see J. K. Fairbank, *Trade and Diplomacy on the China Coast,* I, 196ff., 208–209, and Tyler Dennett, *Americans in Eastern Asia,* 144–71.

[7] *Sketch,* 203.

ing the Mexican War, he showed considerable naval valor, which assured his promotion to warranted master on July 15, 1847, and to commissioned lieutenant the following year, on February 5, 1848. His participation in the capture of Alvarado, Laguna, Tampico, Pánuco, and Veracruz added new merits to his record. From these naval engagements he returned home sick, arriving on the *Ohio* in May, 1847. Preble was reassigned to the Gulf and served on the sloop *Saratoga*, coming home ill once again, this time from climatic exhaustion, in March, 1849. When he had recovered, he was appointed executive officer of the steamer *Legree*, surveying Chesapeake Bay, from April, 1849, to January, 1850, when he transferred to the schooner *Nautilus* to survey Sea Girt Shore until August, 1851. In the fall of 1851, he boarded the frigate *St. Lawrence* to escort American contributors to the Crystal Palace in London, then accompanied the U.S. minister to Lisbon.[8] In 1852, he returned to coastal surveying from August to December on the schooner *Gallatin*, and from December, 1852, until March, 1853, he was attached[9] to the *Vermont* 74. As he noted in a letter to his wife dated Monday, August 1, 1853, it was a "chequered existence."[10] In April, 1853, as lieutenant, Preble was assigned to the *Macedonian*, aboard which he was to spend three intense years participating in naval missions in Far Eastern waters under the leadership of Commodore Matthew C. Perry.[11] Preble's role therein has particular significance for the understanding of his diary.

[8] L. R. Hamersly, *The Records of Living Officers of the U. S. Navy and Marine Corps* (cited hereafter as *Records*), 435–36.

[9] *A Naval Encyclopaedia*, 662; *Sketch*, 204–205.

[10] See the diary entry for August 1, 1853. The best concise account of Preble's navy service is in *A Naval Encyclopaedia*, 661–62.

[11] Matthew Calbraith Perry (1794–1858) was the son of C. R. Perry and the brother of Oliver H. Perry, both officers of the U. S. Navy. After many important assignments in naval operations, mostly in Europe and Africa, M. C. Perry took part in the Mexican War. His fame, however, rests on his memorable mission to Japan and his command of the East India Squadron from 1853 to 1856. He negotiated treaties with Japan and the Ryukyu Islands, thus opening them to American and world relationships, a historical accomplishment which he documented with his own publications, ecpecially the *Narrative of the Expedition of an American Squadron to the China Seas and Japan* (cited hereafter as *Narrative*). He died at

The East Indies Expedition was indeed well organized, with a particular view toward its ultimate importance. Among the crews of the squadron were talented officers, well trained in the naval sciences, and such people of specialized scientific bent as Chaplain George Jones, serving on the *Mississippi* and collecting data on zodiacal light (in the diary, Preble refers to Jones with sympathetic recognition). There were officers who, in accordance with the established American tradition of naval diplomacy, skillfully combined their naval professions with political understanding and a vision of future interests in the Pacific. These aspects have an association even today with the Ryukyu Islands (Okinawa Archipelago), which were opened to commerce by the expedition. Although often relating the dull routine of shipboard life, Preble's diary also portrays actions or adds elements to the personalities of the many members of the expedition and reflects upon the condition of American life in China at that time.

The East India Squadron was composed of the following war vessels: the steamers *Mississippi*, *Allegheny*, *Powhatan*, and *Vermont 74*, and the sloops of war *Vandalia* and *Macedonian*. The steamer *Susquehanna* and the sloops of war *Saratoga* and *Plymouth*, already on the East India station, were also added to the squadron, as were the armed store ships *Supply*, *Lexington*, and *Southampton*. Commodore Perry, who distinguished himself during the Mexican War, chose as his flagship the *Mississippi*, which he later exchanged (in Shanghai on May 17, 1853) for the *Susquehanna*. The Commodore was given special diplomatic and naval authority, as he observed, "because much was necessarily confided to his prudence and discretion," not only in the East Indies, but also with the specific aim that the expedition was "to procure friendly admission to Japan for purposes of trade, and to establish at proper points, permanent depots of coal for our steamers crossing the Pacific." On November 24, 1852, the *Mississippi* departed alone from Norfolk and accepted the way of Madeira, the Cape of Good Hope, Mauritius, and Singapore. Other vessels joined her later.[12]

New York on March 4, 1858. See also *A Naval Encyclopaedia*, 643, and *DAB*, XIV, 486–89.

[12] *Narrative*, I, 75–80; see also Preble's diary.

The ways and times of the *Macedonian,* under Captain Joel Abbot, are shown by the diary. Preble left Portland on April 8 and New York on April 13, 1853, and returned to Boston on August 6, 1856. The *Macedonian* was second in importance to the *Susquehanna,* from which Commodore Perry led the expedition. The *Macedonian,* with her outstanding commandant, participated in all of the important activities of the Perry mission, especially the treaty negotiations at Shimoda and Kanagawa. Preble assisted in surveys of the Bay of Tokyo (Edo), Hakodate, and Keelung in Formosa, and his chart of Keelung Harbor was published in Perry's official report to Congress.[13] While in Chinese waters Preble was given command of the *Queen,* chartered from the British by Commodore Perry. This steamer—137 tons, armed with four four-pounders, to which was added one twelve-pound howitzer from the *Macedonian*—engaged in several military encounters, about which Preble remarked:

> Lieut. Preble was actively employed in co-operation with the naval forces of Great Britain and other powers in ferreting out and destroying the piratical hordes then infesting the Chinese waters. For his part in one of these joint expeditions against the pirates' stronghold at Kulan, he received the thanks of his own Commodore [Joel Abbot] and of the English Admiral [Sir James Stirling].[14]

After returning to Boston on August 6, 1856, Preble was given many important naval duties, culminating in the Mobile River blockade of the South during the Civil War. Here, however, in spite of several successes, he suffered an embarrassing misfortune by letting the Confederate cruiser *Oreto* (later renamed *Florida*) escape through his blockade into the Bay of Mobile on September 4, 1862. He was serving on the *Oneida* at the time, and as a first reaction to the event, Secretary of the Navy Gideon Welles dismissed him from the navy on September 20. After his own protest and those of many important citizens from New England, Preble was restored to rank and position on February 21, 1863, by decision of the Naval Com-

[13] *Narrative,* II, at the end of the volume.

[14] *Sketch,* 206–207.

mittee.[15] He held the rank of commander, which he had previously attained on July 16, 1862.

To plead his case of not having been responsible for the *Oreto*'s escape, Preble assembled all the documentary evidence he could obtain and submitted it to Charles Sumner (1811–1874), a prominent senator from Boston, requesting Sumner to intervene on his behalf with Secretary Welles. Preble published a description of the chase of the *Oreto*, along with reports, letters, and other documents showing his proper conduct in the situation. The documents formed the core of his defense, and he justly won his case.[16]

A new appointment came after Preble's restoration: the command of the old *St. Louis*, so well known to him. He left New York on April 9, 1863, and on June 3, in Lisbon, he relieved Commander Marin and assumed his new duties. Considering his removal from the shores of the United States, he desired to "engage in active hostilities against the Rebels" on the home coasts and "to meet any responsibility in [his] efforts towards restoring the Union."[17]

Finally, Preble was ordered to report to Rear Admiral Dahlgren at Port Royal, South Carolina, arriving there on November 2, 1864. The *St. Louis* proceeded to explore the North Edisto River to "sustain the blockade at that point." While on this mission, Preble was directed to take a select number of officers and men from his crew and report to the Admiral at Port Royal, there to join and co-operate with an army force in assisting General Sherman on his march through Georgia. In the Battle of Honey Hill on November 30 and during several encounters in December, 1864, Commander Preble and his men distinguished themselves in the Fleet Brigade's actions against the Confederates.

Upon disbanding of the Fleet Brigade, Preble returned to the North Edisto, where he remained until March 19, 1865, when he was transferred to the steamer *State of Georgia*. He then sailed from

[15] See also G. H. Preble, *The Chase of the Rebel Steamer of War Oreto*.

[16] G. H. Preble, *A Letter, With Accompanying Documents, Addressed to Hon. Charles Sumner*. Preble included several of the letters from his naval superiors in the notes and text of his *Sketch*, 216–22.

[17] *Sketch*, 223.

Port Royal to Aspinwall to "cooperate with the Naval Forces at Panama, in protecting the person and property of citizens of the United States in their transit over the Isthmus."[18]

At the news of the assassination of President Lincoln, Commander Preble transmitted to Secretary Welles $103 subscribed by the crew of the *State of Georgia* for the national monument to the "Martyr President," as Preble expressed it. A short time later, Preble was relieved from the special command at Aspinwall, arriving in New York on August 29, 1865, and from there went to his home in Portland after an absence of two and one-half years. On October 14, he was made general inspector of supplies at the Boston Navy Yard, a position he held until July 5, 1867, when he became equipment officer there, receiving, in the meantime, a promotion to the rank of captain on March 16, 1867, retroactive to January 29, 1867. On August 1, 1868, Captain Preble proceeded, via the Isthmus of Panama, to San Francisco, where he reported to Rear Admiral Craven, commanding the North Pacific Squadron, and assumed his duties as Craven's chief of staff. On December 19, he was given command of the *Pensacola,* Pacific Fleet, under Admiral Turner, who succeeded Craven in June, 1869.

Preble was promoted to commodore on November 2, 1871, and to the distinguished rank of rear admiral on September 30, 1876. On February 25, 1878, Admiral Preble retired in order to devote his time to the writing and research he so desired. He realized his writing plans in his new home at Boston,[19] and it should be added that he quite early took an interest in historical studies and became a member of several cultural and learned societies, namely:

> On March 6, 1843, he was elected a member of the Naval Library and Institute at Charlestown Navy Yard, became librarian and curator for 1858–59, and was finally made vice-president in 1866–67.
>
> He was elected an associate member of the Portland Natural

[18] *Ibid.,* 228.

[19] See also William Preble Jones, *John Preble of Machias (1771–1841) and His Descendants,* and W. P. Preble, *A Genealogical Sketch of the Preble Families.* For an intensive study of the Preble genealogy, see G. H. Preble's *Sketch.*

History Society in 1852, was its vice-president on 1856–57, and became a corresponding member on January 1, 1863.

On October 9, 1854, he was elected an honorary member of the Portland Rifle Corps.

On June 6, 1866, he was elected a resident member of the New England Historical and Genealogical Society and became a life member on July 1, 1869.

On August 6, 1866, he was elected a corresponding member of the Maine Historical Society.

On February 21, 1868, he was elected a corresponding member of the State Historical Society of Wisconsin.[20]

George Henry Preble died in Boston on March 1, 1885, closing a life deservedly honored and rich in eminent services rendered the United States at a time of great national changes. The diary he left his wife represents one of the periods of his naval career, an important era in the history of the Pacific during the opening of new countries to American commerce and in the first years of peculiar association for missions, trade, and diplomacy in China and Japan.

The Diary: 1853–1856

The diary of Rear Admiral George Henry Preble was copied from the original kept during his participation, aboard the *Macedonian*, in Commodore Matthew C. Perry's East Indies Expedition. Preble intimates in the dedication that the diary was compiled from letters he sent to his wife, Susan, and is therefore dedicated to her. This is only a part of the whole truth.

On December 22, 1852, Commodore Perry issued an order "forbidding communications to the public prints at home touching the movements of the squadron, and prohibiting also such information through the medium of private letters to friends." Secretary of the Navy John P. Kennedy had directed, Perry announced, "that private notes and journals kept by any members of the expedition should be considered as belonging to the government . . . ."[21] Preble did not

[20] *Sketch*, 233.

[21] *Narrative*, I, 88.

think the order prudent, certainly not in the nature of a requirement by Secretary Kennedy, nor did he believe it sufficiently justified.

As is evident, Preble kept a regular diary under the guise of letters to his wife. Moreover, he did so deliberately, writing an account almost every day in covert defiance of Perry's directive, an order which Preble sincerely disliked and with which he expressed his disagreement in the diary. The very character of the day-by-day record proves it was not letter writing—although this aspect can be discovered as well—but a genuine diary. Preble himself wrote on July 16, 1854, that "my fatigue and the prostrating heat have compelled me to forego the pleasure of keeping up my daily diary of events," and on August 8, 1856, already in Boston but still aboard the *Macedonian*, he noted: "Too happy to write diary."

In his *Narrative of the Expedition of an American Squadron to the China Seas and Japan*, Perry largely ascribes to himself the success and results of the expedition. Thus any other observations or records of events could be quite different from those which the "Old Bruin," as Preble was wont to call the Commodore, might wish or personally present in his own account. Preble's diary is just such a document. His description of daily assignments and his often detailed observations, along with many brief notations of happenings during the negotiations with the Japanese, add considerable information to the report Perry submitted to the President and the Congress of the United States. These and other aspects make the diary a most valuable research tool in the study of American expansion in the Pacific, for without it there is less complete understanding of Perry's accomplishments and insufficient knowledge of daily developments in the opening of Japan and the Ryukyu Islands to intercourse with the Western world.

A number of nineteenth-century New Englanders appear in Preble's account, shown with interesting relatives and friends closely interrelated in the typical fashion of old families, so characteristic of life before the Civil War. Here, too, is to be seen the adventurous spirit of those Americans who went abroad to seek their fortunes. It is Preble, however, who dominates the narrative with observations collected in the faraway and exotic countries where the United States, in its varied free enterprise, was rising to political and economic prominence.

The diary is rich in its presentation of American life in the Far East, particularly China. In part, it is a gallery of the first American businessmen, diplomats, and missionaries, a strange association of God and mammon. A long line of residents in Canton, Macao, Ningpo, Amoy, Foochow, or Shanghai; rich, princely merchants; adventurous sea captains and their romantically named sailing vessels; learned and zealous missionaries—these constitute a most interesting picture.

George H. Preble appears in the diary as a good husband and solicitous father, a deeply religious and serious man. His love of reading is reflected in quotations of verses and proverbs and references to books. His language has its own quality: concise, literary yet colloquial, in simple terms expressing the deep tensions of a cultivated nineteenth-century American. It satisfies the reader. His sharp observations of life at sea, of the "angry sky" and "blue waters," of the daily work aboard ships are pleasant and solid.

On the *ex libris* of the diary, which reposes in the library of the Massachusetts Historical Society and is catalogued as "027. 29f.," is this inscription: "Given by Susie Z. Preble, January 6, 1919." The donor was Susie Zabiah Preble, the only surviving daughter of the G. H. Prebles, born in Portland on September 1, 1850, at 62 Danforth Street, on the corner of Tyng Street. She also donated to the Society an extensive collection of the papers left by her distinguished father.

The diary is a bound volume, now in poor condition, of blue, good quality paper, written with a neat hand. It opens with four unnumbered pages, followed by 555 numbered pages. Page 558 is written but unnumbered; the next two pages, 559 and 560, are also unnumbered but blank. These are followed with a continuation of the diary on three unnumbered pages, 561, 562, 563, interrupted again by five blank, unnumbered pages: 564, 565, 566, 567, 568. The next two pages, 569 and 570, are written on; the two after that, 571 and 572, are pasted with three newspaper cuttings representing Japanese types. The last page of the volume, 573, is pasted with a newspaper cutting, "Export of tea and raw silk to Britain." To the back flyleaf there are pasted sketches of Japanese wrestlers and a program of an "Ethiopian Concert" on the steam frigate *Powhatan*. The contents of the volume are as follows:

Facing page 1	a reprint of the Chinese characters for G. H. Preble's name, with description;
[1]	dedication, "To My Dear Wife";
[2–3]	"Officers Attached to the U. S. Ship *Macedonian,* New York, April 10, 1853";
[3]	"Armament of the *Macedonian,* 1853";
[4]	pasted on, a cutting with the Tokugawa crest;
1	the diary proper begins: "New York, Sunday Evening, April 10, 1853, My Dear Wife";
58–59	inserted between, color lithograph by E. Brown, Jr.: "Debarcation in Japan of boat-howitzers as part of escort for Commo. Perry U.S. Special Envoy and Comdr. in Chief of Naval Forces in E.I. Seas";
199–200	inserted between, a concert program;
203	two cuttings pasted on, "Notes on Japan, Temples, Religion, etc.," *Boston Journal,* by G. H. Preble;
226	sketch of a hill resembling a man, Port Lloyd, the Bonin Islands;
230	in the text, a drawing of a Japanese coat of arms;
240	in the text, a sketch of a rock, resembling a huge finger, in the sea near the Bonin Islands;
241–42	inserted between, a color sketch of the coast of Shimoda;
267–68	inserted between, a rubbing of Japanese gold coins, made in Hakodate, 1854;
274	in the text, a sketch of a waterspout;
310–18	on each page in the text, sketches of rocks in the sea near the Ryukyu Islands;

332 pasted on, a newspaper cutting showing the port of Canton, 1854;

333–34 inserted between, a lithograph of the Canton fish market;

352 pasted in the text, Preble's paper stamp with the inscription "Liberty and Truth";

353–54 inserted between, a concert program printed on yellow silk;

360 pasted in the text, a Chinese good-wish card with the translation "Let the seas be like oil";

361 pasted in the text, a red card, written in Chinese, expressing the sympathy of the residents of Canton Bay;

370 pasted in the text, a reprint of four Chinese seals;

371–72 inserted between, an invitation to a ball at the Hongkong Regatta Club, November 17, 1854;

385–86 inserted between, an invitation to a ball at the Zetland Lodge of Free Masons, Hong Kong, December 13, 1854;

387 pasted on, a lithograph showing summer house and pagoda on the island of Whampoa;

405–406 inserted between, "Syllabus of a lecture on the Early Writings of Charles Dickens," February 5; 1855;

431–32 inserted between, a short letter to Mrs. G. H. Preble with sentiments before sailing from Hong Kong to Shanghai, Good Friday, April 6, 1855;

457–58 put loose between, a later photograph showing the river at Canton;

459–60 inserted between, an invitation for dinner on board the U.S.S. *Macedonian*, June 28, 1855;

464	pasted on, an envelope and a name card of the Chinese maritime commissioner in Ningpo;
500–501	two unnumbered pages;
519–20	inserted between, an invitation for dinner with Sir John and Lady Bowring, Hong Kong, December 25, 1855, at the Government House;
521–22	inserted between, a plan of Lt. G. H. Preble's cabin on the *Macedonian*, with a drawing of the furnishings;
536	pasted on, poem, "Go Sheet," by G. H. Preble;
[562–63]	pasted in, "Abstract of the Cruise of the U.S. Ship *Macedonian*";
[564–65]	inserted between, an engraving from a newspaper showing Japanese samurais.

The Opening of Japan

A DIARY OF DISCOVERY IN THE FAR EAST, 1853–1856

To My Dear Wife
This Diary, extracted generally verbatim
or with but trifling alterations and additions
from my letters to you and compiled from them
at your request, is dedicated to your perusal
by
Your ever affectionate Husband
Geo. Henry Preble

Officers Attached to the U. S. Ship Macedonian
New York, April 10, 1853

Captain	Joel Abbot	Died in Hong Kong, Dec. 14, 1855
Lieuts.	L. B. Avery	Resigned Dec. 1854, afterwards shot himself
"	W. Gwathmey	Rebel
"	G. H. Preble	
"	E. Y. Winder	Rebel
Actg. Master	John Walcutt	Dropped from service Sept. 1855
Purser	R. T. Allison	Rebel
Surgeon	R. Woodworth	Died
Ast. Surgeon	J. C. Gilliam	Lost in the Levant
2nd Let. Marines	J. H. Jones	
Pass'd Mid	John Watters	
" "	J. G. Sproston	Killed in Rebel War
Actg. M. Mates	Chas. W. Abbot	Since Paytos USN
" "	John R. C. Lewis	Grand Nephew of Geo. Washington
" "	Lawrence L. Lewis	ditto ditto
" "	W. S. Hambleton	Left at St. Helena, and died on passage home
Capts' Clerk	N.M.W. Abbot	Died May 31, 1853
Boatswain	J. C. Hayden	
Gunner	Hamilton Bell	Run at Manila, Aug. 1854
Carpenter	Dave Jones	
Sailmaster	Chas. Y. Frost	Lost in the Levant

Armament of the Macedonian, *1853*

2.10 inch	shell guns
16.8 "	" "
4.6 "	shot guns 32 pdrs.

The Diary: 1853

The Diary: 1853

New York, Sunday Evening, April 10, 1853

My Dear Wife,

I arrived here this morning by the Providence and Stonington boats and lost no time in going on board the *Macedonian*,[1] and ascertaining the state of things, though I could not report until tomorrow. I find her ready for sea, and Capt. Abbot[2] says he hopes to sail tomorrow. She will, however, be delayed, I think, until the next day, if not longer. She will touch at Madeira, the Canaries, and at the Cape of Good Hope on her way out, so a letter via England to the last named place would probably meet me there. In Boston I saw Chas. H.[3] and breakfasted with him. Zabiah[4] could not see me as she was ill.

[1] There were three U. S. vessels named *Macedonian;* Preble's sailing ship was the third. She was of 1,140 tons; built in 1832; launched in 1836; razed in 1852; in ordinary at Norfolk, Virginia, 1874; and sold, December, 1875.

[2] Joel Abbot (1793–1855) was commander, U. S. Naval Forces, East India, China and Japan seas, 1853–55, and captain of the *Macedonian* from October, 1850. He died at Hong Kong on December 14, 1855. Born into a prominent Boston family, he was made midshipman on June 18, 1822; lieutenant on April 1, 1828; commander on December 8, 1838; and captain on October 3, 1850. For more information, see *DAB*, I, 14–15. There is much about him in the diary, especially the entry dated December 15, 1855. Preble sometimes spells his name "Abbott," a confusion which can also be observed in Perry's official report.

[3] Perhaps Charles Harris, a relative of Preble's wife, Susan. See *Sketch*, 243 n.4.

[4] Zabiah May (b. 1794), daughter of Jeremiah Gore and Thankful Harris, married Henry Smith and had thirteen children by him; Preble does not give their names in the *Sketch*. In 1870, she was living in Boston, a widow. *Sketch*, 245.

He is building a barn, and they are preparing to move into his house in Dorchester. John Smith,[5] he told me, would close up his partnership concern next July. A good name, I should say, for Aunt S. John S. was disappointed at not obtaining an office from Washington. I found no one at home at Dr. Flint's[6] but H. Gurney.[7] The Doctor and Aunt Sarah[8] were out riding. I dined at Mrs. Oxnard's,[9] and saw her on my forenoon call but she was confined to her bed with a sick headache at dinner time. Silsbee[10] took my daguerrotype, for which I am to send him an equivalent from China. I left it at Mrs. Oxnard's to be forwarded, and hope it will please you, though I was too much hurried to have him sit me more than once. My cold is improving; the weather here I find is much milder than it is East. We had a rough night in the boat to Boston, but I slept through it all. I do not yet realize that I am away from home more than a day or so. It will come upon me by degrees, as the days linger on and only too soon. With a fine ship and pleasant companions I ought not to complain, and doubtless am envied by many in the service. God bless you. My loving thoughts are all yours and homeward.

[5] Preble does not mention John Smith in the *Sketch*. It seems, however, that Smith was his relative. Boston genealogical sources indicate many John Smiths, none of whom can be associated as a relative of Preble.

[6] John Flint, M.D., of Boston married Sarah Harris. *Sketch*, 245.

[7] Alpheus Gurney married Eliza (b. 1800), daughter of Jeremiah Gore and Thankful Harris; she was a near relative of Mrs. G. H. Preble. *Ibid.*

[8] Sarah Harris, born July 19, 1806, was the aunt of Mrs. G. H. Preble. *Ibid.*

[9] Mrs. Oxnard, born Charlotte Farnham, was married to Henry Oxnard on May 5, 1819. Henry was born on January 6, 1789, and died on December 15, 1843, at his residence on Mt. Vernon Street in Boston, leaving two sons, Enoch and Stephen, and a daughter, Mehitable. The *Boston Daily Advertiser* (December 18, 1843) speaks of him with great praise. See also *Sketch*, 146–48.

The Oxnard family of Boston and Portland was rather large. It was intermarried with the Prebles when Martha Preble (1786–1860) married Edward Oxnard, her cousin, on July 26, 1819. *Sketch*, 148–50; see also G. H. Preble, *Martha Preble Oxnard Eldest Child of Brig.-General Jedidiah Preble and Mehitable Bangs, 1754–1824*.

[10] Silsbee, Case and Company were the famous old Boston photographic artists at 299½ Washington Street. In 1858, the "principal photographic operator" was Mr. G. M. Silsbee. For references, see their *Glance at the Progress and Position of the Useful and Beautiful Arts*, the only known copy of which is owned by the Massachusetts Historical Society.

New York, Tuesday, April 12, 1853

I enclose two hundred dollars. I have had to borrow it, as the navy agent has no funds and the Purser[11] is not allowed to advance. I could not and would not go to sea without making some provision for my family, and at last borrowed some. Our mess bill I find is enormous, viz. $250. The permission to allow two thirds of my monthly pay I have not yet received from the Secretary.[12] If it does not come before we sail, I shall leave you half pay and make up the deficiency by another allotment as soon as the permission is received and will send you more money before we sail. I have been and am still sadly perplexed by these sudden and unexpected orders.

April 13, 1853

These must be my last words and *adieu,* and I regret they have to be few and short. We sail, or are to be towed to sea at 8 o'clock. I have not more than half completed arrangements but hope to be settled down in a day or two. I am in such a turmoil and perplexity I don't know what to do, or which way to turn, but your love, and love for you shines through it all and is my star of hope and promise. We do love each other—don't we, Susie?[13] Robt. Boyd[14] has just left me; he

[11] R. T. Allison; see note 38 below.

[12] John P. Kennedy (1795–1870) was the secretary of the navy from July, 1852, to March, 1853; it was he who decided to organize the Japan expedition. Kennedy's MSS, preserved in the Peabody Institute, contain valuable material for the study of the expedition. See also *DAB,* X, 333–34.

[13] Susan Zabiah (born August 1, 1820) was the daughter of John Cox and Thankful Harris Gore of Portland. She was married to George Henry Preble on November 18, 1845. Her mother was the first wife of Jeremia Gore. *Sketch,* 200, 243.

[14] Robert Boyd was apparently from Portland, to which his father, Joseph, came in 1784. In 1796, Joseph Boyd married Isabella Southgate, by whom he had one son, Robert. William Willis, *The History of Portland, from 1636 to 1864,* 790–91. From the *Portland Obituary Scrapbook,* VII, 83–84, we learn that "Captain Robert Boyd, U.S.N., a veteran officer in the U. S. Navy, died in Brooklyn, Wednesday night of heart failure. He was born at Portland, Feb. 22nd, 1834, and was 56 years of age. He belonged to the third generation of the Boyd family in America, his grandfather being Robert Boyd, who came here from Scotland in 1756. His father was also Robert Boyd. The deceased was a cousin of Major C. H. Boyd of this city. The funeral will probably be in Evergreen cemetery, in the old family lot."

brought on board a package for young Robbie.[15] He tells me he has been house visiting today. The mail has just come on board with the needful authority and I enclose an allotment for ninety dollars a month. I breathe freer. Write to Madeira by the next two English steamers. God bless you and our darling little ones. Who are never absent from the thoughts of your affectionate husband.

Wednesday Evening

I wrote you a hurried letter this morning. I will now endeavor to write you a hasty postscript while the ship is in tow of the steam tug. I have had a lifetime of thoughts and anxiety crowded into the last few days, and shall be glad to get into blue water, since I have to leave home and wash them out in a measure. Explain to everyone the manner in which I was hurried away, as an excuse for leaving so much for you to settle and attend to. I have reserved to myself $40. per month of my pay, which I hope will pay my future mess bills and furnish such renewals of clothing as may be required and other necessities. We hope to reach Madeira on the 10th of May, and thence visit the Canary Islds; touch at Gable Bay,[16] Cape of Good Hope, call at the Comoro Islds.,[17] and thence to Hong Kong, China; such is the projected route. I find myself the 3d Lieut. on board, like the ship, have a fine room and pleasant messmates. Keep me informed all about Harry the bold, and little Susie,[18] and ask them, for my sake, to be good children and mind mama. I am called on deck. God bless you and good bye.

At Sea, Sunday noon, April 17, 1853

With my first Sunday at sea, I resume my old habit of writing you the events of the week. I can scarcely realize, I am on the broad At-

[15] He was perhaps a son of Robert Boyd.

[16] There were two routes from New York to China; around South Africa or around South America. The first was shorter, and the Azores were a meeting place for American ships.

[17] The Comoro Islands, between Madagascar and the African continent at the northern entrance of the Mozambique Channel, are a group of volcanic islands belonging to France.

[18] The children of G. H. Preble and Susan Zabiah Cox: Henry Oxnard, born January 4, 1847, at the Hall House, 80, Cumberland; Susie Zabiah, born September 1, 1850, at 62 Danforth Street, Portland, Maine.

lantic, eight hundred miles from home, with my face and pathway to be continually turned from you for two years to come, perhaps three; a sickening, saddening thought as I write it, yet all is for the best; and hard and cruel as it now seems. Bye and bye, we shall discover it is for our mutual good. Having to go to sea, I could not ask a finer ship, more agreeable mess mates, a cruise more interesting or healthier climates than we expect to visit. Surely these are blessings to be grateful for. Still my thoughts linger behind, and my heart is sore as I think of our long separation. I would be with you and our dear little ones, those twins of our affections.

It is a week this morning since I arrived in New York. We took our departure in a thick fog and saturated by a misty, drizzly rain, which soon changed to cold weather and favorable winds that have lasted until now, and continue. The ship sails well and we anticipate a quiet passage to Madeira. Your letter of the 11th reached me as we were getting under way and I hope that another may welcome our arrival at Madeira. I think I have not informed you that another Lieut. was ordered to the ship with instructions to leave Washington by the 3 P.M. train of cars, it being then one o'clock, and proceed to New York and report, and only to be excused from going in the ship if I had reported, and there were four Lieuts. on board. He reached New York the day after I had reported and was only too happy to find me on board. Woodhouse[19] was in New York fitting out his Schooner, but I had no time to hunt him up. Robt. Boyd, when he came on board the morning we sailed with the package for his son, was the best home face I saw. I hope Mrs. Oxnard has sent you the daguerrotypes, and that it pleases you. I wish you would write to Harriet Preble[20] and inform her of my sudden departure,

[19] He was, perhaps, Captain Philip Woodhouse, a New Yorker, of the *Queen of the West,* a packet ship. A. H. Clark, *The Clipper Ship Era* (cited hereafter as *Clipper*), 41, 43, 48.

[20] Harriet Preble, the eldest daughter of Henry Preble and Francis Wright, was born September 26, 1795, at Lewes, Sussex, England, and died a spinster at West Manchester, Pennsylvania, on February 4, 1854. "A gifted and pretentious lady," she was schooled in Paris. She played the piano, sketched scenes from life, maintained the friendship of distinguished literary persons in both France and the United States, and was admired by many people. *Sketch,* 271–74, and a portrait. For an extensive biography, see R. H. Lee, *Memoir of the Life of Harriet Preble.*

which left no time for leave-taking or little writing. I shall read this evening, as we agreed, the 1st Psalm and 2d chap. of *Matthew*, and continue each Sunday, counting the weeks of absence by the chapters. It will be pleasant as aforetime to know our thoughts, as well as our hearts, are united.

I began this at noon, it is now evening, and blowing a moderate gale, which is hurrying us on our course. May a kind Providence watch over and protect you in my absence, and return me to you in its own good season.

At Sea, Sunday Evening, April 24, 1853

Another week has come and gone without furnishing any novel or exciting incident. The weather and winds have been rough, chilly and boisterous, and frequently wet and rainy. We have had, however, occasional glimpses of sunshine and a milder climate. We have made good progress on our course and are 2200 miles from New York and within 200 of Flores and Corvo, two of the Western Islds., and hope to sight them tomorrow. Our ship has astonished us with her fast sailing, which is the more remarkable, as formerly, before she was razeed, and the change in her battery, she was considered a dull ship. We now anticipate anchoring at Madeira next Thursday, and will remain there three or four days before sailing for Palma Island. I think from thence the Capt. intends running down to the Cape de Verdes. We hope he will, as he has decided to go direct to Macao without stopping at the Cape of Good Hope, a long three months of ocean before us. The best way to send your letters will be by English mail to Hong Kong, China, care of Rawle Drinker & Co.[21] The postage, 45 cts., must be prepaid. Write at least once a month that way. Another good way to write is via California. There are regular packets from San Francisco to China by which the letters will be forwarded. Via England the mail is very regular and received in about sixty days after date; through France via Marseilles, the route is quicker but the postage is double. Occasionally you can try

[21] In 1851, Rawls, Drinker and Company, a well-known American trading firm in Hong Kong, was under the management of Sandwich Drinker, who was a friend of Townsend Harris. Eldon Griffin, *Clippers and Consuls*, 280.

sending a letter through the Naval Lyceum at N.Y.[22] or the Naval base and Institute at Boston,[23] but I would not advise much use of them. I cannot hope to hear from you at Madeira as our passage promises to eclipse that of a steamer, but I shall look for letters awaiting me at Hong Kong. It is all like a dream to me yet. I cannot believe I am 17 days from and 2500 miles dist. with a prospective absence of three years. Yet the reality stares me in the face. Mine is a cruel life, and I wish I could loose myself from it, but "I am bound and fast bound so"—that from it I cannot go.[24]

Our Capt. has brought two of his sons with him. One as his clerk,[25] the other rated a Master's Mate, but studying medecine[26] with our Surgeon[27] to fit him an Asst. Surgeon in the Navy. The old man has another son, a Purser,[28] on board the *Marion*,[29] whom he is expecting

[22] The U. S. Naval Lyceum was organized at New York Navy Yard on November 28, 1833. Matthew C. Perry, at that time master-commandant, presided at the first meeting. The Lyceum was incorporated by New York authorities in 1835 and later became the basis of the United States Naval Institute. In 1836–37, it published bi-monthly *The Naval Magazine*, which contained articles by many well-known contemporary writers, such as James Fenimore Cooper. Through its library, the Lyceum took charge of letters to and from various foreign naval stations. It was reorganized in 1871. *A Naval Encyclopaedia*, 514–15.

[23] Boston Base, which has connection with Preble's life, was formerly in Charlestown, a suburb of Boston. *A Naval Encyclopaedia*, 88.

[24] See Byron's *Mazeppa*, lines 539–41: "The earth gave way, the skies roll'd round, / I seem'd to sink upon the ground; / But err'd, for I was fastly bound."

[25] N. M. W. Abbot was taken on board the Macedonian by Captain Joel Abbot, his father, with the expectation that the sea climate would benefit his poor health. He died on the way to China, May 31, 1853, and was buried on Prince Island; see Preble's diary, entry of June 5, 1853.

[26] Charles W. Abbot is not included in L. R. Hamersly's *List of Officers of the Navy of the United States and of the Marine Corps from 1775 to 1900* (cited hereafter as *List*. He was a student of medicine and accompanied his father, Joel, on the cruise to the Far East. He is mentioned later in the diary.

[27] Robert Woodworth was made assistant surgeon and attached to the *Macedonian* on February 23, 1835. Made surgeon on December 1, 1846, he retired on May 13, 1867, and died on March 17, 1870.

[28] John P. Abbot was made purser on October 1, 1852; he resigned on September 1, 1856.

[29] The U.S. Navy sailing vessel *Marion*, 566 tons, had 16 guns and was built in 1838. She was broken up and made a steamer of 919 tons, with two screws, in 1874.

to meet among the Islands, and still another son[30] who is a lieut. on board the *Dale*.[31] The clerk seems in the last stages of consumption and is the merest shadow of a human being. Yet his father seems unaware of his feeble state and talks of his recovery. His appearance is so ghastly and deathlike it is disagreeable to me to see him about. Our ward room mess promises to be an agreeable one. The 1st Lt.[32] was my mess mate on board the *St. Lawrence*.[33] You may remember my telling you of a Southampton maid who followed one of the officers to the U.S. It was our present 1st Lt. who was the magnet of attraction; and it appears from a daguerrotype he showed me, she is now a mother. He leaves her an allotment. I know no more as I asked no questions. G—y [Gwathmey][34] the 2d Lt. is an amiable, pleasant fellow. He too was ordered to the *St. L*[*ouis*],[35] but did not go in her. W—der [Winder][36] the 4th is married, but has no children. Though younger than I am, his hair is perfectly white. He is our caterer. W—cutt [Walcutt],[37] the Master, is a jolly, good-natured

[30] J. Francis Abbot was made midshipman on December 27, 1837; passed midshipman, June 29, 1843; master, October 14, 1850; lieutenant, April 22, 1851; reserved list, September 13, 1855; commander, reserved list, April 4, 1867. He died in 1870.

[31] The U.S.S. *Dale,* a sailing vessel of 675 tons, eight guns, was built in 1839 for use by naval militia in Baltimore.

[32] Latham B. Avery was made midshipman on December 19, 1831; passed midshipman, June 15, 1837; lieutenant, September 8, 1841. He resigned on September 28, 1855, and shot himself in December, 1855.

[33] The U.S.S. *St. Lawrence,* a sailing vessel of 1,726 tons, was built in 1846, launched in 1847, and used as marine barracks at Norfolk in 1874. She was sold in 1875.

[34] Washington Gwathmey was made midshipman on July 21, 1832; passed midshipman, June 23, 1838; lieutenant, June 28, 1843; dismissed, April 17, 1861.

[35] The *St. Louis,* a vessel of 830 tons, 18 guns, was built in 1828 and served the naval militia in Philadelphia.

[36] Edward L. Winder was made midshipman on April 29, 1836; passed midshipman, July 1, 1842; master, October 25, 1849; lieutenant, April 20, 1850; dismissed, April 22, 1861.

[37] John Walcutt was made midshipman on March 2, 1840; passed midshipman, July 11, 1846; master, January 30, 1855; dropped from service, September 28, 1855.

individual. The Purser,[38] in looks and manners, though with much more character, resembles Chas. H. W—th [Woodworth] the Surgeon attached to the Florida Sqdn.[39] When I was and is a bachelor and gentleman. J—s [Jones],[40] the Marine officer has been everything by turns and nothing long, except nine years married. He is a great talker and always ready to do a kindness. The Asst. Surgeon G[illiam][41] is a Virginian and in the same condition I was when I made this cruise ten years ago—engaged to be married. The Purser's wife is the daughter of Chief Justice Taney.[42] We muster four bentincks[43] and five free rooms; but I am the only one who has a child to solace and to bless. Those dear treasures, how I wish I could annihilate space and fold them in my embrace.

Funchal, Isld. Madeira, May 1, 1853

We are just now the usual bustle incident to anchoring, and with sails furled, and quietly resting in that midstream after a pleasant and speedy passage. The packet sails for England tomorrow and I cannot let her go without my last words. Resuming my last *Sunday Journal.*[44] At day light on Monday the 25th we sighted Corvo and Flores, two of the Azores, and sailed along to the Nth of them within good viewing distance of Corvo so that we could readily distinguish

[38] Richard T. Allison was made purser on October 30, 1849; dismissed from the U.S. Navy, May 6, 1861.

[39] See the biographical sketch of Preble in this volume.

[40] James H. Jones was given in the "List of Officers" in Commodore Perry's *Narrative,* II, 413, as first lieutenant on the *Macedonian.* His name is in Preble's "List of Officers" as second lieutenant; not indicated on the *Macedonian.*

[41] James S. Gilliam was made assistant surgeon on April 26, 1847; resigned, December 2, 1858; reappointed, March 11, 1869; lost in the Levant, June, 1861.

[42] Roger Brooke Taney (1777–1864) attorney general, secretary of the treasury, was chief justice of the U.S. Supreme Court, beginning in 1836, having been nominated by President Jackson. For details of his life and a bibliography, see *DAB,* XVIII, 289–94.

[43] Bentincks are triangular courses. The Bentinck boom is a spar across the foot of the foresail. Gershom Bradford, *A Glossary of Sea Terms,* 14.

[44] *Sunday Journal.* Perhaps Preble meant one of the American or English Sunday weeklies; however, there is no such known journal in the American or British press union catalogues in the years 1850–60.

the characteristics of its scenery. On Tuesday morning, soon after midnight, we found ourselves entangled between Graciosa and St. George, two Islds of the same group, having been set to the Sth by a current, not allowed for in our reckoning, and hauled to the Nth until day light, when around to the Nth and E[t] of Graciosa—a fertile and beautifully cultivated Isld. The lofty peak of Pico, and those of Fayal and St. George were seen in the distance. At noon we were up with Terceira, an island I visited when a keeper on board the old U.S.S. *St. Louis*.[45] At daylight on Wednesday (the 28th) we saw the high and large Isld of St. Michael[46] half enveloped in clouds and mist, and coasted along its Eastern Shore, about five miles dist. The features of its landscape, a mingling of the grand and beautiful seldom surpassed. From St. Michael, light and fair winds, and pleasant weather accompanied us, nothing unusual occurring until the morning when at day light we decried this island, and anchored at 11 A.M.

Being Mayday and Sunday—it is a *fiesta* on shore and a thousand flags are flying over the city. Many of my messmates have availed themselves of their privileges to go on shore, but I am detained on board until tomorrow, as I have the day's duty.

Our sail along the island as we approached the anchorage was very beautiful this morning. I could not realize that such verdant hills could be the abode of such starvation as has been represented. They appear pictures of fertility. The scenery is grand and beautiful. The highest peak is higher than the loftiest of the White Mountains, and our ship is anchored within ten miles of its summit, whereas you cannot approach the water level of the White Mts.[47] much nearer than sixty miles. The peaks of Madeira are green and fruitful to their very apex's, while those of the White Mts. are bald, grey stone in summer and snow-capped in winter. It was a pretty sight as we glided rather than sailed along this morning to see the mountain rills bounding toward the ocean, mere threads in size, and leaping hundreds of feet,

[45] Preble refers to his return from Lisbon to New York in July, 1851, after conveying U.S. Minister Charles Haddock (1796–1861), whom President Fillmore appointed in 1850 as chargé d'affaires to Portugal, where he remained until 1854. *DAB*, VIII, 76.

[46] São Miguel.

[47] Mount Katahdin, Maine, 5,268 feet, is the highest elevation in the state.

one precipice at a single bound. And it was pleasant to hear the fishermen greet us as "Bueno Americanos,"[48] as we floated along; an exemplification of the old adage: The road to a people's heart is through their stomachs. It is now sixteen years since I last visited Madeira. Yet I can recall and recognize the prominent features of its landscape, and see no change in the appearance of the town either for better or worse. Most places in the possession of the Portuguese seem finished according to their ideas, and at a stand still.

When I take a shirt from my bureau it is an amusing lottery—at one time long tail, liberal collar and extension wrist bands, at another, laconic shirts, little or no collar and sleeves, shortened up to the elbows. My collection is a relic of past fashions.

At Sea, Sunday afternoon, May 8, 1853

Last Sunday we had just quietly "furled our canvass wings" and anchored in the Funchal Roads. Today we are steering towards the Cape de Verds, with a light wind fanning us along and pleasant weather, one day out from Palma, one of the Canary group of Islds. After writing you from Madeira I was twice on shore, and find I did the Portuguese injustice. Funchal considerably improved according to my recollection. The streets are cleaner and better paved, and there is an attempt at a bit of a square or *aleymada* planted with oaks, which is new. We were very kindly and hospitably entertained at Madeira by our Consul, Mr. March,[49] who literally kept open house for us. We came in and went out as we chose. It was at Madeira that your Uncle Josiah[50] died; I made an unsuccessful attempt to find his grave. The stranger's grave yard is a pretty place and is planted with cypress trees, but has few monuments or headstones that tell the brief history of its tenants. We remained at Madeira three days, sailing

[48] "The good Americans."

[49] John Howard March of New Hampshire received a recess appointment as consul to Madeira on October 21, 1816, was confirmed by the Senate on December 17, 1816, and left his post about January 1, 1859. Before his appointment, he had resided in Madeira as a merchant. His date of birth has not been established. Cf. National Archives, *Records of the Department of State, Pers. 1816*.

[50] Josiah Cox, son of John Cox, was born on January 23, 1785, married Susan Greenleaf, daughter of Joseph and Susan Pearson, and died of cancer on July 29, 1829. His widow died on December 17, 1850. *Sketch*, 241.

on the morning of the 4th inst. and arriving at Sta. Cruz, Palma, on the morning of the 7th. We left there a young man we brought from Madeira as a passenger. An Austrian named Oscar Pfeiffer, the son of Ida Pfeiffer,[51] whose "voyage of a lady around the world and to Iceland" has within a year or two been so extensively read. The young man is a pianist and as he understood no English, and but little Spanish and was seasick withal and we had no instrument for him to play on, we did not find his companionship much of an accession, though as gentlemanly and agreeable as a dumb man well could be. I made but one visit on shore at Santa Cruz de la Palma, had quite a surfeit of it in a few hours, and was glad to return on board. It has the appearance and characteristics of all Spanish towns that it is furnished with a fine but still incomplete Cathedral and a pretty little *aleymada.*

The numerous pestilences have destroyed the life of the place, and greatly reduced the number of its inhabitants. I took a walk over the hills back of the town and found heaps of cineria and ashes perforated with caves and dens in which live the most wretched and poverty-stricken of the inhabitants. I was told that over seven hundred of these troglodytes died during the last pestilence, and no wonder. A few years back Palma was a sailors' paradise from the numbers of women easily obtainable for their sensual pleasures, but the plague has performed its silent work with them, so that few remain. The Canary group of Islands, of which Palma is a member, were accidentally discovered in 1330 by the crew of a French ship driven thither by storms. After several attempts at Colonization by the Spaniards, a French gentleman, John De Béthencourt, took possession of several. His heir sold their sovereignty to the Spaniards, who

[51] Ida Laura Reyer Pfeiffer (1797–1858), an Austrian traveler and writer, was born in Vienna and in 1820 married Dr. Pfeiffer, a Polish lawyer from Lwów (Lvov). She made two trips around the world and published accounts of them in German: *Eine Frauenfahrt um die Welt* (1850) and *Meine zweite Weltreise* (1856). Her books were translated into several languages. Preble refers to the following two books: *Journey to Iceland and Travels in Sweden and Norway* (London and New York, 1852) and *A Lady's Voyage Round the World* (New York, 1852), translated from the German by Mrs. Percy Sinnett. See *Allgemeine deutsche Biographie,* XXV, 791–92, and *Webster's Biographical Dictionary,* 1174.

finally effected the conquest of the Islands towards the close of the 15th Century after an obstinate defence by the natives, styled Guanches.[52] The mummies of these aboriginals have been found in the caves in modern times in such a state of dissication as to weigh only 6 to 8 lbs. each.

The Canary bird is still a dweller of his native wilds in the Islands, but I have learned to my surprise that his natural plumage was and is a grey or brown, and that their present bright color is derived from frequent crossings. I have always imagined the reverse. The birds derive their name from the Islands. The name of the Islands is derived from the number of dogs found upon Palma at the time of their discovery.

It is now six o'clock and I have just been on deck to look at the Peak and the Isld of Tenerife, which though one hundred and thirty miles distant is distinctly visible, and if we had daylight might be seen several hours longer. The Peak is over 12,000 feet high, the height of three Mt. Washingtons above the level of the sea, and still another beneath it and is covered with snow. The sides of the mountain exhibit the five zones of cultivation. Our course is now towards the Cape de Verds, but Capt. A[bbot] is undecided whether to stop

[52] Guanches, Guanchis, or Cuanchos were the aboriginal natives of the Canary Islands, especially Tenerife, before the final Spanish conquest in 1495 by Alonzo de Lugo, under the sovereignty of Ferdinand and Isabella, and after the Treaty of Alcaçova, between Portugal and Castile, in 1479. See Friar Alonso de Espinola, 1594, *The Guanches of Tenerife, The Holy Image of Our Lady of Candelaria* (London, The Hakluyt Society, Second Series, Vol. XXI, 1907), translated by Clement Markham.

Jean de Béthencourt (*ca.* 1360–1422), a French explorer from Normandy, tried to conquer the Canary Islands in 1402, 1404, and 1406. Henry III of Castile gave him the title "King of the Canaries" under his suzerainty. He left the Canaries to his nephew, Maciot de Béthencourt, when he died at Grainville-la-Teinturière. His unreliable account has been translated into several languages.

The date 1334, and not 1330 as Preble mentioned it, belongs to the discovery of the Canaries by a French vessel. For a short bibliography, see the following: *Encyclopaedia Britannica*, Edition XI (1910), V, 174; *Grande Enciclopédia Portuguesa e Brasileira*, V. 687–88; and P. Bontier de J. de Verrier, *The Canarian, Or the Book of the Conquest and Conversion of the Canarians in the Year 1402, by Messire Jean de Bethencourt* (London, The Hakluyt Society, Vol. XLVI, 1874), translated by R. H. Major.

at any of that group or at Prince's Island. He says he will govern his movements as he finds the winds.

One month of the thirty of my absence has gone. God speed the others to their close, and reunite us in peace and happiness.

At Sea, Lat. 9.37 Long. 17.40 W. May 15, 1853

No event worthy of record has relieved the monotony of sky and water the past week and I have only to mark another milestone of time in my journal of absence. Fair winds, a smooth sea and pleasant weather have blessed our progress since we left Las Palmas.

By running your finger over the map of Africa you will find us today about 300 miles to the Westward of Sierra Leone, the grave of L.E.L. and full 1500 from Prince's Island, our anticipated destination.

The winds get daily lighter as we approach the line. We entered the Tropic of Cancer on the 10th and Old Sol makes himself felt. The thermometer today has been up to 90° and the pitch melts in the seams of the deck. I am now fairly embarked in my sealife and habits, excepting that I have abandoned smoking entirely as too expensive a habit to indulge in for the present. I have smoked but two segars since we left New York, and am astonished how little I miss the luxury.

Since leaving Palma our horizon has not included a single sail, and we passed the De Verdes[53] without sighting them. We have sailed 4500 miles since leaving N.Y., an average of 150 miles for every day at sea.

At Sea, May 22d, 1853. Lat. 20. Long. 15.31 W.

The past has been a week of calms and sweltering weather, and we are only 225 miles nearer our destination than we were last Sunday. One sail, a small schooner and plenty of Dolphins have been seen. A huge shark was cruising today in our wake, and Mother Carey's[54] chickens have been picking up crumbs of comfort under the ship's stern.

[53] Cabo Verde, or Cape Verde, is the westernmost point on the African coast. Adjacent are some small islands, which Preble apparently calls "De Verdes."

[54] Here Preble drew a parallel, using the name of Wilson's petrel (*Oceanites oceanicus,* Kuhl), or Mother Carey's chicken, also named long-legged storm petrel and common stormy petrel.

At Sea, May 29, Lat. 2.14.N. Long. 0°.24.W.

The calms and sultry weather was succeeded last Monday by drenching rains and squally weather with much lightning, which lasted until Thursday. Since then we have enjoyed cool and cloudy weather and a pleasant breeze which has brought us within 500 miles of Prince's Island.[55] This morning a brig showing Am. Colors passed us bound to the Wst. S. The Capt's son is failing rapidly and his death may take place at any moment. Since yesterday he has not left his cot. The Capt. told him of his approaching dissolution, and he received the information with the greatest calmness, only expressing a wish that he could see his mother once again. Since then he has noted in a little book how he wishes his effects to be disposed of and has arranged and labelled many of these mementos with his own hands. His father wished him to read some appropriate books, but he said no, they would only trouble him, his mind was made up and his opinion formed on those subjects, and his time was too short to convince or change him now. Though only sixteen, he seems old in thought, feelings and knowledge—a veritable Paul Dombey—whose expiring light, like the last flicker of a candle gleams the brightest.[56]

We are now three or more days sail from Prince's Island and as we are to wood and water there, are not likely to get away until towards the middle of June. You may calculate our arrival at Angjer Isld[57] of Java about the middle of August, and at Macao where we are to find our letters from home, a month later. Last Sunday when I wrote I was used up with three watches and the hot weather; a return to four watches, and the cool weather brought by the rains, has restored strength and amiability. I talk of cool weather although the ther-

[55] Prince Edward Island, together with near-by Marion Island, in the Indian Ocean, about 1,500 miles southeast of the Cape of Good Hope, belonged to the British sovereignty until 1948, when, on January 4, they were transferred to the Union of South Africa. They were discovered in January, 1772, by Marion du Fresne, a French navigator.

[56] Paul Dombey was a hero from the novel *Dombey and Son* (1848), by Charles Dickens. Paul Dombey, Sr., is a man of pride and strong nature but financially ruined and with family perplexities of a petty character.

[57] Anjier Lor, or Anjier, Java (Lat. 6° 2′ S.; Long. 105° 57′ E.). It was a port of call for many a clipper ship sailing from Boston to Canton and is known in the "Clipper Literature."

mometer has not been below 80° since the 13th. Yet it is cool on deck and in the air and breeze when the sun is clouded. At night in our rooms beneath two decks, the confined and heated air occasions disturbed slumbers. A few nights since, a mess mate waked me and told me not to hallo out so. I was dreaming in a confused way, either of committing a murder or of being the victim of one. My suffering was as intense as if real and I was thankful for having the vision dispelled.

It is wretched to think I have to wait five months before I can hear from you. This living upon remembrances of the past and anticipations of the future has too much in it of the hope that maketh the heart sick. Yet there is no doubt it adds to the pleasure we have when permitted to enjoy each other's embraces. It is Byron I believe in his *Corsair* who says, Nought can sanctify the joys of home, "Like hope's gay glance from ocean's troubled foam";[58] a singular statment from one who himself never enjoyed the delights of home.

Prince's Island, Sunday Afternoon, June 5, 1853

The Capt's son who was so ill when I last wrote died on Tuesday exactly at noon by the sun (as so often happens). His body has been encased in lead, so that it can at some future time be removed to the U.S. It is a providence he died before our arrival here where his remains can be quietly interred and where he has a brother on the station who can disinter them.

This is a most beautiful and picturesque Island. Its hills are thrown up in such fantastic shape it seem as if Dame Nature must have made it in a frolicsome mood. Hills rise up so abruptly a thousand feet or more you are ready to swear they were tossed up instantaneously, as a child throws up its ball, or a fountain spouts upward a jet of water, with this difference, these hills remain a congealise jet of stone—a fixed and solid fact. The whole Island as seen from our ship, with the exception of the perpendicular basaltic sides of some of the hills, is a mass of living green from its topmost summits to the very waters edge. A picture of living tropical luxuriance, while down

58 "Oh! What can sanctify the joys of home, / Like Hope's gay glance from Ocean's troubled foam," comes from Byron's *The Corsair*, Canto III, 565–66.

its precipitous hillsides glitter and flash numerous water falls for hundreds of feet. A great drawback to our enjoyment of its scenery has been the heavy and continual rain that has poured down since our arrival. In my experience I never have known so much water to fall in the same time, yet the Negros say it is not the wet season. I do not see how there could well be a wetter one. It has literally poured down in sheets of water for hours together for at least half the time, and has rained hard as they would say in the U.S. for the remainder. The windows of the heavens have been truly opened, so that we feel quite competent to judge of Father Noah's shower. We clewed[59] up our sails when we came in and let them hang from the royals[60] down as it was raining, and we have never seen a time to find them since. Occasionally to relieve them of the great weight we let go the headlines and clewlines and release the water that has collected in their folds and which comes down a deluging avalanche on deck. I doubt whether a ship of war ever laid at anchor so long with sails tossed before. Within ninety miles of the Equator the weather is warm and a pair of flannel trouwsers, a flannel shirt, a tarpaulin hat and coat sans shoes or stockings complete a very satisfactory and comfortable uniform for our watch keeping. The naked full dress of the natives is sensible and healthy, however shocking to the good taste and ideas of civilization and propriety.

The Island is small, being only ten miles long and we are told of a Portuguese town on the other side of it but here at West Bay, as our anchorage is called, probably because situated on the N.E. side of the Island, and as far as we can see, it is all as it fell from the hands of nature. Opposite our anchorage a Portuguese flag hangs over a delapidated stone wall and negro huts, dignified with the name of 'the Fort.' A Fort minus the guns. Near at hand too, it is the house and negro quarters of Madam Ferraise[61] whose settlement with the house of one 'Mafia' in the next cove, and one far distant on the hills,

59 "Clew up" means to draw the lower ends of sails to the upper yard or mast, ready for furling.

60 A royal is a sail immediately above the topgallant sail; the royals are skysails, ordinarily being the topmost sails.

61 Madam Ferraise was perhaps the owner of a brothel.

comprise all signs of human life and civilization within our view. The trees on shore are alive with troops of frolicsome and chattering monkeys, small and grey, and flocks of whistling and screaming parrots.

Prince's Island is only resorted to by the cruisers of the English, French and U.S. Squadrons on the coast of Africa for supplies of wood, water and refreshments. The wood is cut upon the mountains and brought down upon their backs by the negros for one cent a stick. Good water is abundant. Provisions and fruit we have found rather dearer than in more civilized places where the value of money is better understood, and change to be had. Most of the tropical fruits are found here in their seasons and we have at this season found and enjoyed—The Alligator Pear-Pineapples, Bananas, Plantations, the Sour Sop, Custard Apple Limas, Cocoa Nuts, Papaws Cocoa, Cucumbers and Green corn. Of course we have had to pay for them and the wretched half naked ragged negros have revelled in our money. Eggs—25 cts a dozen, chickens and Ducks 1$ each, and other things proportionate. Even the wood costs 10$ the cord.

We hope to resume our voyage in a day or two and are only waiting for our supply of wood, which has to be cut and brought down from the mountains and comes aboard slowly. As we do not expect to touch anywhere you may expect to receive my next letter from Angjer Isld of Java where with good luck we hope to rest ourselves in about sixty days. And you may hope for your next letter about November unless we meet a ship at sea and can send sooner.

At Sea, Sunday June 12th 1853

We sailed from West Bay last Tuesday and we are now only one hundred and fifty miles away from it, having had nothing but a continuance light, baffling and headwinds. We have had several good looks at the coast of Africa, and on Thursday saw a French Brig of War. On Friday we crossed the Equator without being visited by Neptune, but are still almost in hail of his special cruizing ground, being only forty-six miles South of that invisible line. The weather astonishes us—though immediately upon the Equator, the very name of which seems to give forth a scorching heat, yesterday and the day before were so cool, that we found our thick clothing comfortable all the day, and our pea jackets and overcoats indispensible to our night comfort.

After the weather is disposed of, one day at sea is like another in its occupations and amusements: that to journalize them would be monotonous. The Purser [R. T. Allison] and I have become inveterate chess players, and fight our ten or twelve mimic battles daily. Smoking for the present I have in motives of economy abandoned, except on Sunday when I limit myself to a single segar after dinner, which from my week's abstinence is all the more enjoyed.

At Sea, Sunday June 19th, 1853

We are today in the region and under the influence of the S.E. trades, two hundred and ninety miles distant from St. Helena where the Captain now proposes stopping, if the winds will allow us to do so, without much effort. I think he wants to send home notice of his son's death. The wind now surges us directly toward that island and our hopes and prayers are for its continuance. The week has been an uneventful one, and my time has been divided between routines of duty, chess with our purser, and the perusal of some odd and old numbers of the *London Quarterly Review.*[62]

I continue to like our Capt. who improves upon acquaintance—minding his own duties, and not interfering as is too often the case with the duties of those under him. He is a plain common sense New England man, making no pretensions of show or humbug. We all sympathize with him in the death of his son, whose loss is a living sorrow to him. A few years since he had an amiable and lovely daughter burnt to death. Five years ago today my dear Mother died. How time flies! His wings have certainly not been leaden.

St. Helena, Tuesday June 21st 1853

We arrived here very opportunely today for the ship *Lanark*[63]

[62] The *London Quarterly Review*, or *The London Review*, was founded in February, 1809, was widely read by educated English-speaking persons and was popular among American readers. See also *British Union-Catalogue of Periodicals*, III, 95.

[63] The brig *Lanark* was a British ship built in 1846 by Alexander Hall and Company to compete with the American opium clippers in China. *Clipper*, 59.

sails tonight for Boston and will take our letters. We also send by her Young Hamilton,[64] one of our Masters Mates, whose return home is recommended by our Surgeon. It is melancholy to think he leaves us to die, perhaps never to reach home again, as he is consumptive. He was placed on board by his father who hoped the voyage might recover him, but he has grown worse, and the Doctors have no hope for his life. We do not make a long stay here but will leave tomorrow or next day in persuance of our cruize.

At Sea, Sunday June 26th, 1853
Lat. 25.45 S. Long. 2.24 W.

The past has been quite an eventful week, and I find it pleasant to seat myself here for my weekly gossip and share its recollections with my darling. We were all very glad, when in consequence of our neighborhood to St. Helena,[65] and the wind pointing us directly towards it, and from some hints thrown out by myself, Capt. Abbott decided to anchor in the wadstream of the "Prison Isle."[66] It was really astonishing when the announcement was made how many before unthought of reasons were to urge our stopping, until it seems a neglect of duty to pass it bye. The Master wished to rate his chronometers by the Time Ball dropped from the Observatory each noon. The Surgeon required vaccine matter. The Ship wanted wood and water. A sick officer whose lungs were too delicate for the Cape weather should be sent home, and last though not least, an opportunity to send letters home would be afforded and there was every probability of our obtaining late news from the U.S.

So much for the reasons which were found to present with our inclinations. Moved by these considerations and the wind driving us

[64] W. S. Hambleton, acting master-mate on the *Macedonian,* apparently was not a regular navy officer, for he is not in the available standard lists of the U.S. Navy. Preble noted on his lists of the officers attached to the *Macedonian* that Hambleton "left St. Helena, and died on passage home."

[65] The island of St. Helena is situated in Lat. 15° 55′ S. and Long. 5° 46′ W., a distance of 1,200 miles from the Cape of Good Hope. Napoleon was taken there on the H.M.S. *Northumberland* on October 15, 1815.

[66] For the private life of Napoleon on St. Helena, see the still valuable book by B. E. O'Meara, Napoleon's surgeon, *Napoleon at St. Helena.*

in sight of the Island, we steered for the Port and on Tuesday noon anchored off Jamestown, and sailed again the following forenoon, in continuance of our cruize. We were fortunate in finding there the Ship *Lanark*, Capt. Knapp of Boston[67] and bound to that port. By her we sent our letters, and Mr. Hambleton the sick Officer. When we first anchored it was the Captain's intention to sail again in the evening, and I had duty to keep me aboard until 4 P.M. I had no hope of visiting the shore, and anticipated a lasting regret, at being so near, yet miss seeing the grave and prison of Napoleon, and that another might not have the same regret kept his watch from 4 to 1, to allow him ample time for the excursion. Fortunately the ship was detained until the next forenoon, so that at the expense of a few hours stolen from mornings sleep, after keeping a midnight watch I was able to make the excursion and at the most favorable hour, that of sunrise. I will tell you presently about it, but first, let me give you my impression of the Island—we approached it.

When I first went on deck Tuesday morning, a thin haze half obscured it, but as we approached from the Nth and Est, and the sun burst away the mist it appeared a huge high rugged and precipitous rock, rising from the ocean in gloomy rudeness—desolate grandeur and naked sterility, causing us to exclaim well may it be called "the barren and rocky island of St. Helena."

As we advanced, the prospect improved, the mountain assumed more varied hues and picturesque shapes, and their splintered summits wore even a verdant tint from a scanty vegetation which covered them, while the elevated plain about Longwood,[68] and the bright green of the valleys, here and there revealed a striking con-

[67] Previously, William Knapp was the captain of the *Hornet*, remembered for her race with the *Flying Cloud* between Sandy Hook and San Francisco in 1853. The voyage was made in 105 days, and the *Hornet* came in forty minutes ahead. C. C. Cutler, *The Story of the American Clipper Ship: Greyhounds of the Sea* (cited hereafter as *Greyhounds*), 253, 462, and *Clipper*, 59.

[68] Longwood, formerly the British governor's country seat at St. Helena, was given to Napoleon as his residence-prison. For his sympathies toward the exiled Napoleon, O'Meara was removed from St. Helena on July 25, 1818, sent to England, and summarily dismissed from service. O'Meara's antipathies for England made him a Liberal and a partisan of O'Connell. O'Meara, *op. cit.*, I, xxiii–xxv.

trast to the iron grey hue and dry furrows of the hills and mountains that descended to its rocky coasts. Jamestown[69] is so situated in a long and narrow valley, shut in between two steep mountains that we did not see it until we had nearly reached the anchorage. The points which jut out on each side forming the arms of its wadstream are strongly fortified.

These batteries, the Government House, the Church with its steeple surrounded and in part hid by trees, the slated houses, with their neat appearance and neutral colored walls and the rude and rough mountains, which form the framework—make a pleasing picture. At the head of the valley is seen 'The Briar's'—Napoleon's first residence[70] on the Island—easily recognized by one who has seen the numerous engravings of it. An Island more prisonlike in appearance than St. Helena cannot be imagined. It is a prison on a magnificent scale, worthy to cage an Emperor whose rifles at one time threatened to control the whole civilized world. A prison sitting solitary on mid-ocean walled and surrounded by thousands of miles of living waters—its iron-ribbed mountains a substitute of iron bars. The whole island is scarcely thirty miles in circumference and contains only 30,000 acres of land susceptible of cultivation—all else is barren rock and volcano debris. The present number of inhabitants on the Island is said to be 6,000—who are treated like exotics fed from the products of other lands, the island not being able to support half that number from its own resources. Frequent supplies are brought from the Cape Colony and elsewhere and there is a law which prohibits a man from killing his own ox, without permission first obtained from the Governor. The soldiers of the Garrison are supplied with salt rations as when embarked on board ship. Of water fortunately there is plenty. It tumbles, of the purest quality, down the mountain sides and is conveyed through pipes to the shore where it is taken in boats, purposely constructed, to the shipping. Provisions of all kinds are of course very high and ships with difficulty get supplied.

[69] Jamestown is the only city on the island and is the port and capital of St. Helena. It is surrounded by the precipices Rupert's Hill and Ladder Hill.

[70] Briar, an estate located about one and one-half miles from Jamestawn, belonged to Mr. Balcombe, an English resident of St. Helena. O'Meara, *op. cit.*, I, 8–10.

When our officers returned from the shore exhilarated by their rides, and visit to Longwood, it was late in the evening and it was ascertained the ship could not sail before nine the next morning so with sudden resolve it was agreed by the 1st Lieut. and myself to rise at early daybreak and go on shore, trusting to obtain horses to take us to Longwood, see what was to be seen, visit the vacant tomb, and return to the ship before the hour assigned for her departure. In persuance of this resolve we left the ship at half past five the next morning after having fortified ourselves with a cup of coffee, and on reaching the shore readily found the horses, and were mounted and off before daybreak. It was my third attempt at equestrian performance—and my first within eight years—my latest ride having been at Saldanha Bay[71] and my only other performances on the occasion of my visiting Lady Hester Stanhope,[72] the holy city of Jerusalem, and the classic city and suburbs of Athens. My skill is reserved for great occasions.

Having but scant time and a full six miles before us we started off at a brisk trot, Avery leading and I bouncing, jolting and rolling in the rear. My horse seemed to know the inexperience of the rider, and required the aid of frequent whippings to urge him on. The jolting I got was awful. The road from Jamestown winds up by inclined planes the hills on the left of the singular and beautiful valley through which the town is prolonged, and as we ascended, and the day broke, we had a fine bird's eye view of the whole town, bay and shipping. As we proceeded ascending hill after hill around which the road wound, new and striking scenes opened at every moment. Now looking down upon the calm and majestic skybound ocean, with the clouds below us tossed upon its surface and anon the view was broken

[71] Saldanha Bay is an inlet on the southwestern coast of South Africa, 63 miles from Cape Town. With the growth of Cape Town, it was rarely visited.

[72] Lady Hester Lucy Stanhope (1776–1839), an English eccentric, was the eldest daughter of Charles, third Earl Stanhope. William Pitt was her uncle. After an original, often daring life in Pitt's household and various encounters on her wanderings in the Levant, as well as a rich social life there, she died in misery on Mount Lebanon on June 23, 1839. For more detailed information and a bibliography, see *Dictionary of National Biography* (cited hereafter as *DNB*), XVIII, 899–901.

by the grandly sterile hills, evidently the result of a frightful struggle of nature—their only clothing a few straggling pines bent down limestone direction by the constant force of the trade wind, while in the sheltering valley was seen a most beautiful oasis of trees and flowers, the result of the uniform climate and more beautiful and lovely in contrast with their surrounding, dreary, parched and stony arid eminence. Just as the sun appears more bright when emerging from a cloud, or a smile is more bright and beautiful when the offspring of a tear. We observed the tomb shaded by its willows in the valley on our right, but deferred our visit to it until our return from Longwood, wishing to reach the latter by sunrise. Continuing on therefore, we had the satisfaction of seeing his glorious orb emerge from his ocean bath, and gild the reposing clouds beneath as we descended from the last hill that brought us to the gate leading to the exile's island residence. Longwood is 1762 feet above the sea, but being lower than the surrounding hills, its view is circumscribed by them, though glimpses of an ocean horizon are here and there to be seen. To the right of the house extends a long and level plain overlooking the sea and scantily covered with trees, which gives the name to the estate. It was towards its seabound extremity that Napoleon extended his morning rambles, and looking out upon the sea, which said to him "this far shall thou go and no farther," was used to stand and meditate.

So old, shabby and delapidated was the building at which we dismounted, that we could not realize it had ever been the residence of the once mighty Napoleon. The pencilings upon the lentils of the door and the 2 shillings demanded from us by the ragged boy who acted as janitor, and showed us a board on which was a tariff of prices of admission soon convinced us we had reached the object of our excursion and John Bull was as ready to turn an honest penny as any Yankee.

In a few minutes a respectably dressed female came along to show us the place and receive the shillings, without which 'open sesame' our ride was naught. Having paid 'the consideration' we were permitted to enter the old house in which for near six years the Captive Emperor resided and where he died.[73] The new house was not com-

[73] Madame Bertrand was the wife of General Comte Henri Gratien Bertrand.

pleted until after his death. The old house is now a farm building. The first room we entered would be the hall or entry way with us but was used by the Emperor as a billiard room, but at the time of our visit contained a few agricultural impliments and heaps of straw and litter. The next room entered from it, was his drawing room and dining room, and is the size of our little talk parlor, and lighted by two windows; like the entrance hall it was filthy and barnlike, and contained some rakes, cornshellers and other agricultural machines. The plastering broken from the walls and in a wretched state of delapidation showed the beams. It was in this room that the great Napoleon died. Here his spirit passed away in the midst of a tempest —while his fleeing visions placed him again at the head of his armies. His head reclined against one of the windows, and the stone against which it rested has been piously taken away by the French. The next room is somewhat larger. I should say about the size of our front parlor—this was his bed chamber, and is now a stable for horses. The windows have been walled up and a pavement supplies the place of the removed flooring. The kitchen is in a similar state of delapidation and the whole house has been desecrated to the various uses of a farm yard. The Emperor's fish pond in close contiguity to the house is about the diameter of a generous rain water cistern, but not so deep or capacious. The whole aspect of the place attests the truth of the poet, "Great Caesar dead and turned to clay stop a hole to keep the wind away."[74] A portion of the building has been torn down, and across the yard we saw another delapidated building, which the woman told us was that occupied by O'Meara, his physician.[75] We asked her what the Frenchman said to all this desolation: "Oh," she replied, "Some cry and some swear"—tears and curses from them I think are quite excusable. From the old house, after pencilling our names on the walls, we bent our steps to the new which is a handsome frame building, plastered on the outside and large enough to have accommodated the Emperor and his adherents had it been finished. It is now

[74] William Shakespeare, *Hamlet,* Act V, scene 1: "Imperious Caesar, dead and turn'd to clay, / Might stop a hole to keep the wind away."

[75] Barry Edward O'Meara was born in Ireland in 1778 and served in the British navy as assistant surgeon. In 1815, he sailed on the *Northumberland* to St. Helena, where he was Napoleon's personal physician. O'Meara, *op. cit.*, I, 7–9.

barren of everything, except a few ragged curtains, and we were told has never been occupied unless by officers of the garrison. The bathing tub used by the emperor has been removed to it and is the only thing that connects him at all with the place. Another open sesame judiciously applied enabled us to refresh ourselves in the emperor's bath. Close at hand to the new house is the cottage that was occupied by Gen. Bertrand, surrounding which there is a pretty shrubbery and several flower beds planted by the Gen's Lady;[76] from the one we cut a cane and from the other gathered bouquets, and having seen all that there was to be seen remounted to return after and further payment of shillings to the boy who held our horses. Quitting the main road on our return we descended a beautiful valley to the Emperor's tomb, which is about a mile and a half from Longwood. There we found an old talkative negro and his wife to show us the place, and another tariff board stating admittance to the show was to be had for 1/6th. With the old negro we descended into the empty vault or pit, which is about twelve feet deep, and stood upon the spot where had rested the coffins (for he was buried in four). Here we procured a bit of the lime stone wall that surrounded the coffins and a slip of willows which overhangs the tomb (the latter I intend for a penhandle), a sprig of cypress, a bunch of flowers from shrubs planted by Madam Bertrand and a cane from the shrub nearest the grave—also a bottle of water from a spring close at hand, which was dug out at the request of Napoleon, who preferred the water to any other and had it conveyed daily to Longwood for his use. It is clear and limpid and I drank a tumbler full on the spot, and pronounced the Emperor's judgment excellent. The sight of the tomb was selected by Napoleon, and was daily his favorite resort accompanied by a guard. The old woman told us he fell asleep one day over his book, and dreamed that Josephine appeared to him, and promised to visit him in his grave if he chose that spot—a very natural legend to grow out of his preference for it. The old negro was eloquent as to the disposition of the body—the oft told tale run glibly from his tongue. "His head was placed to East," said he "likewise his feet to West, etc, and his cocked hat lay across his breast."

[76] Madame Bertrand was the wife of General Comte Henri Gratien Bertrand (1773–1844), who attended Napoleon at St. Helena. O'Meara, *op. cit.*, I, lxxix–xc.

On leaving the grave we returned to Jamestown with all convenient haste, and reached the ship at 9, well contented at having accomplished so interesting and pleasant an excursion. I will say nothing of my being thrown by my vicious horse as I was remounting him at Longwood, the only inconvenience from which was a bruise. On our ride to Longwood—a stout boy asked us if we wanted any lads like him on board. Avery told him yes, but he must be on hand to go aboard at 9 o'clock, as we sailed at ten—and sure enough—we found him at the landing waiting for us bundle in hand, and he is now with us and a hindrance.

Finding there was still an hour or two before the ship sailing, I went on shore again to look at the town, and breakfasted at our consul's, and was introduced to his daughter just returned from a visit to Boston, and full of what she saw and enjoyed there.

At noon our ship was underway, and at sundown we had the body of the island in sight astern, and some thirty miles to the North. The *Lanark* sailing with us was probably as far from it in the opposite direction with our letters.

Tonight (21st) we have been admiring what all acknowledge to be the most beautiful sunset they have ever witnessed. First, the sky was of a most beautiful and serene blue, and resting on it thousands of fleecy white clouds; as the sun went down, the blue changed cameleon like to the most beautiful and delicate purple-violet and rose blush hues while the little fleecy clouds changed to all imaginable colors from deep purple to a brilliant red, with their edges tinged and tipped with gold. The sight brought on deck all hands both officers and men. And we stood as it were spell bound watching and admiring it for nearly two hours until the veil of night shut it from our sight. It was beyond description beautiful—serenely beautiful and grandly sublime. Throughout the day, Cape Pigeons, Cape Hens, and albatrosse have been hovering about the ship, no new sight to me but were seen for the first time by the Captain and several of the officers, myself and the Master being the only officers who have been around the world, or made a cruize to the East Indies. I believe I am the oldest Lieut. in the wardroom, both my seniors in rank being a year my junior in age. The Surgeon and marine officer in the mess count more years than I do. The junior Lieut.

Winder is however white headed and would be thought much older, his hair having been changed by sickness. We are a very harmonious duet and I hope may so continue to the end. It is difficult to coop together in almost the close communion of man and wife eight men of various tastes and intellects without some jangling.

At Sea, Lat. 31.44 Long 6.486, Sunday July 3d, 1853

Rolling in the calm that follows a storm and sighing for that "soft and gentle breeze"—that was "the fair one's cry" having had enough and more than enough of the "snorting gales and white waves heaving high." A revolution has occurred in our mess—the cook and steward condemned for incompetency, and suspected of dishonesty have been deposed and John Agni, a Chinese, and pantry boy has been promoted to the cook's place, and the Ship's cook assistant one Mason, a black, shines *pro temp* as Steward. From time to time, when the ship was arriving at or leaving port, silver forks and spoons have been missing and though suspicions of theft were entertained, still their loss might be from carelessness, but when on leaving St. Helena two silver watches were missing from the Master's room, there could be no doubt a thief was about and as the steward is was ascertained spent money on shore he could not account for having, suspicion fell on him; and it was soon discovered that he and the cook were carrying on a lucrative business in selling coffee to the men, we concluded to dismiss both, and trust to luck and the boys. In the joint labors of Agni and Mason we have found a very good substitute for the Sicilian and the Portuguese messes of our ex-rascals—besides a saving of 30$ a month we paid them extra for supposed but undiscovered merits.

The evening following this mess revolution, while sailing along with a fine increasing breeze, and rejoicing in our pleasant prospects, we were struck by a heavy squall, which parted the main brace and brought our main yard in two pieces on deck. When you are informed our main yard is ninety feet in length and five and a half feet in circumference or 22 inches in diameter, and a tough yellow pine stick, you can imagine the great force the wind must have exerted to break it squarely in two pieces; after this accident the wind gradually freshened to a SW gale, with frequent squalls of rain and hail which continued until yesterday, since when we have been rolling in this calm. All this time until last evening when they got it aloft again, the carpenters have been employed in fixing the main yard and rendering it serviceable—no mean job to work at in a gale of wind.

To my personal discomfort just previous to the accident I had obtained the services of the carpenters, to make some improvements in my little room and had succeeded in having everything pulled to pieces in order to a reconstruction when they were called off to this more important work, leaving me and my surroundings in admirable confusion. The weather grows cool and the days shorten as we advance to southern latitudes. By your next spring we will have seen three consecutive winters: the one last past with you, our present winter here, and the next northern winter in China. I often wish myself where my heart is, but have not lost faith in my motto whatever is, is best, and shall endeavor to do my duty—trusting that a kind, protecting providence is reserving me for better times and happier hours.

At Sea, Lat. 38.30 S. Long. 22.30 E.
Sunday, July 19, 1853

Today we are to the Sth of the Cape of Good Hope or of 'Storms,' as at first more rightly named, and are enjoying (?) true 'Cape' weather—that is scudding under close reefs before a SW gale which since last evening has been hurrying us—12 knots an hour towards our destination. With the wind we are having the usual high sea at home in this region, and are rolled and tossed about until our very bones ache. The squalls that hurry over, increasing the intensity of the wind, are accompanied by heavy rains, so there is no comfort on deck or below and the wardroom is all afloat—from the sea that is jerked in at every plunge through the rudder casing. There is nothing like 'still life' on board. I write with my chair lashed, feet well braced, candlestick tied up, and ink and paper convulsively grasped in one hand, while my pen resting at each successive roll, is guided in the other by jerks. Last Sunday we were rolling and slatting our sails out in a calm. Since then the wind has performed the circuit of the compass—and we have had every variety of weather. The weather has been coolish, but not uncomfortably so, the therm[ometer] averaging 56°—rather cooler than your July I fancy. The albatross and Cape pigeons are our constant companions, and increase in numbers about us daily. Their motions are watched with the usual interest, and our youngsters have been making unsuccessful efforts to catch them.

Our mess is reduced to primitive feeding. Our standing dish that portion of the hog named after Noah's second son, probably because it was his favorite ration when adrift in the Ark. A cup of coffee in hand, and a corn dogger in these piping times, we consider ourselves lucky to get down our throats without accident to our dress or the deck.

At Sea, Lat. 37.30. S. Long. 53°. E.
Sunday July 17, 1853

We have had a continuation of the weather described last Sunday, only worse and more of it. Yesterday it blew harder and there was a heavier sea on than I remember ever to have seen, and we hope the gale reached its climax. Scudding as we were before the wind full fourteen miles an hour, it was fearful to hear its howl through the rigging and to witness the force with which it struck our top sail. The whole ocean was streaked into a white foam, and the wave crests were blown away like smoke. It still blows heavily, but we have made a little more sail, and our spirits go up with barometer, which is on the rise, and we hope for a better time coming. This gale is one you read of in books, but seldom meet with in a sea experience. Our ward-room has been ankle deep the whole week from the leak around the rudder casing, and sleep has been well nigh an impossibility. Yesterday we had frequent squalls of hail—the stones, larger than buck-shot, cut like knives.

On Wednesday we spotted the Am. Ship *Versailles* 72 days from Boston bound to Australia.[77] It was blowing too hard to send a boat or we might have got news eighteen days later than any we had on board. We passed her very rapidly, and in two hours she was hull down astern.

[77] The *Versailles,* Captain Frost, left Boston for Shanghai on June 25, 1852. *Greyhounds,* 469.

At Sea, Lat. 37.55. S. Long. 80.40 E.
Sunday July 24, 1853

With the exception of one day of pleasant shine, the past week has been but a continuation of the discomforts of the two preceding it. Last night we passed between the Islands of St. Pauls and Amsterdam without seeing them and are rejoicing that hauling to the Nth we shall soon find better weather. Since last night at sundown a furious gale has been chasing us right astern, to which we can show but little sail, and the sea being more mountainous than ever, we are proportionately wet and uncomfortable. We have not set a regular table, excepting once or twice for three weeks, but have breakfasted, dined and supped, as best we could in our own rooms.

At Sea, Lat. 21.S. Long 103.E.
Sunday July 31, 1853

It is pleasant to get once more into a mild climate and to enjoy the genial sunshine. Next Sunday I hope to write from Java Head—as we are fanning along through the trade winds. All the anti-tropical birds, with the exception of a few Cape pigeons, who still linger in our wake, have left us. With the good weather the purser and I have resumed our game of chess and all are fast forgetting the rough experiences of the last three weeks. Our thoughts now turn to our arrival at Canton, and anticipations of our letters. We are now less than 1000 miles from Anjiers, but about 2400 from Canton, and have sailed some 15 to 16,000 miles since we left New York—which is equal to 140 miles of travel for every day of absence. In the last month our average has been over 200 miles a day—certainly not slow travelling. This nomad life is not at all suited to my domestic tastes. I feel a growing desire to fulfill my phrenological developments, which a Phrenologist once told me would "prevent my ever leaving home on any long journey."

Indian Ocean, Lat. 18.S. Long. 104.E.
Monday August 1, 1853

This, your birthday, my dear Susie, induces me to add another few lines to your letter by way of remembrance. I have been endeavoring to recollect whether I have ever been at home on this anniversary[78] since we first met in 1835 and can remember only two occasions, viz., the year of our engagement, 1841, and the year we commenced housekeeping in 1847. This shows I have not had a year of uninterrupted home comfort since I entered the Navy. In 1836, 7 and 8 I was on board the Frigate *U[nited] S[tates]* in the Mediterranean. In 1839 and 40, attached to the W. India Squadron. In 1841 just happily through my examination as a Mid, I was at home—but after settling my fortune in your smiles left before the month was out to participate in the Florida War. In 1842, on board the Brig *Jefferson*[79] in Florida. In 1843, 4 and 5 on board Sloop *St. Louis* in the East Indies. In 1846 on board Schr. *Petrel.*[80] Mexican War, 1847, at home and sick. In 1848 on board Sloop *Saratoga*[81] in the W. Indies. In 1849 on board *Legree* surveying the Chesapeak. In 1850 on Long Island, Seagrist Shore, attached to the surveying Sch. *Nautilus.*[82] In 1851 on board the frigate *St. Lawrence* to world's fair and Lisbon. In 1852 commanding Schr. *Gallatin*[83] on the Coast Survey, and today here—an epitome of eighteen years' chequered existence. "All's well that ends well." "There's a sweet little cherub that sits up aloft and looks out for the life of poor Jack."

Anjer's Roads, Isld of Java,
Sunday Augt. 7, 1853

We arrived here yesterday in 44 days from St. Helena, a distance of 6355 miles and all things considered a good passage. We are to sail again tomorrow, that is if 14000 fath. of water and 10 cords of

[78] For the date of Preble's service in the U. S. Navy, see the biographical sketch in this volume.

[79] In the *General Navy Register* it is said that the *Jefferson* had eighteen guns and was built in 1814 but in 1821 was sold, "or broken up, or unfit for repair."

[80] On May 30, 1846, Preble was ordered to join the schooner*Petrel,* 74 tons, one gun (twenty-four pounds), on which he was acting master; being invalidated, he left her on May 31, 1847. See *Sketch,* 205, and *A Naval Encyclopoedia,* 662.

[81] The U.S.S. *Saratoga,* 1,025 tons, four guns, built in 1842, was given to the Public Marine School, Philadelphia.

[82] The schooner *Nautilus* is not in the *List;* she might have been rented from a private company.

[83] The schooner *Gallatin* was used for the coast survey. Preble served on her.

wood can be procured today. We find here three Am[erican] Whaling vessels, but to our great disappointment no opportunity for forwarding the letters we have penned on the passage; the weather is too hot for writing here—my thoughts stick perspiringly, hinder my pen, as the sweat pours from my brows.

Straits of Sunda, Tuesday Augt. 9, 1853

We commenced our voyage to China this morning, the tenth anniversary of my appointment as an acting Lieut. on board the *St. Louis* when bound on a similar cruise. While at Anjier I was on shore three times and took several pleasant strolls along the shore and rural walks in the neighborhood with our purser. His tastes and domestic attachments assimilate more nearly with mine, than any other of my messmates. We saw several novel things the others I am sure did not. The village of Anjer is, to my mind, quite prettily laid out, its principal streets crossing each other at right angles; and there is a small but neat fortification, which is garrisoned by a company of soldiers. In public buildings are a Mosque without a minaret and a market. Its most interesting feature is an immense Banian Tree, near the Fort, which shades the landing and from the top of which is displayed the Dutch flag. The boat landing is in a canal, which runs by the rear of the Fort, and appears to be an extension of a mountain stream. Excepting the Military Comdt and the Capt of the Port, who is an officer of the Netherlands Navy, the inhabitants are Malays or Chinese. Their dwellings are of a frame work of bamboo, covered with a matting, or the braided leaves of the plantation or banana. The houses of a few of the well-to-do people are made of brick, with covered portiers both front and rear supported by four brick pillars. Thus constructed and stuccoed and white washed as many are, they have a neat and tasty appearance. All are one storied —and those we entered had the thatched roofs concealed by a neat figure matting, which served to keep the apartment cool, and prevented the dust from shaking down. The windows are unglazed and have solid wooden shutters. The floors are of brick or earth. A house generally consists of one principal room and a bed room, and the roof is extended over the walls to cover and shelter the porticos. In the rear of the house are detached buildings for kitchen, stables and other domestic purposes. Wm Penn[84] our "comprador" said his house was "A No. 1" and that he was not ashamed to invite us to it —and for want of a tavern to go to, we availed ourselves of his no doubt selfish hospitality. Penn is blessed with two wives which but for their betal stained teeth might have been handsome, but being as they were, we did not break the 10th Commandment.[85] His portico was furnished with three round tables of teak wood which he told us he bought number one cheap at an auction and the principal room was ornamented with six looking glasses, two Yankee clocks, a settee, several arm chairs, a large round table, a side board and many minor accessories of use or ornament. In honor of our arrival Penn shone out in a coat ornamented with Am. Navy buttons and I believe he considered himself as our representative at Anjier.

To the left of the village there is a beautiful and extensive grove of Cocoa nut trees, which extends for more than a mile along the beach. The trees are in rows at regular intervals, and there being no undergrowth this grove furnishes a most agreeable, cool, and shady walk. For a three cent piece a native was persuaded to climb a tree and throw us down a green cocoa nut, the cool sweet milk of which, so grateful and refreshing in a hot climate, can only be appreciated by those who have enjoyed the luxury. To the right and left of the village, and in front, winds the main road to Batavia, and which extends the whole length of the island—a distance of eight hundred miles. Its construction is said to have been at the expension of the lives of twelve thousand natives. It is a broad and smooth carriage road fenced on each side by a mound of earth, planted on top at an equal distance with a small shrub tree that gives it a pleasant perspective. Scattered along its island side at both extremes of the main village of Anjier are numerous rural Malay villages—each consisting of a single street of such houses—having a gateway at each extremity and path ways leading into the main road. Whenever we

[84] William Penn, unknown; but there was in Batavia, Java, a William Fitz Paine (1783–1834), who was unmarried. Marriage was sometimes rather complex in the South Seas. A man might have children by several wives living in the same household. R. B. Forbes, *Personal Reminiscences*, 335.

[85] The Tenth Commandment: "Thou shalt not covet thy neighbor's goods."

approached or entered one of these villages it appeared at once deserted except by its canine inhabitants, who literally 'dogged' our heels and with furious barkings escorted us from gateway to gateway. The women left their spinning and weaving and other household employments in haste and retiring to their dwellings, shut the doors in our face. The men were perhaps away at their labor in the fields. In the same way, when crossing the fields, the women fled at our approach like startled deer, and even the Buffalos seemed to partake of their terror, for as they snuffed our coming, they would rush around and around their tethers until they broke loose from them, and then scamper away, stopping occasionally at safe distances and look back and point their heads at us, and then away again. Towards a Malay, they exhibited no such terror. It was evident our smell and appearance was not to their brute taste. The houses of these rural communities had such a small garden or breder in their front, and along the street was a row of sugar cane. In the village of Anjer, though it was scarce a quarter of a mile dist. from the nearest of these villages, we did not seem to disturb the women, but were permitted to see them at their daily avocations without interrupting them.

On our first visit to the shore, we were attracted by the sound of discordant and monotonous music, and turned into a bye street to ascertain what it means and whence it proceeded. We soon came to where a dozen or more Malays were beating upon a rude kind of tambourine, and accompanying it by singing in a yar-yar-yar manner, something we could not pretend to understand. Over the way, on the opposite side of the alley a company of both sexes and all ages was assembled at a feast given as we afterwards were informed by a man and woman on his recovery from a sickness The feast was chiefly of rice, tea and fruit. We were civilly invited to a seat, when a cup of tea and some bananas were placed before us. We, of course, to avoid offence partook of this simple hospitality and then shaking hands with our entertainers, bade them good day and resumed our rambles, which we extended a long way up the beach in search of red coral and shells, and returned over the fields gathering flowers and seeds until the hour and our appetites informed us it was dinner time on board.

The next day the Purser and I were again on shore, and attracted as before by the sound of music, were fortunate in being the spectators of a curious wedding. The music today was of a better and more varied sort, for besides tambourines and single headed drums, there was several performers upon instruments resembling those glass harmonicons on which strips of glass suspended on tapes are struck with a cork hammer. This Malay harmonicon was of stouter make, of metal, and the strips or keys 8 to 10 in number were suspended on springs, and after being struck by the hammer their vibration was checked or stopped as required by the left hand of the performer.

When we first became observers of this ceremony, having no idea of what might have preceeded our arrival, the Groom and his Bride were seated on the same mat facing each other, their heads meekly bent down, and their hands carelessly clasped in front, with those parts of their persons that were unclad, viz., face, neck, arms, etc., painted with red, green and white spots—very much as our cook ornaments a ham with dabs of red and black pepper and salt. Two old women were busy in twisting up into knots behind, the long, flowing black hair of this Malayan Adonis and Venus. This done, using some dirty looking water from a vessel at their side, they with other friends proceeded to wash the face, arms and breast, etc. of the presumed happy pair. Having rubbed and scrubbed until spite of anticipated happiness, many wry faces were made by our friends at this rough usage. They ended this part of the ceremony with a copious flood of water over both. This washed away all vestige of the painting, but left I noticed a red mark upon their flesh, where it had inflamed it. Thus cleansed and washed the couple stood up, with bended heads and folded hands, their long and glossy black hair falling loose upon their shoulders. They were then wrapped and enclosed in a sheet or cloth of coarse fabric, presented by the two old women officiating, with water from cocoa nut ladles, of which each drank, first from the one and then from the other ladle, and the bride squirted the water from her mouth into the bridegroom's face, which caused a great laugh among the spectators. Whether it was done in spite, fun, or was part of the ceremony, I had no means of ascertaining. The groom, happy man that he was, took it in good part and smiled as he wiped away the joke, or insult. A young woman now stepped forward and removed the bridegroom's wet trowsers. He, quite modestly, holding his loose wet robe about his loins, while she helped him on with a dry pair of green color. Some changes from wet to dry clothing were at the same time made by another assistant in the dress of the bride—after which both squatted cross-legged upon the mat, still enclosed in the same sheet. The old woman brought some rice and both partook from the same dish—while more of the same article was sprinkled upon their shoulders, the old woman muttering all the time what we supposed a prayer, and a group of younglings, which might be their brothers and sisters, standing around. The cloth was now removed, and the young bride's hair was again twisted up and decorated with ribbon and flowers and at the same time some gay clothing placed around her. On the head of the bridegroom was set a flat-topped paper cap, and the bride's forehead smeared with white paint. At this point of the ceremony the old women commenced throwing water at and over each other and then sprinkled the byestanders amid shouts of laughter until the water in their vessel was exhausted. The Purser and I did not entirely escape, though he sheltered himself behind a gilded screen, and I fled ingloriously up the alley. The contracting parties next stood up and accompanied by their friends and followed by the two old women, who sprinkled rice over their shoulders, moved across the enclosure, to the portico of a neighboring mat house (their future residence) and again seated themselves side by side on the platform. A young woman now wrapped a shawl around the bridegroom, and stuck a handsome kris or Malay knife between its folds—another at the same time redecorated the bride twineing more ribbons in her hair and placing a silver bracelet upon her wrist, removing all the flowers and ribbons with which she had previously been adorned. Learning on inquiry that the remaining ceremonies would last two hours, and included a feast to which we were not invited, and after it the happy pair would retire to their private enjoyment, we took our leave at this stage of the proceedings, and resumed our rambles after shells and flowers. One of the old women asked us if we would not like to take a wife—pointing to a bevy of perhaps not unwilling damsels. We made her to understand we were both already blest with such encumbrance and shook our heads in a most decided negative. No priest seemed to have a part in this Malayan ceremony nor did we see any male except the bridegroom assisting at it. The little boys about Anjier are usually in a natural full dress, and the little girls are clad all the same excepting that occasionally you see one with a silver shield fastened by chains covering those parts that our civilized delicacy forbids should be seen. The women about Anjier keep their breasts covered, otherwise men and women dress so alike it is difficult to distinguish the sexes. The children are bright sturdy little bipeds without dress or feathers, and show remarkably white teeth. The teeth of all adults are much disfigured by the universal custom of chewing the betal nut and leaf—which stains them and gives a black and decayed look. The Mosque which we visited has four plain walls with looped holes for windows and had no adornments. A pulpit faced the entrance and over it were some Arabic inscriptions. It had a thatched roof and earthen floor—but the latter was spread with mats. On each side of the doorway there was an elongated drum which the Doctor[86] said "would be hard to beat" as the heads were shoved in. At the time of our visit the Mosque contained but two worshippers—a man and a woman who were bowing their heads to the ground, and with great earnestness going through all the genuflexions of Mohammedan worship.

In front of this Mosque there was a stone tank of dirty water where all the worshippers put off their shoes and bathed their feet before entering the sacred enclosure, and in the rear of the Temple was a small burial place. The Market of Anjer is held under a series of mat sheds, and is well supplied with preparations of the betal and rice, and fruit and vegetables, but we did not see any meats. The fish market, contiguous, was well furnished and in variety.

Coming from a forty-four day sea voyage, and a prolonged diet of ham, we were well prepared to enjoy the fruit and poultry for which Anjer is ever famous. Hectameters of chickens have been sacrificed to our insatiable appetites since our arrival, and from the cackling and crowing about our decks now [that] we are at sea, it requires but little imagination to suppose oneself near a farm yard. Another mess revolution has installed Dr. W[oodworth] as our caterer, whom we hope will both feed us better and more econom-

[86] Surgeon of the *Macedonian* was Robert Woodworth, see note 27 above.

ically than our last—a goodly supply of Ducks, Pigs, Turtles, Chickens, sweet and irish potatoes, oranges, pumettas, cocoa nuts and bananas, gives us this hope.

The Straits of Sunda,[87] through which we are beating, separates the Islands of Java and Sumatra, and the Indian Ocean from the Java Sea. They have some very peculiar land about them. Crackatoa Point rises a smooth cone from the water. Two little islands have appropriately the names of "the Cap" and "the Button." Another Island directly in the center of the straits has the equally appropriate name of Thwart-the-Way. Many years ago a cousin of mine, Chas. Preble,[88] a brother of Mrs. Nonnely and Mrs. Avery,[89] was drowned in these straits by the capsizing of the Brig on board of which he was, when all on board perished.

China Sea, Lat. 1.30.S. Long. 107.15.E.
Sunday August 14, 1853

After beating about in the Java Sea since Tuesday, bothered by shoals, headwinds, squalls and calms—often anchoring from one or the other or all of these vexations—we passed through the Straits of Gaspar last evening and, Java Sea and those straits astern, entered upon the China Sea this morning. As we are only 1800 miles from Macao, we hope to get there in ten or twelve days—I say only 1800 miles because the distance is but the tithe of the eighteen thousand we have already accomplished. We are now fluttering between winter and summer, expecting to cross the Equator for the second time tonight. The day has been warm, clouded and showery like many a summer day at home, but though the thermometer stands at 83° in the shade, the air is cool and refreshing. A smooth Sea has enabled us to keep open air so that a fine breeze has ventilated our little cabins, and enables us to use them with comfort. The North Star will soon

[87] Soenda (or Sunda) Strait, between Java and Sumatra, is fourteen miles wide at its narrowest part.

[88] In the *Sketch*, 312–13, Preble gives his name as the son of John Preble (1771–1870) of Machias, Maine, and Esther Collins. He was born on July 12, 1809, and married Sophronia Merrill on September 21, 1835. There is no indication of the date of his death.

[89] Mrs. Nonnely and Mrs. Avery are not mentioned in the *Sketch*.

again be shining over both of us—a connecting link with those we have left behind us, whose reappearance we shall gladly hail.

China Sea, Friday Augt. 19, 1853

I may call this anniversary, dear Susie, our good Friday, since on this day twelve years ago we happily became conscious of each other's love, though no words were then spoken, in the woods at Gorham. Then were revived in my breast hopes that had long fluttered between doubt and fear. Our walk and silent talk by the mill stream can never be forgotten.

Today we have been making a glorious run, and are in Lat. 10° N. between 7 and 800 miles from Macao—about 9 A.M. which is about your 8:30 P.M. we sighted a singular little island called Lapata from its shoe-shape and passed within half a mile of it. When first seen from the Nth it looked like a square rock or cube of stone, but as we approached and passed its Eastern side, the cube lengthened out into not a bad resemblance of a lady's slipper.

A few miles from it are two remarkable lumps of rock and earth called the 'Catroichs'—one of which resembled a fortress perched on a round hill. All these rocks are the homes of myriads of birds, and the recess of their cliffs was alive with them. The nests of the esoulent swallow, so esteemed by the Chinese, are found among them, and we saw several of those tiny architects. While admiring these bold little islands—front works to the mainland, pushed out into the ocean—our purser was unsentimental enough to wish he had the guano they contain, on the farm he has not yet bought, but which it is his daydream to purchase at the end of our cruise.

China Sea, Sunday Augt. 21, 1853
Lat.15.50.N. Long. 113.40.E.

With the sun nearly vertical we have luxuriated in a fair wind and smooth sea which has driven us 200 miles a day on our course, so that at noon today we were only 400 miles from Macao and got soundings to confirm our position on Maceles Field Bank in twelve fathoms of water. Our lead brought up a sizable piece of Coral from the bottom. Anticipating a continuance of the good weather and favoring winds, we hope to anchor at Macao on the 24th, so that I have pleasant thoughts of reading your letters on the 25th, so peculiarly our anniversary, when the doubts and fears and hopes of the 19th were made a happy certainty. It is 136 days today since I said good bye—and I have averaged in my travels 140 miles a day for every day of my absence. Some would call that rapid travelling but in our impatience to reach our station and obtain our letters we seem to have been moved by leaden wings.

At Anchor, Mouth of Canton River,
Thursday August 25, 1853

Not at Macao yet, and the date of our arrival seems very uncertain. We made the land and received a pilot on board night before last, when sixty miles only distant. Last evening we anchored 32 miles from our port—got underway again this morning, and after a hard day's work under a boiling sun, are again at anchor 16 miles off without a breath of wind, and a strong tide against us.

This slow work almost in hail of letters and news is quite disheartening. The more that we have been hoping to receive our mails, and send our answers by the mail steamer from Hong Kong on the 1st. If we continue becalmed, our purser has volunteered to take a boat tomorrow and go into Macao for our mails. We are having very hot weather, and I have suffered a good deal from the heat. I have repudiated all clothing but a thin pair of drawers in my state room, and yet with the air port open, find the heat almost unsupportable. Earth, air and ocean seem to reflect the heat of the fiery furnace to which Shadrack[90] and his companions were condemned, and which you may remember was seven times heated. Our jobs comforter of a pilot tells us he was once three weeks in getting from where we now are to Macao—all on account of this "weather pigeon" which he says he *sabes mucho*.

At Anchor Cum-sing Moon
Sunday August 28, 1853

We anchored here last evening, and received our mail; my latest letter is dated May 5th, but some of my messmates have dates to

[90] Shadrach, Meshach, and Abednego were thrown into the fiery furnace. See Dan. 3:12–30.

the 16th of June. We find at anchor here the *Southampton*,[91] *Susquehanna*[92] and the *Vandalia*.[93] The *Mississippi*[94] is up the river at Whampoa,[95] the *Powhatan*[96] at Hong Kong. The remainder of the Squadron at Shanghai and elsewhere. Commodore Perry is living on shore at Macao[97] about twenty miles from this anchorage. He has visited the Bay of Jeddo—and received the President's letter at Uraga to Japanese Commissioners appointed to receive it,[98] and returns in March with his whole squadron to receive the enswer—and a favorable one is anticipated.

Cum-sing Moon, Sept. 1, 1853

The hot weather we experience in this most wretched of places wilts me right down, so to use a homely expression, "I feel like a well soaped rag after a hard day's washing." It is indeed intensely hot—and we occupy our staterooms panting and sleepless, sighing

[91] The *Southampton,* an American sailing vessel of 567 tons, four guns, was built in 1842.

[92] The *Susquehanna,* a steamer (paddle) of 2,213 tons, 23 guns, was built in 1848 and sold on September 24, 1883.

[93] The *Vandalia,* 981 tons, eight guns, was rebuilt in 1874. She was wrecked during a typhoon at Samoa in 1889.

[94] The steam vessel (paddle) *Mississippi,* ten guns, was built in 1841 and destroyed on March 14, 1863. She was Commodore Perry's flagship during the expedition to Japan.

[95] The port of Whampoa, on an island in the Pearl River about ten miles from Canton, was the center of early foreign and American commerce with China. Griffin, *op. cit.*, 242–45. For a contemporary sketch of Whampoa, see *Greyhounds,* facing p. 101, and especially the illustrations in James Orange, *The Chater Collection,* sec. VII.

[96] The *Powhatan,* a steamer (paddle) of 2,182 tons, 17 guns, was built in 1850 and sold on July 30, 1887.

[97] Commodore Perry liked to stay at Portuguese Macao in the house owned by Mr. Spooner, director of the American firm Russell and Company. See *Narrative,* I, 139–40.

[98] Commodore Perry delivered two personal messages to the envoys of the shogun, the "emperor" of Japan: the first, July 7, 1853, requesting personal handling of President Fillmore's letter to the shogun in Edo; and the second, dated July 14, 1853, when he gave the President's letter to the shogun's representatives in Uraga, Lord Toda of Iwami and Lord Ito of Izu. *Narrative,* I, 244–63; see also M. C. Perry, *Commodore Perry's Landing in Japan.*

for the midnight breeze that comes in and fans us to sleep until morning. The aim of our life here is to keep cool and avoid exciting topics of conversation. Of course in a squadron like ours, where ship visiting takes the place of shore going, all sorts of galley news gets adrift. Every officer who comes on board has some new yarn about the ship and her destination. I have it however from Capt Abbott that he expects our ship to remain here until October—then go to Manila—perhaps Como. Perry may go in her and thence in March sail to join the squadron to be assembled in Jeddo Bay.

Cum-sing Moon our anchorage is a great opium depot, and there are now stationed here five receiving ships where it is stored under the English flag and one under the American. From them it is taken to the Chinese boats and smuggled all over the Empire. A wretched village has grown up on one of the Islands forming the harbor—a paradise for sailors who love rum and women, but a curse to every one else, and even to them would they realize it. Yesterday one of the men of the *Susquehanna* coming off to the ship drunk jumped overboard and was drowned—and two little boys from our ship, who had been on shore and tested the *samshee*[99] as the vile rice rum is styled, attempted the same feat in their crazedness, but were picked up by one of our boats after swimming nearly a mile. The meaning of Cum-sing Moon I have been told is "the Star of the beautiful gateway" or "the Gateway of the beautiful Star" but on our charts it is translated "The Golden sunborn Pass"—high sounding titles it has no shoe of deserving.

My letters to you are the only journal I shall keep this cruise, partly because the weather promises to be too hot for comfortable pen work in my room, but principally because Commodore Perry has issued his vermillion edict, that all journals and diaries are to be sealed and delivered up to him on and at a certain date—an infringement of our private rights we are not disposed to tolerate.

Cum-sing Moon, Sunday Sept. 4, 1853

This morning we had the usual Masters around the Captain, and some twenty or thirty "Gene orders" of the Com'dre's were read

[99] Preble gives the foreign-made name of Chinese rice wine, which in its original form is *chiu*, or *sam-shu*, and quite often *shao-chu*, or burnt wine.

upon the Quarter Deck—one requires us to deliver up a certain date our private journals, another forbids writing for publication, others relate to exercise of guns, boat signals, etc. While these things were reading in came *Powhatan* and banged away a salute to the Commodore's pennant, it being her first sight of it. The flag ship returned the salute, and the *Powhatan* anchored. This afternoon we have been crowded with visitors from her, most of her wardroom officers being old acquaintances. Joe Adams[100] is one of her Lieuts., and looks, you may tell Mrs. B., fresh and hearty. He says he has seen quite enough of China and the East, and wishes himself in the Mediterranean Ship visiting and gossip in the fashion of the Squadron, and the slightest suggestion or remark, furnishes food for the genuine rumors and magnified and added to at every halting place, returns so disfigured to the innocent originator that he hears and repeats the story, unaware it is his own offspring. The Cast "brick" as these rumors are called is that Com. Perry is to go home and Capt. Abbott to take command of the squadron, which has no better foundation than a playful remark of our 1st Lieut. caught up and retailed, with circumstantial proof, as a fact. We think our separation hard, dear Susie—but there are other officers who can complain of theirs with more reason. The Marine Officer of the Flag Ship was married at Norfolk and sailed for the Pacific two days after in the Frigate *Congress*,[101] and was absent forty-one months; his acquaintance with the lady had not been a long one—and I was amused when telling us last night of his return he exclaimed, "By God, gentlemen, I often wondered whether Virginia (his wife) would know me." Another officer, Doctor Steele,[102] sailed from home a fortnight after his marriage and has already three years on the station with no prospect of immediate return. We are to remain to our present anchorage, so Capt. Abbott says, until the change of monsoon in Oct., when he thinks we will

[100] Joseph H. Adams became midshipman on December 8, 1831; passed midshipman, June 23, 1838; lieutenant, February 15, 1843. He died on October 4, 1853.

[101] The fourth *Congress*, a sailing vessel of 1,867 tons, 44 guns, was built in 1839 and destroyed at Hampton Roads in 1862.

[102] Perhaps he was Thomas B. Steele, who was made assistant surgeon on March 5, 1847; surgeon, August 29, 1860; resigned, April 21, 1861.

sail for Manila with Com'dre Perry, and there is talk of our taking him to Bombay and Calcutta which I do not believe. In March the whole squadron will go to Japan to receive the Emperor's letter. The success of the expedition has so far been beyond the most sanguine expectation. A coal depot has been established at the Loo Choo Islds, [103] and another at the Bonin Islds,[104] both of which we are to visit when the squadron moves North. Our ship is very much admired and visited and is considered the crack ship of the squadron. There are plenty of Officers who are desirous of exchanging into her, but we are all so well satisfied that none can be found on board who are willing to exchange. Commodore Perry is to visit and inspect the ship this week and we are preparing for his reception. He is a 'big gun' out here, and lives in a fine house at Macao fifteen miles away, little caring about the drear monotonous anchorage here. We would have a much livelier time at Macao or Hong Kong neither of which are far off. I made a great mistake in leaving you an allotment. Spanish dollars in which we are paid are worth 40 per cent here and seventy-five at Hong Kong, and by buying bills on England, I might have made all that profit and sent you 140 to 175$ where I now leave you 100$. The reason Spanish dollars are so valuable is that the Chinese will take no other currency, and perhaps the rebellion in the Northern provinces has something to do with it.

Cum-sing Moon, Sunday Sept. 11, 1853

The mail which arrived on Friday brought me several letters from

[103] The Ryukyu or Luchu Islands, between southern Japan and Formosa, are today generally known as the Okinawa Archipelago.

[104] The Bonin or Ogasawara Islands remain under Japanese sovereignty. They are 335 miles northwest of the Marianas and comprise four groups: Perry (Muko Jime), Kater (Yome Jime), Reel (Chichi Jima), and Coffin (Haha Jima). In 1823 and 1824, two American mariners, Captain Coffin and Captain John Ebbets, visited the Bonins. The islands were visited by a Russian, F. P. Lutke, in 1828 and by the British geographer F. W. Beechey in 1827. Beechey claimed the islands for Britain. Sir Richard Collinson visited the Bonins in 1853, the same year Commodore Perry stopped there with the intention of adding them to the United States' Pacific possessions. The Japanese asserted their ownership in 1861. *Encyclopaedia Britannica,* XVI, 726; *Narrative,* I, 196–304.

Portland dated the last of June. The reported loss of the ship with half the officers and crew drowned and which occasioned some anxiety to our friends, had fortunately not even a shadow of foundation, and is supposed by Capt. Abbott to have been maliciously inspired.

On Tuesday Com'dre Perry came up from Macao to inspect the squadron and was received with manned yards and a salute of fifteen guns, higher honors than it is usual for a Commodore to receive.

We had on our cocked hats and full buckram to receive him as a matter of course. The 'Great Chief' looked at our cabin accommodations and said he intended taking a cruise with us. Did I tell you in my last [letter] that the first Chinaman who came on board when we anchored presented a certificate that he, 'Sallie Preble,' was an excellent washerwoman, and could supply a bumbrat without fear of his smuggling liquor. I was glad to find our name in such good repute in these celestial regions and gave 'him,' for Sallie in this instance is a 'him,' and not a her, my washing—alas for his reputation, they are returned to me worse washed and more pounded than were even poor clothes before. 'Sallie' obtained the baptismal name of Preble from our ship of that name, which was on this station not long ago.[105]

Cum-sing Moon, Sunday Sept 18, 1853

The weather continues very hot, but we are anticipating cooler weather next month when I hope to enjoy something besides a profuse perspiration and the hum of Musquitos. The annoyance of the one by day is being continued by the other at night. The Court which has been in session on board the *Vandalia* was adjourned the other day by the President with the usual form "the Court is dissolved *sine die*," when a member wittily remarked, the members have been dissolved long ago, and another said, while trying others we have been very much tried ourselves. Mr. Bittinger[106] the chaplain of the *Susquehanna* gave us a sermon last Sunday:

[105] The second *Preble*, a sailing vessel of 566 tons, 16 guns, was built in 1838. She burned at Pensacola on April 27, 1863.

[106] Edmund C. Bittinger was made chaplain on September 30, 1850; served on the *Susquehanna* in the Far East; on the retired list, March 19, 1881. He died on August 2, 1889.

"My timbers, what lingo he could and belayed—
Why, twas just all as one as high Dutch."[107]

He talked of the heavenly city (allegorically of course) as having walls of precious stones and gates of pearls, which the sailors equally as a matter of course took literally, and he threatened "hell fires" and other kindred tortures to unrepentant sinners—adding that, "one look of a dying man no matter how wicked his life had been, one repentant expiring look was sufficient to ensure him all the joys of immortality." A consoling belief that—for where is there ever a dying man, who does not at that moment of his dissolution, repent and regret the evil doings of his past life or who would not give the whole world in exchange for his own soul? I cannot believe in the quick pardon anymore than a kind and merciful father condemns his children to eternal punishment for the misdoings of a life, which has been well described as a point between two eternities.

Cum-sing Moon, Sunday Oct 2d, 1853

Wind, weather permitting we are to sail in the morning for Hong Kong. There are no regrets at our intended departure, none I think care ever to see this sun-bright, shadeless opium pest house again. Last evening we were enlivened a little by the attack of a Portuguese Govt. Lorcha upon a horde of pirates which resulted in the capture of three of their vessels, though the villains themselves escaped to the shore. The Portuguese Lorcha sailed this morning with her three prizes. The only vessels of the squadron now in port with us are the *Powhatan* and *Mississippi,* the rest of the squadron is up the river at Whampoa—to look out for Am. interests, should there be a revolutionary outbreak at Canton. The rebels have possession of Shanghai and seem to be making successful progress all over the Empire. China is in a most unsettled condition, and there is no foretelling what innovations upon 'old custom' may be forced upon these celestials. Our sick list is on the decrease, and having sent our sickest men to the hospital, we have not now more than the average ailing ones on board. Capt. and Mrs. Endicott[108] and Mr. and Mrs. De Silver

[107] This is an odd quotation, mixed up either by the preacher or by Preble.

[108] In 1828, Captain Samuel Endicott was the master of the *George,* built at Salem

of Hong Kong[109] visited on ship yesterday, and we had a nice time, it being the first time we had spoken to a European woman since we left St. Helena. Mrs. Endicott has an infant not more than four months old and looked quite matronly. Capt. E. is of the Salem family, their residence is at Macao, but they have fine quarters on board the *Old Lintin Opium* receiving ship,[110] and he is said to have made a fortune of two or three hundred thousand dollars. The quantity and value of the opium used by the Chinese is incredible. In this harbor alone four to five stout ships are permanently anchored, with cargo that throughout the year average from 2 to 3 million dollars. Capt E. told me that only yesterday he sold 300 chests which at their average value at 500$ each would amount to $150,000. And while I was talking with him he sold ten more—a chest contains about 133 pounds or one tael of opium. The drug is put up in dry balls, the size of a large flea, or small Dutch cheese. To prepare it for smoking it is dissolved in water and boiled down to the consistency of thick tar, and it is always smoked in a reclining posture. The use destroys the body of its wretched indulgent, but there it stops—unlike liquor which is a raging devil to the annoyance of others.

Harbor of Victoria, Hong Kong,[111]
Sunday Oct 9, 1853

Leaving Cum-sing Moon on the 3d we anchored here on the 6th,

---

in 1814 for a privateer. After the ship was condemned in Rio Janeiro in 1837, Endicott was engaged in making money by selling opium in China. Griffin, *op. cit.*, 245 n.; *Greyhounds*, 85, 395.

109 Robert P. De Silver was appointed U.S. vice-consul in Macao on February 7, 1849; he was also a keeper of the naval depot. With the transfer of the depot in 1854, he went to Hong Kong without permission from American authorities. He left as vice-consul Mr. S. B. Rawle. In 1856, Rawle was made consul, a post he held until his death in 1858. De Silver resigned on November 5, 1855. Griffin, *op. cit.*, 278–79, 362.

110 This vessel is apparently little known and is not noted in the standard reference work on American or British opium ships. There was a sailing vessel called the *Linten*, about which little is known. *Clipper*, 236. The name *Old Lintin Opium* might have been given to the old receiving ship used as quarters for Captain Endicott.

111 For a pictorial and topographical study of Hong Kong as it was during

and were greeted with the melancholy news that Mrs. Boyd's[112] cousin Lt. Jos. Adams of the *Powhatan* was both dead and buried; his death having occurred within 24 hours of our departure from Cum-sing Moon—though we left him, as it was supposed, convalescing from a sudden but slotic illness. It is difficult to realize that one we saw only a few days since, so full of life and enjoyment of this world's pleasures, should now be tenanting a cold and silent grave. He was buried at Macao, and the officers propose to raise by subscription a monument over his remains.

The N.E. monsoon set in the day we arrived here and the change from intense heat to cool weather has been too great for comfort. In twelve hours the thermometer fell from 90° to 64. It has had the good effect however, of banishing the sickness from our ship. Yesterday I was on shore and enjoyed a long and delightful walk. At 5 P.M. I dined with Mr. De Silver and after an evening promenade returned to tea and music—and as it blew too fresh to return to the ship, quartered at the Hotel for the night. Today, after our usual Sunday ceremonies I called with a party of our officers upon the Capt and Doctor H.M.S. *Mindoro*,[113] now a Hospital hulk but known to us as the identical ship on board of which Key wrote our national hymn, "The Star Spangled Banner," while he was detained as a prisoner on board, during the attack upon Fort McHenry by the

Preble's visit, see Orange, *op. cit.*, sec. VIII, plates 1–52, with explanations, 347–68. Hong Kong, a British crown colony, was acquired from China in 1842 and was composed of Kowloon Peninsula, New Territories, and Hong Kong Island; the total area amounted to 391 square miles. Hong Kong, situated on the eastern side of the estuary of the Pearl River, was the residence of American "princely merchants," as Preble called them.

112 Perhaps she was Mrs. F. Boyd, wife of a partner in Boyd and Company, Boston shipbuilders. Preble's scant information makes it impossible to know who she was. It should be observed that the Boyd names of the time—John J. Boyd of New York, F. Boyd and Company of Boston, and Boyd and Hincken of New York—are all connected with ships sailing to China during the 1845–55 "tea rush" in America. The Prebles had many relatives and friends in Boston. See also *Greyhounds*, 115, 400, 406, 416, 431.

113 The *Mindoro* was a gunboat of 142 tons, three guns. She was transferred to the Asiatic station by the War Department.

British fleet.[114] The raising of our flag on its walls the morning after the bombardment furnishing the occasion of this patriotic outburst, commencing, "Oh say can you tell by the dawn's early light etc."

Hong Kong is a very pretty town and has been built out of my remembrance since I was here in 1845. The No. of European residents at this time is stated at 5,000, and of Chinese more than 16,000. Pretty well for a city that had no existence prior to the English War of 1840.

Hong Kong, Monday Oct 17, 1853

The mail steamer *Singapore*[115] took our letters for the United States on Tuesday, and the next day the *Pottinger* arrived bringing me letters from home via Cape of Good Hope to May 11th and a letter sent to Madeira and returned to the U.S. and remailed at Boston Augt. 3d.

Yesterday I attended service at St. John's Cathedral and took a delightful ramble over the hill with the Purser and my friend Gwathmey. The services at the Cathedral were as usual, only there seemed to me more getting up and sitting down than customary. The sermon was preached by a Mr. Odell and was a funeral discourse on the death of Dr. Morrison,[116] who has been the colonial physician

114 Francis Scott Key (1779–1843) wrote "The Star Spangled Banner" on September 14, 1814, during the British fleet's bombardment of Fort McHenry near Baltimore. It was immediately a popular song. He published it in his collection of songs, *Lord With Glowing Heart I'd Praise Thee* (New York, 1857). See *National Cyclopaedia of American Biography* (cited hereafter as *NCAB*), V, 498; *DAB*, X, 362–63.

115 The *Singapore* was perhaps a German ship which Preble mentions again later.

116 Robert Morrison (1782–1834) was one of the most prominent British Protestant missionaries in China. He studied astronomy and medicine, but he excelled in Chinese studies. He translated into Chinese the New Testament and several religious tracts. His fame rests in the compilation of the *Dictionary of the Chinese Language* (1815–23), in six volumes, and in the Chinese translation of the Bible (1823). He was respected by all for his high ideals and scholarship. He arrived at Canton via America in 1807 and died there in 1834. *DNB*, XIII, 1008–1009; K. S. Latourette, *The Great Century in Northern Africa and Asia, A.D. 1800–A.D. 1914*, 296–300, with bibliographical data. For a portrait of Morrison, see Orange, *op. cit.*, 370. See also Arthur W. Hummel, *Eminent Chinese of the Ch'ing Period (1644–1912)*, I, 361, 403; II, 967.

and a man very much esteemed in the community. One little incident worthy of remark attended the services—a multitude of small birds, 'winged worshippers' as our poet has called them, were flitting, twittering and chirruping over our heads during the whole service, in pleasing symphony to the praise and prayer of the devout worshippers beneath.

In 1844, I remember listening to an Am. Baptist Missionary who preached in a small chapel to a smaller audience. The change in this place since then is exemplified in this stately Cathedral which cost to erect over $45,000, and has the spacious palace of the Bishop at its side, who, from being the humble Mr. Smith, Episcopal Missionary,[117] is now styled "Lord Bishop of Victoria," and receives a salary of 5,000 pounds.

From the Harbor 'Victoria' makes a fine show and looks an assemblage of public buildings, from the houses, very generally having pillaried verandahs and porticos—though the numerous government buildings and barracks built with the Chinese ransom money help out the panorama very considerably. After our long ocean passage and continued imprisonment at the hot anchorage of Cum sing-moon, Hong Kong seems a new introduction to the world and society. The De Silvers promise to be a pleasant acquaintance. Mr. D[e Silver] is the brother of my friend, our consul at Macao. I made the acquaintance today of Miss Mary Rawle,[118] a pleasant and agreeable old maid of five and thirty or forty. Her father, now a fine old gentleman of 70 or 80, was an acquaintance of mine in 1845. His granddaughter, Mrs. Williams, whose husband is the head of the American firm, Williams, Arthur & Co.,[119] is a very pretty, pleasant and lively little

[117] George Smith, bishop of Victoria, was born in 1815; ordained, 1840; went to China in 1844 and as a result published a report, *A Narrative of an Exploratory Visit to Each of the Consular Cities in China, and to Islands of Hong Kong, and Chusan* (London, 1847); consecrated Anglican bishop, March 29, 1849; resigned his see in 1865; died in Kent, England, December 14, 1871. He is the author of five minor works on China and Japan, written from a missionary's point of view. *DNB*, VIII, 447.

[118] When R. P. De Silver left the U.S. consulate in Macao in 1854, he appointed as vice-consul Mr. S. B. Rawle. In 1856, Rawle was made consul. His post was unsalaried at that time. See note 109 above and Griffin, *op. cit.*, 190, 278–79, 362.

[119] Williams, Anthon and Company, an American trading firm established in

body, and we hope to have a good time when they all come on board tomorrow to see us.

My life has been preserved today by one of those kind providences which are often so palpable. A party of us consisting of Purser A[llison], Dr. Gilliam, Lt. Jones, and Winder and myself. Came from the ship and walked to the Victoria Library to enjoy an hour's quiet reading. We were soon stretched out on easy chairs and couches conning our books. Having finished my examination of one pamphlet, I got up from my sofa on the verandah looking toward the harbor, to return it to a table spread with others some ten feet distant, and was returning to my seat with another when I saw the marble paved verandah falling in and my poor messmate, Winder, precipitated to the basement below a distance of fourteen feet. He was completely covered and surrounded by the broken beams and masonry. My own feet were arrested on the very door sill from which the verandah separated, and I saw the sofa on which, but a moment before, I had been sitting, slide down into the abyss—but, fortunately, it struck against a side wall and thus providentially covered and protected the head of my messmate from being broken. Had I been sitting on it that end must have fallen on his head and destroyed his life, if not my own; as it happened, his arm was broken by the marble squares of the pavement, and he did not escape without other bruises and scratches. Lt. Jones, feeling his chair slipping, succeeded in springing from it into the room, and escaped. Imagine the breathless feeling with which I saw the floor give way to my very feet, and poor Winder falling. Looking down immediately after and asking him if he was much hurt, it was a great relief to hear him reply "not much, old fellow, but I believe my arm is broken"—though he fainted immediately. It was a compound fracture and will take three weeks to cure; fortunately Dr. Gilliam was at hand to take him to the ship, and the Capt. has given up to his use one of the cabin state rooms, where he can have more air and light than in his own little back room.

South China, was particularly interested in the camphor trade in 1840. Griffin, *op. cit.*, 285.

The accident caused much talk on shore. The seeming solid marble pavement of the verandah was supported on beams of wood which the industrious white ants had treacherously eaten away until the slight jar of my raising from my seat was sufficient to throw the whole fabric down.

Hong Kong, Tuesday Oct. 25, 1853

I suffered sore disappointment today when the mail arrived without bringing me any letters or newspapers, while the countenance of all my messmates around me were radiant with their happy news from home. I was glad to borrow a newspaper and retire to my room to hide my disappointment. We learn by this mail that Young Hambleton[120] who left the ship at St. Helena died on his passage home about a week before the ship he sailed in arrived at New York. This makes the eighth death from our number since we left the U.S. Two days ago, one of our sailors on shore, and of course drunk, died while breakfasting.

[Hong Kong] Oct. 30, 1853

We are to sail from here tomorrow for Whampoa and in a few days thence to Manila, at least that is the project. From Manila we are to return here or go to Loo Choo, as may happen. Today I have been on board the French Commodore and English Admiral with Capt. Abbott's compliments; and this afternoon, the Admiral, Sir Fleetwood Pillers, a son of Lord Exmouth of Algerean notoriety, calls to see the Capt and admire our "noble ship" as he called her. Sir Fleetwood was promoted a Port Capt in 1806 when he was but 16 years of age—and this is the first time he has been to sea for thirty years. He commanded a Line of Battle ship when 18 and is a hale, hearty, bluff old gentleman now.

Blenheim Beach, Whampoa, Canton River
Sunday November 6, 1853

Sailing from Hong Kong on Monday, we anchored here on Tuesday evening. Commodore Perry came up in the *Powhatan* on Friday, and she is anchored near us. On Thursday I went to Canton with

[120] W. S. Hambleton is indicated by Preble in the list of officers attached to the *Macedonian* as "Act. M. Mate." See note 64 above.

the Purser in a "Fast Boat," and returned Friday evening from a very pleasant excursion. We left the ship at 10 A.M. and reached Canton at one—and resolving to remain all night, dismissed our boat, and came down in the little Am. steamer, *Spark*,[121] with a party of gentlemen who were invited to some theatricals on board the *Susquehanna*. 'Olo Acosos Hotel,' the only apology for one at Canton, is miserable indeed, and we gladly accepted an invitation to the hospitable table of Messrs. Russell & Co.,[122] sleeping only at the Hotel. Canton has not changed much since my visit eight years ago—except that the English factories then burnt have been rebuilt. The gardens, fronting the European Settlement, extended and embellished, and a pretty little Episcopal Church with a turret has been erected in front of the factories on the dividing line between the English and what is known as the American grounds. Our flag staff, which we defended when I was here in the *St. Louis*, still rises proudly from the center of the grounds and the staffs of England, France and Denmark have been since erected on either side of it.

A long boat house, over which are the rooms of the Canton Library, Masonic Lodge and a Billiard room, extends over the water and occupies the place of the wall, and great sheds of the Chinese guard, beyond the entrance towards old China streets.

The Chinese part, old and new China streets, etc., remain unchanged and there is the same curious variety of mat-covered boats.

121 There was a little steamer *Spark*, one gun, owned by the U.S. Navy. She was purchased in 1831 and sold in 1833.

122 Samuel Russell and Company was the largest American trading firm in Canton. It was founded in 1818 and established in Canton in 1824 as Russell and Company. The company traded in general merchandise, tea, shipping services, and opium in the beginning. It was headed first by P. S. Forbes, then by his brother, R. B. Forbes. From 1844 until 1852, the Shanghai branch was headed by J. N. A. Griswold. There were several other partners, such as R. S. Sturgis, Edward Cunningham, R. W. Spooner, Fredrich Reiche, George Griswold, S. S. Gray, William H. King, and others. The partners quite often served as the U.S. consuls or vice-consuls in Canton, Ningpo, Shanghai, Macao, and even Hong Kong. For lists of the Partners of Russell and Company, see Griffin, *op. cit.*, 245–46, 306 n.; see also Fairbank, *op. cit.*, I, 226, 373, *passim;* Samuel Couling, *The Encyclopaedia Sinica*, 489–90. A very important source of information is a book by one of the partners, R. B. Forbes, entitled *Personal Reminiscences;* see also Dennett, *op. cit.*, 71–72.

Old Nirgua, who painted my miniature and copied your daguerrotype, still lives and paints, though there are now other painters superior to him. Several of the English and Am. residents now have their wives and families with them forming a very agreeable society. While Mrs. Parker,[123] who was then the first and only woman who had the courage to live here with her husband, still holds her place in the society.

On my return, I stopped with the Canton gentlemen aboard the *Susquehanna* to see the theatricals and was highly amused and entertained. The scenery and acting were very creditable and I have seen worse acting on the stage at home—for instance, the acting at Lancaster hall before I left when we went to see Mrs. Forrest. The audience comprised deputations from all the ships, and the European residents at Canton and Whampoa. The first performance was a farce called 'Family Lars'—and a pretty young man was dressed to personate Maria, and did it very well, though his walk and sea roll, though concealed by petticoats, could not be mistaken. Following the farce came a song or two and then Bombasto Furioso, admirably performed and dressed; following this we had more songs, and another farce, written by one of the men and displaying considerable wit and humor, finished the performances.

Dr. Wheelwright,[124] whom I saw on board the *Susquehanna*, gave me all the particulars of Joe Adams' illness and death and told me, at his request, he had written to Wm. Foster[125] to break the news to his sister. He says he has never seen such coolness displayed by any man. Twenty-four hours before his death both he and Dr. Maxwell[126] thought him convalescing. A post mortem examination dis-

[123] Mrs. Peter Parker was the former Miss Harriet Colby Webster of Augusta, Maine. She was married to Peter Parker on March 29, 1841, and was the first American woman to reside in Canton. *NCAB*, X, 285.

[124] Charles H. Wheelwright was made assistant surgeon on October 17, 1839; attached to the *Powhatan* during the Japan expedition; surgeon, April 5, 1854. He died on July 30, 1862.

[125] There was a Captain William L. Foster, master of the *Morning Star*, a California clipper of 1,105 tons built by T. B. Waters and Company of Boston in 1853. *Greyhounds*, 429, 495, 501; see also *Clipper*, 233, 346.

[126] Charles D. Maxwell was assistant surgeon, September 6, 1837; surgeon,

closed that a portion of his bowels had thickened and ulcerated, and that one of the ulcers had punctured through, and the blood discharging through the aperture had literally filled him up. He dictated the disposal of his property, and it was copied and brought to him to sign, but as he was asleep, it was thought best not to disturb him, and from that sleep he only awoke to the convulsions which preceded death.

Blenheim Beach, Whampoa, Canton River,
Sunday Nov. 13, 1853

Another mail was received today, and I was again disappointed, though schooled by my last disappointment, I did not feel my lack of letters so much as I did when I was so confident of receiving some by the last mail. Knowing your punctuality in writing, I do not allow myself to think that is any ill health that has prevented your writing, but rather something wrong in the address has prevented your letters reaching me.

A newspaper informing me of the death of my friend, the Hon. John Anderson, is all the item of Portland news I have been able to glean from our files.

It is, at last I believe, definitely settled that we are to leave here tomorrow morning for Hong Kong, take in provisions and sail for the North, rendezvousing at Napa, Loo Choo,[127] until the arrival of the squadron, when we are all to go to Japan. It is, however, a profound secret, whispered to me but not to be repeated out here. Commodore Perry specifies the 20th as the day we are to sail from Hong Kong, but no one thinks we can get our provisions and other stores on board and sail before the 23d. Even with that delay, we cannot expect another mail, and I must live for months on that hope deferred (for letters) that maketh the heart sick. The Russian Squadron was, at last accounts, at Nangasaki,[128] and the French Squadron

October 18, 1849; retired, October 21, 1868. He served on the *Powhatan* during Perry's expedition to Japan. See also *Narrative*, II, 411.

127 Naha, or Napa, is the port of Okinawa, Ryukyu Islands.

128 Admiral Evfemii Vasilevich Putiatin arrived at Nagasaki with his squadron on August 21, 1853. G. A. Lensen, *Russia's Japan Expedition of 1852–1855*, 7–10.

has also gone to the North.[129] The knowledge of this has hurried our Commodore's movements, as it was his original intention to return to Japan in April. We expect cold and stormy weather and plenty of it, and have been getting our stores ready for it. Here we have weather which is as fickle as a coquette. The thermometer stands in the day at 84° and perhaps before night falls to 64° or vice versa, rendering a complete change of dress indispensable. I was on board the *Powhatan* this forenoon and saw them packing Joe Adams' wardrobe to send home by a merchant ship. The officers of the squadron have already subscribed $175 for a monument over his remains, and Mr. Heine[130] is to make a drawing of it and the cemetery at Macao to send to his sister. I put on board the ship *Courser*[131] today a small box of tea, which I hope you will like; it is a mixture of pecoe, oolang and souchong,[132] selected by an experienced tea-taster, 'Mr. Sloan,' and costs him more in specie than the best qualities imported for sale in the U.S. and is of fresh—of this year's crop. Remember me in every cup of it you drink. I visited Canton again last week. I left the ship at 4 A.M. by which you will see I was no sluggard. Reached the city at 8, and left again at 7, in the evening, but owing to adverse winds and tides, did not reach the ship until 2, the next morning. Our boat voyage up and down was without interest except that once an alarm of 'pirates' was raised, when we seized our muskets and made such other warlike demonstrations, that the pirates (?) pulled back in such haste as showed him more frightened than we were.

[129] Two boats of the French Asiatic squadron, the *Colbert* and the *Napoleon III*, were watching Putiatin's Russian squadron. *Ibid.*, 101–102, 136.

[130] Commodore Perry took two "artists" to sketch people and places during the expedition: W. Heine and E. Brown, Jr. Many of the fine illustrations in his report were executed by them and signed "from nature by Heine Figures by Brown." *Narrative*, I, p. iv.

[131] The *Courser* was a California clipper of 1,024 tons, built at Boston in 1851. Her first master was A. L. Richardson and after 1852, Captain William Cole. She was lost on April 4, 1858, near Pratos Shoal. *Greyhounds*, 415, 455.

[132] Souchong, from the Chinese word *siao-chung*, "small sort," is one of the finer varieties of black tea. Oolong, or onlung, from the Chinese word *wu-lung*, "black dragon," is a dark variety of cured tea. Pekoe, from the Amoy dialect word *pek-ho*, "white down" or "hair," a superior kind of black tea, is so called from the leaves' being picked while young, with the down still on them.

Our boat people were greatly alarmed, and up and down, had eyes and ears open for both banks of the river, anticipating a pirate behind every bush, or to see one emerge from every creek we passed. The robberies of native boats are frequent, but I cannot learn that recently any Europeans have been attacked. Plunder being the object of the rascals, they do not care to incur danger. What do you think of a boy two years older than our little Harry, that is eight years old, pulling an oar in a boat all day long can earn his living! Such is the sight here, by no means uncommon. I was in a sampan the other day, where a girl of that age handled an oar for full six miles, with the strength and skill of a man. I felt ashamed of my manhood, allowing myself to be carried with such luxurious ease, at the expense of so much labor from so young a specimen of the weaker sex, but I did not offer to take her oar notwithstanding, and I doubt my ability to fill it with so much muscle if I had. Generally the little sampans are managed by females; the larger Fast Boats contain a family, each member of which young and old, regardless of sex, takes a turn at the oars. Like the snail, they carry their house with them, or rather the house is gifted with locomotion and carries them. It is also their temple, for every boat, no matter how small has its 'boss' place, or house where they offer up their worship. We hire for the ship a Fast Boat, for which we pay $30 a month, ready at all times to do our bidding. It is a fine, commodious boat with large mat sails, and supports the following population: an old man and his wife, his sons and two young lads of 16 or 18; in all, seven persons all fed, clothed and lodged on our $30. Sampans with a crew of five or six can be hired for $10 a month, which is even cheaper. Do not send me any newspapers by mail with the ends covered. Our Commodore has had to pay $25 for a bundle so done up although it was opened in the presence of the Postmaster. They would not deliver his letters and dispatches, until he had taken the package. In going up river the other day we passed the dead bodies of two Chinamen floating down and our boat men burnt some press stick, as a mass, or to light them through the shadows of death.

Hong Kong, Nov. 18, 1853

"Our Anniversary!" Was it Tuesday or Wednesday that we were

made one flesh? Joking aside, I really have forgotten the day of the week, though I remember it was a day that made me the happiest of mortals. It is Friday today and therefore, however out of season, 'Good Friday' to me; it would be good indeed if I could annihilate the miles of ocean that separate our bodies, not our hearts, and seated by your side, love, recall the events of the intervening years.

> "Come a health! and it is not to be slighted
> with sips a cold pulse or spirit suppine
> All the blood in my heart seems to rush
> to my lips to commingle its flow with the wine."
> "Then with three, as is due, let the honors be paid
> Whilst I give with my hand, heart and head
> Here to her, the fond mother, dear partner, kind maid
> Who first taught me to love, woo and wed."

You may be sure your health has been honored today and drunk in the best wine the ship afforded.

We left our anchorage at Blenheim beach on Monday and anchored here the next morning. We have the *Susquehanna* here with us, but the Commodore is at Macao. The *Mississippi* and *Powhatan* are still up the river. We have loaded our ship with provisions, but the Commodore is now in no hurry to have us sail, his cause of uneasiness having been removed, and everybody on shore advising him not to expose his squadron to the boisterous weather of the approaching month. The store ship *Lexington,*[133] which sailed for New York on the 18th of June, 154 days out, thus has not yet arrived, and you lost nothing by not writing by her, as we have dates to Sept. 7, by the overland mail which I hope you will avail yourself of in the future. The Commodore has chartered a small steamer called the *Queen*[134] for $500 a month which has given rise to small joking that

[133] The *Lexington* was an American steamer attached to the Japanese expedition under Lieutenant, commanding, John J. Glasson. *Narrative,* II, 410.

[134] The *Queen* was a private ship owned by an Englishman, W. A. Bowra of Hong Kong. Before returning to the United States, Perry chartered the *Queen* and put her under Preble's command for participation in Sir James Stirling's organized sea force against the Chinese pirates and Taiping rebels. Primarily, the *Queen* was to protect American citizens in China. Preble's diary supplies interesting information about the *Queen's* participation in the coastal war against the pirates. Commodore Perry,

he has engaged to keep the Queen at that price, not dear for so exalted a mistress. It is a little singular to have under our republican flag a vessel so styled.

Mrs. Parker desires to be remembered to her cousin, Mrs. Dr. Gilman.[135]

The Doctor[136] has cut the missionary and seeks to shine as a diplomat. He has built himself a fine house, and is reputed to have increased his worldly wealth materially. What he wants is children to give his house a domestic appearance. He is now almost the only European resident who was here in 1844. Mr. Forbes[137] who then had just come out (after failing in business at Rio de Janeiro) to take the place of a junior partner in the house of Russell & Co. has just gone home, the senior partner, and with a large fortune, some say 700,000$. I hear also of another fortune made in the same time.

---

in his official report, did not dwell upon her brave service. The *Queen* was captured by Chinese soldiers in 1857; the captain and several Europeans were killed and the vessel burned. See Orange, *op. cit.*, 92.

[135] Jos. Taylor Gilman was a partner in Russell and Company from 1843 to 1845; see Griffin, *op. cit.*, 306 n.

[136] Peter Parker (1804–1888), a medical missionary in China, came to Canton in 1834 and in 1835 founded the famous Ophthalmic Hospital, known by the popular name "Dr. Parker's Hospital." He is the founder of the Medical Missionary Society in China. Parker gave much time to American consular and diplomatic problems and carried on an extensive correspondence with the Department of State, advising on American expansion into the Far East, especially when he was acting U.S. commissioner in China from 1855 to 1857. His energy and wisdom contributed to the somewhat better establishment of United States interests and diplomatic relations with China. Latourette, *The Great Century in Northern Africa and Asia,* 301, 303; Griffin, *op. cit.*, 40, 129–33, 360; Couling, *op. cit.*, 424; S. W. Williams, *The Middle Kingdom,* I, 333–37. For Parker's consular activities, see references in Fairbank, *op. cit.*, I, 165–66, 389, 400, 415.

[137] Robert Bennet Forbes (1804–1889) was a man of many enterprises; sea captain, China merchant, shopowner, and writer. At the beginning of his business career, he worked with Perkins and Company at Canton, and when the company merged with Russell and Company in 1830, he worked for the latter but refused to trade in opium. In 1839, he became head of the company until 1840, when he returned to Boston. He played a prominent role during the Opium War. He returned to China in 1849, serving as American and French vice-consul and director of Russell and Company. In his old age, Forbes published many pamphlets, some relating to China commerce. *DAB,* VI, 508–509; Griffin, *op. cit.*, 40f.

When we were here in the *St. Louis*, 'Tom Hunt' as he is called was on board the good ship *Hervgua* as a mate, a coarse, illiterate fellow who could not put two words of English together properly. He left the ship and commenced trading in a small way and finally started in business as a ship chandler at Whampoa on board a chop boat or old hulk and is said now to be worth 2 or 300,000$.

Sunday Nov. 20th, 1853

The ship has been reported ready for sea and we may soon expect the Commodore's orders to send us off. The thought of leaving without any news from home makes me homesick.

"This ship no lingering hopes endear
No fond resemblance chains me here
* * * * Day by Day
I wear the cheerless hours away
O! when will time consenting give
The Home in which my heart can live."

Hong Kong, Saturday Nov. 26, 1853

Provisioned for a six month cruise we still await our orders. It is a pleasant place to wait at, and we feel in no hurry to buffet the boisterous winds and weather of this season. What would you think of your Lily's pulling at an oar from our ship to shore, full a mile distant! Yet I saw a little bright-eyed 'cow child,' celestial in our 'Fast-Boat.' It is true the wee little thing had her cousin of 14 to guide and help her at the oar, but hers was no child's play. She rose to the oar, and laid back on it like no tyro, and put upon the stroke all the strength her little frame was capable of.

You often have asked me to write a book but I feel none of the vanities of authorship, and never aspire to anything higher than an expression of thought or opinion, in the ephemeral columns of a newspaper. If I thought by accident I could make anything by it—to help our scanty means—I might consent like Dogberry[138] to "write myself an ass." I did think once of compiling a Nautical Dictionary or Cyclopedia of Nautical Knowledge, and may do it yet, if I can master my natural indolence for the requisite research and investiga-

[138] Dogberry is an absurd character in Shakespeare's *Much Ado About Nothing.*

tion. It would I fear be a labor of love, rather than profit. I have often lamented my indifferent memory, but my mess mates think differently and refer to me for dates and general information as the Encyclopedist of the mess. If I have improved my memory it must be from my habit of noting down in my reading any little anecdote or incident which particularly strikes me. I am surprised myself to find how many odds and ends of knowledge I have stowed away to serve their turn. If I had the power of saving to reproduce what I have seen, in my short but eventful life, I could no doubt as you say make an amusing book, being as I am. I have the ore but need the Jeweller's art to set it with jewels.

Hong Kong, Sunday, Dec. 4, 1853

The mail from England arrived late last Monday evening. It was blowing a gale at the time, so as to render communication with the shore impracticable, and I turned in feeling a consolation that I had nothing to expect, and pitying the impatience of my messmates. It was an agreeable surprise to be awakened early the next morning and have your letter dated from Augt 19th to Sept 6th put in my hands. I was wide awake in a minute and eager in its perusal, not stopping for the ceremony of dressing. I can now proceed to sea with a light heart.

The distressing accounts of pestilence at New Orleans, which I had read in the papers, caused me to tremble for our friends there. I notice the scourge has also been decimating the slave population of the plantations. I hope it may show to the slave holders the unstable nature of that property, and assist them to thinking of a scheme of general and gradual emancipation that all friends of humanity must wish for. I am no abolitionist as the term is understood, but favor the enforcement of all laws sustaining rights guaranteed by our Constitution, but I feel and see the evils of slavery upon both races and hope to see the slave owner himself, ere many years assisting to remove its incubus from our land. It is a mockery to our free institutions that it exists in our midst, and morally, politically and practically, like the Ivy on the oak is destructive of them. I hope ere I die to see our whole country—a free union—one and inseparable. Our latest dates by this mail are Sept. 24 from the U.S., and Oct. 8

from England. I was glad to hear all were well when you wrote, and to receive all the interesting items of news concerning my friends which you communicate.

Commodore Perry has issued an order forbidding any writing for the press, and requiring all Journals, private or otherwise, to be given up to him at a specified date. A very impolite order I think, for, of course, no one will keep a diary under such requirement. My letters to you will be my only diary, and Col. Seaton, of the *Nat. Intelligencer,*[139] whom Arthur writes me, is desirous I should correspond for his paper, must take the will for the deed.

Hong Kong, Dec. 10, 1853

The mail by the *Malta* closes tonight. The *Plymouth*[140] arrived from Loo Choo and the Bonin Islds. yesterday. She brings us the intelligence of the loss of one of her boats and a boat crew at the Bonin Islands in a typhoon. The party in charge of Lieut. John Mathews, [141] left the ship on a touring expedition, and were caught by a sudden gale in which it is supposed all perished. The ship dragged from her position with twenty-one feet of water, with five anchors ahead, and was saved from shipwreck by a providential shift of wind. I was on board the *Plymouth* today. She has been thirty-two months in commission, and her officers are expecting to go home as soon as the result of the Japan "pidgeon" is known—even then they will have been 3½ years before they can be paid off. The Commodore says she shall leave the squadron about the 1st of May and gives Capt. Kelly[142] the choice to remain at Shanghai, to look after

[139] The *National Intelligencer* was founded as a triweekly at Washington, D.C., by Samuel Harris Smith on October 31, 1800. John Gales joined it in 1807, remaining until his death in 1860; another partner was his brother-in-law, William W. Seaton, who edited the journal until 1865. It was a daily from 1813 to its discontinuance in 1869. S. N. D. North, *The Newspapers and Periodical Press*, 33.

[140] The *Plymouth,* a sailing ship of 989 tons, 20 guns, was built in 1843 and destroyed at Norfolk in 1861.

[141] John Matthews was made midshipman on February 22, 1838; passed midshipman, May 20, 1844; master, August 30, 1851; lieutenant, July 13, 1852. He was a lieutenant on the *Plymouth* and with his companions met death in a gale off the Bonin Islands on October 25, 1853. *Narrative,* II, 408–409, 411.

[142] John Kelly was commander of the *Plymouth* during the expedition to Japan. He was made midshipman on February 1, 1814; lieutenant, January 13, 1825; com-

Am[erican] interest in that troubled quarter or go up to Japan. The *Saratoga* has been over three years in Commission already, and it is arranged that she take the Commodore's dispatches from Japan to San Francisco, and then return via Cape Horn. The *Mississippi* will land the Commodore at Panama, and also return via Cape Horn. Our ship and the *Vandalia*, being sailing ships and the last comers, are likely to be kept upon the station after the Expedition has accomplished its object, in which case Capt. Abbott will hoist his flag as Commodore. The *Lexington,* not yet arrived, is now 176 days out, and we begin to be anxious about her safety. She has on board a vibrater-engine and passenger car complete and a magnetic telegraph and other presents[143] calculated to astonish the brother of the sun, moon and stars. Our latest rumor is that the Emperor of Japan is dead,[144] and the whole nation mourns his loss for a year, and that no business can be accomplished until the days of mourning are accomplished. It is thought to be a ruse to evade our negotiations.

Hong Kong, Dec. 12, 1853

The mail steamer took her departure yesterday with my letter, and today we have one arrived which brings me yours of Augt. 10th, which somehow got into the French closed mail and was sent back to England and forwarded thence. By this stupid blundering its dates have been anticipated by the previous mail. The sight of your well known hand writing and its little items of local intelligence did me good, however. Direct my letters in the future to the care of Mister A. H. Fryer & Co., Hong Kong, which is the business address of Mr. De Silver I wrote you about. I dined at their house today and had for dessert a cake and plum pudding sent to them from England by the overland route; the freight on them must have been many times their value, but Mrs. Hal, as she is called, or "Mrs. Smily Hal" in contradistinction to her sister-in-law at Macao, who is

---

mander, September 8, 1841; captain, September 14, 1855; commodore on retired list, July 16, 1862. He died on February 6, 1863. See also *Narrative,* II, 411.

143 Concerning the presents brought by Commodore Perry for the Japanese authorities, see *Narrative,* I, 357–58.

144 This is a reference to the death of Shogun Iyeyoshi Tokugawa (b. 1792) on August 15, 1853.

Courtesy Massachusetts Historical Society

Lieutenant George Henry Preble, U.S.N., at the Time of the Perry Expedition

The Chartered Steamer *Queen*, Which Preble Commanded, at Canton

"Mrs. Smily Bob," was frantically delighted at the remembrance. "Mrs. Hal" is yet a bride having been married rather less than a year. Her husband was attracted by her good looks and sprightly manners when passing through England, and recalling them on his arrival in China sent back to offer his hand and heart—was accepted, and she came out in charge of Capt. Buchanan[145] of the *Susquehanna*, and who on their arrival took the part of a godfather, and, as they say, gave her away. She is an ambitious, contentious little body, fond of show and dress, and very desirous of shining in the aristocratic circles of the colony, which her husband's occupation of shop keeper excludes her from. At present they are a pair of turtle doves (De Silver being a very amiable man) and I hope they will long continue such.

I notice what you say about . . . Theology is one thing, Religion another. The first is a curious inquiry to be pursued and investigated. The other a practical, working fact which should enter into all our employments, directing them, and us, in a spirit of love and forbearance. The very best of us fall far short of the requirements of a practiced, everyday, work day religion. The sentiment of all religions, Pagan, Jewish, Mohammedan and Christian is the same, that is the adoration of some superior power, spirit or intelligence from which is derived innumerable benefits.

The religion of Confucius is the most artless of any. It prescribes reverence to an Invisible Being, residing in the visible Heavens,[146] and distributing thence happiness or misery to mankind. It enjoins no particular worship to him, so that priests, temples, sacrifices and

[145] Franklin Buchanan, an officer of the Confederate Navy, was born about 1800 at Baltimore. He was made midshipman on January 28, 1815; lieutenant, January 13, 1825; master-commandant, September 8, 1841; first superintendent of the Naval Academy, 1845–47; captain, September 14, 1855; entered the Confederate service, 1861; commanded the *Merrimac* in the attack on the Union fleet at Hampton Roads. He blew up his ship to prevent her being captured; made a rear admiral; commanded the ironclad *Tennessee* in Mobile Bay, August, 1864, and was defeated there by Admiral Farragut. *A Naval Encyclopaedia*, 95.

[146] At the bottom of p. 86 of the diary, below the words "visible Heavens," Preble noted: "afterwards Admiral in Rebel Navy." The note refers to Captain Buchanan. See note 145 above.

rites are foreign to it. The moral part consists in honoring the servants of the Supreme Invisible Being, the spirit presiding over mountains, rivers, forests, etc., and in the performance of duties necessary to the welfare of the public and every family. Moral virtue is inculcated both by precept and example, and the most sublime ideas of a Supreme Being under the name of "Shang-ti" are entertained. Many heathen rites and ceremonies have crept in and obscure the purity of the original faith. Such is the state religion of China at the present time, though the followers of Buddha and Tau[147] have probably the greatest number of votaries. At Canton and Macao there are quite a number of Parsee merchants.[148] "Fire worshippers" who in their long gowns and high glazed caps form a noted object. I always understood that they worshipped the Sun as a God and Fire as his emblem, until my last visit to Canton when an intelligent Parsee told me it was a Mohammedan slander, that they worshipped the sun only as the work and emblem of a superior being, his highest and most glorious creation, and that in the same sense they adored the trees and everything in nature, the work of his hands. That is, "they looked through Nature up to Nature's god." A Parsee belief is nearer Christian and a Christian nigher a Parsee's than I have ever imagined. Come to sift beliefs, would it not be difficult for a Trinitarian to explain his idea of the personality of the triune deity, or the Unitarian to describe the personality of his one God, since both believe the Deity to occupy all space, controlling alike the hearts of men and angels.

Hong Kong, Sunday Dec. 18, 1853

The Commodore arrived yesterday in the *Mississippi,* and has, as usual, brought with him an excitement. We are ordered to hold ourselves in readiness for sea at a moment's notice and have the un-

[147] Taoism, derived from the word *tao,* "the way," "the virtue," "the principle of life," is a religion supposedly founded by Lao-tzu (b. *ca.* 604 b.c.). For a short presentation of Taoism, see Couling, *op. cit.,* 287, 544–48; for its philosophical aspects, see Fung Yu-lan, *A History of Chinese Philosophy,* I, 153–55; 177–79, *passim;* II, 169–70, 240–43, *passim.*

[148] The Parsi, or Parsee, merchants were Zoroastrians of Persian or Indian origin.

pleasant anticipation of passing our Christmas, so near at hand, at sea. Today the *Mississippi* returned to Macao to convey the Hon. Humphrey Marshall,[149] our commissioner to China, to Canton. I attended services at the Cathedral in the forenoon and heard the Bishop of Victoria preach from the text, "I am determined not to know anything among you save Jesus Christ and him crucified."[150] The reverberations of the church prevented my hearing all of the discourse, but my companions, who were Episcopalians, pronounced it excellent. What I did hear seemed to me commonplace, perhaps through my prejudice against the good sense of the preacher whom I remembered on the *St. Louis* as the young missionary, Mr. Smith, who took that walk with us in Henam, and was so prejudiced against Unitarians, not counting them as Christians; aside from his discourse, I had little satisfaction in the services; they were to me so formally devout and theatrical. The frequent getting up and sitting down, the assistant preacher in one pulpit and the Bishop in another. Their several genuflexions at particular parts of the creed, etc., the deep based Amens and responses of the hired clerk, who gave the cue to the congregation, and the obtrusive manner in which the 'three persons' were intruded, jarred upon my ideas of the simplicity and humility of Christian worship. I endeavored to convey myself away and to imagine the solemn and impressive words of our good Dr. N[ichols][151] in the 'Old Jerusalem' of my childhood.

The Cathedral here is a fine Gothic building, with stained glass windows, which were opened today, and as before, when I attended service here, little swallows and sparrows were twittering and flitting

[149] Humphrey Marshall of Kentucky was appointed U.S. commissioner and consul in Shanghai on August 4, 1852; he stayed until January, 1854. Griffin, *op. cit.*, 358.

[150] I Cor. 2:2.

[151] The Reverend Dr. Ichabod Nichols was born in Portsmouth, New Hampshire, on July 5, 1784; appointed minister at the First Congregational Parish, Portland, Maine, 1809; died January 2, 1859. A prominent man and a well-educated member of Portland society, he was a Harvard graduate and religious author. Cf. Willis, *op. cit.*, 653–59.

about overhead, praising their maker in the artless happiness with which they moved and sang.

The Bishop is said to be a very excellent man in private life and very charitable. His salary, which is about 15000$ with a place to live in, is a great change from his small stipend as a missionary. He is the youngest of the Bench of Bishops and signs himself George of Victoria, that is, Lord Bishop of Victoria,[152] a rather more sonorous title than Rev. George Smith, by which I formerly knew him. He has written a book on China, which I saw a few days since at the Library. In it he mentions our walks at Henam with Dr. Parker, Capt. McKeever,[153] Dr. L.[154] and myself, but without mention of names, but speaks of the old woman praying by the wayside.

We dined two of the officers of H.M.S. *Winchester*[155] and our friend Fryer in our mess, which with our usual Sunday ceremonies and church on shore has made it rather an occupied day. The Purser was called away from the dinner table to see the Commodore, and is ordered to make out his drafts on England which he goes tomorrow to Canton to negotiate.

Today has been peculiarly calm, placid and balmy, like one of our Indian summer days. The Capt. says it is a weather breather, and I hope it may be the breeder of many just like it—cool and strong winds are more appropriate to the season. When you receive this, we will probably be at Loo Choo, where all the squadron is to rendezvous previous to going to Japan. We expect to sail from here on the 24th to reach Japan in March or April and return to China in June. My

[152] On the establishment of the Victoria (Hong Kong) diocese and the activities of its first bishop, George Smith, see G. B. Endacott and D. E. She, *The Diocese of Victoria, Hong Kong*.

[153] Isaac McKeever was made midshipman on December 1, 1809; lieutenant, December 9, 1814; commander, May 27, 1830; captain, December 8, 1838. He died on April 1, 1856.

[154] He was most probably Arthur M. Lynah, assistant surgeon on the *Mississippi*. *Narrative*, II, 411.

[155] The H.M.S. *Winchester*, a launch, belonged to the squadron organized by Sir James Stirling, commander-in-chief of the British navy at Hong Kong. Grace Fox, *British Admirals and Chinese Pirates, 1832–1869*. 125.

friend, John Goldsborough,[156] is on board the *Saratoga*, has just lost all his curios, the gatherings of his four year cruise. He stored them with a friend at Hong Kong, and, anticipating the *Saratoga* would be sent home without returning here, ordered them sent to Shanghai. On the passage the Lorcka they went by was taken by the pirates and Goldsborough's shawls and Chinese treasures are probably enriching the wardrobe of some Chinese Medira.[157] Rather hard is it not?

The eccentric Commander of the *Southampton* reports having seen a volcano boiling and smoking out of the sea near the NE[st] end of Formosa which he has named for J. P. Kennedy, the late Sec'y of the Navy. He also picked up at sea a tiny canoe filled with natives, who replied to all questioning, I alla-bar-boo, and whom it is thought were blown off from an island of that name, near 2000 miles from the place where they were recruited.

What an artificial state of existence is mine, and how unsatisfactory that so much of my limited three score and ten must be passed in the same way; up late, turned out early, sleep irregularly interrupted, and drifted hither and thither by sudden summons, thousands of miles away from a home that is the haven of all my hopes and fears, perhaps after years of absence to return to it for a few months to taste its pleasures and comforts, just enough to realize them and then be sent off on another tour of wanderings. How I wish I had no future absences to dread, and that this was to be my last. We have the finest ship in the squadron, and the happiest mess—and I must be content.

Hong Kong, Dec. 22, 1853

Capt. Abbott has reported the ship ready for sea, and we are reported to be in readiness to sail by signal, without further notice.

9 P.M. At Sea. The Pilot left us about an hour ago, and we are

[156] John R. Goldsborough was made a midshipman on November 16, 1824; passed midshipman, April 28, 1832; lieutenant, September 6, 1837; commander, September 14, 1855; captain, July 16, 1862; commodore, April 13, 1867; retired, July 2, 1870; died, June 22, 1877. He served on the *Saratoga* during the expedition to Japan. See also *Narrative*, II, 410, and *Records*, 76–77.

[157] Preble's comparison is with Medea, a legendary Greek sorceress who plotted against the lives of her lovers-husbands, with whom she adventured much.

now fairly embarked on our voyage to Loo Choo and Japan. The Fast Boat family which has attended the ship for the last three months, Sam Fun, Betsey, Amoy and the old man and woman all came in for a share of our regrets; they were always so smiling, good-humored, and ready. They volunteered to accompany us out and take the pilot back, not anticipating so rough a sea, and were sea sick enough to be glad when the time came for them to chin chin us with fire crackers and say goodbye. The weather for the season may be called pleasant, still there is nothing agreeable in a misty atmosphere, strong head wind, and a cross sea and rolling swell. We anticipate constant headwinds, rough and stormy weather, but hope to make the passage to Loo Choo in twenty days.

At Sea, Friday Dec. 23d.

The wind has been high and sea rolling, and the ship has been dancing a sort of sea polka all day, which renders writing a matter of difficulty; one's thoughts have to be divided between providing for the safety of the inkstand, the stability of the candle and care for the pen and paper, as well as the subject.

We have had specks of the Coast of China in sight today and numerous fleets of Chinese fishing boats and junks, and passed a barque struggling like ourselves against wind and weather. Several of my messmates have retired to their rooms—not sea sick (?) but fatigued and sleepy after a restless night. A noble great Turkey graced our dinner table today, which only needed some of your stuffing to be perfect, and the steward made us a sponge cake which almost rivalled Mrs. B—s. These with roast beef, bananas, oranges, sweet and Irish potatoes made up a nice bill of fare to all well enough to enjoy it. The Captain's chinese boy broke a demijohn[158] of molasses today and spilt it all over him, which with his sea sickness made him a lazy table object. The wind has been going down but the sea does not subside as fast as the wind, and it has been good exercise to keep on our feet.

Saturday Dec. 24, 1853

Another rough and stormy day beating against the head winds and pitching into a head sea under double reefed top sails and reefed

[158] A demijohn is a bulging, narrow-necked bottle, with a capacity of one to ten gallons, often encased in wicker and with wicker handles.

courses. Passed an English steamer which we imagined the one from Hong Kong with our letters. Surrounded all day by numerous fishing boats and sighting the Chinese coast on every inshore tack. Our mess chat has been of home and former Christmas merry-making. I have the mid-watch and shall commence my Christmas at the beginning. I do not wish you here to share it with me, but I do wish I was where I could give you the earliest greetings. Last year I came home from Washington bringing my detachment from the *Marion* and orders to the *Vermont*.[159] How improbable then, that today I should be aboard the *Macedonian*. I should like to hang myself in your stocking tonight—could you have it better filled?

Sunday evening (Christmas) Dec. 25, 1853

It has been wet and stormy, but like Mark Tapley,[160] we have been exceeding jolly under the circumstances. We sighted 'Pedro Blanco' or White Peter alias White's Rock today, which stands like a sentinel 20 miles from land. It probably gets its name from the white bird that encrusts its top and has trickled down its sides. We were enabled to correct our position by it, the thick weather having prevented our getting any observations of the heavenly bodies since the pilot left us. As the rock is just fifty miles east of Hong Kong, we have gained just so much and no more towards our port notwithstanding our three days hard work and many discomforts.

My Bible reading today speaks of the marriage relation as of God's appointment and says what God hath joined together no man should put asunder—how[ever] without wishing to be profane it seems to me the Secretary of the Navy has put us asunder pretty effectively.

At Sea, Wednesday Dec. 28, 1853

Ever since Christmas when I last wrote, we have been struggling against heavy gales and made of course but little progress. This forenoon we had a glimpse of sunshine but it has all clouded over again and with three reefs in our topsails and another in our cornices we are prepared for a blowy night. This afternoon Capt. Abbott, finding

[159] The *Vermont*, 2,633 tons, 16 guns, was built in 1848 and became receiving ship, New York, 1874.

[160] Mark Tapley is a character in Charles Dickens' *Martin Chuzzlewit* who takes credit for being cheerful in dangerous circumstances.

we could not pass to windward of some dangerous islands and shoals close at hand on which many ships have been lost, kept away for them to pass to leeward. At 3 P.M. we had them in plain sight—a long low and pretty island, surrounded by coral reefs. We passed about eight miles from the island but the green water on the shoals and the breakers were much greener. These islands and shoals are called "The Praters" or Silver Island. Yesterday and today we have had a ship in company under close sail struggling like ourselves against the gale, we hoisted our ensign other stranger did the same but we were able to make out her nationality, though we judged her to be English. At the rate we have gained towards Loo Choo since we left Hong Kong, it will take us sixty days to get there, but we hope today we are having the dawning of better luck.

Good night dearest. You open your eyes to the morning light as I shut mine to my evening slumbers, so that while one watches the other is dreaming.

December 31, 1853

Ever since my last date it has been blowing a gale, and old Boreal seems to be taking a final blow out to close the year with today, and has brought our noble ship down to the smallest quantity of canvass. We are now nine days out and only 200 miles from Hong Kong. In present weather I see no end to our voyage, but we may struggle for months like the *Flying Dutchman*,[161] or until a change of monsoon. We are somewhere near the S. end of Formosa and the Bashee Islds. if you look at the map and run your finger up to Loo Choo you will perceive what a long passage we have before us.

Yesterday a singular appearance of water attracted our attention; all about us was a heavy breaking white capped sea, while half a mile off, extending in a N.W. and S.E. direction beyond our sight was a belt of smooth water, apparently about half a mile wide, in which the surface of the sea appeared to be depressed a foot or more below the general level; beyond it to the horizon was the same angry sea

[161] The *Flying Dutchman*, 1,257 tons, one of the beautiful California clippers, was built in 1852 by William H. Webb of New York. She sailed under Captain Ashbel Hubbard. She went ashore on Brigantine Shoal, New Jersey, and was lost, February, 1858. *Greyhounds*, 240, 292, 470, 472; *Clipper*, 216, 344, 354.

that surrounded us. We were near enough to see that it was not a shoal, and attributed it to a current, but how caused or how running was a matter of speculation. We first noticed it at about 4 P.M. and coasted along it until sunset shut it from our sight.

I attempted a game of chess today with our Purser, and our first mishap was a salt water baptism down the hatch, almost a regual immersion, soon followed by a lee lurch, which proved a Waterloo defeat for both of us, sending kings, queens, knights, clergy, and soldiers all in a heap and tumbling their castles on top of them.

The Diary: 1854

The Diary: 1854

[At Sea], Sunday January 1, 1854

We have been favored with a pleasant day for the commencement of the New Year, and all feel encouraged by the most auspicious opening. The old year ended in a nasty wet and disagreeable watch which I kept on deck, making and taking in sail and hauling upon the breezes. It was the winding up of our bad weather. We have now our royals set to a fair wind, and our apartments and the main deck are dry for the first time since we left Hong Kong. Tomorrow we hope to be in the Pacific. A ship was seen from aloft this afternoon, but has passed out of sight. Flying fish, Porpoises and chocolate Albatrosses have been sporting about us. The contrast between today and yesterday, after a few hours of sunshine, is very striking.

Our clean white decks, and the men in their Sunday monstrosity clothes, look comfortable, and the call of "all hands splice the main brace," has made our jacks smiling and happy. At 3 P.M., after our tight days of discomforts, we were only 330 miles from Hong Kong, scarcely more than a day and a half run with a good breeze. Sent a bottle adrift today, freighted with our latitude and longitude, a gift to Mr. Maury[1] and science.

I have the mid watch tonight, and shall end the first day of the first week of the first month of the New Year with waking thoughts of my absent darlings and prayers for their health and happiness.

[1] Matthew Fontaine Maury (1806–1873) was a naval officer and noted oceanographer. Among his several works, he published in 1851 *Explanations and Sailing Directions to Accompany the Wind and Current Charts.* From Preble's text, it could be inferred that he collected data for Maury. *DAB*, XII, 428–31.

Homes, well loved group! It's Sabbath Day
  Its tunes I seem to hear
Though boone full many a league alone
  They come distinct and clear
Oh Sabbath night! Oh treasured home!
  Fond pride of memory's train
And thoughts of yesteryear
  Shall bring my youth again.
When Sabbath bells have ceased their sound
  And the hours of day are past
And twilight draws its curtain round
  And shadows gather fast
Where is one spot and one alone
  Round which our hearts must cling
And fondest memories one by one
  Their choicest treasures bring
That spot is home its sacred walls
  Admit no discord then
Nor crowded marts, nor festive halls
  Nor gayest haunts of men
Can know a joy so real and pure
  None such to them is given.
Might joys like these for age endure
  This earth were quite a Heaven.

At Sea, Monday Jan. 2d, 1854

We have had Formosa 'the beautiful' island in sight all day, and towards sundown the two small islands of Botel Tobags and we are now running through the Bashee Channel into the Pacific. The Captain and Master are on deck, and keeping an anxious look out for some rocks and reefs which I hope we may not plunge upon. We saw the smoke of a steamer this afternoon and two water spouts; my ears are afflicted like Job, with sore ribs, and I have a stye on my eye from writing by candle light—no additions to my comfort. Last night a block fell from aloft, and struck down a man at my side senseless. The Doctor cannot tell yet whether the man will live or not. The block weighed ten pounds and fell a hundred feet. Though the man was standing not six feet from me, the block fell so quietly, I was not aware of the accident until I heard someone exclaim, "there's a man killed," and saw them stoop to pick him up.

Tuesday Jan. 3d, 1854

Another double reefed and rainy day, but we had a fine run to the Est during the night, and are now in the Pacific. In my morning watch I was kept busy reducing sail, and bracing the yards to sudden shifts of wind. Tonight I have 'a sleep in' and wishing you a good night shall tell my boy Anthony Boyden to call me at 7 bells tomorrow morning.

Wednesday Jan. 4, 1854

The seventh anniversary of our dear little Harry's birth. I have just come down from a calm and drizzling watch, protected from the wet by my painted suit. In the mess we had an animated discussion as to Henry VIII's originating the reformation in England, and whether or not he was the head and founder of the English church.

Thursday Jan. 5th, 1854

Light airs and showers of rain all day, but now a breeze has sprung up which is promising a very quiet day. At noon we were 370 miles from our destination but have to sail three times that distance to reach it. Doct. Woodworth tells me he has two men on his list he fears will not recover.

Friday Jan. 6, 1854

A pleasant but foggy day which has bothered the master about fixing the position of the ship. The moon has been showing herself through the rugged and hurrying clouds this evening. I believe we are about 300 miles from Loo Choo.

Saturday Jan. 7, 1854

After a foggy morning we had a very pleasant day, and the air has been and is clear, cool, invigorating and delightful. We saw today the little island of Hoa-pin-san, and discovered by our bearings we had been drifted since our last observation by the currents 27 miles to the Nst and Est. Tonight is the night when sweethearts and wives are toasted, and as I have no wine—here's to your health in a bumper [of] "medicated Compound of Sasparilla,"[2] which the Doctor has furnished me to relieve my Job-like afflictions.

Sunday Jan. 8, 1854

A pleasant day, devoted to the usual Sunday duties, reading, writing, and quiet, and thoughts of home.

Happy the man whose wish and care
  A few paternal acres bound
Content to breathe his native air
  In his own ground.

Blest who can unconcernably find
  Hours days and years slide soft away
In health of body, peace of mind
  quiet by day.

Whose herds with milk, whose fields with bread
  Whose flocks supply him with attire
Whose trees in summer yield him shade
  In winter fire.

Thus would I live, unseen unknown
  Thus unlamented let me die
Steal from the world, and not a stone
  Tell where I lie.

Sound sleep by night, study and ease
  Together mixed; sweet reconscription
And him incensed, which most doth please
  With meditation.[3]

At Sea, Monday Jan 9, 1854

240 miles from Loo Choo today at noon and hastening towards it with a fair wind, the first we have really had since we left Hong Kong. Ten knots (i.e. nautic mile) an hour is fast shortening the dis-

[2] "Sasparilla"—from sarsaparilla, a medicinal preparation used as an alternative and tonic.

[3] Horace, *Epodes*, Book II: "Beatus ille que procul negotiis . . . ."

tance between us and our destination. Today the ther[mometer] stands at 61°. Yesterday and today I believe have been the coldest days we have had since leaving the U.S., unless one or two days off the Cape of Good Hope were colder.

Tuesday Jan 10th

Nearly as far from Loo Choo as we were yesterday! After obtaining a position to run for it with prevailing winds as advised by the books, the wind has hauled to the S.E. and threatens to blow a gale. Well, what matter, since I'm kept away from home, how and where I'm flung about on the earth's surface, [just] so I get my letters. The Doctor tells me he has a man very sick with chronic diarrhea. The man knocked down by a ten pound block a few nights since is in the fair way of recovery. Some people have hard heads.

Wednesday Jan. 11th

Rolling along under reduced sail before a N.W. wind waiting for daylight to shape our course of Napa Kiang.[4]

This morning at daylight we discovered the volcanic and dome shaped Island of Cleopatra,[5] which is about 2000 feet high, and soon after had the wind all around the compass and the heaviest sheet rain we have experienced since leaving Prince's Island. In the afternoon it cleared up and the wind became steady enough to allow of our making sail on our course; a little before sundown we passed Sulphur Island, which in outline resembles a patent metallic coffin. The whole shop was impregnated with a sulphurous odor as we passed under its lee. It was very evident that the island was in active volcanic action, and some fancied they saw it smoking. We saw a junk today struggling against the elements, and passed a sealed bottle, which our [sailors] assert is the one we threw overboard eleven

[4] Naha River is the influx into the port of Naha.

[5] The islands Cleopatra, Sulphur, and Montgomery constitute a group of islands named by Basil Hall the Montgomery Islands, Lat. 127° 55′ E, Long. 26° 55′ N. He shows them on a map in his *Account of a Voyage of Discovery to the West Coast of Corea and the Great Loo-choo Island*, Appendix, facing p. xix. The islands of the Ryukyu Archipelago have several variants of local Chinese and Japanese names or those given by European explorers, Captain Hall in particular. Many of the old names have been changed.

days since, and that it has beaten us in the passage. We are now running for the Montgomery Islands, and after sighting them will wait for daylight.

Harbor of Napa Kiang, Thursday, Jan. 12th, 1854

We anchored here about noon. It seems quite comfortable to be again in port. The *Vandalia* is here and the *Supply* arrived a few hours before us, though she left Hong Kong a week after us. By the *Supply* I received your letter of April 12th enclosing one from Gov. Stevens[6] accepting my offer to accompany him on his railroad explorations across the Rocky Mts. Though old, your letter was acceptable, and home feelings were kindled by the sight of your well known handwriting. My duties have kept me very busy today, but tomorrow if pleasant I shall go on shore to see the strange sights of this strange people. A deluge of officers from the *Vandalia* and *Supply*[7] is upon us, and I must do my share towards entertaining them.

Napa Kiang, Friday Jan 13th, 1854

Yesterday a canoe came off with a 'Yellow Cap' mandarin bearer of the Mayor of Napa's card to our captain—a piece of red paper a foot and more square containing that official's name and titles in choice Loo Chooan. Our Capt. took it, looked at it, turned it over, looked at it again, and then naively exclaimed, "Why there is nothing on it"—not supposing the insignificant character in the center of so large a paper could mean anything.

The Mayor sent as his apology for not calling personally that "he had the itch." A very sufficient reason we all concluded. It is said to

[6] Isaac Ingalls Stevens (1818–1862) of Andover, Massachusetts, was governor of Washington Territory from March 16, 1853, to March 4, 1857. He was also a territorial delegate to Congress and is noted for his survey of the North Pacific territories, as well as for his wars with the Indians. See *DAB*, XVII, 612–14, and bibliographical sources.

[7] The *Supply*, a sailing vessel of 547 tons, four guns, was purchased in 1846, laid up, New York, 1874. She was part of Commodore Perry's expeditionary force to Japan. Perry established an American base on Okinawa from May 26, 1853, to July 17, 1854. G. H. Kerr, *Okinawa: The History of an Island People*, 307–41, with illustrations.

be a prevalent disease and we are cautioned not to shake hands with any of the people no matter how high may be their rank—as the complaint is universal. The usual salutation is "kotowing"—bowing very low as in the Eastern Salaam and doubling your two hands and placing them together, and shaking them at the person you know or recognize. His honor the mayor sent the Capt this morning a present of pigs, poultry, goats and vegetables very acceptable after our sea voyage.

This morning I left the ship with a large party of our officers in the 10 o'clock boat to visit 'Napa.' We pulled around the point into Junk river or Harbor, where the commoners of the place find shelter, and passing the town, pulled up to the 'watering place,' and then returning to the town, landed and explored it; then walked to Mr. Bettelheim's,[8] the missionary, and from his house to the landing place near our ship: in all, a distance of over six miles. The country is in a state of garden-like cultivation; the people are numerous, and the place curious and peculiar. The rock seems all of coral formation and reminds me of those about Anton Leizondo and Vera Cruz. The rocky head lands of the Island are very much worn and gouged out by the action of the sea, and two of them bear the name of 'Capstan' and 'False Capstan Head' bestowed by the English Surveyors. The town or city of Napa is built along the banks of a little river,[9] and every house with its ground separated from its neighbor and enclosed by a wall of rough stone reaching as high as the roof. The entrances of these enclosures were usually closed, and the women and female children ran away at our approach or if unable to avoid us, turned their faces to the walls as we passed. Looking behind us we

[8] Bernard Jean Bettelheim (1811–1870), M.D., a Hungarian Jew, became a zealous Protestant missionary in the Ryukyu Islands and resided in Naha, Okinawa. On May 2, 1846, the Bettelheims, along with Miss James, a Colonial Infant Society teacher, arrived as English citizens and were located in a Buddhist temple, Rinkai-ji, on an island in Naha Harbor. This was their first home. Later they were moved to another temple, Gokoku-ji, until June, 1854. At the request of the regent of the Ryukyus, Commodore Perry took Bettelheim to Ningpo, China, on July 17, 1854. He died in Brookfield, Missouri. E. R. Bull, *Okinawa or Ryukyu, the Floating Dragon*, 121–22; Kerr, *op. cit.*, 279–96.

[9] Napa Kiang, or Naha Gawa.

often caught them peering at us with genuine feminine curiosity. In the market place the women left their wares and fled from us. It was amusing and yet annoying to see such crowds of people run as hard to escape from five or six who thought themselves passably good looking. Certainly some of these wrinkled old beldames had no occasion for alarm, and very few of the young maidens could be called even pretty.

There was very little for sale in the market, and nothing curious to buy.

Some boxes of a rough lacquer, a few pieces of coarse cotton cloth of Loo Chooan manufacture, some crockery and pottery with vegetables and other articles of diet, comprised about all we saw. Many of the venders decamped locking their boxes. In the river fronting the town were four junks of large size and many smaller craft. A small ferry boat was plying from bank to bank crowded with passengers. We visited the principal Temple dedicated to Confucius, and which has a large copper figure of the sage supported on each side by another idol of smaller dimensions. Within the enclosure of this Temple there was a Dragon boat and a great bell. One of the party climbed up into the shrine and thoughtlessly and irreverently plucked a tablet out of the sage's hand—examined and put it back, then pulled to our horror the old gentleman's nose, and descended.

The Keeper of the Temple made no objection to his sacrilege, and Mr. Bettelheim tells us they have so little reverence for their gods that in the Capital Shuda[10] the children stone them. Mr. B. lives with his wife and children in a Temple that was given up to them for their abode. Near his residence on False Capstan head there is a fortress and Temple, and in the latter which we opened and examined we found several Buddha idols. We also visited another Temple near the market.

Uninvited and without ceremony being told to do so by Mr. Bettelheim we pushed open doors and entered people's houses. After the women had made their escape to some inner sanctuary the men would welcome us, and offer us tea and sometimes a pipe. The tea was served in little cups unsweetened and without milk. Smoking

[10] Shuri Castle is in Shuri, or Shuda. It was the residence of the Ryukyu kings.

seems to be a general custom, and the only English words many could command was "American tobacco" begging some. We made a blind beggar boy rich in the article, but I fear it was taken from him. Their own tobacco is very mild and put up in papers in shape and size like a common brick.

The Loo Chooans pay an annual tribute of $10,000 to the Emperor of China, and a number of youths are annually sent to Pekin to be educated. There is said to be a Japanese viceroy and some Japanese soldiers and priests at Shuda, but if so they are kept very secret for they have not been seen by any of the Europeans or Foreigners who have visited the island from Capt. Basil Hall's[11] time until now. They carry on a trade with both China and Japan, and since the arrival of the *Vandalia* three junks have arrived from Japan. The day before we came in a large junk sailed for Hong Kong, availing of the favoring monsoon. The people on shore today were very curious in their inquiries about the Chinese rebellion. The Masonry of the Loo Chooan houses, the wall which surrounded, and the bridges are all constructed of the coral rock, neatly dressed and faced, but put together without cement. Some arches we saw are beautiful specimens of masonry, but only a few of them had keystones.

Their way of making salt is peculiar; a low and level flat near the bay is used by them as a salt pan. Salt water is thrown upon it and evaporated. It is raked over several times, and the salt that has collected is scraped up with the earth in heaps over little vats. More water is thrown upon the heaps and the salt collects, by its own gravity, in the vats. At least that is as near as I could make out the operation. The several ranks of the people are distinguished by Red, Blue, or Yellow Caps, and by the color of the pin with which they fasten up their hair. The silver pins are the gentlemen or little better. The yellow pins little better than their serfs. There are a great number of tombs in sight of our ship, larger than those we have been

[11] Basil Hall (1788–1844), a British naval officer, is celebrated for his cruise in the sloop *Lyra* in 1816 with Lord Amherst's embassy to China. This exploratory cruise is described in his *Account of a Voyage of Discovery to the West Coast of Corea and the Great Loo-choo Islands*. He also published accounts of his travels to Chile, Peru, Mexico, and the west coast of North America. *DNB*, VIII, 942–43; *Encyclopaedia Britannica* (1956), I, 99.

accustomed to see in China, and of the same horseshoe shape. Their new year commences like the Chinese with the first new moon which happens this year on the 29th inst. and is celebrated with a grand Fair which I hope to attend, and, where aided by Dr. Bettelheim, I hope to purchase something curious as a memento to this visit.

Capt. Basil Hall, who was the first to visit and describe the Loo Chooans, makes them to be veritable acadians, but he was a well known romancer, and Dr. B. assures was never permitted to land at Napa, and did not see so much of the place as I have on my first morning's ramble. There would be no difficulty in opening trade with these people, if it were not for the Japanese spies, who are said to be everywhere, and overlook, note and report the minute particulars. There is in the Foreign Grave Yard on shore a Tomb created over the remains of a French Missionary[12] to Japan, who died here in 1848 and another of the surgeon of the *Victoriese,*[13] each has a large wooden cross at the head of the grave, which is evidence the Loo Chooans do not entertain the hostility to that emblem of our faith the Japanese are said to. A sailor from the *Mississippi* and one from the *Susquehanna* are buried in the same enclosure, and I fear we may have to add another one from our ship.

Capt. Pope of the *Vandalia,* whom I met on shore, today enquired the latest news from down east, but he had the latest dates. Com. Perry hurried the *Supply* to sea when the mail was hourly expected, saying the next ship would bring up the letters soon enough. So much for his phelinks! I suppose it is all for the best I did not get Gov. Stevens' letter, and that I am here, but I think I would have enjoyed the adventure.

Saturday Jan. 14, 1854

It has been a beautiful day which I improved by making an excursion to Shuda—accompanied by Purser Allison and Doctor Gilliam.

[12] Father Mathieu Adnet (1813–1848), a Frenchman, died in Naha after a two-year stay on Okinawa. His tombstone is still preserved. Bull, *op. cit.,* 129.

[13] The *Victorieuse,* a French corvette under the command of Rigault de Genouilly, took part in various actions (after 1846) in China against the Taipings and in Korea in defense of French missionaries. Cf. Ch. Dallet, *Histoire de l'église de Corée,* II, 336–39.

We landed from the ship at 10 o'clock, and returned in season for our usual mess dinner at 3 o'clock. In a straight line from the shore to Shuda the distance may not be more than two miles, but following the road is mad to exceed two and a half. The road is beautifully paved with black lava and coral, and the views from it are very fine. The whole surface of the country is occupied. Hills and valleys are alike in a state of garden-like cultivation, and where the hills are too rocky or sterile for any other purpose, they are honeycombed with the tombs of the dead. Rice, beans, sweet potatoes, wheat and sugar cane seem the principal product of these fields. The fear expressed yesterday we noticed again today; the women and children abandoned their houses, and fled across the fields at our approach, or cowered behind the bushes and stone walls, occasionally one bolder than the rest, or because she thought escape impossible, would simply turn her back on us as we passed.

Whenever we looked back, we could see crowds following us, but only point a finger at them, and they were off like a shot. We walked over the Capital Shuda but saw but little—the houses being all shut up behind their high stone enclosures; we opened doors and intruded ourselves into several of these without seeing anything to reward our pains. The Regent's Palace is enclosed by a Fortress, which covers the top of a high hill, around the base of which the Capital of Shuda is clustered. We walked all around the Fortress only to find it inaccessible to our further researches.

We saw, however, in our rambles, a pretty artificial lake or pond surrounded by winding walls of stone, and crossed by bridges, with a small temple in one part approached by a bridge.

We also happened upon a large horseshoe-shaped enclosure of stone, at [the] back part of which were three tombs, each of them as large as a house devotes to a living inhabitant. They were all in a row, adjoining each other and were ornamented with grotesque lions carved in stone. Nearby was a Buddhist Temple, in which were two idols seated in a lotus leaf, and a third mounted on a dog. One of those in the lotus leaf was seated on a white elephant. The shaven priest or Bonze who attended this Temple lived in a house adjoining, where he offered us tea, water and a pipe. He refused our money, but accepted a segar and politely accompanied us to the gateway, where he kotowed us out. From their neighborhood to the palace and extraordinary size and style, we imagined them to be the tombs of the Vice kings or regents. It was only by climbing a high wall and after crossing what[14] we supposed some gentleman's private grounds that we chanced to see them. The rock on which the Palace and the Fortress of Shuda is built reminded me of the Acropolis at Athens but wanted its beautiful marble Temples. Shuda like Athens lies all around her Acropolis. The masonry here reminds me of the description I have read of the dwellings of the Mexicans or Peruvians in the time of Cortez[15] and Pizarro.[16] We saw from a hill some children studying their books in a field below us, but on our approach they all ran away. The teachers, however, entertained us with tea and pipes, and before we left, the children came crowding back to see us. Several fine enclosures and houses we hoped to enter, and knocked for admittance at, were closed against us.

I have learned today that Metsa is the Loo Chooan for 'water' and 'cha' which is the same in Chinese—for tea. Tobacco they call as we do, tobacco.

Napa Roads, Island of Loo Choo
Sunday Jan. 15, 1954

It has been raining in pleasant showers all day, just enough to purify the air and make the cultivated shores near us look refreshing. Dr. Bettelheim preached on board our ship today an extempora discourse from the Text, "Behold I bring you good tidings of great joy, and which shall be for all the people."[17] He said we had brought him good tidings and he thought he could not introduce himself for the first time better than by proclaiming the good tidings of great joy—which were for all the people. Spoke of the joy of receiving a letter from an absent friend, and how much more should be our joy at receiving good tidings concerning our Heavenly friend and benefac-

[14] Here Preble skipped a page in the diary. The text, however, is complete.

[15] Hernando Cortes (1485–1547), the Spanish conqueror of Mexico, landed in Mexico on March 4, 1519.

[16] Francisco Pizarro (*ca.* 1471–1541) was the Spanish discoverer and conqueror of Peru.

[17] Luke 2:10.

tor. It was an ingenious and animated discourse to which his foreign accentuation and broken English gave additional force. Reading the Hymns was rather a stumbling block to him but he showed he conceived their sense. Doc B. is a converted Jew, and now an enthusiastic missionary. He has been here for eight years, subjected to constant espionage and several times imprisoned and beaten. His labors have been rewarded by only one convert, who was murdered when his heresy became known. Dr. B. has his wife and three children to share his voluntary exile, two little blue-eyed girls and a boy. At times they have been a year without communication with the world beyond the island, but since our Expedition the communication has been more frequent. We brought him up letters from England, and toys and presents for the children. The smallest girl with a shyness almost equal to a Loo Chooan brought me her new doll to look at. Madam appears a sensible pleasant woman, and the Doctor speaks six languages. At present he is our Chief, I may say only means of communication with the natives, and through him we obtain pigs, poultry and other mess necessaries. Some call the Doctor a humbug and say he resides here from avaricious motives, but I reserve my opinion until I see and know more of him. It seems cruel to doubt the sincerity of one who has isolated himself from the rest of the world, subject to persecution and martyrdom, as he has done. He is supported by a society of British Naval Officers, and his salary is said to be only 500$. He lives in a deserted Temple, which makes him a comfortable residence rent free. The officers of the *Plymouth* have presented him with a silver Goblet[18] which cost about $80, in recognition of his services when they were here last winter. In his house he has the engraved portraits of Com. Perry and Queen Victoria hanging cheek by jowl.

Monday Jan 16th

Eight hours on deck today in the rain, and the rest of the day in taking comfort below, have not furnished me with any incident worth recording. Purser A. went out today with his gun and brought back a bag full of game. The natives saw him shoot with astonishment. You

[18] See the picture of the goblet in Bull, *op. cit.*

know that not a gun, sword, pike, arrow or arms of any description has been seen on the island. It is rumored there is a Japanese garrison shut up in the Fortress of Shuda or somewhere but no one has ever seen them. The walls and Forts of Masonry are well adapted to defence though not against cannon or musketry. When or how these curious islanders were disarmed, and whether by Chinese or Japanese conquerors, we have been unable to ascertain.

Tuesday Jan 17, 1854

I enjoyed another ramble on shore today and an hour or two of pleasant conversation with Dr. Bettelheim and his lady. The Doctor is a manifest destiny man, and believes there is a Divine Providence working by direct interposition to bring Japan and its tributaries—these 'Isles of the Sea' into the Christian fold. He says the correct name of the Capitol is Shu-Lie,[19] a Head mile, that is, it is the starting point for measuring distances throughout the Island.

When Dr. B. first arrived, the natives brought him two cows to get vaccine from small pox, as is evident from the seamed and scarred faces we have seen, being one of the plagues of the Island. Two years after, when the disease was epidemic and making frightful ravages, he succeeded in procuring some lymph with which he first vaccinated his two children, and then others until he checked and arrested its fatality. Since then the mandarins have given up the sick to his care and through care for their bodies, he hopes to influence their minds. The native Doctors came to see him vaccinate, and now he has six assistants among them who use his lancets.

However much he may have benefited this people in this way, I do not believe his missionary efforts have advanced the cause of Christianity one step. It is an uphill battle to convert a people who are indifferent to their own religion. Once the Doctor succeeded in distributing quite a lot of tracts printed in Chinese. But they were all gathered up in a few days and returned to him by the authorities. He thinks, however, a few may have escaped their notice, and be yet abroad to leaven the whole lump of this heathen population. Our Master, who was a little drunken at the time, said to Mrs. B. this morning, "You have been eight years here you say, and how many

[19] Shu-li is the Shuri of today.

converts have you made?" "Well," she replied, "We have been able to influence four, but can scarcely claim to having made one convert." At which our Master exclaimed, Depend on it. In Adam your business don't pay. Why your average success has been but half of a half Christian in a year.

In my walk through Napa and the market this morning the same fear was expressed by the women and children which I have mentioned on former occasions, but the children, grown bolder, ran after and picked up the small coppers we dropped behind us. The market women covered up their goods and left their stalls, but we took the liberty of peeping under their covers; sweet potatoes seems to be the chief article of traffic, but we saw some white radishes 18 inches long and as big around as a Paten bottle. In the fish market were some flying fish the size of a mackeral, and two or three kinds of shark with several baskets of a sea weed which appears to be used as an article of food. We saw several men and women today who appeared to be afflicted with elephantiasis.

The windows here are all 'glazed' with oiled paper which admits the light but affords no look out. Since the arrival of our squadron we have furnished Dr. B.'s windows with glass, which it its first introduction for the purpose to this island. We have also furnished him with chairs and other comforts. Among the latter I suspect was some whiskey—real monongahela—with which he regaled us today.[20]

Wednesday Jan. 18, 1854

Purser A. went out with his gun this morning and returned this evening with cur low, spoonbills, doves, woodcock, cranes and plover, a full load of game. He is a keen and untiring sportsman and enjoys the exhilaration of a tramp after birds.

In an odd note of the *Living Age*,[21] I was reading today there is an article on the Human Hair which I found the following very applicable I think to a person you and I know very well. In all the galleries of Europe there is not a painting by any old master of a female

[20] Monongahela whiskey was produced in the nineteenth century in Monongahela, Pennsylvania.

[21] Its full title was *Littell's Living Age*. It was founded in Boston in May, 1844, and discontinued in August, 1941. *British Union-Catalogue of Periodicals*, III, 69.

head in which black hair is depicted; poets and painters both delight in golden or sun locks or auburn ringlets "thus you see your hair has the recommendation of high art and poetry" but here is another extract still more appropo, "There is a kind of hair full of graceful waves, which in Ireland is called 'good-natured hair'; there is something quite charming in its rippling line across the forehead. Art has attempted to imitate it, but the eye immediately detects the imposture. It no more resembles the real thing than the set smile of the opera dancer does the genuine play of the features from some pleasurable emotion of the mind. This buckled hair is, in short, the same as that denounced by the early Christians under the name of the 'malice of the devil,' a term which it well deserves." After this I think you will hold your good natured auburn locks in more esteem.

Thursday Jan 19th

We are having a N.W. gale today which has obliged us to let go a second anchor, and the ship rolls and pitches, but we congratulated ourselves on being in port.

I read today that the custom of giving and wearing wedding rings originated with the Romans, and that they placed the ring on the fourth finger because it was believed a nerve reached thence to the heart. The Romans were right; don't you feel so darling?

Friday Jan 20th

The gale has abated and I have brought a wearisome and monotonous day's duty on deck to a close. Our Marine Officer was kept out of the ship last night, and various were the conjectures as to where he found shelter. He returned this afternoon when it was discovered he had been housed on board the *Vandalia.*

For want of other amusement we sealed the door of his room and affixed to it a paper offering a reward for any information concerning him, and made up a mock inventory of his effects. To assist the joke I got off the following doggerel. You must know he is particularly sensitive about his grey hairs and bald head, and being thought as the Chinese say an 'olo' man. Anything for a laugh to enliven one of the sixteen thousand odd hours that must elapse before we hail Columbia again.

"Oh Jones! Old Jones where hast thou gone
Thus wandering from us all alone
Why leave us thus to speculate
Upon thy unknown mysterious fate
We fear that on the road to Shudi
Drinking too deep Loo Chooan saki
That thou old man alas didst get high
And in the fields sought thy repose
Or somewhere else! Where heaven only knows!
Perhaps inflamed by amatory desire
Enticed by a Loo Chooan Deliah
You in her arms reposed last night!
Grey—'olo' man—immoral wright!

We hope our surmise is not right
A friend suggests how hard it rhymes
You slept last night at Bettelheim's
We know 'twas your 'manifest destiny'
That with him you should take your tea
Another friend suggests the regent
Has poor old Jones to prison sent
Others believe with brother 'Reed'
You went on board to take your feed
Wherein thou art. Do pity our distress
I mean your friends in this our wardroom mess
And let us see again—gray bald old Jones
And joy anew in his soft dulcet tones."[22]

Napa, Loo Choo, Saturday Jan 21, 1854

Yesterday a man named Levins, who has been sick for sometime, died on board, and I went ashore this afternoon and attended his funeral. He had been dying for three days previous and our surgeons were astonished at the tenacity with which life clung to him. He was conscious to the last and died with all the calmness of a Christian philosopher. It seems to me that when made aware of the certainty of

[22] At this point in the diary, Preble mistakenly numbered the page "121½."

death, we reconcile ourselves to the inevitable, and meet it calmly. This is often seen in last moments of criminals before execution. It is particularly my experience with sailors, who certainly are not the most moral of men, and generally have sins enough to remember to make a deathbed terrible, if it were not for this apathetic calmness.

Returning to the ship to dinner, we were about discussing the dessert, when we were electrified by the announcement that three steamers were in sight, which we knew must be the *Susquehanna, Powhatan* and *Mississippi,* though full two weeks sooner than we expected them. By the squadron I have received your letter of Oct 25th and hope to have another by the Store Ships, *Southampton* or *Saratoga,* expected tomorrow. It grieves me to hear of the dropping off of so many of the old standard inhabitants of Portland, viz., Mr. Man, Anderson, Gerrish, and now Mr. Staley. Henceforth they will be remembered only by a few friends and in the hearts of their children. We who have been youngsters are growing old to supply their vacant places.

Henry's saying "he feared he would be a girl before he was born," though undoubtedly original to his young brain, has not been unthought of. It was only the other day in reading some remarkable instances of memory, one said "He recollected being afraid before he was born that he would be a girl." Next to was the instance of the man who recollected "the Doctors knocking the snow off the heads of his boots the night he was born."

Loo Choo, Sunday Jan 22d, 1854

F . . . k C . . . k[23] is here on board the Store ship *Lexington* or rather the wreck of what is left of him, for he is disagreeably disfigured by disease and is said to be very intemperate. What a change from the handsome manly boy we knew, and how it must grieve his mother's and sister's hearts. It is reported the Commodore sent his Chaplain[24] on board to take his pledge that he would stop drinking.

[23] In Perry's official report, there is no sailor on the *Southampton* or any other ship of the expedition who could be identified as F . . . k C . . . k.

[24] There were two chaplains in the expedition: George Jones, attached to the *Mississippi,* and E. C. Bittinger on the *Susquehanna.* Both were considered by Commodore Perry as his chaplains. *Narrative,* II, 411.

I regret he is in our squadron, and hope it may not be my disagreeable duty to sit on his Court Martial, should he, as seems likely, be tried by one.

I learn today that our ship, with the other sailing vessels, will sail in a week for Japan, leaving the steamers to follow. The Commodore has been hurried up by receiving orders to send the *Susquehanna* home, and he has today had Carpenters on board the *Powhatan*, measuring to see if the *Susquehanna's* deck cabin can be shifted to her. The *Susquehanna* is to accompany us to Japan, and as soon as the Treaty is concluded, will go to Bombay, to bring to China the new U.S. Commissioner Mr. McLane,[25] and then return home.

All hands today are engaged in discharging the coals from the *Supply*, and are to be kept at work all night, and she is to sail at once for Shanghai to take in another load—a good opportunity for us to send letters, which will not be neglected by me.

Among other local events of the day, I may mention the birth on board of a pretty, lively, frisky little kid, which the men have already in training for a pet. Its mother was sent off by the Mayor of Napa the day we arrived, as a present to the Captain.

How would you like to be served as the Marquis de Argenson served his Mistress—as an evidence of my love and affection? The Marquis de Voyer de Argenson[26] had an actress named Mademoiselle Lehan for a Mistress. She died one day, and a Christian burial was not allowed to players, the Marquis had her body burned to ashes. Being an alchemist, the idea occurred to him to heat the ashes, and by that means a small quantity of glass was produced, which he caused to be made into two rings. One of these rings was in the pos-

[25] Robert Milligan McLane (1815–1898) was a noted lawyer, congressman, and diplomat. In 1853, he was nominated U.S. commissioner to China and also to Japan, Siam, Korea, and Cochin China. He tried to maintain American interests in Canton in co-operation with the diplomatic and consular agents of Great Britain and France, but was unsuccessful in his relations with the Chinese. J. H. Latane and D. W. Wainhouse, *A History of American Foreign Policy, 1776–1940*, 336–37; *DAB*, XII, 115–16; H. B. Morse, *The International Relations of the Chinese Empire*, I, 412–15.

[26] Contemporary to G. H. Preble was Marquis Marc René de Voyer d'Argenson (1771–1842), who was aide-de-camp to Lafayette. He was known for his democratic tastes and manners. See *La grande éncyclopédie*, III, 838, with bibliography.

session of M. de la Borde,[27] Chamberlain to Louis XVI. It appeared like common glass.

Perhaps you would rather be remembered as I have lately read a modern blue beard sought to keep his loves in remembrance. The story goes that he was three times married, and that he had the bodies of his first two wives embalmed and one placed on each side of his bed. The story said, however, that the third lady, before she consented to share his couch, compelled him to remove his old favorites. These stories may make you laugh—as they did me.

Monday Jan 23d, 1854

The Commodore, wherever he goes, keeps everybody busy. Our boats have been discharging the *Supply* and she is to sail on Saturday. Our Carpenters have been knocking down and building up Cabins on board the steamers, and our other mechanics have been busy at work so that but little bread of idleness has been eaten today. Capt. A[bbot] sent me to see the Commodore this forenoon on a matter of duty, and I was very graciously received and recognized. It is the second time I have said how do you do to him, since our arrival out. The two missing store ships and the *Saratoga* have not arrived but are hourly expected. I hope for a letter by one or the other.

Tuesday Jan 24, 1854

The two store ships arrived today noon, and the *Saratoga* reported outside. She will have a rough time of it tonight, for it is blowing a fresh gale from the N.W. The weather has prevented our boarding the store ships to ascertain whether they may have brought us any letters. I am a rough-looking fellow now, for I have not touched razor to my face for more than a month; yet if I were to haul alongside of you, in spite of the 'bore's' bristles, you would find a spot to kiss, I fancy. My mess mates say my hirsute beard is improving, but to myself I look like an Orson[28] that would frighten a city damsel, and only fitted to live with Satyrs. While I wear my beard long, I have my hair cropped short and shampoo it every morning.

[27] Charles Borde (1711–1781) was a poet and writer of significance.

[28] Orsino, duke of Illyria, is a character in Shakespeare's comedy *Twelfth Night.*

Courtesy U.S. Navy

he U.S.S. *Susquehanna*, Commodore Perry's Flagship during the Expedition, from a Watercolor by Clary Ray

A Japanese Junk

The Commodore is arranging a tour up the island for next week to last five days. I am a volunteer, but as our ship is expected to go to sea, I fear there is little chance of my making the excursion. I learn that one of our ships is to remain at Jeddo through the summer, and another is to be sent to the sea of Ochosths to land Lt. Bent[29] of the *Mississippi,* who proposes to travel from Ochosths to Tobolsk and Smolensk, and has written to St. Petersburg for the necessary passports. He explained to me today his projected journey, which I thought would be novel and interesting, but attended with danger and difficulty. The ships of the squadron are crowded full of everything necessary for a prolonged visit to Japan. Our ship has full eight months' stores and provisions on board, and water excepted, we could keep the sea that long.

Purser Allison writes long and fine letters to his wife as I believe I have before mentioned. He has been counting his lines and letters today and says he gets 82 lines on a page letter paper size, 12,296 words. He has seven sheets of a letter (56 pages) of that sort now ready to send off. His wife seems to return to him line for line and letter for letter. I thought I was a wearisomely long correspondent, but I find my letters do not exceed 2,980 words on a sheet, only 600 more than our Purser gets on a page; still I think mine are fine enough, and I would prefer you paying postage rather than for spectacles. The Purser expects to save enough from this cruize to buy a farm and resign. He takes his absence very hard, but I believe I love you as much as he does his wife, though I do not let my absence worry me as much. There is no rose in creation for him out here.

Loo Choo, Wednesday Jan 25, 1854

I have shivered through this raw, cold and blustering day without much improvement either of mind or body or estate. Yesterday we buried one of the Engineers of the *Susquehanna* named Crosby,[30]

[29] Commodore Perry does not include the name of Lieutenant Bent in the official list of officers belonging to the several ships composing his naval expedition to Japan. *Narrative,* II, 410–14.

[30] Eli Crosby was made third assistant engineer on September 22, 1849; second assistant engineer, February 26, 1851. He died on January 24, 1854.

who died from the effects of constipation too long neglected. This evening the gale begins to abate, but it has blown hard through the day, and an angry sea sends its snowy foam over the reefs which protect this anchorage. That ship outside must have had a disagreeable time of it. She is thought now not to be the *Saratoga*[31] but a Merchant ship chartered to land a missionary here on her route to San Francisco.

Reading Abbott's Napoleon in the May no. of *Harper*[32] today, I came across the following which shows me that great people act just like common folks: you and I, for instance, sometimes. Abbott says that when Napoleon was called by his valet in the morning, the Empress would say with a smile, will you rise so soon? Remain a little longer. Well if I do, you will not sleep will you? Was His Majesty's usual reply. Then he would roll her up in the coverlid laughing and tickling her on the cheeks and neck.

Thursday Jan 26, 1854

Again I draw my curtain and shut myself in my little stateroom to write my darling. How such a misnomer came to be applied to a little room 6 feet long, eight feet wide and six feet high, and when cleansed of its contents—viz., drawers, berth, bureau, washstand, trunk, chair, book and etc., just 288 cubic feet of air—I cannot imagine. The English name of cabin is better. The blowy weather continues but the Commodore has made signal to the sailing ships, us included, and supply excepted, "to complete our wood and water, and be in readiness to sail as soon as the weather moderates."

Our marine officer has been endeavoring to outdo the Purser and has actually got ninety-two lines upon a page of his letter. This has occasioned a talk about fine writing, and I told them of seeing at Lowell's[33] last year 75 words written on the 1/625 part of an inch,

31 The *Saratoga,* an old American packet ship, was under the command of Captain Benjamin Trask. *Greyhounds,* 136; *Clipper,* 43; see also note 81 under the year 1853.

32 See John S. C. Abbott, "Napoleon Bonaparte," *Harper's New Monthly Magazine,* Vol. VI (May, 1853), 749–62.

33 Preble refers to James Russell Lowell (1819–1891), a prominent American poet, essayist, scholar, and diplomat.

which they could not credit. I told them also of Mr. Lowell's writing the Lord's Prayer[34] plainly and legibly without magnifier within the circumference of a three-cent piece. This being also doubted, I undertook the same and send you the result. The weather has prevented my going on shore today to say goodbye to Loo Choo.

Sir Thos. More when confined in the tower and deprived of pen and ink, wrote his Margaret,[35] "This letter is written with a coal but to express my love a peck of coals would not suffice." I am not brought to the same strait, but I can say a peck of living coals would not express the glow and fervor of my affection for my absent darling.

Napa Roads, Loo Choo, Friday Jan 27, 1854

The gale has abated and we have so far completed our wooding and watering that we can sail tomorrow if the Commodore wishes. The *Lexington* brought us some newspapers which we received this morning. The *Southampton* we have not heard from—but if she had brought any letters today they would have been sent on board. F . . . k C . . . k I am informed looks wretchedly; what a melancholy case of self-destruction his is. A young man prematurely old from disease and offensive to the sight—perhaps it is better he should drink himself out of the world than linger in it to be a monument of his own shame and sensuality. From my recollections of his early and promising youth and friendship for his father, I wish I could do something for him, but alas he is beyond advice or control. I tremble for the purity and innocence of our noble little boy when I think of

[34] Correctly, "A Prayer," by James Russell Lowell; cf. *The Poetical Works of James Russell Lowell,* I, 46: "God! do not let my loved one die but rather wait until the time . . . ."

[35] Margaret (married to Mr. Roper), the eldest daughter of Sir Thomas More (1478–1535), was a child of his first marriage (to Jane Colte, *ca.* October 1, 1505). She was most beloved by her father, who corresponded with her during his imprisonment in the Tower of London. Preble refers to a letter sent from the Tower in 1534: "If I would with my writing, (mine owne good daughter) declare how much pleasure and comfort your daughterlye loving letters were unto me a peck of coles woulde not suffice to make me the pennes . . ." Cf. E. F. Rogers (ed.), *The Correspondence of Sir Thomas More,* 540.

all the temptations and allurements he will be subjected to and over which we can have so little control. We must trust him to a kind providence aided by such advice and influence as it is in our power to give. I would rather he proved good than proved great and honest, trustful, industrious, loving God and doing good to man, rather than gifted with the wisdom of Solomon, and having his weaknesses.

Saturday Jan 28, 1854

It is pleasant to set down to this my evening remembrance after an active day's duty on deck, and throw aside its cares and vexations for a little love chat. Our boats and men are working night and day to discharge the *Supply*. We are to sail on Tuesday for Jedo Bay accompanied by the squadron of sailing vessels. I have been annoyed today by the conduct of our Master[36] who is a very clever fellow when himself, but occasionally as today makes too free with the bottle. Every situation in life has its peculiar cares and anxieties, and mine can claim no exemptions.

Napa Road, Loo Choo, Sunday Jan 29, 1854

For a wonder we have had a pleasant day, and we have enjoyed it, from its rarity. After our muster and inspection I went on board the *Mississippi* to church and heard a curious discourse from Chaplain Jones[37] from this text—"On shore yesterday at the hospital I saw a man who had fallen from the mizen top of one of these vessels and

[36] He was John Walcutt, acting master of the *Macedonian;* see also note 37 under the year 1853.

[37] George Jones (1800–1870) was born in York, Pennsylvania, graduated from Yale College in 1823, and received his M.A. in 1826. He was made chaplain on April 20, 1833, and during Perry's expedition was attached to the *Mississippi.* He died in Philadelphia on January 22, 1870. He is the compiler of the third volume of Commodore Perry's report to the Congress, *Observations on the Zodiacal Light,* and the author of the documentary *Sketches of Naval Life* (2 vols., 1829) and other books of lesser value. He was on a cruise in China in 1844–45 as a navy chaplain and was the first chaplain of the U.S. Naval Academy at Annapolis (February, 1851). He retired in July, 1862, but during the Civil War served as a chaplain in Washington and at Gettysburg. His merits are mostly connected with the scientific studies of the zodiacal light. *DAB,* X, 170–71; *List,* 301; *LBD,* IV, 433. See also C. M. Drury, *United States Naval Chaplains, 1778–1945,* 141.

broke his leg." His application was, as in the physical world any endeavor to counteract the laws of gravitation either by design or accident is attended with pain and suffering and perhaps death, so in the spiritual world, any offence against God's laws are equally punishable. His application was clumsy but effective, and he closed by quoting as the summary of all God's laws, the new commandment.[38] To love God with all our heart and our neighbor as ourself. Before the seamen he read very impressively the Chapter on Charity—"If I have all these and have not Charity, etc."[39] He stopped his reading and defined Charity as love, and said, without love and the emotions produced by it all of which are described in the chapter, religion was nothing. His whole service was liberal Christianity and therefore pleased me. I saw Dr. Bettelheim among his auditors and could not but hope he would carry away a little charity and love for these poor Loo Chooans he so despises. I hear that Dr. B. will leave the Island as soon as the new missionary has been initiated and there is talk of the *Supply*'s taking his family to Shanghai.

Allowing him all due credit for sincerity and enthusiasm, Dr. B. seems to me about the worst kind of a person to have sent among such a people. From his supreme contempt for them he knows less about them after his eight years' residence than some would acquire in as many months. He will not allow them the commonest virtues and attributes all they do to deceit and hypocrisy—even to the cultivation of flowers around their dwellings. His own grounds are as barren of flowers, shrubs or vegitables as the day he arrived. His chief work has been a translation of the Scriptures into the Island language and the construction of a Loo Chooan dictionary.[40]

Have I ever told you that the married women of this island have the backs of their hands tatooed in blue ink. The origin of this custom is said to be that many, many years ago a beautiful Loo Chooan Maid

[38] John 13:34: "A new commandment I give unto you, That ye love one another; as I have loved you, that ye also love one another."

[39] I Cor. 13:4–5: Charity suffereth long, and is kind; charity envieth not; charity vaunteth not itself, is not puffed up . . . ."

[40] Bettelheim translated into Ryukyu six chapters of the Gospel according to St. John. Bull, *op. cit.*, 122.

was married to a young man to whom she was tenderly attached. Soon after their union the young husband left his bride to go to China in the annual Junk, and remained away for a long time without being heard from until all but his devoted wife gave him up for lost. Being very beautiful the widowed wife was much sought by the young men of the village, and urged by the parents to choose a new mate. She persisted in the belief of her husband's return and resisted all entreaties, and, as one of her chief beauties was the pretty and delicate hands, she disfigured them by dipping them in lye or tattooing them. In commemoration of the lovely Loo Chooan maid's constancy, and to evidence their unalterable affection for their husbands, tattooing the hands of married women became from that time a common custom.

The boats of the *Vandalia* which have been up the island surveying its coasts returned today, and the officers say their excursion has been very pleasant. One of them told me they discovered a manufactoring of gun powder, but it was of so poor a quality that he put some in his pipe and smoked it without its exploding! They also discovered where iron has been mined and sulphur and what they think is slaty coal. We have had a crowd of officers aboard from the other ships all day, to say goodbye.

Monday Jan 30, 1854

We are under sailing orders and are to sail at daylight tomorrow. We are anxious to be off while the good weather continues. I went on shore this morning to take my fare well of Great Loo Choo. As an amusement I scattered some Chinese cash, of which there are 1400 to a dollar, among the urchins, of whom I soon had quite a crowd following me. One daring little rascal even thrust his hand into my pocket, but I soon stopped that boldness—which was more than I had bargained for. The *Saratoga* has not yet arrived. The Steamers are to sail from here about a week after us. A few mornings since in washing me, I hauled off with my towel my wedding ring. It is the first time it has been off my finger since you placed it there. If at all superstitious I should take it as a bad omen, but it is not my custom to borrow trouble of that kind. Still I wish you were here to replace it.

At Sea, Tuesday Jan 31, 1854

We got underway in company with the *Lexington* and *Southampton* this morning at daylight, and have been coast[ing] along the shores of the Islands that form the beautiful Loo Choo Archipelago all day. We beat the other ship with ease and are therefore anticipating a long passage. The distance we have to go is about nine hundred miles. We have had a very pleasant day and the fair wind is giving us a good shove up the coast. It is rumored that Commodore Perry has offcial information from the Governor of Java of the death of the Emperor of Japan,[41] and it is surmised the report is thrown out to excuse and delay our negociations. I am not sanguine we will obtain any practical result from our present display of force, but every visit from a ship of war breaks down another barrier of Japanese exclusiveness. Something was attained last summer when our squadron advanced farther than any foreign ship of war had ever advanced before. When the cordan of boats was forced off, and a force landed; and the President's letter given into the hands of a High Official appointed to receive it. This time we expect to complete a survey of Jeddo Bay and astonish 'the little pig tails' with our railroad and electric telegraph. If unsuccessful in negociating a treaty of commerce we hope to get the privilege of asylum for our whalers in the ports of Japan.

We have enjoyed a bright, clear and sunny day with the ther[mometer] at 70. As I came down the ladder just now I saw the beautiful new moon over my right shoulder. The moon is a pleasant companion to our night watches, and calls up a thousand home feelings and associations of the ocean wanderer.

We seem to have been on a whaling ground today, as all day long these monsters of the deep have been 'blowing' and sporting around our bows.

Happening to look at the log slate on board the *Mississippi* yes-

[41] Iyeyoshi (1792–1853), twelfth Tokugawa shogun, became shogun on September 2, 1837. He died on August 15, 1853, exactly one month after Perry's departure from Uraga on July 15. His successor was Shogun Iyesada (1824–1858), who held the office until July 4, 1858. For the date, see Tsuji Zennosuke, *Dai nippon nempio* (Tokyo, 1941), 371–74.

terday, I noticed the name of Joseph Preble Seaman[42] transferred to the *Susquehanna*, and learned he was an old man who had passed all his life in the service and now was quite superannuated, but had always been an efficient and subordinate seaman. I was glad to hear of the good character of one of our name, though in a humble capacity, and must enquire more about him.

At Sea, Wednesday Feb. 1, 1854

Another pleasant day that has advanced us merrily on our course and materially shortened the distance from Jeddo Bay. We, with the *Vandalia,* have been sauntering along under easy sail, while the two other store ships have had all their canvass spread. We had some lightning last night, and the weather now looks a little wild, with a falling barometer and gradually shifting wind so that it is easy to predict a N.W. blow ere long. During the night we coasted the fine large island of Oasima—which was discovered a few years ago by the ship *Preble* and named for her. Soon after, it was seen by the Am[erican] Ship *Montauk*[43] and named for her. Several parts of it seen at other times have been named Crown and Bungelow Islands, but the generally adopted name seems to be that given by the French to a small island discovered by them in its vicinity and called 'Oasima' —evidently of Japanese origin, 'Sima' in their language meaning Island. It is a square Island extending a degree of Latitude and Longitude and is doubtless thickly populated. We saw lights on the shore last night. Soon after leaving its northern extreme we came up with a dome-shaped rock in Lat. 28.41 N. Long. 129.45 which is not on our charts, and we have therefore named it, "Macedonian Rock." If favored with a continuance of our present winds and weather we will be half way to Jedo Bay tomorrow night.

At Sea, Thursday, Feb. 2d, 1854

I have just come down from deck after standing a two hours watch enlivened by showers of rain. The Store Ships have been crowding

[42] There no mention of Joseph Preble, seaman, in the *Sketch.*

[43] The *Montauk* was a clipper ship of 540 tons built in 1844 by William H. Webb of New York. She made a "short" passage from New York to Java Head in 77 days, and 87 days from Macao to New York in 1846, under Captain William McMichael. *Greyhounds,* 101, 102, 114, 399; *Clipper,* 63–64.

their canvass all day, while we and the *Vandalia* have been jogging ahead of them under easy sail, seven knots an hour. At noon we were nearly midway between Loo Choo and Jedo Bay. The wind, still fair, has shifted from SE to SW. and is gradually veering to NW. I knew this morning we would have rain by the pains and aches in my bones. They are an infallible barometer. I expect when I get to be an old man, if I live so long to be so gouty and rheumatic as to be scarcely approachable.

So I warn you, Susie, that you may be prepared for my ill-tempered humors and love me none the less if 'I am cross' and find fault and scold, knowing under all my crabbedness is concealed a warm heart, full of love for you.

Friday, Feb. 3d, 1854

We have our expected weather—a raw, cold North West wind attended by rain, fog and mist. I got a thorough wetting in my watch this forenoon, and by the sound of the wind and rain, seem likely to get another soaking in my watch which is approaching.

Ideas of napping and comfort are comparative, and dependent upon the tastes and habits of the individual. I heard a sailor today say, "New York is the cheapest and pleasantest place to live in I know of. There are places there where you can buy a glass of liquor for a cent, and down in Five points a gallon for nine cents. Where can you find another place as cheap as that?" His ideas of happiness were very simple, but not very commendable. Perhaps viewed by other eyes than our own, our ideas of happiness may seem as fallacious. Anyhow I wish I was at home again and in the enjoyment of our idea of happiness.

I wish I was a girdle
   About your dainty waist
And that your heart now beat against mine
   In sorrow, joy or rest
That I might know it beat alright
   I'd clasp it round so close and tight.

And I would be a necklace
   All day to fall and rise

Upon your balmy bosom
  With your laughter or your sighs
And I would lie so light, so light
  I scarce should be unclasped at night.

In my watch last night I saw a beautiful meteor of a bluish color. It coursed from the N.E. to the S.W. point of the Heavens and exploded and disappeared about 15° above the horizon. It startled everybody on deck, several of the sailors exclaimed what is that, and some compared it to a brilliant blue light though not so lasting; others to a blue rocket, and sudden flash of blinding lightning.

Some porpoises and a solitary chocolate albatross have been about the ship, and this afternoon a piece of squid such as the sperm whale feeds on floated by us, at least six feet square looking like a piece of fat pork streaked with red meat; it is the first I have ever seen.

At Sea, Sunday Feb. 5, 1854

Last night was boisterous and scattered our squadron so that at daylight the vessels were widely separated, and today we have been sailing around gathering them together as a hen does her chickens under her wing against night fall. At 8 this morning we were several miles ahead of the *Vandalia* and still farther from the *Lexington*, so we talked, stared across the V's bow then ran down before the wind and passing her, to the *Lexington*, hauled by the wind on the other tack under her stern and making sail and signal to the *Vandalia* to do the same in four hours run the *Lexington* out of sight astern, and repassed the *Vandalia*, and recrossed her bows. A better evidence of our superiority in sailing could not be given. At noon we made the Islands, southward of Jedo Bay, about eighty miles from our proposed anchorage, and are now working between them, the wind having hauled ahead. Just at sundown we tacked near a very remarkable rock not down on our chart and which from its shape we named House Rock. Though some incline to call it 'Abbott's Monastery.' The outline shows its shape bearing E.N.E. We have the 'Pope'[44] and an Abbott in our squadron—so we may claim to be 'Catholic.'

[44] John Pope was born in Sandwich, Massachusetts, on December 17, 1798. He was made midshipman on May 30, 1816; lieutenant, April 28, 1826; commander, February 15, 1843; captain, September 14, 1855; retired, December 21, 1861; com-

Monday, Feb. 6, 1854

Tantalized all day with a sight of the "Empire of a Thousand Isles," but unable to gain an anchorage. All day is blew a gale from the N.E. with thick rainy weather so that it was dangerous to run, having land all around and close to hand. This evening we are surrounded by dense banks of clouds, and rolling in a perfect calm, as far away from our anchorage as last night. Today Comd. Perry was to have left Loo Choo, with the Steamers, but Capt. Abbott does not expect him before the 22d. We were amused tonight listening to a song composed by one of our darkies, about the *Macedonian, Vandalia,* pigs, poultry, sailing, Loo Choo, Japan, quick passages, etc., etc.—a veritable *altra podrida* none but a negro would have thought to do into rhyme.

Tuesday Feb. 7th, 1854

The tide drifted us last night into a large deep bay, to the west of Jedo Bay, and since daylight we had drifted about in it becalmed, and had ample opportunity to admire its bold and rugged scenery. The hill tops are covered with snow, and one magnificent volcanic cone apparently twelve or fifteen thousand feet high, has presented a sublime appearance. Talk to me of the grandeur of the pyramids after seeing this creation of Almighty Power. The difference between this snow clad pyramid 12,000 feet high and the Master effort of human power 600 feet in altitude conveys a slight idea of man's insignificance when brought into comparison with his maker. This evening I was called on deck to see a lesser mountain on fire. The lava streaming in a broad sheet of flames down its sides to the sea, was reflected on a bank of clouds resting over it. We have drifted rather too close of Cape Nalgasaxa[45] which forms the S.W. entrance to the Bay of Jeddo and have our boats out to pull us away from it. I hear the men singing as they labor at the oars. We hope to gain an anchorage tomorrow and are heartily tired of boxing about at the mercy of tides and currents in the dark—in these almost unknown

modore on retired list, July 16, 1862. He died on January 14, 1876, in Dorchester, Massachusetts. He commanded the sloop *Vandalia* in the East India squadron, 1853–55, and was several times cited with recognition in Perry's *Narrative.*

[45] Cape Nalgasaxa, or Nagasaka, Izu Peninsula.

seas—with no correct charts to guide us. We speculated today on the comforts of a journey over the snowy hills in a cage should we chance to be shipwrecked. P.S. Our volcano has gone out, and proves only to have been some burning bushes, but while it lasted it was as grand a volcanic spectacle as could be scared up.

8 P.M. The calm has suddenly turned to a N.E. gale with cold and cutting winds and rain from the icy hills. We have reefed down to it and are prepared for a blowy night.

Wednesday, Feb. 8, 1854

The gale abated this forenoon, so that we managed to make a little sail and collect our scattered squadron. This evening we are about five miles from where we were last evening at the same time. The thermometer at 50° seems freezing. The volcano Fusi Yama was sublime today showing in clearest outline the whole of its symmetrical snow-clad peak.

At Sea, Thursday, Feb. 9, 1854

One of my mess mates truly characterised the weather this evening when he called it 'disgusting.' We have been contending against strong winds and tacking and wearing every half hour since I wrote last evening. I was reefing, furling and tacking throughout my watches and have halloed myself hoarse. I kept the mid watch last night, and have the same watch tonight. Mr. Watters[46] having gone on the list with a cold, and changed the regular routine. You little think what a wetting I am to get and what an anxious four hours I am to have on decck. It is blowing very heavy, and under greatly reduced sail, the ship is plying between two points of land about fifteen miles apart, waiting for day light and better weather. The rain is falling in torrents only interrupted by squalls of hail and sleet very cutting. The night is so thick and dark we can only see the land when in dangerous proximity to it, and have to wean ship every few minutes, to keep in mid channel. There is a good round moon, which occasionally

[46] John Watters was made midshipman on February 12, 1846; passed midshipman, June 8, 1852; master, September 15, 1855; lieutenant, September 16, 1855; lieutenant commander, July 16, 1862; commander, July 25, 1866. He died on January 22, 1874.

throws a glimmer of light through the heavy clouds. It is the only smiling thing in our present fortunes.

Friday Feb. 10, 1854

What with rain, hail, wind and land all about we had an awful night last night. None of the sea officers slept much I can assure you, and I doubt whether our Purser and Surgeon were altogether easy and to sleep inclined. The 1st Lieut kept the deck all night, and so relieved me as well as others of the wettings and anxieties we expected in our watches.

The rain ceased about daylight, and the gale soon after abated. As the sun rose and cleared the clouds from the hills it disclosed them glistening with a mantle of new fallen snow. We have now tolerable weather, have made more sail and during the day have gained perhaps ten miles. Since Sunday noon when we made the land we have gained just sixty miles, which is just as long as we were in sailing from Loo Choo to our then position—some 8 to 900 miles.

Porpoises and whales have been rolling and spouting all around us, the day long. With no fires, and the thermometer 46° we find it very cold.

Before sundown I saw a beautiful cascade tumbling from one of the snow clad hills into the sea, and hoped to have seen it closer, but we tacked away from it. Several Japanese Junks the first we have seen passed us going seaward, which we take to be a sure sign the weather will soon moderate and be pleasant. They were a good deal after the fashion of Chinese junks, but had canvass sails. The news of our coming must have ere this been conveyed to the Emperor.

On shore [Tokyo Bay], Saturday Feb. 11, 1854

Alas for the poor *Macedonian*, she is hard and fast on a coral reef, and with a gale of wind in prospect. Heaven only knows whether she will ever float again. This forenoon in beating up the bay, we mistook the entrance to the Bay of Jedo and when running along to find it, about half past one struck on this reef, and thumping over some shoal coral patches brought up where we are now. Since that time we have been lightening the ship of shot, sand coal and provisions, and the spare spars, and are preparing our guns to be thrown overboard if necessary. The *Vandalia* is near us and assisting with her boats. We are now waiting for the tide to rise hoping then to be able to move her.

Sunday Feb. 12th 1854

This morning we were visited by some Japanese, two sworded gentry, who informed us the *Southampton* had arrived in Jedo Bay, and offered their assistance in getting our ship from her perilous position. They were accompanied by an interpreter who spoke English.

After working all last night and today in the storm rain and cold, we were able about three o'clock to heave the ship off and get her afloat. Soon after Com. Perry with the three steamers hove in sight, and anchored near us. Seeing our distress, he sent the *Mississippi* to our assistance, and she giving us a long towline, towed us out to a safer anchorage nearer the Commodore. We have been ever since and are still employed in getting our things on board and in their places. Tomorrow at daylight Com. Perry proposes to tow us into Jedo Bay, apparently considering we have no need of rest after our hard work.

Bay of Jedo, Monday Feb. 13, 1854

I was too busy to day, as we came up the Bay, to what was named last year American Anchorage, in tow of the *Mississippi* to look much at the scenery, but what I did see pleased me.

The Forts are well built and numerous but we did not go near enough to see the size of their guns, or whether they are armed or not. We left our Anchorage this morning, but did not get anchored here, and our decks cleared much before the sundown. Each of the Steamers took a sailing ship in tow, and we have the whole squadron assembled with us, except the *Plymouth* left at Shanghai for the protection of our merchants and the *Saratoga* and *Supply* which are even expected to join us. The Japanese have probably never seen in this Bay as fine a squadron as the three noble steam Frigates *Mississippi*,

Susquehanna, Powhatan—sailing sloops *Macedonian, Vandalia* and *Saratoga* and Store Ships *Supply, Southampton* and *Lexington*—will present.[47]

The six hours sleep I got last night was sound and refreshing but I feel tired enough after my arduous duties the last few days to enjoy all the rest allowed me last night.

American Anchorage, Jedo Bay, Tuesday Feb. 14, 1854

Valentine's day, though I had forgotten it until I commandeered for you this valentine. Some Japanese have been on board the *Powhatan,* which wears the Commodore's flag, today to make arrangements for the future negotiations. The Bay of Jedo expands almost to the dimension of an inland sea. Its northern shore is not visible from our anchorage. The shores we see are broken up in rounded hills of moderate elevation behind which towers in majestic sublimity the snow clad symmetrical peak of Fusi-Yama. The shores seem less cultivated than I expected but numerous fishing boats on the Bay, and the close clustered villages in every recess of the shore attest a numerous population.

The Commodore has forbidden any boats communicating with our ships, and no attempts have been made to surround us with a cordon of boats as was done on his first visit. The Japanese wish the Commodore to go back with his squadron to Reception Bay, Uraga, where they received the President's letter last year but he has told them, it is not his custom to leave an anchorage he has once taken. I have been notified I am to be one of the Surveyors, and that we are to make a reconnaissance tomorrow. The *Vandalia* and *Southampton* will anchor farther up the Bay, to cover our work, and afford shelter for our boats and crews if necessary at night. We anticipate cold work but it will give us a good opportunity to see the shores of this novel country. Our running aground was oweing to the errors of our charts. One of the masters mates was permitted to keep my watch last night, and an all night in has completely recovered me from my fatigue. Whispering the sweetest of Valentines I will bid you good night.

[47] Perry returned to the Bay of Edo (Tokyo) on February 13, 1854. The *Saratoga* arrived on March 4, and the *Supply* on March 19. *Narrative,* II, 328.

Jedo Bay, Wednesday Feb. 15, 1854

This forenoon our surveying party pulled along the shore preliminary to commencing work. The cliffs where exposed seemed composed of clay and sand in alternating layers, which are generally horizontal, but occasionally dip gently towards the North, and are thrown upward on the Southern extremity.

We saw and passed numerous populous villages. The houses were all of one story, and have a high steep roof, thus covered with thatch, and the side walls are of matting strengthened by bamboo. We noticed large piles of fire and brush wood and numerous stacks of grain, which looked like barley. Some of the trees and shrubs are stripped of their foliage while others again are in full leaf and bloom, among the latter [an] abundance of camelias. We also saw some walls of well built masonry of dressed and cut stone and on the hills what our sailors call a dungaree fort, which I believe is merely an enclosure of canvass screens, ornamented with the arms and heraldry of some noble, and enclosing a camp of his retainers. It is not intended for deception, as was at first supposed, but really at a distance might be taken for a whitewashed fortress flanked with towers and showy banners. The soldiers and boatmen wear motley garments that remind one of the clown at a circus or look like patchwork. I am informed they represent this heraldry of the great lords of whom they are the retainers. We pulled several miles along the shore, and after my return I went as a whaleman would say "gamming" on board the *Susquehanna* and *Mississippi*. Tomorrow we are to commence the survey of the Bay in earnest. I rejoice to learn we return on board our own ships at night, and will not sleep on board the *Vandalia* or *Southampton*, as was first planned.

Jedo Bay, Thursday Feb. 16th 1854

I have been out all day on surveying duty and after my long confinement in a boat feel quite tired in body, and my eyes are weary from angling with a sextant. I occupied stations close beneath the hills and shores, and have been nearly all day within thirty feet of several projecting points and cliffs, but did not land, as that was contrary to the Commodore's orders. We were tantalized at seeing numerous and large flocks of wild ducks float by our boat, as it was also against orders to shoot them. You know I am not very skillful with a musket or much of a sportsman. Yet they came so near the boat and swam so compactly that I believe I could have bagged several dozen, that would have proved very acceptable to our mess in the present ebbtide of our stores.

The Cliffs over my boat, were crowded all day with curious inhabitants of both sexes and all ages who beckoned us, and invited us by all manner of signs to land, shaking their necklaces at us in answer to our waving our handkerchiefs. Several fishing boats came alongside our boat, and the boat's crew opened trade with Japan exchanging their biscuit and tobacco, for rice, and a light for their pipes. I gave one some cheese; he seemed delighted with it, and gave a crumb of it to each of his boat companions.

They wished me to allow them to look through my spy glass and at my sextant, but that I did not feel authorized to allow.

It has been a mild hazy day but now it is raining merrily the rain sounding over head like an April shower at home. Two of our officers are detained by it on board other ships. We have a stove up in the wardroom and Captain Abbott has come down to warm himself, so I must close my writing and step out into 'the country' as the general apartment outside my stateroom is called and entertain him.

Am. Anchorage, Jedo Bay, Friday Feb. 17, 1854

It has been a wet and stormy day which has interrupted our surveying, but our chief came alongside this evening to say our party would land, and that we recommence, weather permitting tomorrow morning at 7 o'clock. I intend takeing some 'cash,' that is the Chinese coin, along with me, of which I must have about a peck that cost me five dollars, and see if I cannot purchase something.

This evening it has cleared off and the weather is beautiful. Mount Fusi's[48] conical peak showed as clear as a bell at sun down. Our Barometer fell today to 29.48 which is lower than it has been before and we anticipated a tremendous gale, but after a smart blow from S.W. which shifted suddenly to the Nth it went up again. A sail was reported in sight at sundown thought to be the *Saratoga*, but it may have been only a Japanese Junk loaming in the fog. The Commo-

[48] Mount Fuji, or Fujiyama.

dore is sick a bed, and that and the weather has delayed our treaty makeing. The Japanese urge him to go to Uraga where he was received before, and say they have been at great expense in erecting buildings, and made great preparations for his reception there. He refused to leave this anchorage, and says to them when he came before he brought a letter, with orders from his Master the Presdt of the U.S. to deliver it, and he had no choice but to deliver it wherever he could. Now the case is reversed he comes to receive a letter, and he will only receive it where it is convenient to himself either here, or he will go to Jedo. Meanwhile his boats must continue the survey which the Japanese wish suspended until the negociations are completed. I shall rejoice when the diplomacy is finished. I have no faith that our commerce with this people will be worth much for a long time. How can it be until new wants are created? Excluded and self relying for two hundred years they want nothing that their own Islands and hands do not produce, and having only mined, labored and manufactured for themselves, have nothing to export. No doubt the new riches will come and a trade spring up but it has all to be created. The simplest way to treat with them I am convinced would be to land and walk about without fear. If anyone is maltreated, with our force at hand demand ample reparation. Japanese exclusion I believe is altogether due to the rulers. We had abundance of evidence yesterday that the people were ready and eager to communicate with us and buy, sell and barter but are prevented by the Officials and through fear of their spies.

The retainers of a great chief, in their heraldic dresses, bring one back to the feudal ages. I saw the retainers of one chief yesterday wearing cloaks of broad red and white stripes, with a blue patch on the shoulder so that they looked not unlike a walking regiment of American flags. The retainers of another chief wore cloaks with blue and white checks, six inches square—walking chess boards. A great many indeed most of the two sworded gentry wear black silk capes with the arms of the chief to whose family they are attached, embroidered and printed on each shoulder in a white circular spot about two inches in diameter. The men shave the sides of their heads, and tie up their black hair in a little cue or pig tail, which is brought forward towards the crown of the head and chopped off square at the end. The women wear their hair, which, as well as the men is invariably a jet black, long and turned up on the head similar to the jug handle fashion that prevails in China. In order not to disturb it once it is done up, they have when they lie down little bamboo pillows on which they rest the backs of their neck and high enough to clear the back of their head from the floor or couch. They carry their children on their backs, and it is funny to see the bright eyed little things heads showing over the mothers right shoulders.

The shores of the Bay are very broken and hilly and extending arms or capes and points, from numerous little bays and coves within it, such as the one we are at anchor in; nearly all these coves embosom villages, some only a few fishermens huts, but frequently a large town of many thousand inhabitants. These projecting capes, are generally cliffs of clay or sandstone, that have been washed off perpendicular their tops usually crowned, with a tall and rank grass or grain and dark spruce or pine trees. Many of the trees have shed their foliage, though some have not. Generally the hills look brown and sear. The lower lands in the valleys afford the contrast of a bright and cheerful green, and are probably planted with rice.

Our stove with its gas smoke and heat is a nuisance and drives me out of my room to get a breath of fresh air on deck. In consequence of the smoke below, I smoked a pipe on deck—"Jones' Meerschaum"[49] the first time I ever smoked one, or Loo Chooan tobacco which is very mild. I smoke but very little now, but if I were at home could enjoy reading the newspapers, and smoking a good Havana segar—such as you like the fragrance of. Goodnight I go:

"In dreams to meet that as of old,
Then they soft arms my neck enfold
And thy sweet voice is in my ear,
In every scene, to memory dear
I see thee still!"

Jedo Bay, Feb. 18, 1854

I have been absent from the ship all day in my boat surveying and

[49] The trade name of a fine pipe tobacco popular during the middle to the nineteenth century.

feel too weary and achy for anything but sleep and almost too much for that. At first it was pleasant enough, but in the afternoon there arose a rough irregular sea which tossed the boat about so, where I was anchored as a station point, that I was actually seasick, and had to lie down on her bottom. When I reached the ship I was so benumbed, that I could not walk, and Neal Dow,[50] to the contrary, experienced very restoring effects from a stiff glass of brandy and water prescribed by our Doctor. My station today was near what we have called 'Perry Island.' I found it fortified and garrisoned—and the whole garrison some 60 to 100 was drawn up with flying banners to look at us and possibly oppose our landing. I am too tired! Good night!

Jedo Bay, Sunday Feb 19, 1854

It has been a beautiful mild and pleasant day, "A day lost to us surveyors" some one said, but I am glad such respect has been paid to it, for I was tired out and needed the Sabbath's rest and quiet. Like a good Christian I attended church service on board the *Mississippi* in the forenoon. Some chickens and other delicacies were sent on board today by the "Japs' for our sick. Commodore Perry has informed them he must know the determination of the Emperor[51] by Tuesday or he will move his squadron up the Bay as near to Jedo as he can get it. Everything seems favorable for our negociations, and it is rumored through the squadron, that the Emperor is inclined to grant all the President has asked.

There has been a great no. of visitors on board our ship today and a proportionate quantity of idle gossip. Now that they have gone, and we have shrunk again into ourselves, I am quietly occupying my state room, and shall read as we have agreed between us, including

[50] Neal Dow was born at Portland, Maine, on March 20, 1804, and died there on October 2, 1897. He is known for zealously advocating prohibitionism and for the introduction of the Maine prohibitory law in 1851. He was a poor mayor of Portland (1851) and not the best brigadier general nominated by the Gulf Department (1862). As the Prohibition party's candidate for the presidency of the United States in 1880, he lost the election. *DAB*, V, 411–12, with extensive bibliography.

[51] Neither the United States government nor Commodore Perry realized that in Japan there was a strange dualism of emperor and shogun (the military ruler). The Commodore actually negotiated with the shogun, not the emperor.

those chapters I omitted last Sunday when we were pulling our noble ship off the rocks.

Miss Bremer[52] in one of her stories asks a linguist if it was known with certainty in what language Adam declared his love to Eve! Yes was his reply. It was the very language in which she answered him. Can you tell me the language in which two happy creatures, made theirs known on that blessed evening so many long years ago? I am sure I cannot but that I shivered and shaked and was made happy. Happy night! Happy hour!! Happy moment!!! production of so much good and so much happiness since.

Jedo Bay, Monday, Feb 20, 1854

We have had warm and pleasant weather for our surveying and I was absent from the ship from 7 to 7, a greater part of the time stationed within a few feet of 'Town' Point to be angled on and to angle from. We gave that name to the station because of a large town close behind it. The inhabitants crowded the hill, and beckoned us on shore, and by the most unmistakable signs invited our intercourse with their women. One female went so far as to raise her drapery and expose her person to us. They are either a very lewd and lascivious people, or have catered before this, to the passions of sailors. The married women, or those that have children, in order to render themselves less attractive to all but their husbands, stain their teeth with a mixture of urine and iron filings. When they laugh, which they often do, it creates a very disagreeable impression; our sailors call these black teethed ladies—'walking ink bottles.' To inexperienced eyes the dress of the two sexes is so much alike, that but for the manner of wearing their hair, and this custom of staining the teeth, it would be difficult to tell male from female.

Incited by the friendly demonstrations made to us all day, towards sundown I pulled along the shore, and landing at a point cut from a tree thirty feet high a branch of Japonica[53] full of flowers and buds.

[52] Fredrika Bremer (1801–1865) was born in Finland but moved to Sweden and was known for her Swedish novels, in which she advocated the emancipation of women. Her stories were made popular through translations by Mary Howitt. Miss Bremer published a utopian story connected with her observations on the United States. *Encyclopaedia Britannica* (1956), IV, 90.

[53] *Camellia japonica,* a native of China and Japan, has various cultivated forms.

I have trimmed it off for a cane. Coming from Jedo Bay, and the first cane cut in Japan, may give it an intrinsic value to some of my friends. The people followed one boat along the shore, as did also two Custom house boats, wearing the flag black and white stripes matching us and them, but as soon as I landed the people fled.

Tomorrow Lt. Jones our marine officer and one of the Lieuts go to Uraga in the *Vandalia* to form part of a suite to the Flag Capt [Adams][54] who is to have an interview there with the Prince.

Jedo Bay, Tuesday Feb. 21, 1854

We started to survey this morning, but the weather assuming a threatening appearance and soon blowing a gale from the S.W. forced us to return to our ships. The *Vandalia* got under way, with Capt. Adams and his suite for Uraga, but came to anchor again a few miles from the squadron. Some letters came on board from the Flag Ship today, that had been mislaid and lost sight of by the Commodore, but I was not one of the unfortunate fortunates to receive one. I dined today on board the *Mississippi,* and did such justice to a chicken pie, that I feel dyspeptic tonight. Tomorrow will be one of the days we celebrate.

Jedo Bay, Am. Anchorage, Thursday Feb 23d 1854

I was detained on board the *Southampton* five miles up the Bay, last night and so prevented from writing. We commenced our survey as usual, when suddenly there sprung up a gale from the S.W. and as I was in her neighborhood I scud for her. At first I inclined to go on shore and trust to the hospitality of the inhabitants, but the store ship was near, and on the whole I concluded would be the safer and pleasantest asylum. Presently the other surveying boats came along side, and we remained and made the best of it. This forenoon the gale shifted to the Nth and Est—and running down before it flying, at times the boat fairly jumping out of water. I got on board ship about 11 o'clock. I had hardly told my adventure, before at 12

[54] Henry A. Adams was made midshipman on March 14, 1814; lieutenant, January 13, 1825; commander, September 8, 1841; captain, September 14, 1855; commodore, retired list, July 16, 1862; died, May 11, 1869. He was attached to Perry's expedition as second in command to the captain of the fleet. In the *Narrative,* Perry refers to him in several places with recognition and satisfaction.

I was called to keep a watch, one of the watch officers having taken sick, and another gone on the *Vandalia* to Uraga. Yesterday our ship, with the others saluted in memory of the 'Great and Good.' The thunder of our eight and ten inch guns must have astonished this peculiar people.

The *Vandalia* remains at Uraga; on her return the Squadron will proceed up the Bay eight or ten miles near to Jedo, or as far as our survey has extended. Yesterday I landed for a few minutes on the beach and picked up some sea worm shells, valueless except as an index to what may be obtained by dredging the bottom. I also found a live oyster and swallowed it, but it was too coppery to be palatable. I taste it now. One of the Japs broke off a branch of Japonica at me, and the people on the cliffs loaded the boat with branches and flowers they threw into her, which certainly has a friendly look. All underneath the pine trees that crown the hills I notice the fields are brilliant with crimson flowers.

Am. Anchorage, Jedo Bay, Friday, Feb. 24, 1854

This forenoon the steam ships and store ships got underway and went up the Bay, and we are now anchored ten miles to the Nth of this anchorage and that much nearer Jedo. Our ship is ordered to wait the arrival of the *Saratoga* and then join the squadron. The *Vandalia* passed up from Uraga this afternoon and sending us our officers on board they are now giving an account of their interview with the Jap. Prince and other high officials. They were well received, and the only obstacle now to negotiating a treaty is the Commodore's refusal to treat at Uraga. The Emperor, who by the way is not dead has altered the law forbidding intercourse with foreigners, so far as Americans are concerned. When the treaty is signed, the Officers can come on shore, and the shops, with all they have in them will be open for our purchases. This is agreeable news, but better still is the news, that the *Southampton* is to go to Shanghai for coal, and give us a good opportunity to forward our letters, and receive others on her return. The Lieut. Gov. of Uraga told some of our officers of course through the interpreters, that when the Treaty was signed we could have plenty of Japanese wives, but said their women did not like mustachios, and hoped when the officers came to see them they would shave them off. From this we have decided that henceforth in Japan, the morality of an officer is to be known by the length of his mustache. The other ships having left my duties on the survey are temporarily suspended.

Am. Anchorage, Saturday Feb. 25, 1854

The 38th anniversary of my birth, and my third year beyond the meridians of those allotted to men. I wish I could recall all my idle and waste moments, but the dead must bury its dead—the past belongs to the past, only the present and future is our own. I wish I was where I could receive your congratulations at having closed another year in my book of life and opened a new one. I should prefer being in Casco Bay[55] to being here in Jedo Bay. Keeping watch is not half so pleasant, as it would be to watch Harry and Lily. I should prefer surveying no. 62 Danforth St. and its precincts, to surveying the shores of this inland sea. I know you are thinking of me tonight. I have passed a quiet day—when not on watch, and looking at the gulls—in reading and writing. Last night was the coldest we have experienced. The thermometer fell to 31° and ice formed. Today we have been eating oranges grown on the shores of the Bay, and the air has been delicious. We have every reason to be satisfied with the rigor of a Japanese winter, so much dreaded.

Among the presents received by Com. Perry, was a box of obscene paintings of naked men and women, another proof of the lewdness of this exclusive people. My messmates who went to Uraga speak in high terms of the manners and polite hospitality of the officials they communicated with, and also praised the finished workmanship of their arms. Their match locks have superb barrels, something like a smooth bore rifle. The reason they assign for not having adopted flint locks is that the Islands do not produce flint and a good reason for a people as exclusive as themselves. Now they are likely to jump at once from matchlocks to percussion caps. The men who have been on board of our ship are very fond of sweetened whiskey, which we treat them with, rather than exhaust upon them our small stock of wines. Their own liquor, called *Saki,*[56] a wine or spirit or brandy

[55] Cos Cob Bay, Connecticut.

[56] Sake is Japanese rice wine.

made from rice, differs from the Chinese *Sameoshu*[57] and the *Arrechi*,[58] made from the same vegetable, and is thought by some of the officers quite palatable. Our Looking glasses and Spy glass are objects of admiration, but they seem most pleased with our boats. Leather-watches and trinkets may prove articles of profitable traffic when trade is opened.

Heine the artist of the Expedition is sketching a Panorama of it to exhibit when it returns. One of his scenes will be "the *Macedonian* ashore"—and the *Mississippi* hauling her off near enough to the truth for a picture. Commodore Perry ordered the artist to sketch his landing last July, and to put him in the center of the picture—ignorant that by all the rules of perspective, that would give him the most insignificant place. A match story is told of Com. Elliott's cursing a trombone player and threatening to flog him for a lazy rascal because he did not play more than half the time while "that little fellow with the flute was twice as industrious." On the trombone's saying he played his part, the Commodore grew furious and said: no you don't you lazy whelp you, for I've been watching you.

Sunday Feb. 26, 1854

I have the dyspepsia to night, which may be accounted for by a cold, and is not the result of over-indulgence. The disease is disagreeable enough, when you have the satisfaction, that it is occasioned by indulgence of the pleasures of the appetite, but it is hard to have it when on a salt fare.

Monday Feb. 27, 1854

This morning a message came from the Commodore and we got underway, and have been endeavoring all day to work with a light breeze up to the other ships. We are now anchored about four miles from them waiting for a wind and day light. The treaty preliminaries are settled. The Grand Conference and ratification on the part of Japan is to take place next Friday at Yokahama where the squadron is now anchored.

57 See note 99 under the year 1853.

58 Preble undoubtedly did not get the genuine Chinese name of this kind of rice wine.

Our surveying boats have been in sight of Jedo, so we can no longer be reproached for not knowing where it is. While our ship was underway, we had our boats industriously employed in picking up drift timber, large squared logs, which have evidently been used as a barricade of some kind. They are pine and several measure eighteen inches on the side. I counted one hundred and twenty concentric rings or years growth on one of these squared logs. In China one of these logs would be worth one hundred dollars, and such spars may prove an important item in our future trade.

It has been a pleasant day, and is a calm dark night. The surrounding horizon is illuminated by numerous fires on the hills which we suppose are fed from the stubble and coarse grass the inhabitants are burning preparatory to further cultivation. It seems strange to be in a bay alive with boats, which shun us as they would a pestilence. Surrounded by beautiful hills we cannot wander over freely. Sea villages and towns we must not land at and shores we may not touch. Even the wild fowl so numerous, are by the Commodores 'vermillion' edict not to be disturbed, while our messes are reduced to salt beef and tongues, ham and like sea delicacies.

Treaty Bay, Bay of Jedo, Tuesday Feb. 28, 1854

We anchored this morning in 'Treaty Bay' as it has been named. Off the town of Yokahama, and about a mile and a half from where the Japanese have created buildings for the Conference between the high contracting powers. The wind and weather is emphatically East, and I have been taking a spy glass view of the place through the medium of a rainy mist. The Japanese are busy putting up a long shed-like wooden 'Palace' for the reception of the Commodore, which after the the negociations are over looks as if it would answer admirably for a coal shed. Having made due allowance for the exaggerations of travellers, I have not been disappointed in Japan or the Japanese, but some of my messmates who took the travellers romances for gospel are egregiously disappointed. I do not see any fortifications in this upper part of the Bay, but there are plenty of canvass screens or 'dungaree forts' which show where soldiers are encamped. Our presents are all to be landed here, and whether we see Jedo except at a distance depends upon our Treaty.

Wednesday March 1, 1854

It has been a sombre drizzly day, but we have been out with our surveying boats placing buoys to enable the squadron to anchor in line nearer the shore and cover the landing which is to take place as soon as 'the shanty' is ready for the Commodore's reception. All the marines and fifty blue jackets from each ship are to be landed as a guard of honor, and as many of the officers as can be spared from duty are to form the suite of our 'Lord High Ambassador.' After the opening day, a guard of marines, and one or more officers from each ship in turn are to form the Commodore's escort. Today the Capt of the *Susquehanna*, assisted by the Flag Capt and others has been entertaining the Gov[ernor] of Uraga, and suite on board the *Susquehanna;* bumpers were drained to Japan and the U.S. and to the U.S. and Japan. Judging by the reports of those who came from the dinner, they had a merry time, and great good feeling prevailed. Some of the Japs even made excursions to the mast heads, to cool off after their libations, and view the surrounding scenery. Our treaty will be cemented under influences displeasing to friend Dow, and I imagine it will be many years before his cold water system finds favor in the "Empire of a Thousand Isles." I was amused at hearing one of our 'old salts' growl out today, "for his part he could any day lick a hundred of such fellows in petticoats, who hid themselves behind canvass forts and used paper pocket handkerchiefs."

Our mess elected the Purser caterer today, and he is now monarch of our empty store room, Dr. W[oodworth] having resigned. A few hams, and one or two kits of salmon we have left and we must be content with the ships ration unless the treaty provides for a poultry trade soon. To add to the misery of a salt ration the Commodore has ordered us an allowance of water though we have 18,000 gallons enough for 60 days on board. It is within the bounds of probability that the Japanese break off negociations with us, as they did with the Russians,[59] and may therefore prove a wise precaution, but it occasions no little growling.

Today being St. Davids day is celebrated by all Welshmen wearing a leek in their cap or hat. The custom originated from one of their

[59] The Japanese broke off negotiations on February 1, 1854, at Nagasaki. For a detailed description, see Lensen, *Russia's Japan Expedition*, 57–64.

kings having gained a signal victory over their Saxon enemies on this day, and to distinguish his troops from the enemies, causing them to wear leeks plucked from an adjoining field.

We had a mess discussion today about the time at home compared with ours here. One of the most difficult things to explain clearly that I know of but I will try. Here we are in Long 139°E of Greenwich, which is about 14 hours 15′ later than the time at home as we came, but 9.45 earlier if counted as we are going. At first sight these differences in the dif[ference] of time seem paradoxical, and you would say one or the other is wrong—not so—subtract one, or add the other to our time and the result is equally 5.45 A.M. for the home time, the way we sailed 5.45 A.M. of this morning, but in the other case 5.45 A.M. tomorrow morning. With us it is 8 P.M., so in either case you are waking to daylight the same day, about the time I begin to think of a first watch or blanket bay. It is actually night here and morning with you which ever way we travel around the world.

Treaty Bay, Thursday March 2d, 1854

My duties have taken me today all about the Bay planting bouys, and on board the *Powhatan* and *Mississippi*. I learned no news, but got very cold as the weather was raw and chilly. That curious original Junius J. Boyle[60] the Commander of the *Southampton* has been boring us with his company today. A little of him is amusing but a surfeit is disgusting. His numerous stories derive their pith from his manner of telling them. It was Boyle, who when one of the lodgers at a N.Y. Hotel where he was stopping, swallowed some campherie mistaking it for gin, proposed to put a wick in him and burn him out. Today some one remarked several of his front teeth were missing. Yes, said he, they didn't like their rations and deserted. I shipped a new crew of forcastle men in New York but as we are here in Japan on salt rations I've given them liberty—locked them up in my secretary—hum! The other day, when driven by the gale on board Boyle's vessel, some one reading his journal, read: —at Gallapagos Islands,

[60] Junius J. Boyle was made midshipman on August 27, 1823; passed midshipman, March 23, 1829; lieutenant, June 21, 1832; reserved list, September 13, 1855; commodore, reserved list, April 4, 1863. He died on August 11, 1870.

date so and so, appointed John Smith postmaster. Yes said Boyle explanatory, you see h–u–m. I went on shore to bury him h–u–m, and after putting him in his grave h–u–m I saw a whalers letter box and pole close by, and I stuck it up at the head of his grave. There being no harm you see I thought I would give him the position.

Treaty Bay, Friday March 3d, 1854

I have been in a boat all day and feel rather tired. Surveying this cold weather is by no means a pleasant duty, yet the excitement is better than our dull imprisonment on board ship. I have pulled all along the shore today and seen some novel sights, which I will take some other time to describe, some winter evening at home perhaps. The *Saratoga* is again reported down the Bay. One of our surveying officers will go down in the morning to pilot her up. It is now thought the first interview will come off on Monday.

Treaty Bay, Saturday March 4, 1854

Last year the people of the U.S. were excited by the Inauguration of a new President, Frank Pierce.[61] This year we are excited by the publishing of the Programme of the Landing. Three officers from each ship will form the Commodores Staff and a military force of 160 marines and 300 sailors, exclusive of the crews of 26 boats that are to cover his landing, will form his guard and escort. He is to land under a salute of seventeen guns from the *Macedonian* the only ship except the *Vandalia* that has a saluting battery. I do not know yet whether I am to land, as we are to draw lots unless my messmate who went to Uraga withdraws in my favor.

At sundown the *Saratoga* was beating up the Bay. I am impatient to see my old friends on board of her. Doct Steele[62] who was my messmate on board of her in 1848, is still attached to her, having seen nearly seven years service in that ship. Goldsborough her 1st Lt joined her in 1850. It is rumored she will take the Treaty to Panama,[63] land there a bearer of dispatches, and continue her voyage

[61] Franklin Pierce (1804–1869) was the fourteenth president of the United States (1853–57).

[62] William Steele was made assistant surgeon on March 5, 1847; served on the *Saratoga;* surgeon, August 29, 1860; resigned, April 21, 1861.

[63] The Treaty of Panama, signed in 1846 by the United States and Colombia,

around Cape Horn to Boston. Madigan,[64] Wayne[65] and Webb[66] all on board of her are friends of mine. This morning I reported on board the *Mississippi* for surveying duty, but the weather was unfavorable—a few flying flakes of snow warned us it would be cold work—so we returned to our ship, and I have been nursing a cold and sore throat, which I hope will pass off before Monday.

The Japanese are an honest people to judge by their acts for they have returned to the squadron a barrel of coal we threw over board when on the reef, a canvass hammock, and a square piece of cotton cloth we had used as a surveying signal. In contrast we the other day picked up 18 logs, which at Hong Kong would be worth 800$ and have cut them up for firewood.

Treaty Bay, Sunday March 5, 1854

After our 'muster' and the reading of several sentences of Courts Martial, this forenoon I went on board the *Saratoga* which came to anchor during the night, to exchange greetings with my old friends. I found her crowded with officers from all the ships who had come to congratulate them on their arrival. They have had a hard time of it, and been in the lower bay since the 13th of Feb., they saw the steamers towing us in on that ship. They left Shanghai with their decks crowded with livestock for the squadron, which as they got short of feed they had to kill, and give to their own crew.

They and the ship are pretty well worn out with the length of the cruise, and look like ancient mariners, Goldsborough showed me a stick on which like Robinson Crusoe he had notched his months of absence, which counted up to forty-three with another to be added on

guaranteed to American citizens the right of transit across the Isthmus of Panama. This allowed the construction of the Panama Railway by John Lloyd Stephens and his company in 1850–55.

64 John Madigan was made midshipman on February 19, 1840; passed midshipman, July 11, 1846; master, March 1, 1855; dropped, September 13, 1855: lieutenant, active list, September 22, 1865; died, October 22, 1870. During Perry's expedition he was still passed midshipman on the *Saratoga;* see *Narrative,* II, 411.

65 William A. Wayne was made midshipman on October 27, 1833; passed midshipman, July 8, 1839; lieutenant, June 4, 1844; resigned, May 1, 1861.

66 William A. Webb was made midshipman on January 26, 1838; passed midshipman, July 2, 1845; master, October 9, 1853; lieutenant, June 12, 1854; resigned, May 17, 1861.

the 12th inst. Except Sir John Franklin's ship,[67] the *Saratoga* is now the longest out on the ocean. They are delighted with the rumor of their return, but should they start as expected as soon as the 1st of April, and touch at San Francisco they are not likely to get to Boston before the end of August which brings them to the fifth year of their cruise.

The Purser and Marine officer of the *Susquehanna* dined with our mess today, and several officers dropping on board to dessert—(desert indeed!) prolonged the festivities. Just now the Capt sent down for us to decide who was to attend the Commodore on Wednesday. As it was Sunday I would not throw dice, so I cut for the chance in a book with Gwathmey, a distinction without a difference you will say but it satisfied my conscience, and I was lucky enough to have the fates decide in my favor, and you may expect a description of the interview from an eye witness. It has been a rainy day and there is promise of a continuance of the same weather. I saw a Japanese map of the Bay of Jedo to day, which was quite correct in outline, as far as we have examined the Bay, but it was without soundings.

Treaty Bay, Monday March 6, 1854

The ship is full of idle rumors about going home, going to the Mediterranean etc none of which I credit. The Japanese have reported their buildings ready, and at their request they have been inspected by Capt. Adams, and pronounced "ollo proper."

Wind, weather, and the Commodores health permitting the Grand interview is to take place the day after tomorrow at 11 o'clock.

Imagine me bearded and mustachioed, a savage looking customer armed with sword and revolver, acting as one of the Flags guard of honor. We are to have some eating and drinking for the Japs have sent off to know how many they are to entertain. The weather has cleared off this afternoon bright and pleasant and we have hopes of a fine day tomorrow.

Treaty Bay, Tuesday March 7th 1854

I returned to the ship late after a hard days surveying, tired, cold

[67] Sir John Franklin (1786–1847) is known for his expeditions through the Northwest Passage to Canada. His last expedition, in 1845 on the *Erebus* and the *Terror*, ended disastrously. No one was saved. *DNB*, XX, 191.

and dyspeptic, and after I had tinctured, soda-ed and walked myself, into more comfortable feelings, John Goldsborough came on board and has kept in conversation ever since.

A jury of Doctors sat on F . . . k C . . . k to day. I learned he has not been condemned to go home, but one of the board has just told me he has a disease of the lungs resulting from hard drinking.

Tomorrow our grand function is to come off. It is repeated the Emperor has asked for a list of the officers, in order to make them presents.

Treaty Bay, Sunday March 12th 1854

I have been so engaged in my surveying and other duties and so fatigued after my return from them, that I have not put a pen to paper since Tuesday. I must now give you some account of Com. Perrys interview with the Japanese Commissioners on Wednesday. The interview took place in the house I have before mentioned, as erected for the purpose at Yokohama, so Treaty when concluded, will be known as Treaty of Yokohama.

As I explained I formed one of the escort. Commodore Perry landed under a salute of seventeen guns from our ship. He was preceded by an Am[erican] Ensign and his own blue broad pennant, borne in the hands of two stalwart six foot negros from the *Macedonian,* and protected by a guard of five hundred sailors and marines. Some thirty or forty officers were drawn up upon the beach in a double line to receive him, and after he had passed between, they formed two and two in his rear and followed him to the Treaty House. Twenty-six boats employed to convoy him and his cortege on shore, drew up along the beach, and after he had landed the launches in charge of Lieut Boudinot[68] fired first a salute of twenty-one guns from their howitzers, in honor of the Emperor of Japan, second, a salute of nineteen guns in honor of the Prince Commissioner.[69] The

[68] W. E. Boudinot was made midshipman on February 1, 1836; passed midshipman, July 1, 1842; master, March 7, 1849; lieutenant, September 5, 1849; resigned, November 17, 1858. He served on the *Powhatan* as a lieutenant. See also *Narrative,* II, 410.

[69] The "Prince Commissioner" was the chief envoy, Towa Izu-no-kami, or Toda, lord of Izu. The vice-envoy was Ido Iwame-no kami, or Ido, lard of Iwame. Perry

first time I imagine in the history of our navy a salute was ever fired by the boats of a squadron. The show on our side was pretty and imposing. On the part of the Japanese it was a disappointment. Their troops consisted of a few companies of archers and spearmen, and sparsely drawn up in a neighboring field were a few others with swords and match locks. They conveyed no idea of splendor, or force. The Reception Hall was scantily hung with crape, and ornamented with screens painted with white storks, a favorite Japanese emblem.

The Commodore and his escort were at first all seated on the left hand side of this hall, and the Commissioners and their suites took seats on the right hand side. After some 'kotowing' on the part of the Japanese interpreters, the business of the day was opened by a mutual interchange of compliments. This politeness accomplished, the Commodore with his Flag Capt., Secretary and Interpreters, retired with the five Jap. Commissioners to a small room at the head of the hall where what they said and did was concealed from our vulgar ears and eyes, while we his lesser satellites outside were treated to a chow-chow or Feast. First they brought us tea and candy, then fish and soup, curiously rather than palatably prepared, next sweet saki—the country liquor made from rice. Some ginger bread brought on with the candy was really good, and about the only eatable thing I remember. Everything hot or cold was served on trays, dishes, cups or bowls of lacquered ware, generally crimson or green or gold. Everybody was disappointed and tired of the pageant before it was over. The greatest part of the Commodore's interview was taken up in obtaining a burial place for a marine who had died that morning on board the *Mississippi*. The Japanese wanted the body taken to Nagasaki, then Uraga, but finally consented to his being buried in one of their own grave yards at Yokohama. After Chaplain Jones had performed the usual burial services, probably the first time any Christian service has been performed on the soil of Japan since the expulsion of the Jesuits 200 years ago, one of their bonzes performed other services over the body, and the grave was left guarded by Japanese Soldiers.

landed at Kurihama on July 14, 1853, and met the envoys, presented them with the President's letter. S. W. Williams, *A Journal of the Perry Expedition to Japan (1853–1854)*, 61–63.

Since the Commodores interview on Wednesday, the Flag Capt. has been continuing the negociations, and it is rumored the Japanese agree to grant all and more than the President asked for in his letter. Two or three ports it is understood are to be opened for our trade. Tomorrow Capt. Abbott is to land with almost as much state and ceremony as the Comd to deliver our presents to the Japanese.[70] They are various and very bulky, and cost over $20,000.

The Japanese have been a greatly overrated people. I doubt whether they will [be] on the whole as a nation [compared] with the Chinese. In some respects they are superior but in others they are far behind the celestials. It is astonishing how travellers have been carried away by their imaginations. All is not gold that glitters has a real exemplification. The Golden pillars and walls of palaces and temples, which have excited the admiration and wonder of travellers, are but wood and plaster—gilded.

The Commodore continues his restrictions and we are not permitted to land freely though I apprehend the inhabitants would offer no obstruction to our doing so. The Japs are watering the ship, and at present our decks are overrun with them prying with curious eyes into everything and noting down the English names of everything. They crowded me out of my room this morning when I sat down to write to you. They gave me their cards and asked for mine in return. I send some specimens with the English sound of their names, written under the Japanese characters. They were delighted with the common ships whisky sweetened with coarse brown sugar which we gave them.

Everyday since the interview, I have been out in my boat surveying, and it has proved cold and solitary work, but it seems good for my health, as everybody remarks I am growing stout, which on salt grub is encouraging. We are now rejoicing at the prospect of having something fresh to eat. The Japs, are to furnish us with fowls eggs etc. in turn according to seniority of Capts., and as Capt ranks next

[70] The presents given by Commodore Perry to the Japanese "emperor," "empress," governmental representatives, and members of the Japanese delegation are listed in Williams, *A Journal of the Perry Expedition*, 131–34; see also a picture of the delivery of the presents in *Narrative*, I, facing p. 357, as well as a list of the presents on p. 357.

to Commodore, our ship will be the 2d supplied. We had it reputed yesterday that the *Supply* was below, and got excited over the prospect of news and letters, but rumor as usual was in advance of truth.

A medical survey has condemned Winder, who broke his arm at Hong Kong last Oct. He is to go home in the first ship to leave, broken over and reset; as the bones have grown to gather away, from his own fault in loosening the bandages.

Treaty Bay, Monday March 13, 1854

It has been a wet and dreary day, but the presents were satisfactorily landed though at some inconvenience to the escort. On Wednesday the Commodore lands again to explain them and lecture on railroads, telegraphs, and revolvers, through the medium of his interpreters. It is anticipated the treaty will be concluded and signed this week, after which we are to be allowed to go on shore and see the Japanese at home. Another instance of this people's sensuality occurred at the meeting today. Capt A[bbott] remarking to the interpreter that it was a rainy day. Yes, said he, a fine day for lieing with the ladies.

Some of the embossed and inlaid work on their sword hilts is really very beautiful. It is rumored the *Susquehanna* will leave for Hong Kong next Monday. Several officers condemned by medical survey are to go home in the *Saratoga*, rather a long and dreary route for them. She will go to Boston, and I shall send you a box by her in charge of Madigan, who belongs to the *Saratoga* and has promised to call and see you as he passes through Portland.

Treaty Bay, Tuesday March 14, 1854

A pleasant and rather exciting day from the number of rumors flying about. About noon the Flag Ship hoisted the cornet and fired two guns to recall "all the boats and officers"—presently the Flag Capt. was seen pulling furiously after a Japanese boat, and waving his cap for it to stop but without success. It was immediately conjectured and reported that the Japanese had refused everything, and the negociations were broken off, and we were to have war to the knife. It seems however permission having been granted to several officers to wander about within certain limits on shore, that Mr. Bittinger the chaplain of the *Susquehanna* and another officer were reported by the Japanese as having gone beyond those limits and were on the road and making tracks towards Jedo. They came on board to ask the Commodore to recall them, saying their presence frightened the inhabitants who were not accustomed to the sight of strangers.

It is now reported the treaty—granting all we have asked—will be signed on Thursday, by the Commodore and Commissioners.

The railroad[71] has been laid down on shore. It is a model road, and has a circular track 350 feet in diameter, and is fitted with a miniature locomotive and tender, and a first class American passenger car about quarter size: The track is only 18 inches wide, but our engineers say the engine has power to drag eighteen or twenty persons. After it has been examined here by the commissioners it is to be taken to pieces and sent to Jedo for the inspection of the Emperor. The telegraph is to be put up between Yokohama and Kanagusha and messages will be transmitted over it in Dutch. The chief Commissioner said to Capt. Adams, he was well aware that they were behind the rest of the world in inventions and improvement and that the time had come for them to open their ports and make Treaties with other nations, but we Americans were in too much of a hurry and wanted everything now, and added it was not easy for them to throw off and put bye in a moment the customs and laws of three centuries. He said the innovation must be gradual, and appear to their people to be conceded and not forced from them—all very reasonable I think.

It is worthy of note that about the time of the colonization of New England, and the settlement of our limited states with its notion of religious freedom, Japan closed her doors to the commerce of the world from the very opposite idea. Now after a lapse of three centuries, the infant settlement has become a giant nation, and this then rich and flourishing Empire reduced to feebleness, by its contracted ideas, is forced to treat with the infant and conform to its more expanded views. Perhaps another cycle of progress on the part of Japan and the U.S. may show another turn of the wheel, and Japan freed from her prejudices and exclusiveness may be flourishing in manly

[71] The miniature railway, one-fourth regular size, is shown in *Narrative*, I, facing p. 357.

vigor, and the United States bourne down by her "peculiar institution" have arrived at a stage of national dotage and childishness. The change would be no greater than, the last three centuries have brought in the condition of Spain, Portugal and Italy.

Treaty Bay, Wednesday March 15, 1854

Well I have seen Jedo, and been at anchor about five miles from it in my boat nearly all day, viewing it through my spy glass. We were some ten miles or more from the ship but by great good luck a breeze sprung up at sundown and enabled us to get on board quick and without much labor.

Situated on low and flat ground but little of the city can be seen from the water but it had the appearance of an extensive and populous place—quite as large as report has assigned it. Its appearance is devoid of picturesque interest or beauty. I could not see a single tower steeple turret or dome. Its only remarkable feature is the palace, which occupies about the centre of the thickly clustered building, and like that of Shudi Loo Choo, appears like a walled city or large fortress. Its walls of a purple color trimmed with white. While at anchor a junk passed us and threw a jug of saki to our men, but I would not allow them to pick it up fearing it might intoxicate them. It was an evidence of friendly feeling at all events. On my return to the ship, I found our marine officer had in my absence been ordered to the *Mississippi*, Major Taylor and Merril's *Gazelle*[72] having been condemned by survey and ordered home.

Friday March 17th 1854

It rained hard all day yesterday, so I went on board the *Mississippi* to plot my surveying work and was detained there all night by a storm.

The Commodore landed again today, but as I was not behind the curtain I cannot tell how much he accomplished. It is rumored they wish to open only one port and under oppressive restrictions. Just before the Commodore landed a gorgeously decorated barge, shin-

[72] The *Gazelle* was a sharp-bottomed clipper packet vessel of 1,244 tons, built in 1851. Her captain was Robert Henderson, Jr., and she was owned by Merril and Taylor of New York. The *Gazelle* was dismasted and condemned in 1854. There was also a British ship named *Gazelle* in 1854. *Greyhounds*, 127, 161, 206, 415.

ing in crimson and gold, ornamented with numerous flags and banners, and over all two large tassels or bullion banners of gold, and canopied with a silk Am[erican] flag, and surrounded on all sides with crape screens bearing the Imperial device, approached the landing, slowly towed by twenty or thirty boats and followed by as many more. It reminded me of the State barge of Cleopatra or the Bucentaura in which the Doges of Venice annually went out to marry the sea, and a model of which I saw preserved in the Arsenal at Venice. I learn this evening it brought down a young prince about 23 years old, but whether he came from business pleasure or curiosity I have not learned. A gentleman from shore who examined, said the barge was lacquered all over inside and out, and had many strange ornamental devices.

We have been crowded today with Japanese Officials in charge of the boats watering our ship. They have been curiously and inquisitively examining everything on board, measuring, drawing and taking the name of everything. I showed one our track from New York to Japan on my general chart of the world. He understood what it was directly and pointed it out to his companions. When I showed them the old bounds of Mexico, and how much we conquered from them by our war they wanted to know why when we took so much, we did not take the whole. One was particularly pleased when I dropped some wax on a card and gave him an impression of my seal; pointing to the arms on his shoulder, he gave me to understand he knew what it was. Their swords are really beautiful affairs, and the embossing and inlaid work on some of them is exquisite. One came into my room and opening a little drawer in my desk, dropped in it one of their oblong bronze copper coins which they call a[n] *oban* [copper money].

He first looked around to see that nobody was looking. As an equivalent I gave him a bit of lead pencil and a piece of India rubber which he seemed to covet. They have a great aptitude at catching English sounds and ask the American name of everything they see, and so pick up a vocabulary of our language. They generally give us the Japanese name, but it sounds so barbarous to our ears, we are not at much trouble to remember it. A Japanese on board today took up a musket, went through the manual, and loading and firing with as much precision as one of our marines. They are the reverse of the Chinese in their desire to learn, and inquisitiveness. There is one difference I notice in their language. While they roll the "r" and give it a full sound, the Chinese cannot pronounce it at all but turn into an "l"; thus for rice a Chinaman says "licee."

Treaty Bay, Saturday March 18, 1854

I have been on board the *Mississippi* all day plotting not treason, but only my work upon the survey. I have been too busy to see anything and all the news I have is what I heard as I bent over my work, or in dineing and supping with my friends. The Commodore has decided the *Susquehanna* shall not sail until Monday week instead of next Monday, and the *Vandalia* and *Southampton* sail tomorrow for a place some sixty miles from here, they propose as one of the ports to be opened.

Our officers will make a reconnoisance and report to him before he accepts the port. The first message ever conveyed by magnetic telegraph in Japan was sent across the wires today from the Treaty House to another House more than a mile distant. It was the compliments of one interpreter to another in Dutch. The railroad is not quite ready but the workmen expect to have the cars running on Wednesday.

Our awnings were covered with a light snow this morning and the weather is decidedly coolish. The distant hills have snow upon them and are more or less covered with it.

Treaty Bay, Sunday March 19, 1854

I was awakened this morning with the joyful tidings that the *Supply* was in the lower bay and coming up. Of course I enjoyed my share of letters in anticipation. At noon our mail was brought on board and I crowded into the cabin with the rest to receive my share. I heard name after name called over until at last there was none left, and none for me, and then I slunk away and hid myself in my own room to conceal my disappointment. I know now why it is. All the letters for our ship addressed as mine were to DeSilver at Hong Kong, remain in his hands, as he had no orders to send them to

Shanghai, whence the *Supply* sailed. I shall not expect to hear from you now before we return to Hong Kong in Oct., a long and tedious time to wait. By the *Supply* we have copies of the Presidents Message in Dec. and Purser Allison has a letter from his wife dated the 11th of that month in which she says his first letter from China reached her on the 18th of Nov. If mine to you was as fortunate, it was a pleasant remembrance for the anniversary of our wedding day. Unfortunate myself I am glad you will be more regularly supplied with news from me.

Monday March 20, 1854

We have had a mild pleasant day which I have rather enjoyed at my work in the Bay. I was absent from the ship thirteen hours and came back both hungry and tired.

Treaty Bay, Tuesday March 21, 1854

It has been blowing a S.W. gale but I managed to get on board the *Mississippi* in the morning and plotted up my yesterdays and some back work. I have just finished packing up a couple of oil paintings to send by the *Saratoga*. In the box with them some flower seeds, some Japanese confectionary and a few other trifles. Henry will like the cloth gaily painted with the London coat of arms and which I found round a piece of Purser cloth for a knapsack. The pictures I think curious and well painted, though framed they cost but five dollars the pair. They represent a water shed in the suburbs of Canton, and show the style of building, and the manner of dress of the common people. In one you see a 'Flower Boat' in the distance with the family at their chow-chow. Commodore Perry is to land again on Thursday when I hope the Treaty may be concluded to his and everybody's satisfaction. It is very tantalizing to be within arms length of so much that is curious and interesting and be kept in our floating prisons on salt rations. The Japs promise us abundance of everything, but bring nothing. They live themselves on Fish, candy, vegetables, tea and saki, and do not kill any animals to eat. Fowls they have for ornament and pets, but not for eating. In all my cruisings along the shore I have not seen a domestic fowl.

Treaty Bay, Wednesday March 22 1854

Jones[73] our marine officer left us today to commence his duties on board the *Mississippi*. Winder also left us today to go on board the *Susquehanna* to take passage to Hong Kong, and thence to a clipper ship to the U.S. So 'we are seven' now in our wardroom mess. I have been out all day in my Surveying boat, surrounded as usual by Japanese boats almost to the interruption of my work. They presented us with oranges, a small salted fish like a sardine, and some crabs. I was again in sight of Jedo, and carried my soundings eleven miles from the ship, and found from 30 to 70 feet of water at the end of my work. I am convinced the whole squadron could anchor within 3 or 4 miles of Jedo without difficulty. Capt. Abbott killed his goat today, and sent some of the meat into the wardroom, where curried it proved very acceptable. The Kid born on board the men have got for a pet. The railroad was in full blast today, and I heard its steam whistle, but have not seen the time table for the arrival and departure of the trains.

On Monday the Commodore will give a grand banquet on board the *Powhatan* to the Commissioners and suite, and they are to be entertained with an exercise at General Quarters on board the *Macedonian*. They assure the Commodore they sent the Russians away without granting them any treaty. While the Russians were at Nagasaki a great storm washed away one of their forts, and its great guns which proved to be wooden ones, went floating over the harbor. The Japanese here told us about it, laughing at the deception.

Treaty Bay, Thursday March 23d, 1854

The Flag Ship made signal to the *Susquehanna*. "Prepare to sail at daylight," and I have been very busy all day in closing my letters to send by. Her sudden departure has taken us all by surprise, it seems the Commodore wishes to get her off to Hong Kong before the treaty is concluded, and intends sending his bearer of his dispatches with the concluded treaty by the *Saratoga* and via the Isthmus of Panama.

[73] He was James H. Jones, second lieutenant on the *Macedonian*; see note 40 under the year 1853.

There is no doubt now, that a treaty will be concluded, and a favorable one. Three ports are to be opened to our trade. All of their ports will afford refuge and assistance to vessels in distress, and we are to be allowed to purchase as much coal as we want. Such are some of its provisions as I understand. There will be great disappointment in the U.S. at the amount and value of the immediate commerce between the two countries, for never has a country been more overrated than Japan. The Japanese are undoubtedly an intelligent people, and may be made something of in time, but are just three centuries behind the age in everything. Coming in contact with European civilization, and refinements, may increase their wants and by increasing their own products and manufactures a profitable trade after a while may grow up. At present they create nothing superfluous, and have no outside wants. Kept on ship board, or skirting the shores of the bay in a boat, I have as yet obtained only a general idea of the people. Perhaps a better knowledge may improve them in my eyes. They eat no meat as it is unclean to be engaged in the killing or slaughter of animals. Fowls are not eaten but kept for their eggs or as pets. Their principal diet seems to be rice and beans and fish. The latter are prepared in a hundred different ways.

Tell Adeline,[74] I have seen here "Camelia Japonica" great trees as large as oaks, and covered with flowers. There is one of this kind, the branches of which hang over the Treaty House. I have told you before of my cutting the first cane cut in Japan by our expedition from a Japanese bush or tree.

Treaty Bay, Friday March 24, 1854

The *Susquehanna* left her anchorage before I had my eyes open this morning, and I hope my letter is now a hundred miles on its way towards you. I calculate it will go by the 7th of April mail from Hong Kong and reach you about the middle of June. It will give you a full account of everything that has befallen me since we left Loo Choo. My messmate Winder took his departure in the *Sus-*

[74] Adeline Preble, G. H. Preble's sister, was the eldest daughter and second child of Enoch and Sally Preble. She was born at Portland on September 1, 1805, and was married to widower John Cox on November 4, 1835, at Portland. One of the three daughters of John Cox by his first marriage was Susan, G. H. Preble's wife; see *Sketch*, 198.

quehanna. Little did he think when we went to shore together at Hong Hong last Oct[ober] for an hours quiet reading at the Library, that the result would be an accident, to send him home eighteen months or two years perhaps before me; he seems to rejoice at his accident, as he was bidding us good bye. I really believe I would be willing to break an arm, if the accident would ensure a speedy return home. I read Bayard Taylors description of Com Perrys July visit this morning. He certainly had his eyes open to see everything there was to be seen.

The Commodore was received with more display and ceremony than he has been this time. The Japanese give as a reason, that then he was received as an enemy, but now he is looked upon as a friend.

Soon after the *Susquehanna* got underway, I was turned out and ordered to hold myself in readiness to command the squadron of boats, detailed to escort the Commodore on shore, and to bring off the Japanese presents. To hear was to obey, though I anticipated more trouble than pleasure from the service, expecting to be detained in and about the boats, having all to do, and able to see nothing. I was therefore agreeably surprised when I reported myself to the Flag Captain, at his saying after seeing the Commodore landed I could leave my command, come on shore and mingle with the escort. At 10 A.M. I formed my boats twenty in number, in a line abreast, and pulled slowly towards the shore. When near the beach I separated the boats in two divisions; one landed to the right the other to the left of the Treaty House. After disembarking the escort of Officers, the Marines, and two bands of music, I hauled the boats out from the beach, and anchored them about thirty yards from it, in the same order. The Marines under command of Jones, were drawn up to receive the Commodore and the officers arranged in two lines for him to pass between.

When all had been arranged, the Commodore in his barge with his Flag Capt. and suite was seen approaching. As he neared and passed between the two divisions of boats I ordered the men to "Stand up and off caps," a compliment he acknowledged by raising his own, and tossing the two bow oars of his barge. As he stepped on shore he was saluted with three rolls of the drums, and the marines presented arms. The officers after he had passed between them, formed in order behind him, and followed him to the Treaty House, where the Three High Commissioners were waiting to receive him and turn over the Imperial presents. I got on shore as soon as my duties would permit, and hastened to the Audience Hall, where I found the presents displayed and the Commissioners explaining them. They were chiefly pieces of crape and silk, and specimens of lacquered ware forming a pretty display, but I should judge of not much value. Not worth over a thousand dollars some thought. I am sure one of our presents Audubon's Great work on Am[erican] Birds,[75] was worth more than all we saw there, and that our miniature railroad engine and car cost several times their value. Every one, the Commodore included remarked on the meager display and the lack of rich brocades and magnificent things always associated with our ideas of Japan. Among the presents was a box of toys, and about the only thing I coveted was a doll with a Japanese face, hair done up a la Japanese and dressed to match. It would have given you a good idea of their style, and been a real treasure to dear little Lily. There were also some pieces of rich crimson crape which I liked. The presents were from the Emperor to the President, except a few presented by the Commissioners to Com. Perry, Capt. Adams, the Interpreters, and the Engineers who put up the railroad.

After looking at the presents in the Hall, we were taken outside and shown a large pile of sacks of rice done up in straw. Each package weighing at least 150 lbs, and another pile of charcoal, also intended as a present to the squadron.

While we were looking at them and I was thinking of getting them off to the ships a procession of fifty athletes filed before us. Without being tall, these men were giants of bone and fat and muscle weighing from 200 to 400 lbs each. As we had seen nothing of the kind before, we received them with exclamations of surprise. They were entirely naked except that they wore a stout silken girdle about their loins concealing what modesty should not expose. At a given signal each of these "strong men" for that is the English translation of their Japanese name, seized two packages of rice, and holding

[75] John James Audubon (1785–1851) was the author of *The Birds of America, from Original Drawings* (4 vols., London, 1827–38; American ed., 7 vols., New York, 1840–44; 2nd Am. ed., New York, 1856).

them above their heads carried them with apparent ease to a place beyond the Commodore and deposited them in another pile ready for embarkation. Several carried a package of rice on their extended arms above their heads—thus—and one caught and carried a bundle along holding it with his teeth. Capt. Adams after the exhibition attempted simply to raise one of the packages from the ground and found it as much as he could manage—and our sailors found them heavy in getting them afterwards into the boats. After this exhibition of strength, the Commodore directed our marines to be manuvered, perhaps to match an exhibition of order and discipline against one of mere brute force. While the marines were drilling I was having rice and charcoal passed into our launches and sent off to the store ships.

When I had it all embarked I rejoined the diplomatic party whom I found watching the locomotive with its tender and car pass around the circular railroad. We then returned to the Treaty House where the electric telegraph was in operation, and several messages were sent over and answers returned in the wires in Dutch to the great wonder of the Japs. After which some of the lesser nobles were amused at receiving shocks from the electric machine connected with it. The Japanese next invited us to the rear of the building and introduced again their strong men this time as wrestlers. For their exhibition a circular area of loose earth had been, within an encloseur of canvass screens, which have been so often described as canvass forts. When we had arranged ourselves, twenty-five of the athletes entered on one side, as naked as before except that around the loins of each was suspended a beautiful crape apron of a bright color having a Japanese device wrought on it, and its edges fringed with a hew silk silver or gold bullion. These aprons were orange, scarlet, crimson, green, blue, white etcetera with the device in a strongly contrasted color. Having formed a semi-circle around the little area, they 'Kotowed' to us and the Japanese Chiefs and filed out on the side opposite to their entrance. When another twenty five similarly attired or non attired entered did as the other party did and also retired. These strong men I noticed were all very much scarred, and had numerous little round patches over fresh sores, which we were told were caused by moxas, they had inflicted upon themselves as a sovereign remedy against or for the cure of pains.

After a few minutes a Master of Ceremonies, seated on the outer edge of the circle, with a nasal twang, that would have done credit to a live Yankee called out two unpronounceable names. In response two of our naked and fat friends disrobed of their gay aprons entered and squatted down in the center of the circle. Then they rubbed themselves under the arms and thighs, with the loose black earth, grunting all the while and carefully removing small sharp stones or pebbles like to bruise or cut them in their falls. They then planted themselves firmly with their hands on their hips, next locked arms, and struggled, the one striving to push the other outside the circle. It was a simple endurance of breath, and feat of strength—not of skill. There was no attempt at tripping with the feet, or what we call wrestling. They would rush at each other, and strive to push the other opponent beyond the circle, butting with their heads, against the adversaries breast until it was black and blue, uttering all the while loud and uncouth cries. The first pushed beyond the bounds salaamed to his victor in acknowledgement of defeat. Both were treated to a sip of saki. When the defeated man retired and his conqueror returned to the arena, and contested with another opponent, and another and another until exhausted by his many victories he was in turn driven beyond the magic circle. Several were conquerors twice, but I saw only one who was the victor four times successively. At first the exhibition was interesting but it soon grew tedious from repetition. I was glad to be summoned from it especially as the weather was chilly, to the Hall of Audience to partake of a chow-chow. When seated each of us had placed before him a small lacquered tray on which was a cup of raw fish or snake soup, a plate of roasted chestnuts or other equivalents, a saucer of hard boiled egg, another of shrimps and lobsters, and a third of excellent raw oysters. A small cup of saki and some fine salt completed our entertainment. I did justice to the excellence of the oysters by eating three saucers full, and found the craw fish and eggs palatable. The saki, especially as it was warm as sometimes drunk in this country, I thought detestable. After this remove, we had another cake confectionary and tea in which they are not much if any behind our civilized notion of such things. Following the custom of the country I pocketed all of mine I did not eat, paper being furnished us for the purpose. We had our chow chow on the tables which in the morning were covered with the presents, they having been hurriedly cleared away. While the Commodore hobnobed, with the three princes in the little room, sacred to their treaty conferences. With this repast our entertainment ended.

The Commodore and his suite returned to the Ships, and Capt. Lee[76] and I hurried off the presents and then embarked ourselves. The presents are all packed in neat pine boxes, and each box had a small tray or borrow for its safe and careful conveyance. The boxes were almost as curious as their contents.

Treaty Bay, Saturday March 25, 1854

We have had a pleasant day. As our survey is for the present suspended I have resumed my duties as a watch officer. We raised a little excitement in the squadron by getting up a race this afternoon between two of our boats, and two of the *Mississippi*'s. In one we were the conquerors, in the other the vanquished. As I promised I will endeavor to give you a more particular account of the Japanese presents. First there was a handsome lacquered stand or book case, furnished with several drawers having white metal or silver handles and mountings. Then several large square lacquered boxes of papers, and smaller ones containing materials for writing. Two lacquered kettles with silver wire tops for holding fire, a curiously shaped writing desk, and an odd shaped thing with an elephant on its top. A couple of dozen lacquered cups and saucers completed the list of lacquered ware. The gilded ornaments were in relief and the color of all was a a rich brown, though some was sprinkled with gold dust. None of it was inlaid with pearl, like the Japanese lacquered ware generally seen. Of silk goods there was about a dozen pieces plain, white or scarlet, and two or three dozen of plaided silks, all very

[76] Sidney Smith Lee was made midshipman on December 30, 1820; lieutenant, May 17, 1828; commander, June 4, 1850; dismissed, April 22, 1861. He served on the *Mississippi* during Perry's expedition. See also *Narrative,* II, 410.

narrow, not over fifteen inches wide. Of crape goods there was a variety. Some of different colors figured in such a way, as to be useful only for window curtains. Several of crimson figured with the same color and others of plain crimson and white, were very fine and beautiful—far superior to the chinese fabric of the same kind—as was the lacquered ware. A piece of purple was particularly admired for its brilliancy.

The crimson and scarlet dyes, were the most rich and beautiful. The boxes of toys, umbrellas, soy, confectionary, shells and so forth are of course undescribable. The bundles of rice and charcoal only remarkable for the neatness with which they were packed.

When exhibited in the U.S. I think these presents will prove a great disappointment to our people, whose ideas of Japan have been so exaggerated. It is to be regretted they do not include some of the rich brocades for which Japan is famed or any of their beautiful copper castings, or inlaid work of gold or silver, or a collection of their coins and arms. Something also that would illustrate the daily life and habits of a people excluded from the rest of the world so many years. The supposition of their magnificence and immense wealth, will I think prove a mistake. And the splendor of their court exists only in the romances of the old travellers and Jesuits. The government is without doubt despotic, but not more so, than were the European Governments in the days of feudalism and chivalry.

Treaty Bay, Sunday March 26, 1854

A windy rainy day, and consequently a quiet one for we have had no visitors, and even our usual Sunday ceremonies have been waved in consequence of the weather.

Treaty Bay, Monday March 27, 1854

Though it has been blowing a stiff and cold N.W. gale it has been a gala day in the squadron. Undeterred by the weather the three Japanese princes,[77] visited our ship, and partook of an entertainment

[77] The Japanese commissioners negotiating with Commodore Perry were Hayashi Daigaku-no-kami, Ido Tsusshima-no-kami, and Izawa Mimasaki-no-kami. Perry did not understand their titles and positions. He noted, for example, that Hayashi, who was "rector magnificus" of Edo University (*daigaku*), was the "prince of

to which they were invited by the Commodore, on board the *Powhatan*. They first came to our ship, and as they reached the deck the *Mississippi's* guns thundered a salute of seventeen guns, which they with childlike eagerness rushed forward on our forecastle to see, the *Miss.* laying ahead of us. They were then shown all over our ship, and inquisitively examined every part of her, an artist of their numerous suite, taking numerous drawings of such things as they particularly admired. After they had seen the ship the drum beat to general quarters, and we amused them with an exercise of our Great Guns, and small arms, showing them how we boarded an enemy, and how we repulsed one attempting to board, and sent axemen into the rigging to chop it away when requisite. Then rang the Fire bell and exercised at fire quarters, drawing water in buckets and throwing it and streams from our force pumps upon the imaginary conflagration. When they witnessed all we had to show them, they left our ship, and went to the *Powhatan*, under a salute of seventeen guns from our eight inch guns. We were to have manned yards always a pretty sight, but the weather was too boisterous. On reaching the *Powhatan*, a flag bearing the Emperor's arms was hoisted at her foremast head, and kept flying while they remained on board and another flag with the arms of the 1st Prince Commissioner, was hoisted at her mast. The Commodore's blue broad pennant kept its usual place at the main mast. Our glorious stars and stripes waved from the peak, and the Union Jack decorated the bowsprit. All of us having received invitations from the Commodore to join in and assist at the entertainment on the *Powhatan*, as many as could be spared from duty, and I was one, hastened on board. After being shown that noble steamer's massive machinery in motion, the three Princes, with their more immediate suite were taken into the Commodores Cabin, and seated at a feast he had spread for them, and Capts and Commanders of our squadron and his suite, as many as the Cabin could conveniently hold about twenty seven in all. On the Quarter Deck another table was spread and ample provisions made for their more numerous and lesser satellites. Our part being to make them

Daigaku." *Narrative*, I, 341, 347–48; Williams, *A Journal of the Perry Expedition*, 128–29, 144.

eat and drink as much as possible, hoping in accordance with the old adage, if they eat hearty they would give us a good name and eating and drinking seem to be important feature in all the diplomatic meetings we have held with them.

Doing my duty, therefore, in obedience to orders, I plied the Japs in my neighborhood well, and when clean work had been made of Champagne, Madeira, Cherry Cordial, punch and whiskey, I resorted to the Castors and gave them a mixture of catsup and vinegar which they seemed to relish with equal gusto. Following the customs of the country I encouraged them to pocket the remnants of the feast. I saw one fellow walk off with a whole chicken done up in paper under his jacket. Altogether it was an amusing and animated scene. I have not enjoyed such a hearty laugh since we left the U.S. The Commodore wanted to put them in a good humor, as he said the success of his treaty depended upon the success of the entertainment, so we did our best and I am sure it could not have gone off more to his or their satisfaction. They were highly amused when we toasted "The Emperor of Japan, "The President of the U.S.," "The Commodore," "The High Commissioners," and "The Japanese ladies." When the band commenced playing, several commenced shuffling and dancing—and to encourage them some of our greyest and gravest officers danced with them. A funny sight to behold—these baldpated bundles of clothes—and Doctors, Pursers, Lieuts and Capts. all jumping up and down to the music.

Yesterday several of the guests before the feast sent their fans on board, to have mottos written on them, and then returned to them at the feast: that being one of the polite customs of the country. Several gave me their fans at the feast for the same purpose and I wrote, "Commerce and Agriculture tend to unite America and Japan," "California and Japan are now neighbors; it is to be hoped that they will pass many social evenings together," etc. By the way they have heard probably from the Dutch all about California and the gold discovery, and it is thought the secret of our success lies in their hope to benefit from a trade with California.

When the Commissioners had been sufficiently mellowed in the Cabin, they were brought on deck to witness a performance by the

Ethiopian Band of the *Powhatan*, who style themselves "Japanese Minstrels." Then enjoyed the imitations of the negro, and laughed very heartily. In his delight one of the Commissioners went so far as to put his arms around the Commodore's neck and embrace him. Some one remarking to the Commodore, that he did not think he would stand that, Oh, said old Perry—if he will only sign the Treaty he may kiss me. After the Exhibition they left the ship and returned to shore, as they came, in their own boats, and under a salute of seventeen guns from the *Saratoga*. The object in firing the salutes from different ships being to show the power of their batteries.

The Court Artist, a Doctor, who had cunning humbug depicted in his own face, made quite an accurate sketch of the negro minstrels[78] and their instruments, perhaps to be shown to the Emperor. A most laughable scene was seeing one of our officers toasting the Japs, who looked like two bundles of clothes, skewered by two swords. On top of the cabins, where they could have a better view of the performance. Following the Princes we called our boat, and returned to our own ship to tea.

Treaty Bay, Tuesday March 28, 1854

This morning the Commodore landed to have another talk with the Commissioners—It has been a cold day on board ship causing us to miss the stove taken down before the General exercise yesterday. We are beginning to get a scant supply of ducks, chickens, and eggs for our messes—a very pleasant change of diet from our long continuance on salt fare.

I was on board the *Mississippi* and *Saratoga* today. Goldsborough has charge of my pictures and will see them Expressed to you. Madigan has a smaller package he promises to deliver in person. They expect to sail about the 10th of next month. The remainder of the

[78] At this point (between pp. 199 and 200) in Preble's diary, there is inserted a printed program of the entertainment Perry presented aboard ship for his Japanese guests. For a historical note on two programs pasted into Preble's diary which were printed on the shipboard press during Perry's expedition, see Robert W. Lovett, "The Japan Expedition Press," *Harvard Library Bulletin*, Vol. XII (1958), 242–52.

squadron, after the Treaty are to go to the Northern Island of Matsania, where a port is to be opened to our whalers.[79]

The Commodore is determined to see Jedo, it is said, before he leaves the Bay. And having the will, I have little doubt but that he will find a way—but quien sabe.

Treaty Bay, Wednesday March 29, 1854

The *Vandalia* and the *Southampton* have returned from the Harbor of Simoda which they were sent to examine, and pronounce favorable upon it. It will probably be one of the ports opened.

The wind at N.N.E. and the ther[mometer] at 42° has quite shrivelled us up today. In order to keep warm, when not on duty I have been rolled up in my blankets, reading—I expect to do some sharp walking in my watches. The Japanese are making us pay for opening trade. In a bill just brought on board they charge us 75cts apiece for chickens, a California price. Judging from their toughness some of the roosters may have crowed over the expulsion of the Portuguese in 1622, and now *Fiat Justicia* are sacrificed to appease the appetites and keep away scurvy from the adventurers of a Western World who are again unlocking the portals of this Empire with the golden key of commerce. There's a flourish of trumpets—quite exhausting to my genius—so I will say Good night.

Treaty Bay, Thursday March 30, 1854

I had a cold, blistering watch last night, the ther. getting as low as 33°. This morning it stood at 37°. Searching weather for such an open, outdoor habitation as a man of war. I said the Cock on our table yesterday must have witnessed the expulsion of the Portuguese.[80] The one we chawed upon this noon judging by comparison must have been the gentleman who crowed before Peter when he denied his master, [81] or one of his contemporaries.

Quite an excitement was produced last evening by a report brought on board the *Saratoga*, that scales and particles of gold had been found in the gizzards of ducks killed on board that ship. It was im-

[79] Hakodate, Hakkaido, on Tsugaru Strait.

[80] In 1637, the Takugawa government closed Japan to all foreigners except a few Chinese and Dutch merchants.

[81] John 18:25–27.

mediately conjectured it had been washed down by the mountain streams and picked up by them with their gravel. There was no doubt of the fact, for the gold had been seen by the person who brought the report. This led to the examination this morning of the gizzards of the ducks killed on board of our ship. When to our surprise and delight, particles of gold were discovered as large as a pea and the thickness of a thick wafer one of this shape and size [Preble inserted a diagram here]. While considering the extraordinary richness of the country where the poultry were fed upon gold the illusion was destroyed by the Purser of the *Saratoga* who informed us that on submitting theirs to the test it proved to be copper. Trying ours' with acid, we found a similar result. The Metal however was of extraordinary fineness and resembled in color and appearance pinchback or Jewellers' gold.

One of our officers just returned on board says the Treaty is to be signed tomorrow, and that the *Saratoga* is to sail on Saturday. We will know tomorrow, as Capt Abbott's son Chas. is to go home in her as Capt Adams' clerk, and Capt Adams' son come on board of us to take his place.

Treaty Bay, Friday March 31, 1854

Eureka![82] It is finished! The great agony is over! In vulgar parlance the egg has hatched its chicken today. The Treaty of Amity and Friendship between Japan and the United States was signed today to the satisfaction of everybody. Even Old Bruin (i.e. the Commodore) would smile if he only knew how to smile.

After the Treaty was signed and had been given to the Commodore, he expressed to the Commissioners (this was an overheard conversation) his intention of taking his squadron as near to Jedo as he could get them to it. The Japanese stoutly objected saying their law was against it. The Commodore said in reply he was aware of that and every other objection, as their laws had been his study for a year past. They had another law which prohibited ships from passing Uraga, but he had come up to this anchorage and done them no

[82] Eureka, from the Greek, "I have found it," or "That is it," is the exclamation attributed to Archimedes when he discovered a way of determining the purity of the gold in the crown of King Hiero.

damage. On the contrary a treaty of amity and friendship was the consequence. He had even remained on board ship, and respected their laws so far as the land was concerned, though he did think it somewhat uncivil that they had not invited him and his officers on shore. The Emperor and his people had a right to make laws for the land but the sea was free to everybody. The Commissioners then urged that his boats would come to survey, and they did not want the Harbor surveyed. The Commodore told them that was a matter of indifference to him, he had charts enough and survey enough to take him as far as he proposed going, and all he wished was to place his Squadron off Jedo, where the Emperor could see it, and receive a salute. This at once the Commissioners said could not be allowed, but the Commodore finding them obdurate told them his orders were positive to take the ships as near Jedo as possible, and where his Master the President of the U.S. said they must go, there he must take them, and that was the end of it.

A grand reception it is said will be given him at Hakodadi in the straits of Matame,[83] a part that the Treaty provides shall be opened to our Whalemen. We are to go there to survey the Bay before we leave Japanese waters. It is not thought we will remain here a week now that we have opened "the Oyster." Our mess is now so hard up we drink our tea *á la* Japanese and Chinese *sans* sugar or milk; our coffee is 'done and give out' entirely and a few hams and some cans of pickled oyster, so salt we cannot eat them are all we have in our store room save a little strong batter and some flour. These and the ship's ration are now our sole dependence; but for the timely supply of those 'old cocks' we would be hard pushed for something to eat. The last of these we tried we thought must have exercised his juvenile crowing about the commencement of the Christian era. Every succeeding one seems tougher than its predecessor. We know Japan to be a very ancient country, and certainly the one we tried our teeth on today, must have walked out of the Ark before Noah. By boiling them all day, and then working them over in a stew with gravy, rice pepper and other condiments, they are made tolerably palatable and are an improvement on Salt Horse.

[83] Matsumae, on Tsugaru Strait, southwest of Hakodate.

I wonder that Job was not sent to sea, and deprived of all knowledge of his home and family for a twelve month as I am like to be. It would have been a greater trial for his patience than any he was made to endure, and he would have cursed and swore sooner than I did I am sure. The laborer, who sees his little ones snuggly in bed, and meets his family every night at sun down, and spends the sweet sabbath with them is far more blessed in his lot than a wanderer like me laboring on ocean.

Treaty Bay, Saturday April 1st, 1854

The *Saratoga* is to sail as soon as the Commodore writes his dispatches, and I have been all day hard at work writing mine to the friends I love best to remember, and have eight or nine ready. Capt. Adams bearer of the Commodores dispatches will mail our letters at Panama. He says, he expects to rejoin the squadron by the overland route in Oct[ober]. We have transferred all our chronic invalids to the *Saratoga* today and our Capt's son has also gone on board.

It has been given out at the galley today, where all the news on board ship is manufactured, that the *Vandalia* is to go to Shanghai to relieve the *Plymouth*, which is to go to Loo Choo. The *Lexington* is to be sent to the Bonin Islands, another ship to Simoda, and the rest of the squadron to Hakodadi.

Treaty Bay, Sunday April 2d, 1854

A pleasant day, and as usual after muster—a ship full of visitors. It is rumored around the galley today that our ship is to cruize in the Sea of Ochotsk until Oct. Capt. Adams came on board today to say good bye, and told me he expected to be in Washington in seventy days. His son has joined our ship as Capt's Clerk. He seems a clever well disposed genteel young man. When I was at the naval school he was running about the grounds a boy in petticoats. How time does slip up to be sure. Capt. A[dams] says that the Commodore intends the *Saratoga* to sail on Tuesday morning. I have written up all my letters some nine or ten in number and closed all but to you; it is literally casting my bread upon the waters hoping for a return after many days.

Treaty Bay, Monday April 3d, 1854

The Flag Ship signalled to the *Saratoga* this morning to prepare to sail tomorrow morning at 8 o'clock. It has been blowing a S.W. gale, which has prevented all communications with the other ships since the signal.

Since our arrival here, I have wondered that seeing so little I have found so much to say—from day to day. I have written all that I have seen or heard, but I never was in a place six weeks before without gathering more information about it.

Whether it is worth while to come so far to see so little you can judge by my letters. I feel the want and disappointment of hearing from home, but endeavor to be jolly, and laugh at the chronic growling, which appears at our table, with the coarse brown sugar, tea slops, and hard tack to which our mess is reduced.

We sigh for the flesh pots of Egypt, the ducks capons and roasting pigs of China—immortalized by Chas. Lamb. Much as we abused that vile hot hole Cum-sing Moon last summer. We have discovered a worse sojourning place here, for there we received our letters regularly and our mess was well provided. Even Loo Choo improves by contrast. I have procured some of the scales of copper found in our ducks, which I shall send to Dr. Word. Tell him in Japan his profession occupies the third rank in the social scale of Japanese society and its professors are highly esteemed. Those I have seen are shrewd cunning looking rascals—with humbug in their countenance and quackery in their hands. I have seen some of their pills, which are like those of the [old days] and often silvered or gilded. Some of the officials, who came on board in charge of the boats watering our ship, got too much whiskey and were very amusing in their mimery of our names, customs and talking.

One of our crew, the sailmakers mate, met with a laughable accident tonight which had well nigh proved fatal to him. He turned in to his hammock, drunk, and by some means or other swallowed his false teeth. The queer noise he made attracted attention and the Doctor was sent for. The man was likely to choke and already turning black in the face. By pressure the Doctor forced the gold plate on which they had been fastened upward until he could reach it with his hand and pull it out, affording instant relief. The teeth however had separated from the plate, and are doing duty in a comical way in the mans stomach.

Tuesday April 4, 1854

I sent off my letter this morning by the *Saratoga* and saw it fairly dispatched, going on board with it myself and remaining to say goodbye to my friends until she was fairly underway. The squadron cheered her on [her] homeward voyage, and our hands followed her with 'old folks at home,' 'Home sweet home' and kindred tunes. The excitement of her sailing having unfitted me for sober work, I spent the day in visiting on board the *Vandalia* and *Mississippi* and on board the latter was pressed by my friend Wm. L. Maurry[84] our hydrographic chief to stretch a sheet of drawing paper for our chart of the Bay.

Frank Cook went home in the *Saratoga,* a melancholy spectacle, imbecile in mind and body—a victim to himself. Capt Abbott's son also went in her and we have Capt. Adams' son to take his place as Capt. clerk, who seems a clever well disposed genteel young man. He makes me feel my age for when I was at the naval asylum, he was running about the grounds in petticoats a boy of four years, his father being our Executive.

Wednesday April 5, 1854

A cold rainy day. The great and sudden change from hot to cold, has made every one uncomfortable, and the profane ones to curse the climate. It is reported that the *Saratoga* was seen in the lower bay this morning, but I hope she is miles away from the influence of land winds and bounding merrily on her way across the Pacific.

I am thinking of compiling a "Manual of Practical Hydrography," a part of the Encyclopedia of Nautical Knowledge—which I sometime ago thought of compiling—should I ever attempt or complete these projects, I might have leisure and more books for reference than I have at present and it would be a labor of love and self-improvement rather than profit.

[84] William L. Maury was made midshipman on February 2, 1829; passed midshipman, July 3, 1835; lieutenant, February 26, 1841; lieutenant on the *Mississippi* during Perry's expedition; resigned, April 20, 1861. See also *Narrative,* II, 410.

Thursday April 6, 1854

A mild pleasant day. Com. Perry with a small staff of officers, accompanied by a Japanese interpreter stretched his legs on shore today; the rest of us walked up and down the decks, lookers at this land of Egypt. Yesterday the last of our copper fed ducks graced our table; today we are reduced to what Father Noah took into the Ark with him—hens.

In the afternoon a race between our gig and the *Mississippi*'s enlivened us a little and our boat beat of course. Read a novel today called Pen Owen,[85] full of incidents but ever sauced with prozy conversations.

Friday April 7th 1854

A rainy uncomfortable day, ending in a gale from the Nth. Bar at 29.70 and falling. It has been my watch on deck, and like a wild beast in its cage I have been walking forward and back again, back again, forward under the awnings on the only dry spot on deck.

Treaty Bay, Bay of Jedo, Saturday April 8, 1854

The Gale and rain abated this morning as the sun rose, and the day has proved pleasant, but there are signs of another gale brewing. The inland hills this morning were quite white, low down with new fallen snow contrasting with the green and cultivated fields in our immediate neighborhood and along the shores of the Bay. I went aboard the *Mississippi* today to put down my lines of soundings towards Jedo, as the Commodore wanted them by tomorrow morning. We thought him rather jocose this morning when he signaled "Communication with the shore discontinued," as by his written order, all communication has been strictly forbidden.

Today completes my first year of absence from home.

Sunday April 9, 1854

It has been a long foggy cheerless day, and cold and dyspeptic with a mid watch in perspective I am not in the best of humors with myself or the surrounding world. Some movements today lead us

[85] The novel *Pen Owen* (3 vols., Edinburgh, 1822) was published anonymously by James Hook, D.D., dean of Worcester. See James Kennedy *et al.*, *Dictionary of Anonymous and Pseudonymous English Literature*, IV, 319.

to hope we may weigh anchor for 'Jedo' or elsewhere tomorrow; God grant it. A much longer residence here on salt fare would make us fear like Lots wife pillars of Salt, but far from being like Job monuments of patience, though we might rival him in his affliction of sore boils. I was on board the *Powhatan* this afternoon and took tea, but brought away no news. Capt. A[bbott] has gone to see the Commodore by order, which means something.

Am. Anchorage, Jedo Bay, Monday April 10, 1854

Rheumatism and indigestion have conspired to throw me back and keep me quiet, though it has been an exciting day in the squadron. At day light all the ships got underway and moved in the direction of Jedo. Several of the Japanese went on board the two steamers, ostensibly to see the working of their machinery, but evidently very uneasy in mind. When the steamers approached the anchorage off the Capital they declared their intention to "*harri kari*"[86] themselves, that is to rip open their bellies and let their bowels out. The moment the anchor was let go, no matter where they might be at the time, whether in the Commodore's Cabin or on the Quarter Deck. They also said should a boat land, the Three Prince Commissioners would feel compelled to go through with the same pleasant operation. Under these circumstances the Commodore having sighted Jedo, resolved to turn back to the great joy of the Japanese. He did not get however within five miles of the point to which we had extended our survey with the boats. Soon after coming to his decision the Commodore anchored the squadron here. We have had all sorts of agricultural instruments sent on board of us and are now under sealed orders to sail in the morning, probably for the Bonin Islands. Why there should be any secrecy about it, I cannot imagine.

One of the Japs aboard the *Mississippi* gave his long outside garment to day, and long sword to the Purser's son saying he would have no further use for them and prepared with the greatest composure to disembowel himself with the short sword. When the steamer turned back he joyfully received his property again, and has been sick all day from the reaction after his over-excitement. The officers endeavored to reason with the Japanese upon the folly of

[86] Should be hara-kiri, or suicide by disemboweling.

such an act, for a thing they could neither control or prevent. They replied it was useless to reason on the subject, it was Japanese custom, and they must comply. They preferred death to the loss of caste. The officers of the steamer have no doubt they were sincere and that had the Commodore gone on they would have harri karried themselves.

At Sea, Tuesday April 11, 1854

We left American Anchorage at daylight this morning and are now outside the Bay of Jedo, and fifty miles on our passage to the Bonin Island, which notwithstanding the great mystery is as I rightly surmised the object of our cruize. We are to refresh there until early in May, and rejoin the Commodore at Simoda in the 10th of that month in time to participate in the fair the Japanese are to hold there for our benefit, and to accompany the squadron to Hakodadi, the port that is to be opened to our whaleman in the Straits of Matsami.

We left the Bay of Jedo with considerable luck this morning, with a fine fair wind, but soon run into rainy uncomfortable weather—and the rain is now pouring down upon us, and we are enveloped in a thick fog without wind enough to blow a fly from a toper's nose. For myself I am as uncomfortable as the weather having exercised my bowels with pills and salts and senna.

At Sea, Wednesday April 12, 1854

A rough and rolling day exemplifying the words of the old song "A ship is a thing you can never be quiet in, etc." For the first time in my life, I have paid tribute to Neptune i.e. been sick enough to throw up, rather hard after nineteen years apprenticeship to the old Sea God attributable I suppose to the Doctors stuff I have swallowed and the state in which it has left my disordered bowels. Spite of Neptune went on duty and kept my watches. A little while ago Allison caught a swallow and sent it down to me, and it is now flitting about my room quite fearless, but discontented. When we have brighter weather, or make the land, I intend to send it on its way rejoicing. It is a pretty bird, with long sharp wings forked tail, lavender colored head and throat, white breast and battle green wings and back. Its chirrup is pleasant to hear, and I hope to save its life by keeping it captive a day or two.

It is eighteen years today since I received my first orders in the navy to join the Frigate *U.S.* [*United States*] at New York. Do you mind the time, and the pleasant social winter that preceded it? How the little circle that used to meet nearly every evening in school has been scattered. Two of our companions then are not, and of our elders who smiled upon those meetings how many are wanting.

At Sea, Thursday April 13, 1854

The ship has been wallowing about all day but, we have the consolation of knowing it has been to some purpose, as we are 200 miles nearer our port of destination. I was turned out and had to shift end for end in my berth last night, by the decks leaking over my head and the waters drop-dropping into my face so as to give me quite a baptismal sprinkling. The little swallow I have mentioned slept on my pillow, and I found him there when I shifted my quarters—poor fellow—an avalanche of books was soon after hurled upon him and killed him outright. I regretted his untoward fate but after a little sentimental mourning gave his body to the cat, the most humane and useful disposition that could be made of it.

This being the anniversary of our sailing from New York, I celebrated it by a clean shave—the first time since the 22d of Dec. a razor has touched my face.

At Sea, Friday April 14, 1854

I am told today is Good Friday—only good to me that I am one day nearer home. We have been lazing along all day towards an island called St. Peters or St. Thomas now about 10 miles dist. At noon we were 200 miles from Port Lloyd our haven of rest and refreshment. I read today 'Life on the Isthmus,'[87] and the beautiful story of Picciola.[88]

One of our sailors amused me today by saying in my hearing, all

[87] J. W. Fabens, *A Story of Life on the Isthmus.*

[88] Joseph Xavier Boniface Saintine (1798–1865) was the author of *Picciola; Précé-dé de quelques recherches sur l'emploi du temps dans les prisons d'état* (par Paul L. Jacob, Paris, C. Gorselin, *ca.* 1835). It was translated into English by Mrs. C. F. Gore under the title *Picciola, or Captivity Captive* (London, 1837). A new edition, with illustrations, appeared in Philadelphia in 1850; it is perhaps the one Preble read.

the difference he could see between a ship and a penitentiary was in one you are allowed to talk and the other not, and he had tried both. What do you know about a penitentiary said another sailor. Oh said the first, I paid a quarters once to a man to show me through one and saw you in your cell. You be damned, replied the other nothing abashed. It never cost you that much to see one and when there, you had plenty of opportunity to see it, they did not hurry you out.

At Sea, Saturday April 15, 1854

The Capt. discoursed me for three hours in my watch last night, on his son Nathan who died aboard and with an account of his little daughter who was burnt to death by her night clothes catching fire when she was but five years old. Like all parents his loved and lost, are to him prodigies of intelligence. It was no doubt a relief to him to have a patient listener to his description of their excellences. The little girl was evidently the pride and darling of his heart, and her sudden and distressing death must have rent it to the core. Now though many years have elapsed the recollection of it affected him deeply. What parent can ever forget his little darling! Capt. A[bbot] says his little girl was 'a remarkable little being,' and that every one noticed her beauty, and she would come in after playing out doors, and say, "Papa am I pretty, the little boys I play with in the street say I am, and the little girls say so too," and a gentleman I never saw before, the other day took me in his arms and asked my name and said I was pretty. What do they all mean, papa? Am I pretty? Her father told her to be good was to be pretty, and if she wished always to be called pretty she must try to be good. A few days before the accident which caused her death, sitting in her fathers lap, she looked up thoughtfully into his face and said, "Papa my sunday school teacher said yesterday, that perhaps before next Sunday some one of the little girls in her class might be in Heaven. Do you think it will be me Papa?" The Captain says he told her "Well Mary it is possible it may be you. You are in good health now but in an hour you may meet with some terrible accident to take you there." Little thinking how literally his supposition would come true, and that on Thursday she would be a corpse. The accident occurred in this way. Little Mary slept with her grandmother who had for thirty years been accustomed to have a nurse lamp lighted in her bed chamber every night, which she extinguished at day light. For some time previous little Mary had been allowed with her grandmothers consent the privelege of putting it out. And on the morning of the accident in attempting to do so before her grandmother was awake, it caught her light cotton night dress which was almost instantly in a light blaze. Her screams and the unusual light awakened the grandmother to the dangers of her little charge and she was immediately enveloped her in a piece of drugget, but too late, she was burnt to a crisp all over, and had inhaled a volume of flame. Her father and others alarmed by the screams rushed to the scene, and she was immediately laid by them on a sheet, and covered with flour, which the Capt. said he shoveled upon her, but all to no purpose except to relieve her agony. She died early in the afternoon without a struggle, her last words to her father being to keep her "Rewards of Merit" which she had confided to his care. He says that two or three times, during the day, she made every body leave the room in which she was lieing, and when thus left alone commenced praying and continued in prayer until her pains and smarts caused her to call them in to move her to an easier position. This seems scarcely credible of one only five years old, but her father thinks she had heard older people talk of the efficacy of secret prayer and so resorted to it. I cannot but think a childish whim was magnified by the high strung sensibilities of her agonized parents into a prayerful mood that accorded with their own religious belief. This sad tale reminded me of how often we had allowed Henry to put out the light in our bed room without ever thinking it careless or dangerous. Perhaps our 'Lily' who is not so old as was Little Mary may be doing the same service for mama now. If so this accident will be certain, to stop the habit and show you the danger of cotton night dresses for little ones.

Our calm weather continued until noon, when a breeze came up from behind, which at sundown put us under double reefs and now threatens to blow a gale from the Sth.

At Sea, Sunday April 16, 1854

The expected gale has arrived, and our good ship is tossing and rolling and pitching about to no purpose but our discomfort. I wish

I had some of those poets here who sing the pleasures of the sea. "The proof of the pudding is in the eating thereof" as they would find. To my mind the following verses which I find in the "Putnam"[89] for June are more truthful, if less sentimental.

When you're on the land
The sea is every thing thats bright, and broad,
and blue and grand.
Perhaps on some October night, when the
roused South o'erwhelms
With surge on surge, rolled gathering down
the night the shuddering elms,
You have laid fancying what wild joy there
must be in the motion
Of a brave vessel plunging through the
broken coils of ocean;
You're mind ran back and forth again,
like a fly watching spider
Upon a line of Byron of the "steed that knows
its rider,"[90]
And in your bath next morning, you
splash with double glee
Humming dear Barry's Cornwall's song—"The
Sea! the open sea!"[91]
I wish that Barry and Byron both were
only here with me!
All well enough that sentiment and stuff
upon the shore

[89] This is a continuation from previous issues of a comicosatirical poem, "Our Own, His Wonderings and Personal Adventures," appearing in *Putnam's Monthly Magazine*, Vol. I (January–June, 1853), 687–90.

[90] Byron, *Childe Harold's Pilgrimage*, Canto III, stanza 2: "Once more upon the waters, yet once more! / And the waves bound beneath me as a steed / That knows his rider."

[91] Barry Cornwall was the pseudonym of Bryan Waller Procter (1787–1874), a British composer of "pretty songs." His songs were probably known to Preble from *English Songs and Other Small Poems*. His song "*The Sea*" begins: "The sea! the sea! the open sea! / The blue, the fresh, the ever free!"

But when the sea is smoothest its love,
And when 'tis rough my brace of bards,
you'd neither of you sing
Of "hands on manes" or "blue" or "fresh"
but quite another thing—
Flat on your backs in jerking berths you
scarce could keep your place in
You'd moan an [word illegible] sad. Quick
steward! bring the basin!
In this way men are made to say they
like the sea,
Flams says he does, and all the rest
will be as good as he.
I heard a great man once declare that he
had never found
A sailor yet who loved the fate to which
his life was bound.
And when I asked our brown first mate,
a seaman good and brave
On shore as helpless as a fish, a viking
on the wave,
What life would please him most? He
sighed, looked at his tattooed arm
Studied its hieroglyphs a while and
said, "an inland farm."

Just at sundown three Am[erican] Whaling ships hove in sight and we hove to and boarded one the *Rambler of Nantucket,*[92] 30 months out, and were informed one of the other ships was the *Roscoe,*[93] 48 months out. One had caught 500, the other 900 BBls of oil, and both were bound to the Arctic to fill up if possible with common whale oil and finish their cruise.

[92] The *Rambler* was a ship of 1,119 tons constructed in 1854; Captain Allen Baxter was her master. She belonged to Baxter Brothers, Yarmouth, Massachusetts, and Israel Nash, Boston. She was sold to Germany in 1863. *Greyhounds,* 438, 503, 512.

[93] The *Roscoe,* a packet ship, was built in 1836 and belonged to the Black Ball Line of the regular service between Baltimore and Liverpool. *Greyhounds,* 116; *Clipper,* 41, 47.

At Sea, Monday April 17, 1854

We have had a rainy uncomfortable day. In the morning it fairly poured down in sheets and for two hours of my watch I experienced a perfect cataract against which painted coats and tarpaulins were no protection. The thunder and lightning was quite alarming, commencing with its first explosion directly over our main mast, and without any warning coming out of the thick misty shroud which had enveloped us for hours. It was soon followed up by a wind squall which caused us to shorten sail in a hurry. Altogether I had a nasty nervous disagreeable watch. This afternoon we spoke and boarded the whaling ship *Milton*[94] of New Bedford 30 mos. from home, left the Bonin Islds yesterday. We bought from her a couple of BBls of oil for the ship, and two roasting pigs for our messes, a perfect godsend.

We have now a fair and fine breeze, and ought to get in tomorrow, but will we? Aye that's the question tomorrow must answer.

At Sea, Off Parry Group Bonin Islds,
Pacific Ocean, Tuesday, April 18, 1854

I was awakened this morning by the report of two guns fired to bring off a pilot, and hoped to be soon snug at anchor, but on going on deck at 8 o'clock to my watch, found our navigator had mistaken the land, and supposed one of the Parry Group to be Peel Island and had run for it. The error had been just discovered, and we hauled off and have been beating to windward ever since. We now have the Island in sight but our port is full twenty miles dist. We made a fine dinner in our mess today, for the first time in many weeks off, Clam soup made from fresh clams all the way from Boston, and the Whalers pig which proved a fine roaster.

This Parry Group is a cluster of ragged rocks surrounding four or five, that from their larger size may be called islands. Many of these rocks stand up like statues or monuments and two or three are perforated with holes so that you see through them. The larger rocks are covered with a beautiful green but are destitute of trees. Our weather continues watery but is an improvement on yesterday. A

94 The *Milton*, a whaling ship of New Bedford, was built in 1852. *Greyhounds*, 243.

troublesome 'stye' on my eyelid has prevented my reading and writing, and unaccustomed to the situation the little roaster has been squealing in my stomach.

Wednesday April 19, 1854

Our ill luck continues—we are as far from our port tonight as we were yesterday, and the weather has been execrable. The rain has been constant and down pouring, what Harry would call 'spitting weather.' One of my messmates says he don't know of a better place for constant rain, there are so few people here to be inconvenienced by them.

Port Lloyd,[95] Peel Island, Bonin Group,
Thursday April 20, 1854

It was very provoking when we obtained the latitude this morning by an altitude of the North Star to discover we were beating all day yesterday in the rainy disagreeable weather for Bailey, or the Southern Group of islands, supposing they contained our Haven of rest, when all the time it was under our lee. Having no observation consequent upon the thick weather, we passed our port without seeing it. And makeing the Bailey Islds in the position our dead reckoning gave to Peel Isld. they were readily mistaken for it, the latitude placing us 50 miles to windward of our port. At 4 AM we squared away, and about 4 P.M. anchored in the little circular basin in which we now lie, and which is evidently the basin of a submerged crater. The whole island being of volcanic origin. We have made good use of our time, and obtained a supply of turtle yams and sweet potatoes, and have a boat out seeing. Entering the harbor today we had a fine view of a school of fin back whales, gamboling, turning flukes, jumping clear out of the water, and going through other gymnastic exercises, beautiful and wonderful to behold. I was sent by the Capt ahead of the ship in a boat to mark the position of a school near the entrance, and saw as many as a dozen large turtles swimming upon the surface—unfortunately I had no harpoon or turtle plug to strike them with. We purchase them here weighing 300 lbs for three dol-

[95] The harbor on the western side of Peel Lsland, Bonin Archipelago, was named Port Lloyd in 1827 by Captain Beechey, commandant of the British surveying vessel *Blossom. Narrative*, I, 199.

lars or one cent a pound. What a place for Alderman! We have had sunshine mingled with our rain today and there seems promise of better weather tomorrow.

Port Lloyd, Friday April 21, 1854

Had my room cleaned out and painted, and have been exiled from it by the smell of the fresh paint and turpentine.

Our First Lieut has been makeing a holiday or rather a whole day of work of it, and kept all hands busy—wooding, watering, getting sand, hauling the seine, overhauling rigging are a few among the many 'irons' he has had going. Our turtle soup was excellent today and so was our fried fish and turtle steaks. I made a sketch today of a remarkable hill which overhangs our anchorage and will send it to you. It is beyond a doubt the profile of the First Settler, and is I think the most perfect resemblance of the Human face divine I have ever seen, showing hair, military whiskers and eye as well as the mere profile.

Port Lloyd, Harbor Bonin Islds, Saturday April 22d 1854

I have endeavored in the annexed pen sketch to give you a faithful portrait of the veritable oldest inhabitant, and First Settler at Port Lloyd, who for once I have caught napping. I have failed to do justice to the very perfect resemblance to a Human face which the hill presents.[96] The only defective outline in the original being at the top of the nose which as shown in the sketch seems to have been bitten off; otherwise even to the sloping of the eyes and mouth and shirt collar every thing is perfect. The hair and whiskers are brown earth. The nose and chin a barren rock. The top of the head and hair and the shading about the eyes is formed by a light green shrubbery. The bust is a smooth bald hill covered with a close verdure. The head reclines on the side of the hill as viewed from our anchorage about one third up towards its summit. It is certainly a fantastic freak of nature's handiwork. All on board are agreed it is the most perfect thing of the kind that they have ever seen. My duties have prevented my going on shore, but tomorrow, weather permitting I intend to examine the shores and beaches for shells and curios, and

[96] On p. 226 of the manuscript diary is a sketch, executed by Preble in black ink, of a hill resembling a man.

to clamber over the hills with our Purser on a botanizing excursion.

I may be tempted to buy a lot of land here, as one can be had dog cheap, which is perhaps its only recommendation. Commodore Perry has bought ten acres, and other lots for Howland and Aspinwell[97] and several of the officers have purchased lots on speculation. How would you like to settle here? It would be a simple life: You to do your own cooking washing and dressmaking—provided you wore dresses; I to raise my own vegitables catch my own fish fell my own wood and be in all respects a Caleb Quotem.[98] We would be without doubt of the first society. The greatest variety of fruit and vegitables would be ours for the planting. What say—shall I buy and will you come?

The few settlers have formed themselves into a sort of government for mutual safety and protection. They are so few in number that each of them is an officer and some hold two. What a glorious place for the office seeking beggars of the United States if there was only a little more room to the offices.

We sent fifty of our men on shore today on liberty, and they came off at sundown gloriously drunk and sailorly happy—so much for the progress of civilization in this the Bonin Islands.

Had I a glass of wine I would drain it to 'sweethearts and wives' —but you will think the sentiment no less sincere if I quench it in a glass of pure water from the mountain streams.

Port Lloyd, Sunday April 23, 1854

Raining merrily, but who cares under the shelter of an awning. Until sundown the weather was fine and pleasant. The Purser and I landed early in the forenoon on the South side of the Harbor and made a botanizing and geological tramp over the hills. We admired the Panorama, refreshed our thirst from a cascade that leapt lightly from rock to rock and flashing as it bounded onward to the sea, and

[97] Howland and Aspinwell, a New York shipping company, owned several clipper ships, among them the *Rainbow,* the *Sea Witch,* the *Valparaiso,* and the *John Jay. Greyhounds,* 401, 402, 404, 408.

[98] Caleb Quotem, a comic character representing a loquacious "jack of all trades" in George Colman's (1762–1836) *The Review,* appeared for the first time in Henry Lee's (1756–1818) comic opera, *Caleb Quotem and His Wife, or Paint, Poetry and Putty.*

had a very pleasant excursion. We picked some new beautiful and fragrant flowers, the Purser and myself regretted we could not present to our dear wives at home. I brought back with me a branch from a gigantic fern—seven feet long—but for want of a 'New World'[99] or 'Brother Jonathan'[100] newspaper to press it in I have cut off a side leaf, and keep the stalk for a cane.

I brought on board a load of rocks for the geological cabinet of the Potl[d]. Nat. His. Society.[101] My messmates had a fine laugh at me, when one of the men brought down to me a rock weighing near 100 lbs. which I had found on the beach. It was translucent and crystalized in globe shaped masses within, and is perhaps flint, agate or chalcendy. The Island being volcanic its geology is interesting. A metal was brought on board today which has puzzled our minerologists, and is said to be abundant. It is an extremely hard greyish white metal, cannot be melted in the blow pipe, or when heated red hot in a candle, but flies apart in scintillating pieces and has a peculiar smell which some think sulphur others garlic. We intend submitting it to other test. Its specific gravity is greater than iron, but less than gold. My unusual experience today has fatigued me, and I hope to enjoy a refreshing sleep.

Port Lloyd, Peel Isld, Bonin, Monday April 24, 1854

Another rainy day which I have occupied in a very miscellaneous way—labelling specimens for the P. Nat. His. Soc. Sketching the First Settler for Capt Abbot, putting things to rights in my room, playing chess, with the Purser etc. etc. At 2 o'clock I went on shore with the Purser and at the expense of a nice ducking returned on board again at 3, to dinner. After dinner at 5 o'clock went on shore again with the 1st Lieut and Master called up Mr. Avery 'The Governor' as he is styled. Avery's object being to purchase a portion of

99 *New World: A Weekly Journal of Popular Literature* was founded in New York in 1842. *British Union-Catalogue of Periodicals,* III, 365.

100 *Brother Jonathan* was a New York newspaper founded in 1842. *Ibid.,* I, 432.

101 None of the mineralogical and other gifts of specimens collected by Preble is preserved today in the Portland Society of Natural History. The collection was lost in the great Portland fire in 1866.

his territory. The Governor lives in a hut rude enough outside but paneled and painted on the inside. The panels white with a frame of yellow. It is lighted with two port hole looking windows. In one corner of the parlor, which comprises two thirds of the dwelling stood an oil cask, in another corner was a small table and around the room divers sea chests. A small engraving of Genl. Washington graced one of the panels. Fronting the entrance a Yankee clock ticked complacently. Three chairs or stools and a suspicious looking jug completed all that the room contained, when we entered it except the Governors wife and two small children. While there two or three dogs intruded themselves, and seemed to consider us as intruders, and some chickens walked in and out picking crumbs of comfort from the floor. Taken as a whole the Governors Palace looked like a boat turned bottom up and finished into a dwelling and reminded me of one described in David Copperfield, as did Avery of the Canvas clad guardian of Little Emily whose friends were all drawn dead.[102]

A few years since a band of Chinese pirates invaded the island, and besides robbing Avery of 2000$ in money, his savings of many years, carried off his young wife only fifteen years old, whom the Governor still greatly laments though to console himself he has taken for a helpmate a Portuguese woman—eight and forty— who has now a child at the breast, and another clinging to her knees, a proof that the Govn is alive to the necessity of keeping up the population of the Island. 'His Woman' he calls her and I presume with truth, for clergyman or magistrate to make her his wife, are not to be found on his Island domain. Her charms are not likely to cause any undue solicitation and I have no doubt she is faithful.

In the field back of the Governors palace twenty one huge turtles were lieing under the trees on their backs, waiting their turn to be made into soup and blinking out of their cold watery eyes. As our ship uses four daily they will not have long to wait in their uncomfortable position. We hope to take 1 or 200 up to the squadron. The females at this season are full of eggs and it seems a pity to destroy

[102] Emily Costigan, or Little Em'ly, is a character in Charles Dickens' *David Copperfield*. She represents the victim of a deceived love.

them, but necessity knows no law. In the pigsty the Govr had the most villainously ugly faced sow I have ever seen, a present to him from Com. Perry, who brought it up from China. Even the Gov thinks he could not eat the flesh of such an ill favored animal.

Bidding the Governor *adieu,* at sundown we returned to the ship.

Port Lloyd, Peel Isld, Bonins,
Tuesday April 25, 1854

During the mid watch, which it was mine to keep it blew quite fresh, and I had an exciting time. One of our chains parted, by which we lost an anchor and thirty fathoms of chain. On hauling in the chain, we found that it had unshackled. Today was very windy but otherwise pleasant. In the forenoon went on shore for an hour picking up specimens of the geology of the Island for our Portld Nat. His. Society. In my description of the Governor's family last night I forgot to mention a brood of Muscovy ducks, in which their right wing sticks out at right angles to their bodies. The inside of the wing is turned up and out horizontally. We thought they had broken or deformed in that way to prevent their flying away, but the Governor assured us everyone of them was hatched so.

The Purser shot several snipes, and thirty two Canary birds today, which we are to have like the 'four and twenty blackbirds' in a pie tomorrow.

One of our sailors charmed with the Robinson Crusoe like life of the Island has deserted. He has not been heard from for several days, and some think he has fallen from one of the cliffs and got killed. If not hunger must soon drive him to seek the ship again. He was a likely lad, and we regret his making a fool of himself. I occupy my own room tonight for the first time since it was painted, and hope for pleasant dreams. Good night.

Port Lloyd, Bonin Islds, Wednesday April 26, 1854

On deck nearly all day, assisting with my alertness and orders to recover our lost anchor. We think we have caught it, and wait for daylight to heave it up. Our deserter lad was brought on board this afternoon sick and half starved and is paying the penalty of his romance. Two whaling ships were off the Harbor today and we were boarded from one the *Minerva*[103] of New Bedford and furnished with late California and Sandwich Isld newspapers. Our Canary bird proved so good today, we hope the Purser will furnish us with another.

Last evening one of our wardroom boys brought on board a blue pigeon, which he said he knocked over with a stick. It was in color and shape like our domestic pigeon, but twice as large. The boy said he saw great numbers of them. We put it in the pie with the Canarys, and as a Chinaman would say found it "allo proper."

Thursday April 27, 1854

I have enjoyed a very pleasant day, I don't know where or when I have felt such a balmy pleasant atmosphere. It was like the air after a clearing and cooling evening shower following a hot summer day—only a refinement upon that, and lasting the day long. I was called for the morning watch, but at day light was relieved by the 1st Lt.[104] who wished to attend to getting the lost anchor. All his efforts however proved unsuccessful and we have given up all hope and abandoned all attempts to recover it. As all the ships boats were busy, after breakfast the Purser, Gwathmey, and myself got into a canoe and were paddled on shore. The canoes were dug outs and finished with an out rigger fastened to the end of two long arms, which renders them impossible to be capsized. After landing we strolled into the bushes and picked some nice yellow berries not unlike a gooseberry.

The Purser stalked a flock of plover, which excited his sportman ardor, so we returned to the beach and launched a canoe in which he paddled himself off to the ship for his gun.

On his return with Dr. Gilliam and Mr. Lewis, Gwathmey and myself started on a tramp over the hills, while Allison and Gilliam beat the bushes after game. The Purser had recommended to us the beauties of a ravine he had seen the day before, so we ascended it following by the side of a mountain stream, that murmured along or leaped from rock to rock and occasionally falling over a preci-

[103] The *Minerva,* a whaling ship of 240 tons, was built in Baltimore in 1848. Her captain was Richard Ward, Jr. *Greyhounds,* 399.

[104] L. B. Avery.

pice of many feet, at last found its way to sea at the base of the old man of the mountain, whose profile I have drawn for you.

The weather was delicious. The varied foliage canopied over us beautiful, the birds were chirping all around us. The murmur of the stream added to the other harmonies to make our walk delightful. With some toil and trouble we hauled ourselves up by over hanging bushes a steep ascent by the side of a cascade of 50 or 60 feet and stood above it where we had a most beautiful view of the ravine, and the tree clad precipitous mountain bounding it. Looking down the valley as through a telescope—in the middle distance lay our ship in the crater like basin of Port Lloyd, while beyond in the illimitable distance rolled the blue and calm Pacific. We attempted to clamber up the mountain on our right, but after toiling pushing creeping, hauling and cutting our way through the tangled and luxuriant undergrowth we gave up the attempt and regaining the cascade, continued up the valley until we came to another 30 feet fell which we also surmounted and then retraced our steps, downed the valley and returned to the ship with good appetites for our dinner.

The Purser and Doctor after separating from us shot several plover and in searching for shells on the coral reefs had an adventure with a cuttle fish, which stretched its long arms along the Purser's ram rod in an alarming and threatening manner and brought to his mind the story of a naval officer, who was held fast on one of these reefs by one of these sepia and powerless to extricate himself was held fast until drowned by the rising tide.

After an Aldermanic dinner of turtle in more ways than one, Purser A[llison] Doct. G[illiam] and myself accompanied, Capt. Abbot around the point to a beach to the South of the Harbor to call on an old sailor named Horton, and to present him with some of the agricultural impliments we had for distribution. The old man was left here by the U.S.S. *Plymouth* last Oct. at his own request and by the advice of her surgeon Dr. Gambrill.[105] He is 73 years old and when [he] left was troubled with dropsy but the disease appears

[105] Amos G. Gambrill was made assistant surgeon on June 10, 1829; passed assistant surgeon, March 3, 1835; surgeon, February 20, 1838. He died at Hong Kong on February 12, 1854. See also *Narrative,* II, 411.

now to have left him, and he looks and seems a hale hearty old man. With the money he received on his discharge he bought him the house and valley around it for $140. He appears as happy as a lord, his only complaint being that his house is too large. United to his agricultural employments is that of pilot, we paid him 15$ pilotage coming in and will pay him as much more to take us out. It was pleasant to visit the old man and see his arrangements. He came down to the beach as lord of the manor, spy glass in hand to welcome us and conduct us to his hut, and expressed his gratitude for the presents we brought him. His hut built of logs of palm placed on end, was thatched on the outside as well as on the roof, and inside neatly carpeted with a matting made of the broad palm leaf. A canvass screen divided his simple dwelling into two rooms, and the furniture consisted of a few chairs no two alike, a sea chest, a small table, a little shelf desk, over which was displayed his Library consisting of a Bible, Testament, De Aubignes Reformation,[106] two or three small religious works and a Bowditch's Navigator. Directly over the Bible was suspended a pair of pistols and a hatchet. On the desk was his journal which told how the U.S. Ship *Macedonian* 'Capt Abot,' anchored in Port Lloyd April 23. The Whale Ship *Minerva* was outside, etc. Near it was a Child's Newspaper with the old man's spectacles lieing on it and giving the corner a very respectable look. Behind it scrupously clean and neat was slung his hammock, which fitted with stretchers, just like a midshipmans; the old man thought it superior to any other kind of bed. After entertaining us in his house he took us to his outbuildings and turtle pen and showed us a large mass of red earth, which had slid down from the mountains with great noise upon his lot and had destroyed his lemon trees, but providentially as he esteemed it placed within his reach the very soil he needed for his sandy land. Horton seemed contented with his lot, and grateful to Dr. G[ambrill], for the advice which placed him where he is, and full of sorrow at the news of his death at Hong Kong in June, and which our ships was the first to communicate.

[106] Jean Henri Merle d'Aubigné (1794–1872), *Histoire de la Réformation aux XVIe siècle* (Paris, 1835–53); see the one-volume American edition of the English translation, *History of the Great Reformation of the Sixteenth Century in Germany, Switzerland, England* (New York, W. H. Colyer, 1844).

On our return to the ship we passed in the boat through and under a natural arch that has been perfected through the lava cliffs, and thus materially shortened the distance.

The scenery about the entrance of Port Lloyd is grand and imposing. To be appreciated it must be seen in its full proportion. No sketch or description can convey any idea of it. It is wonderful to behold the result of the terrific volcanic action that produced these islands. Such mountains of ashes and stones mixed with cliffs of lava and basalt of variegated colors all deeply furrowed by the heavy rains until made to resemble gigantic walls of rude masonry, topped with the luxuriant growth of the tropics, present a mingling of the grand and beauty rarely excelled. The Island is four miles square, and has scarcely twenty acres of level ground upon it and all around its shores standing up from the sea like statues of women and dolphins are numerous pinnocle rocks.

At Sea, Off Port Lloyd, Friday April 28, 1854

After a day of work we have at last filled our sails and are standing to the Nth and W^st^ towards Simoda. The weather has been like one of those balmy September days we New Englanders enjoy so much. In the forenoon we practiced the crew at a Target using the great guns and making some splendid shots. At one o'clock we got underway and stood out the Harbor. The Master and I went out in a boat to take a sketch of the entrance, and waited outside for the ship to come out and pick us up. Outside the ship was hovel for a boat that was to bring us out some turtle and onions and to receive 400 galls. of Sperm oil from the Bark *Bayard*[107] in the offing, which accomplished at 6 P.M. we filled away and bid farewell to Port Lloyd. We have on board for ourselves and the squadron nigh upon one hundred two hundred pounds Turtles, which sprawling upon their backs between the guns and made comfortable with wet swabs under their heads by way of pillows present an unusual spectacle. These with 100 BBls of Potatoes and onions we are taking up to the squadron will we hope keep off the scurvy which when we left it was threatened.

[107] The *Bayard,* a packet ship of 339 tons, was owned by Daniel Van Dyke of New York. She was built in 1819. *Greyhounds,* 405.

At Sea, Saturday April 29, 1854

The ship with all her light sails and steering sails spread has been fanning along since we left Port Lloyd 5 and 6 miles an hour and the sea has been smooth enough to allow us to have our air ports open. At daylight we had two of the Parry Group in sight but soon sunk them beneath the horizon astern. Some sharks have longingly and lovingly followed us from Port Lloyd, and several chocolate albatross have been skimming about our treck.

My employment today has been drawing and shading two copies of my sketch of Port Lloyd. One for my darling, and the other for the Purser to send to his darling. I have yet to make another for our Master Walcut, who wishes for it to accompany his official report to the Commodore.

Tonight we have all looked at the new moon over our right shoulder and wished for good news from home. It is said the happiest days of a man's life are the least eventful and the soonest forgotten and with a nation as with individuals. A country is even the most prosperous and happy when its history is shortest and most common place.

At Sea, Sunday April 30, 1854

After a pleasant day we are likely to have a rough night; the wind and sea are increasing and hauling ahead. After our usual Sunday services, this forenoon came my watch on deck, and about an hour before noon the lookout at the mast head reported a sail, which proved when seen from deck to be a rock, not laid down on any chart we have on board. We therefore took in our steering sails and hauled on a wind in order to determine its position as near as possible. At one o'clock we were within 8 to 10 miles of it, and our observations placed it in Lat 29.47 N Long 140.32 E, by measurement we found it 269 feet high and about 60 feet in diameter at its base. From our position it looked not unlike a gigantic fore finger, and as discoverers we propose for it the name of "Neptune's finger." We judge it however to be[108] a rock discovered by Capt. Meares in 1788, in the

[108] Between pp. 241 and 242 of the diary is inserted a color sketch of the harbor of Shimoda with the inscription: "I have been kept so busy on the survey, I have been unable to finish this sketch of the Harbor of Shimoda, but it will serve you

same Lat. but placed by him 120 miles to the E^st and called by him "Lots Wife." The nearest land to it is the high and rocky Island of St. Peters 54 miles dist—which we saw at 5 o'clock and passed at Sundown. Tonight we are sailing over an imperfectly surveyed ocean, on which several islands are marked. A good lookout is more important than skillful navigation. In anticipation of bad weather we have doubled our topsails and reefed our courses. It is now raining.

At Sea, Monday May 1, 1854

Rolling, jerking and pitching onward, a raging sea around us, a wild sky overhead. Yet I trust to a kind providence regardful of our safety, and to the strength of our good ship as did Cromwell to his dry powder horns. Providence does not help those who do not help themselves. At noon 180 miles from Simoda and approaching it ten miles an hour by increase of sea and reduction of canvass, now reduced to eight miles. My employment today has been making a nice copy of my sketch of the Entrance to Port Lloyd on drawing paper for the Master, who wishes it for his monthly report to Com. Perry. It makes quite a pretty picture.

Simoda Isld, Niphon, Tuesday May 2d, 1854

Turned out to be a dark and rainy mid watch; ship under double reefs and reefed course running eight knots. At 4 A.M. judged ourselves 70 miles from Simoda, came down and turned in thanking my stars, my wet and cold watch was over. About 9 o'clock, through the gloom, we discovered our Abbot's House, which told us our harbor was not far dist. At noon we were nine miles from the port and had our squadron in sight, but despaired of getting in as the wind was both light and ahead. Fortunately a strong tide caught and befriended us so that by half past three we were boarded by boats from the squadron and at 5 P.M. anchored at the entrance of the Harbor in a spot designated by the Commodore. The land around Simoda has many striking and beautiful features, and is a great contrast to the tamer shores of Jedo Bay. Many of the beautifully green hills are spotted with a dazzling white which looks like snow but I am told is the chalk of which they are formed washed bare by heavy rains.

something of the character of the scenery. I have finished a pencil sketch but it is on thick paper and cannot go in a letter."

We find the squadron without news and starving for something fresh so that our turtles and onions and potatoes are very acceptable. The *Lexington* is to sail tomorrow for Loo Choo. Our ship with the *Vandalia* and *Southampton* are to sail on the 8th and be followed on the 15th by the steamers for Hakodadi; rumor says the *Vandalia* will go thence to Shanghai, and the remainder of the squadron return here by the 15th of June, when there will be a grand bazaar opened by the Japs, at which we are to make our purchases. At present very little can be bought and oweing to a misunderstanding about the value of our money that little only at extravagant prices. The walks about Simoda are so rugged as not to be very pleasant, and from what I can learn the unmarried officers find their amusement in visits to the bath house where old and young, male and female are mingled promiscuously in a state of unblushing nudity to the gaze of strangers. The remarkable sensuality of the Japanese is everywhere evidenced by their habits conduct and actions. After seeing the ship snugly at anchor the Master Purser and myself took a boat and called upon our friends on board the *Supply, Southampton, Mississippi* and *Lexington* to deliver our cumshaws of turtle to them and to get the news.

Simoda, Wednesday May 3^d^ 1854

A cold and rainy day. Some of my messmates went on shore and made a few trifling purchases; was detained on board myself by my duties. The scenery from our anchorage is strikingly picturesque. The hills are charmingly green, and their lively contrast with the white and reddish chalk cliffs and dark lava crags is very pleasing.

Simoda, Thursday May 4, 1854

I have just come down from an arduous days duty on deck to say Ohio to you, that being the Japanese for "How do you do!" Walcut who hails from that state was quite surprised yesterday, at hearing all the little children of Simoda "hallo Ohio" after him, and thought some of his messmates had told them to by way of a Joke.

During all last night we had a very heavy gale from the Nth E^st^ and the Barometer fell rapidly. This morning the sun struggled through the clouds but was washed into eclipse by passing showers. At noon the store ship *Lexington* got underway for Loo Choo, and the Commodore telegraphed to us, and to the *Vandalia* and *Southampton* to prepare to sail Saturday morning for Hakodadi. We had quite a dinner party aboard to partake of our turtle, and a chowder prepared by our 1st Lieut., call it a fish stew and it was good, but as a chowder execrable—Jones of the Marines, Dr. Williams[109] and Lt. Bent[110] of the *Miss.* and Purser Harwood[111] of the *Vandalia* were our guests. In the afternoon the rain cleared off and we had mild and pleasant weather, but the ship continues rolling prodigiously to the Southerly Swell. While we were at dinner the *Vandalia* commenced fireing at a target, and some of her big balls whistled by us to nervous ears in alarming propinquity.

Simoda, Friday May 5, 1854

I approach my altar of remembrance weary and foot sore, and almost too tired this evening to put pen to paper. I commenced the

109 Samuel Wells Williams (1812–1885), a prominent attorney, Sinologue, and diplomat, was born in Utica, New York. In June, 1833, he went to China and there combined learned interests with missionary duties, contributing to *The Chinese Repository* and co-operating with E. C. Bridgman. In 1835, he moved to Macao with his missionary press. Until 1845, he published a Chinese chrestomathy, vocabulary, topographical names, and *A Chinese Commercial Guide;* he was also the author of a well-known two-volume history of China entitled *The Middle Kingdom.* Williams learned Japanese and translated the Gospel of Matthew. He was invited to be official interpreter for Perry's expedition during 1853 and 1854, and from 1856 to 1876, he was secretary and interpreter for the U.S. legation in China. He took part in treaty negotiations at Tientsin in 1858 and was several times chargé d'affaires of the legation. He compiled *A Syllabic Dictionary of the Chinese Language* (1874), wrote several other Sinological works, and was the first professor of Chinese language and literature at Yale University. *DAB*, XX, 290–91; Couling, *op. cit.*, 602–603; Latourette, *The Great Century in Northern Africa and Asia*, 381–82 and bibliographical notes; Morse, *The International Relations of the Chinese Empire*, I, 516, 522; Williams, *A Journal of the Perry Expedition.* See also Hummel, *op. cit.*, I, 429, and II, 790; Dennett, *op. cit.*, 191–92 *et seq.;* C. C. Creegan, *Pioneer Missionaries of the Church*, 292–300, with a portrait.

110 Silas Bent was made midshipman on July 1, 1836; passed midshipman, July 1, 1842; master, January 7, 1849; lieutenant, August 1, 1849; dismissed, April 25, 1861.

111 James K. Harwood was made purser of the *Vandalia;* dismissed, May 31, 1861.

day at 4 o'clock with the morning watch, and after putting the ship to rights, and getting breakfast, went on shore, where I remained wandering about until Sundown, when I returned to the ship. I saw of course many things new and curious to me, took several picturesque walks, visited several temples, and overhauled the contents of several pictures of Japanese Junks exposed to the fury of storms, and half overwhelmed or sinking, and a long board on which was fastened a hundred or more of the little cues worn by the Japanese—a funny sight evidently the votive offering of some crew preserved from shipwreck. A bow and arrows with some masks, and a woman's long tresses, were among the other offerings displayed upon the walls of this temple. There was also a curious chinese pagoda formed of copper cash (tscuhi) nailed through the centre holes to a board. After hearing an old bonze chant his prayers, and dropping a few cash into his money chest we were invited to a seat by his side and took tea with him.

Another of our strange sights was seeing two men confined in a cage not six feet square, said to be two men, who swam off to the *Mississippi* the other night and asked to be taken aboard to go to America, but were sent on shore again.

Perhaps our strangest sight was a crowd of men, women and children of both sexes congregated in a bath house in a state of absolute nudity, not having even Adams fig leaf, and all scrubbing themselves assiduously without regard to each other, or us spectators and foreigners. They all appeared to wash themselves in a little back room, and then came out into the paved room or area around which we stood to rub wipe and dry themselves. The only separation of the sexes I noticed, was that the men kept to the right side of this room, and the women the left. Both would look at us and laugh and point at what every other human I have ever heard of savage or civilized seek to conceal. Laugh. It was disgusting.

In the shops I purchased a dollars worth of sandals worn by men, women and children, but nothing else. Simoda being only a fishing village, the goods in the shops are naturally of the commonest kind, and the prices extravagant.

At one of the Temples, we found Brown,[112] our daguerrotypist taking it, and not to lose an opportunity of being immortalized the Purser. Dr. G[illiam] and I stood among the tombs and were taken with it.

At Sea, Saturday May 6, 1854

At day light I was called by the summons of "All hands up anchor" and soon we were underway and fanned slowly out of the harbor setting every available sail to counteract the swell which set us towards the rocks. After we and our two company keepers, the *Vandalia* and the *Southampton* had cleared the harbor, we hauled on a wind, and getting a fresh breeze passed both before 8 o'clock. During the afternoon we were beating between the island and the mainland and had a fine view of the smokeing volcano 'Oho-sima,' and of two large towns about its base. Towards sundown we coasted along Niphon in neighborly distance so as to see its beautifully cultivated and terraced hills, with numerous villages. We are now making 8 and 9 knots an hour to the Nth and Est of our course, and have left the other ships so far astern they are not to be seen.

Yesterday in our rambles, I saw many beautiful and fragrant flowers, some common with us, others quite new to me. I wish you could enjoy the fragrant bouquet I brought off and which now adorn my bureau. In one of the Temples visited I saw a coat of chain armor, and in another occupied by soldiers as a barrack. There was a carriage for a field piece, evidently designed from a French model or drawing.

At Sea, off E. Coast Niphon, Sunday May 7, 1854

This morning the wind refreshened so that we took two reefs in our topsails and kept them in all day until about an hour since when the weather moderating we made more sail.

We have seen neither of our companion ships today, and hope and think we have beaten them out of sight. The therm has been between 57 and 60 and we have felt rather chilly.

112 E. Brown was employed as "artist" by Commodore Perry. He served as photographer on the expedition to Japan. See *Narrative,* II, 414.

At Sea, Monday May 8, 1854

It has been a calm cool and delightfully pleasant day, and we now have a fine fair wind and with steering sails aboard are sailing merrily our course. At noon we were half way to the Straits of Sangar,[113] and had experienced a N.erly current of forty miles in the preceding 24 hours. We dropped a bottle over board at noon—on a voyage of current discovery—giving our position, and if picked up requesting the finder to send the paper noting the position where found, to the observatory.

Our Bonin turtle still supply our mess with something fresh, though we rather tire from the want of variety. I have had the skull of one big fellow cleaned and intend giving it to the Nat. His. Society.[114] We were visited today by some little land birds and saw two or three plover. Among the events of the day was an alarm of fire in sail room 'a wolf cry,' which called us to quarters to exercise our firemen.

At Sea, Tuesday May 9, 1854

In contrast to our beautiful day yesterday, we have been enveloped all day in a damp and dense fog, and have not seen anything of the outer world beyond our flying jib boom. Of course we only know our position by Dead Reckoning as it is called, which is very uncertain. At noon we got a cast of the lead and let out 750 feet of line without getting bottom.

At Sea, Wednesday May 10, 1854

The fog disappeared this morning as the sun rose and a westerly wind cleared and dried up everything bright and pleasant revealing the northern end of Niphon and the Southern end of Yesso, plain in sight. At sundown we judged we were fifty miles from our port. The crest of the highest hills in sight are covered with snow, and our ther. has stood at 44°. Our Lat today was between 40, and 40 about 180 miles Sth at Portland, and by our Long. 9000 miles to the Westst of it as the crow flies. I have suffered from rheumatism today, I feel I am growing old, Susie, and must take to thick flannels and other old

113 "Straits of Sangar"—Tsugaru Strait, between Honshu and Hokkaido.
114 Portland Society of Natural History.

man comforts. The *Southampton* has been in sight all day and by a lucky shift of wind in her favor is now, or rather was at sundown within a few miles of us. At the same time we saw a ship in shore under easy sail which may have been the *Vandalia*. We have also had several sperm whales cruizing and sporting around us.

Bay of Hakodadi, Isld Yesso, Thursday May 11, 1854

When I went on deck at 4 this morning I found it bright clear cold and pleasant, and the ship just at the Eastern entrance of the Straits of Sangar separating Niphon from Yesso. Giving the ship all drawing sail we squared away and stood in through the straits, and passed through several rushing tide rips, extending across the straits, breaking, boiling and scathing from the friction of counteracting winds and tides. Before noon we came to anchor in this bay in company with the other two ships. The Bay of Hakodadi reminds me of Gibraltar Bay. Its shores are hilly and mountainous and there is the same rocky mew separated by a low vertical ground. The hills are yet bare and yellow not having clad themselves in their summer mantles. The tops of the hills are still thinly covered with snow. The weather judging by my poor feelings for I have not examined the thermometer is as cold as Greenland. Everybody looks blue and shivering and the ship has that cold and cheerless aspect that a barn has in winter when leaving a comfortably warmed apartment you visited. Contributing more than all else to our cheerless condition has been a gale from E.S.E. which commenced almost as soon as we dropped anchor and has caused us to 'bless our stars' that we are not underway. This afternoon some Japs, with their interpreters came off to the ship to know what we wanted. They had not heard of our treaty, and did not believe in it, even when we showed them a beautifully engraved copy in Japanese, but wished us to take what we required, viz. wood, water and provisions and go away. It seems the Imperial messenger sent overland has not arrived.

After their interview with Captain A[bbot] in the cabin we took them into the wardroom and treated them to ships rum, sweetened with brown sugar which made them talkative and communicative. I showed them my chart of the world, the track of the ship from the U.S. to Hakodadi, which they understood and then pointed out to them California, which they showed they had heard of making signs of digging gold. I also showed them the territory we took from Mexico, and their own little Japanese Empire, and pointed out Russia, England, Holland etc, all of which they evidently understood. In appearance these northern Islanders are like those we have seen at Niphon, only they appear more sedate and perhaps more intelligent, probably a favorable specimen of the Yesso-ans. They were all comfortable and amply clad, the retainers in cotton and their superiors in silk. Notwithstanding the inclement weather they all came off without any covering to their bare shaven heads, the only protection being the little well greased national cue no bigger than a pipe stem, which gathered up from their back hair, points forward to the crown of the head like the hand of a dial. Custom and fashion are arbitrary and enable one to submit to the greatest hardships and inconveniences. I showed the Japs one of our big turtles, the first I imagine they had ever seen, as they looked quizically at it and one made a sketch of the animal.

Bay of Hakodadi, Friday May 12, 1854

A raw rainy uncomfortable day. Bar. falling and very low. Capt. Abbot went on shore today to communicate with the authorities, but could not find anybody 'at home.' The Great Man[115] they told him was absent, and the lesser officials were afraid to take the responsibility. As the case stands we cannot go ashore except on business until the arrival of Com. Perry.

Saturday May 13, 1854

About 2 o'clock this morning having the watch I noticed an eclipse of the moon. All through the night it blowing fresh from S.W. to W. the ship rolled and pitched very uncomfortably at her anchors, but as the sun rose the gale exhausted itself. The master sounded out a channel and at 4 o'clock we got underway, and moved to an anchorage two miles closer in where we are much more snug and comfortable. The other ships have followed our example.

Everyone who has been to the Mediterranean remarks the general resemblance to the Peninsula on which Hakodadi is situated to

[115] Daimyô, a local feudal lord.

the Rock of Gibraltar and its low neutral ground and even carry around the bay the resemblance and point to the Japanese towns answering in position to St. Rogue and Algeciras. The highlands of Niphon on the opposite side of the Straits of Sangar answering to those that extend from Ceuta to Tangier on the African side to the Straits of Gibraltar.

Hakodadi—with its wooden houses shingled roofs board fences, stone wharves, wooden warehouses and sea and yellow hills—reminds me of a New England town, wanting however the pointed spires and pepper box bellfrys of our New England temples of worship.

Bay of Hakodadi, Sunday May 14, 1854

A bright and pleasant Sunday. After our inspection and muster a deputation from shore came off to see the Capt and brought with them a present of eleven baskets of fish, ten of herring and mullet, the other filled with fine salmon and salmon trouts, with a few place sculpins and flounders.

They also brought several baskets and packages of onion tops and other greens—all very acceptable. There was herring enough to supply the crews of all three of the ships, and fish enough of the nicer kind for all the officers messes.

Early in the morning we sent our boats in shore to haul seine but only succeeded in catching a few smelts and small fish, with one salmon trout. The 1st Lieut. of the *Vandalia* old Rootes dined with us today, and we treated him to Turtle and salmon. We mourn that tomorrow is the last of our turtle feasts. We saw droves of horses and herds of cattle grazing on the grassy slopes opposite our ship today, and asked the Japs to bring us off some beef, but they said they never killed their cattle but kept them all for agricultural purposes. The boat crews that came off to the ship today were bareheaded and stark naked to their waists when they ceased rowing they donned a loose jacket or 'Japan' of green with a white mark on the back of it—their feudal uniform. With our thermometer at 44° to 48, this shows their endurance. The officers who came on board left their sandals in their boats. They were amused at sight of the negroes we have on board, and were particularly interested in our two ten inch circle guns, which they examined minutely, measured and made a drawing of. I do not think the boats here are of so good a model as those in Jedo Bay, and they are propelled differently. Instead of being sculled at the side, as are those in Jedo Bay, short oars with handles at right angles to the blades are used, and pulled or sculled as preferred.

Hakodadi Bay, Monday May 15, 1854

After attending to the scrubbing, hammocks, and other important duties of ship cleaning in my morning watch, and stowing away a substantial breakfast, I took our little iron dingy and made an excursion around the bay. I endeavored to unite profit with pleasure and catch some fish with hook and line but without success. Our seining party had better luck, and caught with other fish quite a number of salmon. One of which measured two feet ten inches. They also caught several large crabs—one of which I am preparing for our Portland Society—and two of which are now entombed in my stomach. I can attest their good taste and delicate virtue. Our dinner today was an Oasis in the desert of our mess table comforts since we opened Japan. Fried and boiled salmon, turtle soup, Japanese chickens, sweet potatoes, onions and Japanese rice certainly might make even an Astor house gourmands mouth water. Japanese rice is quite a different vegitable from our rice, and in particular excellent tasteing and looking like fine hominy. When boiled it looks as though eggs or butter was mixed with it. These Northern Japanese seem to have more business like habits than those of the Southern Island. They were off to the ship this morning with water before six o'clock, bringing it in buckets holding about five gallons each and fourteen buckets to a boat.

This noon we had a big junk loaded with excellent wood alongside. It was in large sticks chiefly Birch Beech Oak and Maple, all well known woods to us, and was cut into convenient lengths and backed. It seemed to have been cut and seasoned a long time. Each stick was stamped with a Japanese character on its end, and it was counted into the ship, the head man of the junk calling out 'tally' at every ten sticks.

My boat was followed all along the bay by an officer and squad of soldiers, who as we did not land, I suppose thought they had frightened us away. A near inspection of the houses showed me that their roofs one kept down by big stones similar to the custom of Switzerland.

Hakodadi Bay, Tues May 16, 1854

The Japanese have been bringing off water all day and have also supplied us with one hundred small salmon. Our seiners made some successful hauls and beside a multitude of small fish, landed four large salmon, the largest of which weighed twenty-three pounds. They also brought several buckets full of fine large crabs. This afternoon we dug up some beautiful clams, in shape and size like our Quohogs but their shells beautifully polished and mottled with dark and light browns and yellows. My occupation today has been plotting on a chart the track of our three ships from Simoda to Hakodadi. Dr. Vreeland[116] of the *Vandalia* dined with our mess today. This evening I partook of a crab supper, and am all prepared for a nightmare.

Hakodadi, Wednesday, May 17, 1854

The *Powhatan* and *Mississippi* appeared in sight over the neutral ground soon after daylight, and came to anchor near us at half past nine. I have already been officially notified that I shall be called on to assist in a survey of the Bay commencing tomorrow. Our fishermen were out again today, but had fishermans luck; the wind being too strong for their success.

Thursday May 18, 1854

I have just returned in the rain from surveying having been absent from the ship since daylight. I judge I have walked 8 or 9 miles in addition to my other duties and now at 9 P.M. feel too tired to write more about my days adventures.

Friday May 19, 1854

After another fatigueing day on the survey, I sit down to tell my

[116] Benjamin Veerland served as an assistant surgeon on board the *Vandalia*. He was made assistant surgeon on May 9, 1850; passed assistant surgeon, March 30, 1857; surgeon, April 26, 1861. He died on March 20, 1866. *Narrative*, II, 411.

darling of its adventures, and those of yesterday. I was accompanied yesterday by the Purser, and on our way out towards the entrance of the Bay he shot a large Guillemot, a bird something between a Penguin and a Gull but which proved good eating, as also a smaller duck called in California a Pedunk. He also shot a small webfooted bird with a sharp bill, resembling a snipe, but which none of us had ever seen before, intended preserving its skin for the P.N.H. but it got wet and spoiled and had to be thrown away. On nearing our destination I found a long reef barrier extending out from the shore but managed to get my boat inside and beach her, and then marched up to the top of cliff overlooking the reef and raised my signal flag and pole; all my movements being closely watched by a Japanese officer and eighteen soldiers. They offered us no molestation, but on the contrary gave us friendly assistance showing us the path. They expressed their delight at seeing my sextant and the other instruments. After putting up my signal and taking a round of angles from it I returned to the boat intending to occupy another station, but on reaching her, I found the tide had fallen rapidly, and the reef bare a long way outside of her so that there was no possibility of getting her afloat for several hours. During my absence the Purser and boats crew had been wading about the reef gathering the muscles with which it was covered, until they had loaded the boat. Wherever our men straggled they were followed and watched by a party of Japanese soldiers, who were not quite so wet footed in following them up over the reef as our marines.

Seeing there was no possibility of getting our boat afloat for the present, I had a fire built on the beach, and we all enjoyed a feast of roasted muscles, and dried our wet clothing. A tumbling cascade close at hand furnished us the most invigorating and unexceptionable of beverages. Haveing thus refreshed ourselves, the tide being still on the ebb I resolved to walk to the next station, about two miles dist. So marshalling my forces, I led the procession to a station I have called valley bluff, in my surveying notes. First came I with notebook and spy glass closely followed by boy 'Casey' with my sextant and overcoat. Behind him marched a man with a white flag on a long bamboo pole—a signal of peace, and the signal I intended erecting at the station—behind him came a man armed with an axe and hatchet and close in his rear, another with boards, a bag of nails and a shovel, and bringing up the rear one with a bucket white wash and a white wash brush. We were followed and preceded by an escort of Japanese soldiers, but walked so fast we kept those short legged and petticoated gentry on the run all the way, and their officer at last took a horse and galloped on ahead.

Picking our way along the beach, we came to a fishing village composed of a score or two of thatched huts, and mingled among them several Junks and boats hauled up, thatched over and used for dwellings. Our escort had apparently cleared the way for us, for every house was closed, there was not the sign of a living thing or human being moving in its deserted streets.

On the far end of this village, we came to a shallow stream which I was about to wade when our Japanese guard beckoned us further up where we found a line stretched across, and a ferry boat attached, by which we were all ferried over; our guard continueing our guides takeing us thence through the country to the cliff I had pointed out to them as the object of my journey. We soon had the signal erected and after takeing my angles, I stopped to look about me and had quite a birds eye view of the surrounding country. At the base of the cliff I stood on wound a little murmuring stream to the sea, extending snake like up the valley as far as my eyes could follow it. Fronting the beach, and backed against a cliff which formed the southern boundary of the valley, was the village through which I had passed, one broad street extending through it with several smaller ones branching to the right and left. Every house was tightly closed and I saw only two men pass through its deserted streets and vanish into one of the houses. The cliff on which I stood, was a table land, elevated say 300 feet above the sea, extending a long way to the N.W. and covered with familiar wild flowers such as the violet, buttercup and dandelion all in full bloom, with wild rose bushes not in bloom, grape vines, and a variety of herbs, among others that 'mint' which a Virginian so delights in. One tree I saw without a leaf upon it but completely covered with large white flowers similiar to the magnolia of a sweet fragrance. We gathered a nice lot of dandelion greens for our messes, and having finished our 'pidgeon' returned to the boat.

We were not able to get her afloat however until sundown, when we returned to the ship in a smart rain—hungry and drownded. Today I was up and off again at 6 o'clock, and after receiving my instructions on board the *Mississippi,* run a line of soundings from her to the reef and reoccupied the station, and sent the men to pick up a boat load of muscles, while I waited for the weather to moderate (it having begun to blow fresh) and walked down to the beach taking angles at every 300 paces. The weather not inclineing to moderate as I had hoped I started to return to the ship and crossed the bay on my way to look at a cavern on the opposite shore, but found the sea so rough it was dangerous to attempt its examination, and therefore kept off for the *Mississippi* to put my assistant Mr. Walter Jones on board. Running before the wind a heavy sea struck my boat and caused her to breach to and fill. For a moment we were in danger of being capsized as well as swamped but we got the sail down, bailed her out and under more pointled sail soon reached the *Miss.* Here a new difficulty occurred. The rocking sea washed her side. I caught the ladder, the boat was washed away from under me leaving me clinging to it, and in a moment was dashed back again to the great danger of crushing me. Fortunately I escaped with a wetting. It was blowing too fresh for me to reach our own ship so the men were called out and the boat morred astern to wait a better time. About sundown the wind moderated sufficiently to allow us to get to our own ship.

Hakodadi, Saturday, May 20, 1854

Another long and fatiguing day on the survey. I run quite a number of lines of sounding and was absent from the ship from 5 A.M. until half past seven this evening when I returned, stiff tired-eye weary and hungry. The forenoon was calm and pleasant but in the afternoon it blew up very fresh, and a rough sea rolled into the bay nearly swamping my boat several times and thoroughly drenching all hands in her. I landed again at Valley Station this afternoon and put up my flag which had blown down, and was attended as before by a body guard of Japanese soldiers. Since my return, I learn the officers have been on shore, and trade opened. Several trifles purchased at ridiculously low prices have been shown to me.

Hakodadi, Sunday May 21, 1854

A beautiful day, but not like one of our quiet Sundays in New England. After our morning muster I went on shore—and after visiting the Temples, made a tour of the shops, and bought a few Japanese things. My weekdays being all employed on the survey. The greater no of the shops were closed, and all seemed averse to trade—probably not understanding our strange language and strange currency. The people however inquisitively civil, looked at our watches admired the cloth of our coats, and particularly our boots and shoes.

The Great Temple we entered had a handsome and richly carved and gilded altar behind which was a shrine and the image of a Goddess, looking very like the image of the Virgin Mary, the head surrounded by a halo, as in the images in Roman Catholic churches.[117]

The altar stood in a platform elevated a step above the floor of the Temple and was enclosed by a low railing. Its pillars and cornices were all elaberately carved with representations of deer, dogs, monkeys, snakes, hawks and other animals and strange devices. In front of the door way, was a font for holy water. Indeed the whole interior with its appurtenances resembled a Catholic church, so that take a good Catholic into it blindfolded and uncover his eyes, he might believe himself in a church devoted to his own religion.

The smaller Temple, had also its principal alter richly carved and gilded and on its left there was a small room or chapel, the walls of which were shelfed and stored with little tablets, minature tombstones they looked like, a foot long inscribed with Japanese characters, which we are given to understand describes the several virtues of those whose memories they are designed to perpetuate. I hope to see more of Hakodadi after we complete our survey of the bay, but all I expect to do this week is to range the hills beaches and reefs, and examine its botany, geology and archeology, but only as an amatuer. I know little of either as a science but like to look at a pretty

[117] Kuan Yin, or Kwannon (Japanese) is the most important of the bodhisattvas in Chinese or Japanese Buddhism. His full name is Avalokitesvara. He is divinely merciful, saves from shipwrecks, grants children to barren women, etc. The common, and erroneous, English name is "Goddess of Mercy."

shell or flower and examine a curious rock or mineral. I can appreciate botany in the shape of greens, vegitables and soups, and archeology—or rather malancholy is my delight when my attention is called to a clam muscle or oyster pie or soup.

I did not remain long on shore to day, but returned on board to dinner. Since then we have been over run with visits from the other ships—"A ship is a thing you never can be quiet in."

Hakodadi, Monday May 22d 1854

Another day of active surveying duty. I went on shore with my boat at 8 o'clock and assisted Maury to measure his base line. Its length was nearly 9000 feet or about a mile and three quarters. We chained off the distance, sticking a boarding pike into the sand at the end of every chain of 60 feet in order to keep the line straight, and to be sure of its correctness, measuring and counting back again from its end to our starting point. After measuring the base I run a few lines of soundings and returned on board at sundown.

We had two excitements today one at seeing a ship in the offing showing French colors, supposed a man of war, and another at the Commodores signaling "Intercourse with the shore forbidden"—oweing to some difficulty that has grown out of our recent trafficings.

Hakadadi, Tuesday May 23d 1854

Up and off at an early hour, and sounding in the bay until 3 P.M. when I finished a line at the *Macedonian* and came on board and took my dinner. After that function I run a few more lines of soundings, got a good wetting in a smart shower, and took my book and notes on board the *Miss.* to our chief, and reached my own ship again just at sundown. The difficulties with the Japanese have been arranged and they are to hold a daily bazaar for us during our stay where will be exposed for sale at fixed prices, such things as they may have or wish to dispose of. Nearly all of our officers were on shore today making purchases of plaided silks crockery and Japan ware at remarkably cheap prices.

The *Southampton* sailed today for Volcano Bay and is to rejoin the squadron at Simoda after makeing a survey of it. The *Vandalia* is to sail in a day or two for Shanghai.

Bay of Hakodadi, Wednesday May 24, 1854

Too boisterous weather for surveying so I improved the time to take a peep at the Bazaar, but nearly everything had been bought up and carried off before I got on shore. I succeeded in purchasing a few Japanese Picture books, some straw covered boxes and two pieces of silk of which I send you patterns, one pce of 24 yards 14½ inches wide I gave 5$ for, and think it may make a serviceable dress. The other is 18 inches but contains only 10½ yards hardly enough for a dress and cost 2$ I must try to get another piece. I did not know the quantity until I measured it on board.

The officers have a perfect favour for the purchase of Japanese things, and buy everything handsome or ugly, useful or useless curious or ordinary merely because it is Japanese.

I hope to get you a crape dress, but could not find one today of a color that suited me or that I though would suit you—a piece of 20 yds costs about 5$ I could not but think, how Cary B. would delight in spending some of her dollars here. I only wish she had the chance and I was at home.

Thursday May 25, 1854

The weather continueing to unpleasant for surveying I was on shore again today—but the Commodore had monopolized the Bazaar—so that I was only able to make a few purchases from the little shops that are in nearly every dwelling. I could not pattern the silk as I wished, but two pieces of a course blue that are strong and may do for a morning dress or for lineing if for nothing else. This cost less than calico. I also bought some Indian ink and some tea which I must send you before it loses its flavor.

Bay of Hakodadi, Friday May 26, 1854

Another day spent in examining the shops. Everything in the Bazaar Com. Perry had sent up to his quarters for his inspection and purchase, so that little was left from his selection for outsiders. After doing my shopping I took several walks into the surrounding country, and came upon a fort mounting two guns excavated in the side of a hill, evidently recently built to bear upon our ships. The outside embankment was about twenty feet thick, and its entrances, three in number concealed by a board fence or boarding. The guns are hid in houses, which have been built since our arrival. An officer who saw them before they were covered says that they are brass, twelve pounders. The fort was protected in the rear by a ditch which any ordinary leaper could jump over.

Strange to say we have not seen a woman in Hakodadi. The soldiers who attend all our rambles send one of their party ahead to shut the houses, and drive the women in doors. We often notice little holes torn in the oiled paper windows and imagine the sharp eyes of the Japanese fair are peeping through them at the terrible rough bearded strangers.

We notice here that saki which by our experience at Jedo Bay thought us to consider a national drink, is not commonly used as a beverage. We have not been offered or even seen a cup of it. This is accounted for in part from the fact that the climate is too cold for the production of rice, and all that is used has to be imported. Indeed at this time, there is a scarcity of rice and they are looking with great anxiety for the change of monsoon, to bring them up.[118]

Sunday May 28, 1854

Clear and cold so that a fire if we had one would feel nice and comfortable. Took more walks on shore today. The country looked bright and fresh in its spring mantle, and the birds sang gaily from the bushes. We have been astonished to see how quickly the snow has disappeared from the hills, and their dry yellow and fresh sides, have dressed in their summer green. We were closely followed in all our walks, by a squad of Jap. soldiers who shu-shued the women and children out of our path, and closed doors before us. Some of the cherry trees we saw today, were loaded with blossoms as large and double as a monthly rose.

Bay of Hakodadi, Monday May 29, 1854

A pleasant day. Accompanied Maury on shore, and walked with him and Mr. Heine[119] the artist and one or two more. Up to the top of the highest hill on the Peninsula of Hakodadi to get a birds eye

118 At this point in the diary is inserted a rubbing of Japanese gold coins of various denominations.

119 William Heine was an "artist" hired by Commodore Perry. He made several handsome lithographs which Perry included in the *Narrative*.

view of the Bay, and sketched its topography for our chart. It was a toilsome ascent, but the fine panorama we obtained repaid us. Coming down we fooled our Japanese guards by all taking different routes so that they could not follow all the party to their great distress. At 2 P.M. we returned to the ships after a tour of the shops. This evening I was on board the *Powhatan* to an entertainment given by her Ethiopian band. The Governor of Hakodadi and his suite was on board and highly entertained by the performance. In the afternoon we had him on board our ship and showed him our exercises at quarters. The entertainment on the *Powhatan* ended in a supper in the cabin and wardroom.

[Bay of Hakodate] Tuesday May 30, 1854

I have been out on survey all day, and have barely time to say good bye, and close my letter as the *Vandalia* is to sail at daylight in the morning. Good night.

At Sea, Wednesday May 31, 1854

Very unexpectedly we got underway in company with the *Vandalia* this morning for we did not anticipate sailing before tomorrow. The *Vandalia* has my letter to you embracing everything that has happened to me since the sailing of the *Saratoga*. It is now six months since I have heard from home, and the chances are I will not hear for three months more. I am glad you are in better luck. The *Vandalia* soon seperated from us taking her course down through the Sea of Japan to Shanghai, while we are to make our way to Simoda down the Eastern coast of Japan, and to the Sea around by Fatsisio—the Japanese penal settlement some four hundred miles out of our way. Ostensibly to examine and report upon its position, but really that he may arrive at Simoda before us with the Steamers. Today we have been beating with both wind and tide against us, and of course are not much advanced on our journey. A thick fog has enveloped us nearly all day, but obligeingly lifted just at sundown and enabled us to see Cape Nambu plains and correct our position—and save anxious navigation for the night.

At Sea, Thursday June 1, 1854

In a thick fog all day, but at sundown caught sight of Niphon, just

The Delivery of President Fillmore's Letter at Uraga

The Delivery of the American Presents at Yokohama

enough to let us know we might continue beating. Several sperm whales have been spouting around the ship, and have been 'logged' agreeably to Com. Perrys orders. If they only knew I was writing their history perhaps they would have obligeingly come along side and given me the latest and most reliable information.

At Sea, Friday June 2, 1854

Another foggy day. A wet ship and but little or no wind combined with neuralgia, rheumatism and salt fare, are not things to make one amiable.

At Sea, Saturday, June 3d, 1854

Another damp and disagreeable day—and but little wind until sundown, when we tacked the ship to the Sth and since have been averaging 5 to 6 miles an hour on our course. All day when the fog has permitted the high mountains of Niphon have been in sight. The whales continue our company keeping and one came so near the ship he almost blew in our faces. We have been on the look out for our steamers and hoping they would come along and give us a tow.

At Sea, Sunday June 4, 1854

We have had a bright mild cheerful day with a fair wind enabling us to make good progress. All of which is an agreeable change, and has put us in good humor again. Were it not for a sore throat which remains I would forget all about my rheumatic aches, and the dull dismal day preceeding this. When I left the deck at sundown the Mtns of Niphon were in sight and several junks bound to the Nth. At 8 as the wind seemed increasing we reefed topsails, and are now going ten knots S.W. which is our course.

At Sea, Monday June 5, 1854

That troublesome gentleman General Quarters visited our ship this forenoon and we exhibited for his amusement and inspection the effect of two broadsides of loaded shell: one was fired in single guns, but the other the whole broadside at the word fire. To my utter astonishment the noise and concussion from the whole broadside was less than that from a gun fired singly. Explained by the vibration of one discharge encountered and checked by that of another gun, just as the hand stops the vibration of a glass tumbler or musical instrument. The Mtns of Niphon have been in sight all day with plenty of snow lingering upon their highest distant peeks. The wind has been ahead and we have been beating down the coast makeing poor headway, with whales and Junks our companions.

At Sea, Tuesday June 6, 1854

A mild pleasant day, summing up our sailing at noon we found we had gained only 18 miles to the Sth in the 24 hours preceding. After sailing 150 miles, all oweing to the head wind and currents.

At Sea, Wednesday June 7, 1854

Got a thorough wetting in my mid-watch but did not lose my amiability as the wind was fair. This evening some Japanese fishing boats came up under our stern and threw on board a perfect shower of sardines. Afterwards we obtained several baskets full, and in return gave them bread. It was quite an amuseing scene.

Thursday June 8, 1854

It is really too bad to have the dyspepsia after a dinner of pork and beans. That dish I abominate, yet such is the fact. We have had beautiful weather and been in sight of familiar land all day. The Capes of Jedo Bay, and the Islands that lie to the Est of Simoda but for our orders to sail around Fatsisio[?] we could have anchored there tonight or tomorrow morning. Ou-Sima and Volcano Island[120] are both smokeing before us, and show themselves active volcanos though not in violent eruption.

At Sea, Friday June 9, 1854

A summer like day, which with a stiff glass of whiskey prescribed by the Doctor last night has contributed to relieve me of my dyspepsia. At 10 A.M. we saw very distant and dimly the outline of a high Island which we took to be Fatsisio, and have been working nigher all day until at sundown we were within ten miles of it, and had other Islands in sight. Tomorrow we hope to complete our examination of it and turn our ships head toward Simoda, not to be late for the Fair to be held on the 15th. Just before sundown I was called

[120] The island of O Shima, with Mihara volcano, is at the far end of Tokyo Bay.

on deck to look at a water spout, which was in view ten minutes before it drew itself back into the clouds.

At Sea, Saturday June 10, 1854

We have been loitering about Fatsisio all the beautiful day admiring its green and cultivated hills, terraced to their very apex, one little islet, of a cone shape and possibly 1200 feet high and not half a mile in diameter at its base, was terraced and cultivated to within a dozen feet of its pointed peak, and up its scrappy sides close clustering villiages of huts struggled to retain a foothold. On its North side as we sailed around it a precepise of brown rock over grown in spots with mosses—resembled a crouching lion with a crown upon its head. So that numbers of the men and officers simultaneously called attention to the extraordinarily exact resemblance.

The Island of Fatsisio of which this little peak is a volcanic off shoot is about ten miles long by 4 or 5 broad and has the appearance of two mountainous hills—and nearly every part of it is under Garden like cultivation. We stood into a bay on the South side, we thought might afford anchorage and certainly could have made an easy landing there, so that the story that the prisoners are hoisted on shore by a crane is fabulous.

At the distance of two miles we got no bottom with 120 fathoms or 700 feet of line. The Japanese might banish their criminals and traitors to a worse place, such as the Kurile Islands in the cold and rigorous north. The prisoners exiled to Fatsisio are compelled to work for their livelihood, and it is said the silk stuffs wrought and wove by them exceed in fineness and delicacy those of any other part of the Empire, and the Emperor forbids their sale under severe penalties to foreigners.

Harbor of Simoda, Sunday June 11, 1854

This morning after lying bye all night we *bore* up for our port, and at 8 o'clock passed the Broughton rocks our nights bug bear. The weather then cleared up and we had a fine view of the Islands as we coasted along them and luckily a good strong fair wind and favoring tide to take us ninety six miles to this anchorage before sundown. We see here the old *Mississippi, Powhatan, Supply* and *Southamp-*

ton, but have neither visited, or been visited from either vessel. Our old acquaintances, the Japanese Interpreters "Tosenoske" and "Comda-jor-ja"[121] have been off to see us to "present their compliments and wish us a pleasant journey." We could make little that was intelligible out of their broken English. They understood our sweetened whiskey a great deal better than we did their halting tongues.

Simoda, Tuesday June 13, 1854

Yesterday I was so occupied in visiting and being visited that it left me time for nothing else. Even the half hour I wished to devote to my darling was monopolized by a button hole friend. The Commodore has decided to send our ship to Keelung a port on the Northern end of the Island of Formosa. I am to survey and make a map of the Harbor. Mr. Jones the Chaplain of the *Mississippi* goes with us to make a geological survey of its coal mines and the *Supply* is to accompany us to take away a load of its coal as a specimen, provided she can get one.

The other vessels have also their destinations fixed. The *Southampton* is to go to Hong Kong taking on board here two Japanese boats the Commodore has procured and thence to Washington. The *Mississippi* goes to Loo Choo, Ou-Sima (Preble Isld),[122] Amoy and Ningpo; and the *Powhatan* to the Madji cosimas. From Formosa we go to Manila. Finally the whole squadron will rendezvous at Hong Kong where the Commodore will turn over the Command to Capt. Abbott, and go home overland, but send the *Mississippi* home via Pacific and Cape Horn in order to say she is the First Steamer of war to circumnavigate the globe. I was on shore this forenoon for a short walk and plucked wild flowers for my herbarium which you shall one of these days examine over my shoulder.

The Commodore intended extending our cruise to the Islands of Guam and Ascenscion but had to give it up as we have but seven

[121] Tosonosuke and Konda—undoubtedly these names are not exact. For the picture of two other interpreters, see *Narrative,* I, 348; Williams, *A Journal of the Perry Expedition,* 57, gives two other names, Tateishi Tokushiro Mitsusada and Nagashima Saburosuke.

[122] Oshima, or Amami O Shima, is one of three Oshimas mentioned in the diary. It is situated in the Ryukyus and was apparently named Preble Island.

weeks provisions on board ship. With the thermometer at 80° I am quite fagged out.

Shimoda, Wednesday June 14, 1854

A pleasant summer day which I have enjoyed on shore, going early soon after breakfast, returning on board to dinner, and going again after dinner and remaining until sundown which is here, now about seven P.M. I extended my walks into the country and traversed several valleys, their hilly sides all terraced, and in a high state of cultivation. As we clambered over the precipitous sides of the hill, we were astonished to find what we thought from below, their rude and primitive sides, artificially terraced, and full of cultivation. Everywhere we met the same cordial reception from the simple people, whose fault seems to be their extreme, and I may say beastly sensuality. Tea and water were freely offered at every house we entered, and our dresses were most inquisitively yet not rudely examined. They seem to have a very great appreciation of broad cloth, which I presume most of them saw for the first time on our persons. My ever pointed pencil and pen holder, penknife and foot rule were also objects of curiosity and admiration. One old woman to whom I gave a small square of linen from my shirt bosom (which *entre nous* was worn and ragged) could not sufficiently admire its strength and fine thread and motioned enquiry if it was spun. I produced however the greatest astonishment when I took out and showed them my false teeth. When the Japanese publish an account of our visit I expect they will state as a fact that the Americans have a convenient way of carrying their teeth in their pocket when not requiring to use them. During our walks I cutted quite a number of wild flowers, the Japanese urchins assisting who ran before us or followed wherever we strolled.

The women of Simoda do not hide from us as they did at Hakodadi, but come out of their houses to gaze at us, and salute us with "Ohio"[123] and 'obiho' or How do you do,[124] and good bye, as we pass them.

[123] *Ohayô,* "good morning."

[124] "Obiho"—there is no such Japanese word. "How do you do?" is *ikaga desuka* or *ikaga de irashaimasuka.*

Great numbers of these poor creatures are afflicted with opthalmia, caused by their cooking and working over smoky furnaces. Today one of our apt surgeons provided himself with a bottle of zinc water eye wash, which he freely administered. It was quite amusing to see how the fame of it gathered a crowd about us, and the women intercepting our path holding little saki cups to receive the cooling liquid.

It seems to me I have never seen a country so abounding in beautiful wild flowers as this. Here and at Hakodadi there seems an hundred varieties of the rose, though fortunately for us, we do not see them in bloom, but bright altheas, Convolvuluses, Chrysanthisms, Lilys, Flags, Honeysuckles, Jessamines, and hundreds of other known and unknown varieties crowd the hill sides or lurk in the valleys. On our return from our country stroll we stopped at one of the many Temples to rest. These Temples seem as much devoted to eating drinking and entertainment as worship. We were soon surrounded as usual by a crowd of curious persons of both sexes and all ages—asking the name of everything about us, and feeling, gazing and commenting upon all that seemed so odd to them. A little occurance at this temple shows their sensuality. Among the crowd surrounding us was quite a pretty female whose unstained teeth showed her to be unmarried. A few minutes after we sat down a man came up put his arm around her waist whispered a few words in her ear, and they immediately walked off behind a screen within five feet of us. Her companions were not slow, to show us, by the most indecent signs in which the old priest joined, what they had gone for. The women laughing heartily as if it were a first rate joks and no uncommon occurrence to so pervert their Temples. In a little while a woman brought forward a little naked urchin, and made motions laughing all the while, to cut off all that made him a boy. The little fellow demured at such mutilation and struggled strongly against it.

I stepped into the Bath House for just a moment this afternoon to see the shapes and fashions of the people but stepped out again almost as quickly. It is anything but agreeable for me at least to see a dozen or twenty of both sexes, and of all ages in a state of entire nudity, grouped indiscriminately in a small apartment not fifteen feet square scrubbing away as for dear life to say nothing of the exhalations from their damp bodies. Such a scene is I think calculated to cure the most sensual person of all lascivious emotion. From the bath house I went to the stone quarry's hoping to obtain some fossils, and teeth of fossil sharks often found burried in the tufa, the laborers had all left, and we could not obtain any. This tufa is a soft volcanic, which cuts like cheese but hardens with exposure to the air. It is used here for building purposes, tomb stones, lamp posts, etc. Its color varies from greenish, and grey tints to white and granite. Something like our soap stone it is not so soft or greasy feeling.

Simoda

Yesterday some officers of the *Southampton* were lucky enough to witness a funeral procession, and the burning of the body at the close of the ceremonies; a disposition of the body I have not seen in any work on Japan. It is probable the numerous and distinct sects have each their own custom of burial. In this instance the body was accompanied by a troop of friends dressed in white mourning, principally females who expressed a great deal of grief. Ceremonies were performed over the body at a temple, and it was thence taken into the country and placed in a hole dug for the purpose over some faggots and covered with matting. The body was bent up double to occupy the least space, the knees being fastened by cords to the neck and shoulders. It was then slowly burnt or charred over a smothered fire something as charcoal is made.

We can purchase nothing at present from the shops, as trade has been suspended until the negociations now pending and the relative value of our coin, and that of the Japanese is definitely settled. As we are to sail early next week I fear my collection of Japanese curios will be limited to my purchase at Hakodadi. At Hakodadi our silver dollar was valued at four thousand eight hundred cash, while here the Commissioners refuse to value it at more than sixteen hundred. They reason the cash or copper coin is their standard, and that the itzebrac[125] a small silver coin in shape a parallelogram, of which it takes three to weigh down one of our silver dollars, has been arbitrarily valued and has nothing to do with the question, adding we have asked to traffic with them, they not careing to do so but have

[125] Preble mistakenly heard "itzebrac." I could be *ichi ban*, meaning "one piece."

granted our request. If we do not like the prices put upon their goods, we are not compeled to buy them. An arguement which cannot be controverted. The fact I suppose to be that as foreign coin is not allowed to pass in the empire, and as our coin cannot be exported, the Emperor and his councillors have devised this way of obtaining a revenue of 200 per cent on all our purchases.

There are seven prince commissioners now at Simoda arranging matters with Commodore Perry. They occupy all the Temples and best houses, and their numerous retainers are fastened like locust upon the common people. A few days before our arrival the Commodore had another 'grand function' and landed with three hundred sailors and marines and several pieces of artillery to confer with these princes. In return they are to be entertained on board the Flag Ship. The limits of Hakodadi have been fixed at seven *li*, or Japanese miles equal to a circuit of twelve of ours. It was first proposed by them that we should have the privelege of the streets only. Our boundarys around Simoda are to be the same and the Japs will put up gateways to mark the limits. During our absence Simoda has been set off from the Princepality of Idzu,[126] and erected into a Royal city, and our third prince commissioner has been appointed Governor. This looks as if the Japanese are anticepating some profit from trading with us.

Thursday June 15, 1854

Another pleasant day which I enjoyed on shore, in walking about, gathering flowers, and watching the customs and habits of this seemingly simple and good natured people. I discovered today a field of Irish potatoes and some Indian corn growing. It has been doubted whether either were grown in Japan. Indeed Commodore Perry sent the Emperor some Irish potatoes, thinking they would be a great curiosity. I also saw beautiful oranges, lemon, apricot, plum and cherry trees, and what I thought an apple tree. The merchandize for the Bazaar have arrived and are being arranged for sale in one of the Temples. Our Purser has succeeded in purchaseing some very pretty and delicate porcelain saki cups today and has promised me some of them. The finest Japanese porcelain that I have ever seen is

[126] Izu was a feudal state-province in Tokaido, next to Edo (Tokyo) Bay.

very delicately clear and beautiful translucent, but in its shapes and design did not in my opinion compare with that of Serves or Dresden. It excels that of China, but is clearer and manufactured in such small quantities as to [be] insufficient for home consumption, so that a great deal of porcelain is imported from China. The ordinary porcelain and earthen ware which is to be seen in all the shops at Hakodadi and Simoda is course and clumsy.

At a house I visited today I saw them winding the silk from the cocoons a very simple operation, but it was the first time I had ever seen it. The cocoons were first placed in boiling water and stirred about with a stick until the stick caught and drew up several filaments of the silk—these ends were than placed upon a reel and wound off by turning the reel, until the worm in the cocoon dropped into the water entirely denuded of his silky vestment. Before this happened other filaments had attached themselves to those being wound, so that the winding process was about continuous, broken only when a rough or duty thread was wound on a side reel to avoid its spoiling the better sort.

After dinner I had planned for another excursion but was prevented by an invasion from some of the Officers of the *Mississippi* who remained with us until 5 o'clock. After their leaving I went on board the *Supply* and chatted. 8 P.M. when I returned on board. I have already mentioned seeing two men confined in a cage. I have just now discovered their History. Soon after our arrival Capt. Lee received a letter from a Japanese on shore, saying he was tired of Japan and wished to go to America etc. No notice was taken of this letter and soon another was received of similar purport. No notice was taken of this and in a few nights, two Japanese came off to put themselves under American protection and go to the United States. That could not be permitted and they were sent on shore, and for that offence they were caged as we saw them. They have since been sent to Jedo because the American officers went to see them, their enterprising spirit deserved a better result.

Simoda, Friday June 16th 1854

On board ship, it being my relief duty. The Commodore shifted his broad pennant this afternoon to the *Mississippi* and received the seven Princes with a salute and entertained them with the Ethiopian Minstrels, and a supper. We dressed up in our epaulets, and went to quarters a little before sundown, expecting the Japs on board of us, but it commenced raining, and we were anchored so far out, they omitted their visit. A Jap today wrote his name upon his fan and gave it to me. In return I presented him with a piece of salt water soap as of equal value and probably useful to him.

The Japanese derive their principal subsistance from the sea and the earth; animal food is forbidden by many of their religions, and those who may have destroyed life are considered unclean. A butcher is as loathsome to a Japanese as a hangman to us. We have had great difficulty to getting a few fowl and ducks for our messes. They are always brought to us alive and proved exceeding old and tough. The fowls are chiefly gamecocks of beautiful plumage and exceedingly tame. Hens are kept only for their eggs and the cocks to furnish amusement and as timekeepers. The chief dishes at the entertainment we have attended have been fish cooked and uncooked served up in all sorts of unpalatable ways and often sweetened. Spunge and pound cakes and ginger bread, sugar candy and confectionary all very good with tea and saki. At our later entertainments understanding our preferences, they have provided us literally with boiled shrimps and raw oysters. The tea always served without sugar or cream I have found a pleasant beverage. You never enter a Japanese dwelling without being presented with a small cup of it, and a correspondingly small pipe of tobacco.

Saki is a weak and sweetish liquor made of rice and is drunk both hot and cold. It is drunk almost as universally as tea. To me it is exceedingly insipid, and I have never succeeded in swallowing it beyond the demands of politeness. Some of the Officers, better judges perchance, pronounce it excellent. Sea weed enters largely into the food and cookery of the Japs. We used to see long trains of horses leave Hakodadi daily loaded with this luxury. I noticed several varieties of this article in the market, some of which were beautifully and delicately preserved.

At Hakodadi, I do not remember to have seen but one drunken man, and I neither saw or was offered saki there, though so common here and about the Bay of Jedo. We were told it was not much drunk on the Isld of Jesso, probably because the climate is too cold to grow the rice of which it is made. The present of a bunch of edible sea weed is said to be equivalent to wishing the recipient health and prosperity. Before an entertainment it is custom for the invited to send their fans to the master of the feast who is expected to inscribe them with some appropriate sentence, and return them to his guests at the table.

Saturday June 17, 1854

My days duty on board. The purser obtained a dozen or more of delicate little porcelain saki cups for me on shore today. Coming from Japan, they will from their novelty and beauty make pretty presents, though too small and delicate for any practical use. One of the men brought me some California pearl shells, and the Boatswain a strange looking Loophite, which last I have embalmed in alcohol for the P.N.H. Society.[127] The day commenced with high winds and rain but cleared at eight and gradually improved all day. The Bazaar it is understood will be opened on Monday and the whole squadron will sail hence on Thursday, Laus Deo![128] The *Southampton* goes direct to Hong Kong with our letters, and I hope our voyage to Formosa and Manila may prove short and favorable so that we may tread close upon her track. Good Night, by our time it is eight P.M. I have not cyphered out what the time is with you or what the time is by the Japanese 'guy' as Henry used to call the clock. The Japs you must know commence their day at midnight when their clocks strike nine, after having given three prementory strikes, one hour after midnight the clock strikes eight. The next hour seven, at sunrise six, then five and four at noon nine again; one hour after midday eight two hours after mid-day seven, at sunset six, then five and finally four. At midnight the new day commences.

The hours are struck in the following manner: first one stroke, in a minute and a half a second, and immediately after a third. In a minute and a half more the striking of the hour begins, the strokes succeeding each other at intervals of fifteen seconds, except the two last which follow each other more rapidly.

[127] Portland Society of Natural History.

[128] *Laus Deo*, "glory to God."

Sunday June 18, 1854

A delightfully pleasant day, the whole of which after the morning inspection and muster I have improved on shore and in a visit to the *Mississippi*. Every time I go on shore I find new beauties in the scenery to admire. Every turn opens some valley, and discloses some novelty. I rested today at a small temple occupied as a guard house and was quickly beset by a crowd everyone in it urgent to have me write on his or her fan. So I marked A.B.C. etc. on one, our numerals on another, and made a picture primer on a third and so on, for which I received plenty of "Annastors,"[129] or Japanese thanks. Looking about me I found a laughable representation of Com. Perry and two of our officers, which I brought off, though not without some opposition. In a front yard we passed, we saw a dozen or more children playing the game of blind mans bluff, precisely as it is played with us. The bind man had his face entirely covered with a course blue cloth, and was trying to catch the running shouting urchens. When one was caught he took the blindmans place, a shaven headed bonze and an old woman sat in the cottage door enjoying the play. I wish I could send you a big bunch of wild Hydrangia I plucked today as it differs somewhat from ours.[130]

I have often wondered how with such a dense population so many groves of beautiful trees fringing the hill tops should be preserved. This is perhaps explained by their customs of planting a tree at the birth of every male child, which on attaining its full growth serves as a token that the man is marriagable. When the child becomes a married man the tree is cut down and its wood manufactured into various useful household articles.

Monday June 19, 1854

A rainy day throughout. As 10 o'clock was the time appointed for the long talked of Bazaar to be opened I went on shore to be disappointed as the opening had been postponed. I contrived however to have a peep at all the pretty things and found them marked so high

[129] In Japanese, "thank you" is *arigato*. Preble confused the sound of the word.

[130] Hydrangea, a genus of shrubs and one woody vine of the family *Hydrangeaceae*. They have white or tinted flower clusters.

as to preclude my purchase of any but the most trifling articles. For instance, a lacquered box 14 inches square was marked $32. A Japanese ladies' dress $52, a Japanese Genteleman trowsers 25$, a piece of crape $28. A piece of silk in style and quality similar to one I purchased at Hakodati for $5 was marked $12. A lacquered waiter $12 and so with everything. The no of articles being limited and purchases many, it is proposed to number them all and cast lots for a chance. Any officer drawing a number can purchase the article ticketed with the number he has drawn or exchange it with and officer who holds the number of an article he covets or he can decline purchase altogether when the article will be free to be purchased by anyone. After looking at the Bazaar, I went to the shops and bought a few fans and nick nacks and returned on board.

The other day I wrote of the kindness of one of the surgeons of the Squadron in dispensing eye water to the poor afflicted women of Simoda. Alas that I must record that his benevolence was rewarded by his having a valuable signet ring stolen from him.

I learned a legend today of the origin of the Japanese derived from their own tradition. The word Japan or more properly Jepan is said to mean "Source of Day." The legend runs that a certain Emperor sent three hundred youths and virgins to search for a herb which should confer immortality, but likeing the country, they remained in it, and occupied themselves with peopling it with their kind. There is another tradition, that is evidently more fabulous. At a period very remote the legend says the whole earth was covered with water. At length the Creator of the World cast his eyes upon it and directed his eldest son to reclaim and people it. The son took a long pole to sound the depth of the water and discovered the most shallow part where Japan now is. Collecting the earth together from the bottom with a rake, he manufactured the Island of Niphon, and forthwith endowed it with all the production now indigenous. He then divided himself into two beings one male and the other female for the purpose of peopleing the country. The other children of the Creator did the same, but not gifted equally to their eldest brother, they were not so successful, hence the origin of other countries, and their extraordinary inferiority to the favored Islands of Japan.

Tuesday June 20, 1854

A rainy blowy morning but the weather cleared up about noon. The Commodore has forbidden intercourse with the shore until the money question is arranged, which has kept everybody on board. Had it not been so my duties would have confined me to the ship. It is too bad that our dollar has been arbitrarily depreciated 200 per cent by the Japs. In China 1400 cash are equal to a dollar. Here we are allowed 1600 cash for a dollor, but one of their silver itzeboos[131] weighing just one third as much is worth the same. In explanation the Japs say it has a ficticious value because it has the imperial stamp to prevent it being exported. As all trade is conducted through government officials, the reason for and advantage of this depreciation is obvious. The Gov't recoinage of our money in this way is equivalent to an export duty of 200 per cent. I fear there has been a fatal mistake in our treaty negociations. We finished ballasting the *Southampton* today. She will sail in a day or two with our letters and I trust our deliverance is close at hand. It is now eight days since the *Saratoga* sailed for the West Coast with news of our treaty and my letter to you.

The following are the sounds of some Japanese words with their meanings which I have picked up.[132]

Simoda, Wednesday June 21, 1854

A pleasant day and rather tedious days duty on board. Lt. Boudinot an old messmate of mine reported for our ship today which puts us in five watches. This makes the fourth ship we have been messmates together in. This morning considerable excitement ensued from the Commodores signaling "Contract no more bills." "Fair will be opened at 3 P.M. communication allowed with shore at that hour and not before." As regards the Bazaar, the articles are marked so high and so much beyond my limited means that I have given away my chance to purchase to my messmates and have relieved one

131 Should be *ichi ban*, one piece. Preble undoubtedly did not understand the Japanese way of counting silver coin.

132 Pages 291 and 292 of the diary contain Preble's collected Japanese and Shinese words, including numerals and their ideograms.

of them from his duty to enable him to go on shore and make purchases. It is six months tonight since we left Hong Kong to engage in opening this Japanese Oyster; long tedious monotonous and disagreeable has been the interval. We have had but few of the pleasures that civilized people usually live for and been deprived of news from home and shut out from all knowledge of the busy outside world. We have per force been restricted to the absteniousness of an anchorite (I mean no pun) drinking our tea slops improved with brown sugar because we could get no other, and discussing the merits of various kinds of bean soups, and Japanese and American rice and mess pork and salt Junk.

Thursday June 22, 1854

After keeping the morning watch or seeing the sunrise as we say and watching the operation of holy stoning the decks and subsequently breakfasting I went on shore [with] some of my messmates to visit the shops and do up my shopping previous to our departure. Among my purchases was a black silk scarf and numerous trifling articles for cumshaws to friends. By good luck I obtained two silver coins, which I had dispaired of getting. They cost me only a quarter of a dollar and a few navy buttons. There is a severe penalty attached to the exportation or exchange of coins, so that in all our trading not a copper of Japanese money ever crossed our palms. These today were suddenly put into my hand by a ragged fellow, as I was passing along the street, and who seemed well contented with the buttons I at first gave him in exchange but not considering it a fair exchange or honest I gave him more buttons and the only piece of money I had and sent him on his way rejoicing. I gave one of these coins to our Purser the other I shall keep as a lucky penny. These coins and the oblong copper 'Hachser'[133] I sent home by the *Saratoga* are the only coins I have been able to obtain. I bought some Japanese soy today, which is made of beans, but I doubt if it will keep to be taken home. The shopping mania which has seized upon our officers is very amusing. The gallant gentlemen pounce upon everything that in any way represents Japan. Their attics will in a year or two

[133] "Hachser"—*hachisen,* or eight sens in Tokugawa money.

groan under their Japanese barthens. My collection is very miscelleneous and has cost me but little, yet is comprises articles of ornament and things to eat drink wear and smoke.

Simoda, Friday evening June 23d, 1854

All communications with the shore has been interdicted by signal, and the steamships have come out of the inner harbor and are anchored near us preparatory to sailing. As soon as the *Supply* is ballasted we will all be off. I took my letters on board the Flag Ship this evening to be ready for the earliest opportunity. I shall leave the Japs without regrets, and rejoice in the prospect of reaching a land, where news and newspapers prevail and we can learn the movements on the grand chess board of the world, and obtain the more closely interesting news from that dear little world surrounding our own hearths.

Captain Abbott has an order from the Commodore for me to survey the little harbor of Keelung on the Northern end of the Island of Formosa which is to be our first destination. We expect to reach Manila about the 1st of Augt and Hong Kong early in Sept. If we should reach H.K. [Hong Kong] by the 25th of Augt. our anniversary. It will be also the anniversary of our first dropping anchor in Chinese waters a year ago.

A word now about the clothing of these people before we leave them. The rich are clothed in silks and the poor in coarse cotton clothes, sometimes though rarely I have seen furs upon the better sort. I do not remember to have seen a woolen garment of any discription during the winter in Jedo Bay. Our broad cloths excited universal admiration. They often had a coarse article obtained from the Dutch which was used as a covering to their swords. The upper garment is generally black the under dress of mixed colors. Every person of rank has his family arms and the soldier vasals and retainers of a chief or noble have their chieftains arms wrought or stamped on the back or shoulders of their upper garment. The Imperial servants wear three liliac leaves in silver. The gentry and soldier year these devices about the size of a half dollar, very neatly made to look like silver thread. In winter they keep themselves warm by multiplying their dresses, that is wearing one coat over another until they obtain a comfortable temperature. Instead of shoes they wear clogs or wood and straw sandals which are kept fast to the foot by a loop over the foot and between the great toe, and its next neighbor, when socks are worn, they are made like a mitten with a separate caseing for the great toe to accommodate the sandal. A sheet of fine tough and beautifully figured paper is used as a pocket handkerchief by the rich and a plain and coarser sort by all. This paper has almost the toughness and texture of cloth, and this use of it is not so strange as it might seem. The outer storm garment in common use for protection from wet weather is a cloak made of a tough flexible paper, nicely coated with tea oil on the inside and lacquered on the out. The Umbrellas are also of paper and like the Chinese but of fine quality.

Saturday evening, June 24, 1854

It has been blowing a S.W. gale all day which has prevented our leaving our anchorage. We have been rolling and pitching most uncomfortably with two anchors ahead, and the sea has been breaking angrily over some rocks, rather more neighborly to the ships astern than was agreeable. The least dragging of our anchor would have placed us in a perilous position. The wind has now hauled and is hauling to the Wst and is moderating. The barometer is rising and the sky has assumed a more pleasant aspect. We hope now that tomorrow's sun, will see us underway and steering South. Chaplain Jones, and Passed Mids. Jones and Breese[134] have joined our ship. The Chaplain is to examine and report upon a coal mine at Keelung and the Passed Mids. to assist me in my survey.

When we first came to Japan our readings about it greatly impressed us as to its Military Strength and resources. Our experience has shown that both have been greatly exaggerated and overestimated. With the exception of a few cannon, and forts about Uraga, we saw no other defences in the whole extent of the western shore

[134] Randolph K. Breese was made midshipman on November 6, 1846; passed midshipman, June 8, 1852, with service on the Mississippi in the East Indies; master, September 15, 1855; lieutenant, September 16, 1855: lieutenant commander, July 16, 1862; commander, July 25, 1866; captain, August 9, 1874. He died on September 13, 1881. See also *Records,* 159–60. He assisted Preble in surveying the port of Keelung or Kirun in Formosa.

of Jedo bay (which we surveyed for a distance of several miles) excepting such breastworks as were thrown up after our arrival hastily constructed of earth and sand bags to cover encampments of soldiers watching our movements. The soldiers we saw were armed with lances having their handles beautifully inlaid with mother of pearl, Match locks, Bows and arrows and Tower muskets. Their arms were generally covered with mohair or broadcloth cases, and seemed kept in fine order. It was rarely they allowed us to look at them. In addition to their other arms each soldier is provided with two swords. The longest is about a yard in length, is strongly curved and has a broad back. The other is much shorter being little more than a knife. The blades are kept bright and sharp, and are said by the Japanese to be of such admirable stuff and temper that they will cleave a man asunder from head to foot. An experiment I never saw tried. The hilt has a round and substantial guard but is without any bow over the hand. The handle is long enough to be grasped by both hands, which is the manner in which the long sword is weilded. The scabbards are thick and rather flat, and often covered with a fine shaggreen. The handle is frequently ornamented with silk braid and generally has some device or coat of arms beautifully wrought or inlaid in gold and steel under the silken meshes. This cimetar[135] is always stuck into the sash or girdle on the left side with the edge uppermost. The short sword is similarly shaped and ornamented attached to its sheath there is generally a small knife and a pair of chop sticks of steel with handles wrought in embossed gold and steel. The high officers have each a sword bearer, who carries their swords behind them. Lesser officials have a spear bearer, who follows the officer whenever he walks out.

Our Purser remarked today that the military and warlike strength and spirit of the Japanese had long been to Europe like the ghost in a villiage church yard, a bug bear and a terror, which it only required some bolder fellow than the rest to walk up to (us Yankees) and discover the ghost to be nothing but moon shine on the gravestones or a poor old white horse. Our nation has unclothed the ghost and all

[135] A "cimeter," or scimitar, is a short, curved sword. Here Preble used it to describe a Japanese sword.

the rest of the world will cry bah, and take advantage of the discovery.

Hakodadi we found defended by two batteries one of three and three embrasures, the other having but one. These forts were excavated in the hillside, and earthen breastworks about two feet thick. The sides of the embrasures and the inner side of the breastwork itself was kept from washing away by posts and boarding. The guns were housed over and the embrasures boarded up evidently to conceal the battery from our observation. The guns were housed after our arrival but an officer who had previously seen them said they were 12 Pds., Brass pieces. The fort had a new look as though just erected and its rear was protected by an excavated ditch which a smart man could jump over.

Canvass screens or 'Dungaree Forts' as they were called by the Officers of the *Columbus*,[136] who first approached Jedo Bay, supposed to be put up for the purpose of deception and intimidation have proved to be nothing but thin cotton cloths marked with the devices or arms of a chief, and used to surround his camp or station. The device upon the screen is the same as that worn by his retainers.

During our survey of Jedo Bay I saw a great many of these ornamented screens, and always found them enclosing a military station or surrounding the residence of an official.

The Treaty House was hung with purple crape screens having in white on them, the arms of the Emperor[137] and of the Chief Prince Commissioners.[138] The square around the Treaty House was enclosed by white cotton screens having a device in black. The Yard and all the approaches to the house alloted to the use of Commodore Perry during his visit to Hakodadi was similarly hung with white cotton screens, bearing in their centers four black diamonds seperated by a white St. Andrews Cross—which we were told was the device of the Governor.

Notes of What I have seen in Japan: Flowers: Iris, Roses, Azaleas

[136] The *Columbus* was a ship of 2,480 tons, 74 guns, built in 1816.

[137] Most probably it was the Tokugawa crest.

[138] It was the crest of Chief Commissioner Hayashi Daigaku-no-kami. *Narrative*, I, 347–48.

red and white and very abundant near Simoda; Japonicas—the double white red and variagated. Single Japonicas, red growing to the size of a large tree and very abundant about Jedo Bay; Dandelions, in profusion about Hakodadi. Trees: Pines, several varieties and of large size about Jedo Bay; Maple, a tall and straight variety with very delicate leaves and in one specimen dwarfed near Simoda; the Mulberry papyrefera, Bamboo, Wild Cherry, Apple, Pear, Peach, White Ash, Beach, Birch and Cedar. Birds: Pigeons or Doves, living in holes in the sand live cliffs about Jedo Bay; wild Ducks and Geese numerous at Jedo; Crows, Swallows, Sparrows and white Cranes about Simoda. Hawks and several kinds of Gulls abundant in Jedo Bay; Snipe Ploves and Ravens at Hakodadi.

Salmon, Herring, and Mullet with numerous other fish, and blue Muscles were abundant at Hakodadi; and we got Oysters at Jedo Bay.

Cats, Dogs and Horses were among familiar animals, and mosquito and cockroaches for annoying insects. Crabs, Salmon, Trout, Place Flounders, Smelts, stinging Rays, Sculpins, Piques, four kinds of Clams, Ragifast are also found abundant at Hakodadi.

The Houses about the Bay of Jedo at Simoda and of the little villages along the coast are chiefly of wood. Sometimes rough cast and covered with lime or cement and white washed, often chequered into diamond shaped ornaments striped black. Those I saw and visited were generally one storied and I saw none that exceeded two storys. The upper one being a half story or attic chamber. The better houses are substantially and handsomely tiled with slate colored tiles. The poorer houses are thatched with straw. These houses have generally but one room, which divided into any number of apartments by moveable partitions or screens of paper ornaments according to the taste and wealth of the owner. One half of at least two thirds of all the houses at Simoda are devoted to shops where trifling articles are exposed for sale or barter. Mechanics in the same way have a portion of their dwellings converted into work shops. The Japanese use neither chairs nor tables. The floors of their houses are neatly and softly covered with straw matting. Oiled paper set in small panes supplies the want of glass, and the windows are protected from the weather and at night by external shutters of wood.

The dwellings and warehouses at Hakodadi on the Isld of Jesso were chiefly built of wood and shingled, and had their roofs protected from high winds and fires by a covering of stones, the size of a mans head or fist. On the top of each house is kept buckets of water in readiness to extinguish fires, and the same wise fire precaution is seen in buckets, tubs and troughs of water placed at equal distance along the streets. Many of the warehouses have thick and solid walls of stone handsomely covered with lime and whitewashed. The windows of these warehouses are protected by iron gratings and a net work of iron wire, and fire proof shutters.

For what reason I know not but I saw many buildings that at first glance appeared to be rude and miserable wooden structures, which a nearer and closer inspection showed me were solid fire proof stone structures covered with a layer of rough shingles.

In the grave yard of one of the Hakodadi Temples I saw a praying post on which was a flat iron plate inscribed with a prayer. As often as the plate was turned just so many times was the prayer repeated. An original economy of time I imagine no other religious nation has thought of.[139]

The following is from the foregoing and other memerandum furnished by me as the result of my observations on their temples, to the *Boston Journal.*

NOTES ON JAPAN

CONTRIBUTED TO THE BOSTON JOURNAL BY A U.S. NAVAL OFFICER

G. H. Preble

TEMPLES, RELIGION, ETC.

The three temples I visited at Simoda were each approached through an avenue of stately trees, chiefly cedars and cypress, the way being paved with smoothly cut flag-stones. To the right, and a little in front of each temple, there was a collection of closely huddled grave-stones, many of which had offerings of fresh flowers placed by them in bam-

[139] Page 303 of the diary has an insert, apparently put in later and without much connection with the expedition of 1853–56. It is a handwritten note, with the insignia of the flagship *Tennessee:* "The Admiral, Captain and Officers of the Flagship *Tennessee* will be glad to receive Admiral Preble tomorrow, Tuesday, afternoon between one and five o'clock. Boats will be found at the Pegnot Hotel Landing. Monday, 18 July."

boos or stone basins filled with water. Some of these temples had gilded idols with hideous features—others had none. One idolless temple seemed peculiarly dedicated to the patron God of mariners. Its walls were hung with pictures of Japanese junks struggling mid tempestuous waves; on a long board was fastened a great number (I should think one hundred) of the little cues of hair which it is the Japanese custom to wear over the crown of their head, and which must have been sacrificed and offered in grateful remembrance of escape from the dangers of shipwreck, through interposition of the deity to whom this temple was dedicated. Other offerings in this temple, displayed upon its walls, were a bow, a fan, a sword, two masks apparently of savage faces, and a woman's long tresses. Above the latter there hung a rude picture of two naked women, running over what appeared a snowy beach or country.

This temple had the appearance of being merely an entranceway to the courtyard of a large temple which was raised by several stone steps above and overlooked it. In this temple there were several idols. A large, oblong-shaped bell was suspended over a pyramidal structure in the yard between the two temples, and on the right of their approach. At each side of the door-way were wooden chests of goodly size, for reception of the cash offerings of the worshippers. A drum with copper or bronze sides, and several bronze ornaments were on each side and in front of the three principal idols; and some fresh flowers—the red azalia and a beautiful purple lily—were placed conspicuous, in vessels containing water, among the other decorations of the place. Behind and beyond the idols you looked into a room or recess about which were suspended slips of white paper, but I could see nothing else in the apartment. Three or four feet in front of the main altar the floor of the temple was raised a few inches and covered with matting. The walls of the temple were also hung with votive offerings. In one frame I noticed a curious pagoda, made by nailing the copper coin of the country to the board, through the square holes in their centres. Other frames were filled with rude paintings, one of which represented a party of Japanese soldiers in a snowy county, hurriedly approaching a river in which were two or three boats.

At one of my visits to this temple, a shaven headed priest, dressed in a grey colored robe and wearing a sash drawn diagonally across his back, marked with some device, was down on his knees repeating in a sing-song manner some prayers from a book or breviary before him, bowing his head, slapping his string of black beads or rosary, clasping his hands, and occasionally tapping a small brazen drum at his side. Behind him were three worshippers reciting their prayers, bowing when he bowed and coursing the beads on their rosarys. When the priest had finished his services he turned to us, and after bowing to his worshippers and they to him, with an exceedingly benevolent expression he invited us by motions to sit by his side, and on our refusing that, to walk nearer and examine the idols and altar; and when in reply we pointed to our feet and made signs that we could not take off our shoes, he still invited us to a closer inspection of the idols, which we did not see occasion any longer to refuse. He also invited us to his house near at hand, and gave us pipes to smoke and a small cup of universal beverage cha *or* tea, drank without sugar or cream, and really very palatable. These three temples of Simoda are each at the upper extremity of a principal street, are facing towards the sea, and backed up against steep and well wooded mountains. Hung about the interior of the temple I have been describing were several bells exactly like in shape, fashion and sound to our common sleigh-bells, only of larger size. These, I took it, were so placed to be rung to call the priest from his dwelling to attend to the spiritual wants of his worshippers. Besides the three temples I visited, there were several others in Simoda; indeed for so small a place, it seemed richly supplied. One of those I did not see was described to me as approached by one hundred steps. The Japanese do not appear to have any particular regard for the sanctity of the religious edifices as one temple was allotted to the use and occupation of the Commodore, and I saw others occupied by the Japanese soldiery as their barracks. In one of these temples some of our officers saw the carriage of a French field piece, and in another a coat of chain armor.

The principal temples at Hakodado are three in number; the little roadside edifices, shrines and praying places are innumerable. A room in one of the principal temples was allotted to the daguerrotypist and artist of the expedition. The principal altar of this temple was handsomely and richly gilded and ornamented with candelabra vases of artificial flowers, and a profusion of grotesque carving; and the sanctity of the altar preserved from invasion by a light and handsome railing that extended from pillar to pillar and surrounded it. The head of the idol or image that looked down from behind and over all its gewgaws and frippery, was surrounded by a halo, and I think it highly probable that a devout Catholic might have readily imagined the altar one devoted to his own religion, and presided over by one of a thousand and one holy saints of his calender, especially as a stone basin of holy water stood near the entrance to the sanctuary, and on one of the walls hung a clever representation of the fires of purgatory and hell. The chapel, to the right of the altar, in this temple was stored with little miniature tablets representing head-stones, made of wood and richly gilded, having inscriptions and epitaphs illustrative and commemorative of the virtues of deceased persons. Besides these, attached to the temple was a graveyard all crowded with head-stones, which I was told, did not cover the body of the person they were designed of commemorate, but only bore record of his life and many virtues. In some instances the bones had been collected by friends and placed underneath these head-stones. The stones over the Buddhist priests, that were pointed out to us, were supported on a carved lotus leaf, emblematic of the profession, and each stone in the yard had in front of it a little stone basin filled with water for the birds to drink from.

There is no sectarian intolerance in Japan. On the contrary, they esteem it an act of courtesy to visit, from time to time, each other's gods and do them reverence.

Sunday June 25th, 1854

We attempted to get to sea to day but after working from daylight until 10 am against a light breeze we had to give up, and come to anchor, after having been several times in danger of coming upon the rocks. The steamship would not or did not give us any assistance, but steamed off and away. Commodore Perry sending us word to get out how and when we could that he was afraid to trust his large steamers so near the rocks and that the *Supply* our companion sufferer was in his way. His bright intellect seems not to have conceived, that we could have made fast our lines to the *Supply,* and he taken hold of her and towed both vessels out of danger and to sea.

The *Supply* is now waiting like ourselves for a breeze and the other vessels have long since disappeared from sight. I made a call on board the *Supply* this afternoon and borrowed Lyell's *Principles of Geology*[140] to read on the Passage down being very poorly supplied with reading matter.

[140] Sir Charles Lyell (1797–1875), *Principles of Geology; or, The Modern Changes of the Earth and Its Inhabitants Considered as Illustrative of Geology* (8th ed., London, J. Murray, 1850). Of seven other editions, one, the fifth, was published in Philadelphia and Pittsburgh in 1837.

Monday June 26, 1854

We left Simoda in company with the *Supply* soon after daylight this morning and with the following wind have been steering eight miles or more an hour towards our destination. The *S[upply]* continues in company but in the dim blue distance astern. And we will probably lose sight of her tonight. We have at last fairly turned our backs upon Japan to the joy of all aboard. We can truly say we have been twice glad. First when introduced to its novelties and now at leaving them and it.

Simoda, Tuesday June 27, 1854

Our fair wind lasted until noon today. The wind is now ahead but the weather pleasant and we are evidently approaching warmer latitudes. We experienced a current of 42 miles against us yesterday, against which it was fortunate that we had a fair wind to urge us on. I measured our distance from Formosa yesterday, and found it would take us just eleven days of equal fortune of put us at anchor there. In reading and chess the day has passed very quietly though monotonous. It has not been a day to make history out of. Half the Kingdoms of the known world might have been overturned and reestablished since the interruptions of our communications.

At Sea, Wednesday June 28, 1854

Sailing to the Sth all day with pleasant weather and a smooth sea at dinner we had a discussian on Coats of Arms and Heraldry, and Boudinot our North Carolina messmate remarked as we eat our rice that the true way to cook it after boiling was to drain off the water, steam it for a while which expanded and seperated the grains. Our sailors are enjoying a dance on the forecastle. I wish you could see them.

Thursday June 29, 1854

Pleasant with westerly winds but rather warmer than we like for comfort, and there has been that peculiar dampness that is generally expected in the gulf stream on our own coast. I have been reading Lyell's *Geology* which I find as amusing as a novel and vastly more instructing. Since tea the Purser and I have been battling at chess at which we were about equally matched though tonight he beat me two out of three games.

Friday June 30th 1854

With the thermometer at 86° in my room it is difficult to write. Last night after I had settled myself for a comfortable sleep in, the drum beat to quarters and I had to go on deck. After a broadside of blank cartridges and much snapping of primers, the retreat was beat, and we returned to our couches. Last Monday we had a General Exercise, and exploded twenty-five or thirty of our eight and ten inch shells in the air, a practical lesson to Uncle Sam's boys which cost one or two hundred dollars. The sea continues smooth, the sky serene, and southward still we go.

Saturday July 1, 1854

A swelting hot day, and my chief has been to keep cool and quiet. Reading and playing chess. Tonight we have been drinking to sweethearts and wives. Henry, I suppose, is full of anticipation of the coming fourth, and Lily rather in fear of being blown up by his fire crackers.

Sunday July 2d 1854

No change in wind or weather. After muster, and the usual monthly reading of the Articles of War—our Naval Commission service—the bell tolled for Church and Chaplain Jones read the church service, and preached a sermon from this text. "Our Father which art in Heaven." Intended to impress the sailors that absent from earthly friends, they still had a father ever near and as it would be strange in a child not to talk to his earthly parent, it was still more strange if they would not talk in prayer, and tell their wants to a Heavenly father to whom they are endebted for so many benefits and who declared he is ready to grant them who ask, etc, etc. After the sermon Mr. Jones endeavored to have the 157 Hymn song,[141] and it was amuseing rather than musical to hear some of our active young topmen finishing off the last words of a line while some of the older and sedate seamen were quivering in about the middle of it, and the Chaplain as leader of this impromptu choir puzzled to decide whether to linger along for the last to catch up to him, or to rush ahead and overtake the former. Such as it was he raised quite a choir and this evening it has started the men to practiseing Psalm tunes in-

141 It was perhaps "Away in a Manger," taken from the Presbyterian hymnary.

stead of roaring the usual forecastle songs. [To] write in this hot weather is a task, every word is a Shylock that demands its pound of flesh.

Monday July 3d 1854

Nothing has happened today to disturb the monotony of sky and water, good weather, head winds and an adverse current continue to delay our passage. Today for the first time we have had a head sea which gives to our ship a seasick pitching motion. I had my air port taken out this morning to get a breath of fresh air through but soon a fresh sea came galloping in which washed me out, deluged my bedding and forced me to hastily close it again. The Purser figured up our mess bill for the last 4 months and found it amounted to only twenty dollars each, quite cheap living, but then it is three months since I have drank any coffee, for four months we have sweetened our tea with brown sugar, and six since I have tasted milk. Oh, the luxurious hospitality of Japan!

Tuesday July 4, 1854

Never was there a quieter Fourth passed by three hundred Americans. With the exception of reducing sail to a passing squall we have had no excitement. At sundown the crew were given an extra 'tot of grog' and they are now having a lively time singing Psalm tunes under the direction of the Chaplain on the half deck. It is at their own request, as they asked last evening for permission and instruction. The warm weather makes all of us lazy sleepy and listless and I am no exception. Our executive is sick with a light intermittent fever. We have still a head wind and sea.

Wednesday July 5, 1854

Our singers are in full blast again tonight, and as I write are swelling through. "When I can read my bible clear etc." We have been in sight of the Islands of Ceciles Archepalago, six or seven in number and sailing by them all day. One of them is five thousand feet high equaling the highest land in New England or on our Atlantic Coast. The weather continues excessively warm, and a shower at sundown was considered quite a blessing. We have been driven from our apartments today by the turpentine used in clearing the paintwork.

Lat. 29.43. Long. 130.25. Thursday July 6th, 1854

Several volcanic islands have been in sight all day far off to the South[th], among them Ou-Sima or Preble Isld as it has been named, the second in size of the Loo Choo Group. In the last twenty-four hours we have experienced a current of forty two miles, setting us to the E.N.E. Rather discouraging to be set back nearly two miles an hour is it not?

Lat. 29.53. Long. 129.10E Friday July 7, 1854

The current and winds are still adverse. Nothing new divided the day as usual between reading, chess and watchings.

Lat. 29.04 Long 127.14E Saturday July 8, 1854

The Master reported today noon that we are only 320 miles from our port or about the distance that Portland is from New York; a semi favoring current has set us to the Nth & W[st] the last 24 hours: Lat 29.05, Long 125.42. All day we have been sailing over a sea covered with a fine yellow sand or mud and studded with numerous crabs of minute demensions and drift wood all of which we suppose to have been swept down from the Yellow Sea, or great Yangtse Kiang. Some beautiful dolphins have been sporting around the ship.

Sunday July 9, 1854

We have a continuance of pleasant weather, and a fair wind today which we are able to appreciate. At noon our port was 208 miles dist. Chaplain Jones gave us rather a flowery and ambitious sermon today from the Text "I am not ashamed of this Gospel of Christ."[142] The singing [of] Old Hundred[143] and Hebers Missionary Hymn[144] by the crew was really well done.

Monday July 10 1854

With a fair wind and pleasant weather, we have every prospect of being at anchor tomorrow evening. At sundown we passed some

142 Rom. 1:16.

143 "Old Hundred" is a hymn written by Louis Bourgeois in 1551. See *The Hymnal*, 1. *The Hymnal* was published in 1933 by authority of the General Assembly of the Presbyterian Church in the United States.

144 Reginald Heber (1783–1826), bishop of Calcutta, was the author of *Hymns, Written and Adapted to the Weekly Church Service of the Year* (London, 1827), edited by his wife, Amelia. There were many editions of this hymnal.

islands about thirty miles dist from Keelung and are now under reduced sail in order to keep at a safe distance until daylight. An Island we have just passed called Crag Island is so singular in shape that I will sketch its outline. The rock on the left hand resembles a Castle in ruins, and the likeness is all the more perfect from their being two or three perforations through it which look like doorways. I have been preparing the skin of a sea bird today that flew on board our ship for the P.N.H. Society. Our cat had a feast off his body. The bird is new to me, but one of our sailors calls it a Dyke, a bird common to the coast of Africa.

Keelung Harbor, Island of Formosa Tuesday July 11, 1854

We anchored here at 10 o'clock this morning and found to our surprise the Supply has not arrived before us. We have been regaling ourselves after our long abstinence with pine apples, egg plants, cucumbers pumpkins, pigs, poultry and eggs, not that anyone of us have eaten through the whole list, but the sight of all these attainable things is refreshing. I was on shore today for a few minutes but saw only a crowded dirty town which reminded me of a dozen similiar dirty Syrian towns in the Mediterranean. The 1st Lieut has been having one of his holidays, "All hands" under his direction having been busily at work until after dark. Mooring the ship. Getting out the boats. Striking yards topmasts etc. As it was very squally last night Capt A[bbot] imagined a typhoon approaching and wished the ship prepared for it. Tomorrow weather permitting I am to commence my survey of the Harbor.[145]

Sunday July 16, 1854

As I anticipated my surveying duties have kept me at work from day light until dark and my fatigue and the prostrating heat have compelled me to forego the pleasure of keeping up my daily diary of events. The *Supply* has not yet arrived but is hourly and anxiously looked for. One of her officers was to have assisted me on the survey, but with only one assistant I have already accomplished so much that in a day or two I shall not need his assistance. I hope to make a re-

[145] Perry ordered Preble to make a survey of Keelung Harbor, Formosa, a task in which he was assisted by Passed Midshipman Walter F. Jones. Preble's map of Keelung is inserted in Vol. II of Perry's *Narrative*.

spectable chart of the Harbor, and as it is the first I have planned as well as executed without advice or assistance I am bound to be proud of my work. Some of the rocks and points are very curious. A rock which I have taken for a signal or triangulation point, and named "Ruin Rock" is a lump of soft sand stone washed by the rains so as to present a very exact resemblance to a small gothic ruin. On its top there is a cup like pulpit about large enough for three men to stand upon. The annexed sketch shows some of its peculiarities but not all of them. One of its hollow archways has been connected into a small joss house or altar, and in it there is a quantity of bleached bones and human skulls.

At the Western entrance of the Harbor, there is another curious and peculiar appearance. The soft yellow sand stone has been eaten into and washed away by the corrosion of the sea leaving large and dark colored boulders of a harder rock supported on pillars of the softer stone thus creating many fanciful shapes resembling at a little distance and with a slight effort of the imagination images of men, birds and beasts.[146] I have named it in my survey Image Point. The little sketch of one of my signal stations on the preceding page, will give you a better idea of its peculiarities than my description can. The dark parts are round or oval shaped rocks impregnated with iron and stuck here and there in the sand stone like plums in a pudding. The unshaded part is a light buff sandstone. Two points thus abraded by the sea extended their arms to the E^st^ on the Western side of the entrance and between them is formed a beautiful natural dock large enough to hold our ship, and deep enough on one side for her to lie alongside the natural pier. Back of this dock and between these image like projections, there is a level amphitheater with the escarpment of a sand stone hill rising in terraces behind it. The level part is perhaps one hundred feet square, and its natural stone pavement is traversed by seams and cracks which give it the character of a tessalated pavement like the sketch. Dikes of different colored stone six to eight inches in width marking it all over in irregular seams. A small island in the entrance of the Harbor about a third of a mile square is another interesting feature. The whole island is based on sand stone and the

[146] On p. 312 of the diary are two ink sketches of rocks in the sea near Keelung Harbor, Formosa.

northern side including nine tenths of the Island is washed by the sea in heavy gales, and resembles the natural pavement I have already described. The Southern edge of the Island has on top of the sand stone, a coral formation from six to ten feet in thickness, the top of which has decomposed and furnishes a soil for a few bushes, and some grass and weeds. The Island has evidently been elevated from beneath the sea. The coral could not have grown above the sea level. Chaplain Jones has been quite successful in his researches after coal, and the *Supply* will be able to obtain the three hundred tons she is sent after. There are coal beds only three quarters of a mile from Keelung but the best coal is found on an Island, so we are told one hundred miles distant on the east coast of Formosa. Its near inhabitants are represented to us as the savage aborigines and cannibals, and coal can only be obtained thence by stealth.

Keelung being just in the route of steam ships to China from the W. Coast of America, and a good intermediate halting place for steamers of future lines between China and Japan, if coal can be obtained here at all times and of good quality it must become quite an important place. The present inhabitants are a rude thieving opium smoking *sam shu* drinking people. The exceedingly course cotton flags I put up as signals and which I punched full of holes and cut in shreds to render valueless, were stolen nightly from the poles, and had to be replaced in the morning before commencing work.

Capt. Abbot has exchanged presents and civilities with the chief mandarin who is well pleased to have us here as he is expecting an attack from the rebels, and has been fortifying against their expected attack. He thinks our presence will deter them from making any, and of course wishes to be very civil to us.

The town reminds me of several Syrian towns. The streets of shops, being bazaars or under arched footpaths, and the shops very small. The filth, dogs, dark skinned inhabitants, and peculiar dress, many wearing turbans serve to increase this resemblance. A wall or moat surrounds the town, and it is defended by a miserable fort, armed with two immense guns, and three smaller ones, all rusty and cumberous, and on such rotten and silly planned carriages that I would face the guns than stand behind them in action. The towns best defences are the paddy fields which nearly surround three sides of it and extensive mud flats in front which prevents any approach by boats, leaving only a narrow causeway and a gorge between two hills which has been walled up with a high double wall the only way for the approach of an enemy. A handfull of men could defend the place from thousands.

Mess affairs have quite improved since our arrival and we luxuriate on roasting pigs, ducks geese chickens eggs, pineapples bananas and other notions. There is always some unsatisfied longing, and I hear my messmates forgetful of other deprivations sighing for the cool weather we have left behind.

Keelung, At Sea, Sunday July 23, 1854

We sailed from Keelung this morning and are now enroute to Manila. The *Supply* did not arrive at Keelung until Friday, but brought us some old California newspapers she obtained by speaking to a ship bound from California to Hong Kong. Old as they were, they gave us considerable news, for instance that England and France had allied with the Turks against Russia,[147] and that my acquaintance Sir Chas Napier[148] has command of the Baltic Fleet. We also learn that Capt. Wyman[149] of our navy, who was to have commanded the *Vermont* on this Expedition has died at Florence Italy. These newspapers make me eager and longing to satisfy my doubts, hopes, and fears as to all that has happened at home since I last heard from you Oct. 25/53. I have been constantly employed in the past from daylight until dark on my survey which as far as regards the field and hydragraphical work was finished last night at sundown. I have now to map it, and think I have the material for makeing an

[147] During the Crimean War (1854–56), the Turks, the French, the Sardinians, and the English were allied against Russia.

[148] Sir Charles James Napier (1782–1853), British soldier and statesman, was the most prominent general in the British conquests in India, especially in what is now Pakistan, and in the First Sikh War. *DNB*, XIV, 45–54. At Bermuda in 1813, he served against the United States as a lieutenant colonel of the 102nd Regiment. Encyclopaedia Britannica (1956), XVI, 75, supplies the essential bibliography.

[149] Thomas W. Wyman was made midshipman on December 17, 1810; lieutenant, April 27, 1816; commander, February 9, 1837; captain, November 2, 1842. He died on February 24, 1854.

Commodore Perry Meeting the Japanese Commissioners at Yokohama

The Conference Room at Hakodate, with Commodore Perry at the Left

accurate and reliable chart of the Harbor and its shores and neighborhood. Some coal mines having been discovered on the sea coast to the Eastward of the harbor, I extended my survey to include the cave and bay in front of them and so think I have greatly added to the value of my chart. One day last week I visited in company with Capt. Abbot several of the coal mines and crawled into one a hundred feet or more—sufficient to satisfy my curiosity. The coal appears to be of good quality and in abundance. The seams of it are three feet thick and are to be traced for miles. The Chinese do not understand the art of mineing it, and have only scratched out a little of the surface coal and that much broken up. The Northern end of Formosa seems to be well supplied with valuable products such as alum, sulphur, coal and iron. Alum and sulphur is found quite pure and in large masses, and the rocks so impregnated with iron, that my compasses would not travel when placed on them, but the needle would swing around and point along their axis.

In the outer harbor of Keelung, which I included in my survey after the discovery of the coal mines one of its projecting capes had such a remarkable resemblance to a human head that I made a hasty sketch of it and named it Sphinx Head. I might have called it with equal propriety John the Baptist head in a charger. The sketch is not in the least degree exaggerated, and the shading exactly as it appeared when I made the sketch. Hardly less remarkable was the profile face on a crag in the harbor of which I made the sketch on the opposite page.[150] This had a long flowing beard concealing his chin. Altogether the neighborhood is a series of geological wonders. While all of the Island of Formosa around Keelung is a sand stone, a small Island three miles distant is seinite of the hardest kind and evidently volcanic, with the remains of an ancient crater and any amount of volcanic debris.

One of the exciting events this week on board ship has been that Kitty has brought forth a litter of Kittens of which she is justly proud. What is perhaps worthy of note concerning them is that though the father (i.e. Com. Perry's Japanese cat) and the mother are both grey, one of the kittens is stump tailed and black and white.

[150] In the manuscript diary, p. 317, there is an ink sketch of the sphinx head.

At Sea, Sunday July 30, 1854

Another week has run its round and under the influence of the balmy air today I resume my diary. With the exception of one exciting day we have had a very quiet week and are now only about 4 to 500 miles from Manila.

July 23	Lat.	25.20 N	Long	121.43 E
24	"	25.50 "	"	120.50 "
25	"	25.34 "	"	120.42 "
26	"	23.14 "	"	118.50 "
27	"	21.42 "	"	119.27 "
28	"	21.14 "	"	118.51 "
29	"	20.28 "	"	117.36 "
30	"	20.04 "	"	118.49 "

On Wednesday the 26th our Barometer gave indications of a typhoon, and we had commenced reefing our topsails preparing for it, when a sailor fell from our fore topsail yard, struck on the fore chains splitting his head open, and fell into the sea sinking instantly. Our life bouy was cut adrift, and gratings were thrown overboard but he sunk never to rise again and the ship passed on. We were rushing on before the beginnings of a gale and under the circumstances it would have been madness to have lowered a boat and risked lives of her crew in a vain attempt to save the man. All this happened in less time than I have taken to narrate it and was as soon almost forgotten. I for one can not realize that our little community has been deprived of a life. The men went to their dinners and grog a few minutes later as usual, and the occurrence was scarcely a topic of conversation among them except in his own immediate mess.

I was in the cabin at the time at work upon my charts and saw the poor fellows cap float astern, on hearing the noise and rush on deck I looked out the cabin window.

The gale presently increased but the wind was fortunately fair, which enabled us to pursue our course to the Southth. By night we had passed the Southernmost of the Pescadore group in the Formosa channel. The greatest force of the storm according to our calculations passed to the Nth of us. We had however a rough and ugly night, and the weather continued unsettled through Thursday and

Friday, clearing up on Saturday with frequent and copious rain showers. Several sails have appeared in sight to cheer our passage but we have spoken nothing as yet. It is pleasant to have such evidence of our return to the bounds of civilization.

The *Supply* was to have left Keelung the day after we did, and we fear she may have met the gale farther North, and had a rougher experience of it. In the height of the gale on Wednesday we crossed the Formosa Banks, and obtained ten fathoms in our soundings coral bottom. These banks are too extensive to have been thoroughly surveyed and examined, and we felt every moment we were liable to strike on a shoal spot, which would have been instant annihilation to our vessel and crew, but we had to go ahead. I can assure [you] it was with a feeling of relief we found the water gradually deepening and we breathed freer when we struck the fathomless blue again. For three long hours we were kept in suspense.

Today has been delicious though we are making but poor progress towards Manila. The Chaplain is unwell and we have dispensed with the usual service. We have been today and yesterday passing through rapid tides and currents, which crossing the wind at times raise a rough and breaking sea resembling breakers or a shoal or reef. Yesterday in my watch I noticed a remarkable tide rise of this kind extending N. N. E. and S. S. W. as far as eye could reach and beyond. Half an hour later we passed into a surface of water as smooth as a mirror. My watch keeping and chart making has kept me constantly employed, I have no idle moments.

July 31, 1854, Lat. 19.11 Long. 118.08E.

At Sea to Manila,[151] Tuesday Augt 1, 1854
Lat. 18.09 Long. 118.56E.

This being our peculiar anniversary my dear Susie. I write to commemorate it not that much has happened. I opened my airport just now (6 P.M.) to freshen the air in my 6x6 state room and presently a wave came galloping in and deluged it and saturated everything. I shoved the port in again and seizing my tarpaulin and coat, went

[151] The *Macedonian* visited Manila in August, 1854. At a rope factory at Santa Mesa, two Americans had been murdered by the Spaniards. *Narrative*, I, 501; II, 143–49.

on deck to watch and found the rain pouring down in such torrents that southwesters and storm coats were of no avail to keep it out. It blew hard in squalls, the ship was struck aback. I tacked and wore the ship, reduced and made sail again and halloed myself hoarse until relieved and then came below dripping like a mermaid but not so fascinating. Below the atmosphere chilled in by the gratings and tarpaulins which have been flung over the hatches as in that stewed state, which all who go down to the sea in big ships can understand. All this with the ship's rollings, pitchings, groaning and contortions have conspired to render your birthday anything but a day of comfort. The squally rainy weather continues, and I have in anticipation the enjoyment of it on deck again in a few hours. I have been nearly all day 'plotting' in the cabin, not treason but on my charts.

At Sea, Sunday Augt 6, 1854, Lat. 16.17N: Long. 118.55E.

August	2	Lat.	18.13	N.	Long.	119.54 E.
"	3	"	18.01	"	"	118.48 E.
"	4	"	17.14	"	"	119.45 E.
"	5	"	16.28	"	"	119.36 E.

Last Sunday we were only about four hundred miles from our destination, and today after a week of hard work and tedious sailing we are nearly one hundred and fifty. Never have I experienced so tedious and perplexing a passage—a very rough sea, with heavy squalls of mingled wind and rain, with constant head winds and almost constant rain, with light breezes between squalls have accompanied us ever since Tuesday. On Wednesday as I was tacking the ship, another man fell overboard but luckily caught a rope astern, and was dragged on board more frightened than hurt. On Thursday, our pet goat, which was born on board the ship on the passage from Loo Choo to Japan died from the effects of the bad weather and worse diet. After his living six months upon salt junk, bean soup and rice, as unnatural food for him as was Nebucanezzar's, when he was turned out to pasture, we hoped to have kept him through the cruize and on a more natural diet. Alas poor goaty, his was a brief and troubled life. The squalls of wind have been at times very heavy, and have kept our sailmakers busy repairing the sails torn and rent by them. One of these squalls, more heavy than its brothers, nearly run us under, before we could get our sail in and keep her off before it.

The weather has been one continually source of anxiety, and we watch keepers are quite fagged out. We long to get to Manila and are even impatient to leave there in order to get our letters at Hong Kong. The rain has been incessant and down pouring for the last twenty-four hours, and I hear it now patter pattering on the tarpaulins overhead, and see riverlets of it crossing and recrossing our wardroom deck. Everything in and about my room is moldy and damp. Even Harry and Lily's dog daguerrotype has not escaped the insidious cryptogamic fog.

Manila, Sunday Augt. 13, 1854

Aug			Lat.	N.	Long.	
"	7	"	15.30	"	"	119.31 E.
"	8	"	15.08	"	"	119.20 E.
"	9	"	14.25	"	"	119.27 E.

The winds and weather continued to literally 'devil' us to the latest hour of our passage—as we anchored here on Thursday afternoon during one of the worst squalls we had had. I was releived from watch at noon, and saw it approaching and had prepared for it, and well that I did for in fifteen minutes it was over us, the wind howling fearfully and the rain descending in torrents—while it was so dark, that the sharpest vision could not pierce around us, over a few yards. Everything was clewed down and the sails furled until it cleared up, when we found ourselves quite close to the usual anchorage, and dropped our anchor. We find here four Am. ships which were boarded at once for the news.

On board the *Seaman's Bride*[152] of Baltimore I found Leonard Merrill of Portland, the 2d officer, and the *Winged Racer*[153] of Bos-

152 The *Seaman's Bride* was a California clipper built in Maine. Her captain was A. B. Wyman. *Greyhounds*, 445, 513.

153 The *Winged Racer*, a California clipper ship of 1,760 tons, was built in 1852 at Boston. Her captain was Samuel Easterbrook, whose successors were William Homan and Francis Gorham, and she was owned by R. L. Taylor of New York. She was destroyed off the coast of Java by the *Alabama* in 1863. *Clipper*, 216, 344, 355; *Greyhounds*, 485, 492.

ton was commanded by Fredric Gerham—Geo Colmans brother in law. From the *Racer* I obtained files of the *Portland Adv*[*ertiser*][154] and *Transcript*,[155] which were particularly refreshing to my news thirsty soul posting me as they have up to April.

The burning of the Custom House and loss of all the valuable collections of the Natural His. Society, were among the sad items of information. I shall send a box of rocks by the *Racer* for the New Collection, which I see is to be attempted and you may give them all the shells left in the closet.

I have just put up a box for you, and would have made it layer and more valuable had I not feared it would prevent its going duty free through the custom house. You will find in the box two Joss dresses with two scarfs to match two pieces of Japanese Silk and six pens Hdkfs and two cuffs (wrought) for yourself and Fannie, Lizzie, Mary E.P., Anna Boyd, Ellen and Adeline. I expect you will receive these things the last of December in acceptable time for New Years Presents. I expect to send you another package from Hong Kong. One of the Portland news papers reports that my letter from Loo Choo was charged with three dollars postage. I was glad to learn of its reception, but annoyed that the fact was published which I suppose may be attributed to some officious friend who saw it in the Post Office.

We have received a good deal of hospitality from the American residents of Manila during stay, and the weather has cleared up for our special benefit. It rained they tell for twenty days previous to our arrival and it has not rained since. Our arrival created quite a stir, the people thinking we brought news of a rupture between Spain and the U. S. and were the precursors of a squadron to take the place. Capt. Abbot and Avery dined with the Gov'r General today. Friday and Saturday I passed on shore shopping for myself and messmates.

154 The *Portland Advertiser*, a weekly, 1830–1903; title varies slightly: *Portland Advertiser and Gazette of Maine*, *Portland Weekly Advertiser and Star*, etc. There was also a daily *Portland Advertiser*, with varied title, 1831–1909. Winifred Gregory, *American Newspapers*, 1821–1936, 253.

155 The *Portland Transcript*, a weekly, 1837–1910, changed its name to *Portland Transcript* and *The Northern Pioneer*. *Ibid.*, 255.

I send you some of the fruits, reserving to myself a pair of shoulder straps and a thousand Manila segars at eight dollars a thousand. We expect to sail on Thursday the 17th and hope to reach Hong Kong to send our letters by the mail of the 22d. I have had several invitations to dine with the Merchant Princes on shore but have declined them all it so much cooler and quieter on board.

At Sea, Sunday August 20, 1854

We sailed from Manila Thursday noon as anticipated and are now two hundred miles nearer Hong Kong, which is but slow progress to our impatient hopes and longings. I forwarded by the *Winged Racer* a box of rocks for the Nat. His. Soc. addressed to Dr. Wood. While at Manila we exchanged the usual salutes with the city and saluted our Consul on his visiting the ship. Our Gunner named Hamilton Bell, a smart but worthless officer deserted the ship. We did try very hard to find him.

At Sea, Friday August 25, 1854

This is our Friday, our Good Friday, I mean, and therefore to be remembered. It is thirteen years ago today since we first Thee'd and Thou'd each other.

Hong Kong, Sunday August 27, 1854

From Manila to Hong Kong

Lat.	14.23	N.	Long.	120.04	E.
"	14.29	"	"	119.07	"
"	14.32	"	"	117.38	"
"	14.36	"	"	117.10	"
"	15.06	"	"	116.57	"
"	17.11	"	"	115.57	"
"	19.23	"	"	115.11	"
"	20.27	"	"	114.40	"
"	21.50	"	"	114.12	"

We anchored this morning at three o'clock, and at eight read our newspapers, and letters. I have seventeen packages of letters from you and Ellen the latest date being the 1st of June. I have been reading all day when not interrupted, beginning with latest, and have not yet got half through having read back only to March. The daguerreotype came to hand and I am glad to have it, though I consider the likeness of yourself and Adeline execrable. Ellen is better though she looks as tho' she was holding her mouth up to be kissed. Little Lizzie's and Fanny's are capital. Henry's all but the eyes, and a slight movement. Lily's is also good. When I look at it I want to ask you, "Who are you looking at?" and what made you stare so? The artist must have told you to look at a fixed point, and my wonder is you did not look it down.

We have had a continual flood of visitors today from our Squadron and the North Pacific Surveying Sqdr. which is in port, besides gentlemen from shore, Chinese, compradores, and trades people of all sorts. Among my visitors has been Mr. E. E. Upham of Portland[156] as large as life and twice as natural, with his rosy cheeks and 'shining morning face.' He is here as the nominal captain of a ship which he purchased in Califorina. He has an old salt for a mate to wet nurse him. From him I get considerable Portland news which he obtains from his correspondent Mrs. Little.[157] I gave him the paper containing Lord Elgin's reception which was later than his news. Had he arrived in China two months earlier he could have sold his ship at many thousands of dollars profit. He has still a prospect of doing well though the rebellion has stopped trade very considerably. Upham intends returning to China with a load of Chinese passangers.

U.S. Chartered Steamer *Queen*,[158]
Canton, Friday Sept. 1, 1854

This is our dear little Lily's birthday and I must write a word or

[156] The adventurous Mr. E. E. Upham from Portland is unknown, but there was in Portland the Upham family, to which the Reverend Charles W. Upham belonged. As a minister, he married Eben Preble (brother of G. H. Preble) to Miss Agnes Deborah Taylor Archer. *Sketch*, 197. Captain Upham seems to be closely related to Preble.

[157] It is difficult or even impossible to trace Mrs. Little. There were several ladies of the same name in Portland. She could well be the wife of Captain Robert E. Little master of the California clipper *Ino. Greyhounds*, 416.

[158] At the request of American merchants in Canton, who were alarmed by the Taiping Rebellion, Commodore Perry sent the *Mississippi* to Whampoa, near Can

two of remembrance though even so much hurried worried and perplexed with new and important duties. Truly no man knowth what a day or an hour may bring forth. I had not thought when writing you on Sunday evening that within twenty four hours I would be embarked on board the Str. *John Hancock,*[159] with a detachment of sailors and marines, and on my way to Canton to assume command of this vessel, and hear myself constantly called 'Capt Preble' which seems odd after being Mister so long. I feel very much like a football, kicked about without much rest between contending duties.

After a mid-watch on deck during which I managed to glance through some of your letters by the "lanterns dimly burning," I was called up and into the cabin at daylight, by Capt. Abbott and informed that I was appointed to the command of this little steamer, and must be ready with 40 sailors and 14 marines to take passage in the *J. H.* at 7 o'clock Tuesday morning. Monday was a busy day packing up my own traps, and getting my men ready with their arms and clothings. I received numerous packages of magazines and newspapers, which I have not been able to open, and a dozen of your earliest letters are still waiting to have their seals broken. The later letters have satisfied me of your health and of those nearest and dearest and I can afford to wait more leasure time for the perusal of the others.

One of your letters informs me of the death of Cousin Harriet Preble, after I had read it I opened one from her dated in December. It was like one speaking from the dead. I also read that good and kind Mr. Barbour[160] has gone to his happiness; it would be folly to mourn the death of such a man, descending to the grave full of years of usefulness.

ton, to protect American residents and to guard against pirates. Later, when the *Supply* arrived from Amoy, she anchored opposite the city of Canton. Before leaving the Chinese coast on January 14, 1854, Perry chartered the steamboat *Queen* and put her under the command of Preble. *Narrative,* I, 287–88, 302.

[159] The *John Hancock* must have been a local steamer serving Americans in Canton and other Chinese ports. She is not indicated in the published lists of American ships.

[160] Joseph Barbour of Gorham was married to Agnes Deborah, the widow of Eben Preble, elder brother of G. H. Preble. He died in June, 1854, at age seventy-seven. *Sketch,* 197.

I embarked on board the *Hancock* as ordered Tuesday morning but oweing to some breakage or defect in her machinery we did not reach Canton until Wednesday. The whole of that day was employed in making the necessary transfers, and in releiving Liut. Alfred Taylor [161] of his command. He and his crew going back to Hong Kong in the *Hancock*. In the midst of our exchange of command a fire broke out on shore, which has since been ascertained was the work of an incendiary. This caused us to get up steam on board the *Queen*, and prepare to land the men in case of necessity; it was feared advantage would be taken of the confusion for a general outbreak and pillage. The next morning six of the incendiary's were beheaded. The *Hancock* remained all night at the request of our Consul, but the fires went down soon after dark.

The rebel forces are just outside the city beseiging it and yesterday several skirmishes with the Imperial troops were witnessed from the roofs of the foreign Hongs. Three wounded men were brought to Doctor Parker's Hospital and attended to. I called on Doctor P. last evening who showed me one of the balls. It was a cast iron ball an inch in diameter and taken from the man's neck yet the doctor says he will recover. I am now alone in my command the only officer associated with me is an Engineer named Stamen. Mr. Watters was detached yesterday and ordered to the *Macedonian* as her master. Walcott being made an Adj Lieut. My duties of course are increased but, I am gradually getting things in the right way and expect to have more leasure than I want before long. My crew consists of twenty-seven men a part of whom are Chinese. The *Queen* is a steamer of 137 tons chartered by Com[dre] Perry for the protection of our country men at Canton, during the Sq'dns absence in Japan,

161 Lieutenant Alfred Taylor (1810–1891) of the *Mississippi* was commissioned commodore on September 27, 1866. Born in Virginia on May 23, 1810, he was appointed midshipman on January 1, 1825; served on several ships; promoted to passed midshipman, June 4, 1831; served in the navy yards at Portsmouth and Boston, 1833–34; commissioned lieutenant, February 9, 1837. Distinguished for his duty on several ships, he was attached to the steam sloop *Mississippi*, East India Squadron, 1853–55; promoted to commander, September 14, 1855; captain, September 16, 1862; commodore, September 27, 1866; lighthouse inspector, 1868–70. *Records*, 51. Rear admiral, January 29, 1872; retired list, May 23, 1872; died, April 19, 1891. *Narrative*, II, 413; *NCAB*, IV, 220–21.

for seven hundred and fifty dollars a month. She has a battery of four iron four pounders, and I have a brass boat gun 12 pds, on a field carriage on shore and any number of muskets pistols cutlasses and boarding pikes. More than we have men to use them. My apartments are so spacious I almost feel lost in them. The *Queen* was built for a passenger boat at Hong Kong last spring, and therefore new. I have four berths or sitties in the after cabin and eight in the forward cabin, seven of which I am at liberty to use. As this command increases my pay per month twenty-five dollars, I am glad to have it, but have no idea how long it will last. I hope until the *M*[*acedonian*] is ordered home.

Do you remember how desirous I was to get attached to the Ringold Exp'dn?[162] It is man who proposes but God disposes. I now consider it fortunate my wishes were not gratified. There has been a good deal of trouble in that squadron, and now Comdre Ringold has been sent home insane and Lieut John Rodgers[163] has command of it. From wanting a proper head, its usefulness has been impaired and the Expedition came very nigh being broken up in a general row. I have been very much gratified to learn that in reorganizing the Expedition Rodgers desired to give me the command of one of the vessels as second in rank in the Expedition, and that he delayed

162 Cadwalader Ringgold (1802–1867), a distinguished navy officer, became midshipman on March 4, 1819; lieutenant, May 17, 1828; commander, July 16, 1849; reserved list, September 13, 1855; captain, active list, April 2, 1856; commodore, July 16, 1862; rear admiral, retired list, July 25, 1866; died, April 29, 1867. He participated in several expeditions and is especially noted for his part in the Wilkes exploring expedition, 1838–42, as master of the *Porpoise*. On his expedition to the North Pacific in 1853–54, he charted for the first time numerous Pacific shoals and islands. He reached China in March, 1854, and stayed there to protect the Taiping disturbances. He became sick and by decision of Commodore Perry was sent home as insane on September 4, 1854, aboard the *Susquehanna*. Commander John Rodgers took over the expedition by Perry's order. Ringgold later regained his health. A. B. Cole, *Yankee Surveyors in the Shogun's Seas*, 5–9; *DAB*, XV, 617–18; *List*, 463.

163 John Rodgers, who took over Ringgold's surveying expedition to the North Pacific when Ringgold was declared insane, was made midshipman on April 18, 1828; passed midshipman, June 14, 1834; lieutenant, January 28, 1840; commander, September 14, 1855; captain, July 16, 1862; commodore, June 17, 1863; rear-admiral, December 31, 1869. He died on May 5, 1882. See Cole, *op. cit.*, 23–27.

his arrangements, until he could delay no longer, waiting the arrival of the *Macedonian* to tender to me the appointment; probably his and my disappointment will all turn out for the best.

You know again my offer to accompany Gov. Stevens across the Rocky Mtns, and my receipt of his acceptance of my offer at Loo Choo when it was too late. I see now that his party endured great hardships, and that one detachment of it is supposed to have perished in the snows or been murdered by the Indians. It is therefore wise I war prevented joining him. I am having your daguerreotype with Henry on your lap copied in oil. I went to the painter today to see it and think he is making a good picture, a fair specimen of what may be called Chinese high art. Whatever may be thought of the likeness. He had your hair painted 'yellow' but I made him alter that.

Canton, Thursday Sept. 7, 1854

Your portrait was hung up in my Cabin today where I can look at it when I first open my eyes in the morning and when asked who it is I tell them it is My Queen. I have had a picture of the steamer painted which I will send you—the long cabin, with the six windows is all my own. The two after windows separates my bedroom from my drawing room and dining hall, and aft of those again are roomy, bath and washrooms and a water closet. I have orders to go down to Whampoa tomorrow, and bring our Commissioner the Hon. Louis McLane up. The mail will leave Hong Kong on the 11th and here tomorrow so I must hurry my letters to a conclusion. Won't you be glad to have them. I have written Adeline, Ellen and Mr. Cox,[164] a labor I hope they will appreciate.

On Sunday the Rev. Mr. Preston[165] performed divine service on board the *Queen*, and on Monday a Master's mate Mr. J. P. Williams[166] came up from the *Macedonian* and reported to me for duty.

[164] John Cox was born February 13, 1795; married (first time) Thankful Harris Gore, November 4, 1817, who died July 11, 1833; married (second time) Adeline Preble, November 4, 1835, who was living at Portland in 1870. *Sketch*, 242.

[165] The Reverend C. F. Preston was sent to Canton in 1854 by the American Presbyterian Board. William Dean, *The China Mission*, 163.

[166] According to the *Narrative*, II, 414, John Williams was "Rated Acting Master's Mate" on the *Powhatan*. He is not indicated by Preble in the list of the crew of the *Macedonian*.

The picture on the opposing page[167] is an engraving on wood copied from the Chinese drawing sent, and published in *Ballans Pictorial,*[168] May 9, 1857. The steamer in the fore ground is the *Queen.* The group of buildings on the left embraces the Danish Hong and the new French Hong, at the foot of old China street. Here too are the Club House, Boat House, Masonic Lodge and Canton Library rooms, and directly over it indicated by his flag the residence of Doct. Peter Parker.

Commenceing with the smoke stack of the steamer, and numbering to the right an American Hong was occupied by King & Co.,[169] in its rear Dent & Co.,[170] which is a magnificent and extensive Hong. Then comes Powshon Hong occupied by English merchants, Imperial Hong by Wetmore & Co., Americans; Swedish Hong by Russell & Co., Americans; and Chow Chow Hong, occupied by Parsees.

The Episcopal Church forms the boundary between the English and American gardens. All to the right of the picture was destroyed by fire some years since then known as the English factories, and has since been rebuilt. The space alloted to the Factories consists of a strip of land reclaimed from the river, in front of each is displayed the national flag. There are 13 Hongs, including English, American, Dutch, French, Austrian, Parsees, each consisting of four or five houses ranged around closed courts one behind the other. The English Hong far surpasses the others in elegance and extent. These buildings front the South are built upon a flat raised on piles and seperated from the river by a Quay called "Resplendentia Walk." There are stairs where merchandise is shipped and immense native boats are all about.

167 On p. 332 of the diary is pasted an illustration showing the steamer *Queen* in the harbor of Canton.

168 *Ballon's Pictorial Drawing Room Companion,* Nos. 7–17 (1854–59), was the new title of *Gleason's Pictorial Drawing Room Companion,* Nos. 1–6 (1851–54). See *British Union-Catalogue of Periodicals,* I, 282; II, 305.

169 King and Company, an American firm trading in tea and general merchandise, had branches in Canton, Foochow, and Shanghai. It employed three partners: Fred King, David O. King, and William Henry King. See note 107 under the year 1855 and Griffin, *op. cit.,* 143.

170 Dent and Company was a very active British firm in Shanghai and Yokohama. Griffin, *op. cit.,* 322. Fairbank, *op. cit.,* I, 62, 66ff.

Canton, Wednesday September 13, 1854

On Friday morning the 8th I got underway at daylight and went as far as Whampoa where I received on board from the *Powhatan* the Hon. R. M. McLane and suite. Capt McCluney[171] of the *P.*, Mrs. Spooner wife of our Consul at Canton,[172] D. N. S[pooner], Mrs. Hunter,[173] besides half a score of the Officers of the *Powhatan*, and got underway again for Canton where I anchored about 2 P.M. After seeing the vessel secured I went on shore and dined at the Consuls, who entertained the whole party. The evening was agreeably passed in the society of the ladies. Saturday (9th) I was very much occupied shopping for myself and others. Sunday (10th) I had engaged to dine with Capt Abel Fellows on board H.B.M.S. *Comus*,[174] but very unexpectedly while the Rev. Mr. Cox[175] was engaged in Divine Service on board I received a request (order) from Mr. McLane to take Capt. McCluney down to the *Powhatan*, to

[171] William J. McCluney was captain of the *Powhatan* during Perry's expedition. He was made midshipman on January 1, 1812; lieutenant, April 1, 1818; commander, December 9, 1839; captain, October 13, 1851; retired list, December 21, 1861; commodore, retired list, July 16, 1862. He died on February 11, 1864.

[172] D. N. Spooner, the American vice-consul in Canton in 1853–54, was a partner in Russell and Company. Griffin, *op. cit.*, 306, 360.

[173] Mrs. Hunter was the wife of a prominent American merchant and sociologist, William C. Hunter (1812–1891). Her husband was taught Chinese by the distinguished English scholar Robert Morrison, a Protestant missionary. In 1829, Hunter joined the American firm Russell and Company in Canton, where he befriended Robert B. Forbes, director of the company. He is the author of several books and articles about China, especially *The Fan Kwae at Canton Before Treaty Days, 1825–1844* and *Bits of Old China* (London, 1882 and 1885), important for the study of early American intercourse with Canton and China. *DAB*, IX, 408, with bibliography.

[174] The *Comus* was a British vessel stationed with the Hong Kong Squadron. She was under Captain Abel Fellowes-Glisson. See Preble's note in the diary, October 29, 1854.

[175] Josiah Cox, an Englishman, was the founder of the Wesleyan mission in Hankow. He was sent to China in 1853 by the Wesleyan Missionary Society of England. Cf. Latourette, *The Great Century in Northern Africa and Asia*, 310, 325. For more detailed information on the work of the Wesleyans in China, see G. G. Findlay and W. W. Holdsworth, *The History of the Wesleyan Methodist Missionary Society*, V.

make arrangements for going to Macao tomorrow, without detention at Whampoa. While at Whampoa I run alongside of the *Powhatan* and filled up my coal[176] bunkers from hers, exchanged a portion of my crew and returned to my anchorage off the Factorys at Canton about 9 P.M. Rather a busy Sunday. I had passangers both ways to entertain and after my return went on shore to explain to Mr. McLane the arrangements that had been made for tomorrow.

The next morning Monday 11th I read your letter of June 19–24th and a newspaper of July 1st per overland mail. The lock of Lily's hair comes very opportunily to enable the painter copying her daguerrotype to give the true color to his painting. After recieving my letters I got the *Queen* underway about half past ten A.M. and conveyed the Hon. Mr. McLane, the Spooners, Hunters and others[177] to the *Powhatan* at Whampoa and returned anchoring at Canton between 1 and 2 P.M. I also put on board the *Shooting Star*[178] a box for Susie containing silks and gauzes. If Lily is as honest and stubbornly straight as her hair, she is bound to make her way in the world. Her childlike sayings sent me are very amusing but I heard a good one of a child here the other day that is worth repeating. Like all children her awakened sense had been pondering over the power of God, etc., and said to her father 'Can God do anything?' Yes my child was his answer. Well then said the youthful philosopher I should like to see him make a stick with only one end to it. That child was told to hush and sent to bed instantly. It was the young ones version of the impossibility of there being two mountains without a valley between them.

176 Between pp. 333 and 334 of the diary is inserted a color lithograph representing the fish market at Canton.

177 American social life at Canton was intensively pursued by merchants, missionaries, sea captains, and visitors. Eldon Griffin, author of *Clippers and Consuls*, has observed that the American families represented by firms in Canton and other ports of China were so interlocked in their personal, social, and commercial relations that it would require arduous study to establish their biographies. Griffin, *op. cit.*, 243, n.11.

178 The first *Shooting Star* was a tea clipper of 903 tons. She was built in 1851, owned by the Reed, Wade and Reed Company of Boston, and sold to Siam in 1856. Her captain was Judah P. Baker. *Greyhounds*, 161, 179, 417.

As Doct and Mrs Parker had left Canton a day or two previous for Macao my passangers down comprised all of the gentle sex belonging to the European and American population left there.

The gauze dresses in the box per *Shooting Star* are for Adeline,[179] Ellin,[180] our Fanny,[181] and Lizzie Preble.[182] The Shanghai silks you will find useful, and the Japanese will make Henry durable summer clothing. The straw slippers are for your father, and are capital and easy for home service. The little baskets were put in to fill up the box: one for Mrs. Thomas's[183] little girl, one for Lily, and one for little Lizzie. I have, I believe, remembered all the feminine in this package and that sent by the *Winged Racer* excepting Julia and Ellen Rodgers. As Lizzie is in mourning, perhaps you may think best to give the dress for her to Julia, and Ellen R. can be thought of another time. I have ordered a dozen famous kites for Henry.

It seems probable now that I may retain the command of this steamer three or four months. The longer the better as it increases my pay twenty-five dollars a month and there is a feeling of independence in being Capt. of ones own ship.

Commodore Perry left Hong Kong in the mail steamer to return home by the overland route, and his favorite ship the *Mississippi* sailed the same day for the Sandwich Islands and home via Cape Horn; she will be the first U. S. Steamer of War to pass from the Pacific into the Atlantic and the first to circumnavigate the globe. Capt. Abbot or rather Commodore Abbot now commands the U.S. Squadron in the East Indian and China Seas, and the Japan Expedition is dissolved. Mr. McLane has had the *Powhatan* at his entire disposal and goes in her to Shanghai next week. Our squadron

179 See note 74 above.

180 Perhaps she was Ellen Bangs Preble (1808–1867), sister of G. H. Preble. She died unmarried at her brother's residence in Charlestown, Massachusetts, and is buried in Portland, Maine, Evergreen Cemetery at Westbrook. *Sketch,* 199.

181 Fanny Preble, nee Getchell, was the wife of Ebenezer Preble, grandson of John Preble of Machias.

182 Lizzie Preble was probably Lucy (Elizabeth) Preble, tenth child of John Preble and Sarah Frost. She was born on November 15, 1828. *Sketch,* 142.

183 The Prebles maintained friendly relations with William W. Thomas, who had a business in Exchange Street, Portland, from which he was bought out by Eben Preble, elder brother of G. H. Preble. *Sketch,* 197.

proper therefore is reduced to the *Macedonian*, *Vandalia*, and this little chartered steamer.

The Exploring squadron remains at Hong Kong at sixes and sevens, and I esteem it fortunate that I was not ordered to it.

Sunday September 17, 1854

We have been quietly at anchor since I last wrote. The rebels defeated in numerous skirmishes have been driven back to Fatshan, a city ten or twelve miles dist. Thursday last I attended a theatrical performance on board H.B.M.S. *Comus*, and had a 'Codfish' dinner with Goodridge at Wetmores. After the theatrical performance I had to punish two of my men for drunkeness by the liquor embibed by them on board the English ship. One of the sailors of the *Comus* personated a female character excellently well.

Friday I dined at Mr. Nyes[184] at 7½ P.M, what you will think a fashionable hour, I fortified myself with a substantial 'tiffin' at 3 oclock. Dr. Woodworth of the *Macedonian* came up to stay with me.

Yesterday was rainy and I dined at home. Today I have been partaking of the hospitality of Mr. Hunter with a small and agreeable party. Among the table delicacies was a shark's fins and beake de la mar stew. Pineapples from Calcutta, Mangos and Mango tarts, the fruit from Calcutta, and English Yarmouth bloaters. In the forenoon attended Divine Service on board the *J. P. Kennedy*.[185] Tomorrow there is to be a grand concert given by some French people tickets 3$ to which I have subscribed. As the paper was passed around at Mr. Nye's table I could not well help it. Yesterday was a wet and rainy day and today in contrast is delightfully clear and pleasant. The warm weather makes me idle and listless. Talking today with Old Loeque and suggesting some alterations in the picture he is painting for me he says "I painting-too-muchee."

[184] The brothers Parkin and Gideon Nye operated one of the important early American firms in Canton and Shanghai. They traded in tea, opium, camphor, and shipping. The persons mentioned by Preble in the diary as Mr. Nye or Mrs. Nye are impossible to identify, since he did not indicate the first names of the Nyes. Griffn, *op. cit.*, 243–44, 362.

[185] The U.S.S. *John P. Kennedy* was a vessel of 350 tons, three guns. She was purchased in 1853 and sold in 1856.

Thursday Sept. 21, 1854

Monday 18th dined on board and worked on my chart of Keelung all day. It was a pleasant day Tuesday began pleasant and ended in heavy rainy squally weather. I dined with Capt. Gardner of the Comet[186] just arrived at Mr. Nyes. Wednesday was a very dark gloomy rainy day brightened by the unexpected arrival of the 'over land' with our letters and Master Harry's first effort in drawing for Papa. Thank our darling for his little remembrance. You over estimate the interest of my letters. No doubt they are all you say and think to you but judged by a critical world my description would be consigned to the trunk maker. I have none of the vanity of authorship yet if I thought 'that book' you so much desire I would write would sell. I would brave the critics for the sake of the pennies and to pay off those 'old debts' which are your trouble as well as mine. Your letters tell me of weddings and funerals both equally happy and natural occurances. The happiness from the first is always presupposed and that of the last great change is always hoped. I was surprised to learn the death of Miss Susan Boyd.[187] To the young bride the death of dear 'Aunt Susan'[188] who had been both mother and aunt must have been a loss indeed. Sara Dana's death was another surprise and I thought of Sue Gore deprived of so valued a friend. Capt. Hood's[189] and his daughters wedding afforded me equal surprise.

Sunday September 24, 1854

We have had a week of dull rainy weather and the sky remains overcast. We find thick clothing not uncomfortable. Rev. Mr. Beach performed Divine Services on board the *Queen* today taking

186 The *Comet*, a tea clipper of 1,836 tons, was built in 1850. Her captain was E. C. Gardiner. She was burned in 1865. *Greyhounds*, 294–95, 415; *Clipper*, 208.

187 Contemporary with G. H. Preble in Portland was the Boyd family, with whom, apparently, the Prebles were very friendly. See note 112 under the year 1853.

188 She might have been Sarah Gore, daughter of Jeremiah Gore and Thankful Harris and aunt of Mrs. G. H. Preble. Her name is abbreviated and could not be identified with certainty in the *Sketch*, 245.

189 Captain James M. Hood of Somerset, Massachusetts, has built two clipper ships, the *Raven* and the *Rip Van Winkle*, and a bark, the *Rosario*. *Greyhounds*, 161, 413, 416, 417; *Clipper*, 136, 152, 349, 356.

his text from *Romans* v.1st.[190] Therefore being justified by faith, we have peace with God through our Lord Jesus Christ . . . a sermon wholly lost upon poor Jack, who understands better the working of the main top bowline than Justification by faith. There was heavy firing between the rebels and imperialists all night and during the day. I have been writing letters in preparation for the mail tomorrow. The daguerrotype of the family which you sent me I am having copied on ivory by old Loegua.[191] I called on the painter today. He has the dresses painted but the faces of all but Fannie and Lizzie are yet blank. Ellen and Adeline have on a black silk, you a liliac dress, Fanny a light blue, Lizzies white, and Henry has on a plaid Jacket. I hope the painter will be able to secure a good likeness of all, as he says he can. He says "All-ah too much smallo-makee very much trouble pidgeon by-by, many tim tryee makee allo proper—can secure much fino—can secure too much handsome thing number one likeness—you see—you sabee I speakee you very true."

There is little or no business doing here now in consequence of the disturbances in the interior, and the ships that arrive are sent away empty to Manila or Shanghai to load. Not a single cargo of black tea has come down, the chop boats are kept back by the rebellion. The *Queen* has been rechartered and I expect to retain my command for some months. I have not seen Mr. Upham but once, but his ships, the *Alfred* and the *Leonore* are advertised to take Chinese passengers to California. Capt Abbot writes me he will come up with the *Macedonian* from Hong Kong to Whampoa next week. Last night there was much firing in the direction of Whampoa, but as usual in Chinese fighting there was more noise than danger. The rebellion is likely to be as interminable as the wars of the Roses. You mention Uncle Harrod's[192] failure prevents his going to Europe with Mr. Bartlett, is it his failure of health or business?

[190] The Reverend W. R. Beach was sent to Canton by the Wesleyan Missionary Society. He retired in 1856. See Dean, *op. cit.*, 163.

[191] There was a Chinese artist by the name of Loequa or Lam-qua(?), fl. 1850, who painted, in Western style, portraits for foreign visitors in Canton. Two of these are reproduced in Orange, *op. cit.*, sec. VI, Nos. 54 and 55.

[192] Deacon Joseph Harrod married Eliza (1788–1843), daughter of Josiah Cox and aunt of Mrs. G. H. Preble. Hence, he is Preble's uncle. *Sketch*, 241. His daughter was married to a Mr. Bartlett; he later stayed with her in New York.

Every day I see something I covet, money burns in my pocket. Had I a thousand dollars I could dispose of them very satisfactorily to myself in 'cumshaws' for the absent ones.

I saw a novel sight on the river this morning. Hearing a great hulla ballo, I looked out, and about one hundred yards off, saw a boat draped with matting and decorated with lanterns ornamented with Chinese characters painted in black. On the forward part of the little craft half a dozen women were assembled clothed in white, with a piece of white muslin covering their faces, and sack cloth on their heads. They were wailing bitterly, clapping their hands, and bowing down their heads to the dust. A dead body was inside, and under the matted canopy. After wailing an hour or more I saw them whip off their mourning and with it their scornful crys and sad faces, and sit quietly down to their chow-chow chatting and laughing as usual.

Good night dearest.

A voice is wafted towards me
  My name it seems to speak,
I feel a pressure on my hand,
  A kiss upon my cheek,
I know whose is the pressure
  And whose the thrilling tone,
And though my eyes discern you not,
  I know I am not alone.

Canton, Sunday October 1, 1854

My letters and home dispatches were sent by the overland on Monday, and the week has been an eventful and exciting one, as well as pleasant. Tuesday a New York gentleman Mr. J. C. Oliver of New York came on board with a letter from Purser Allison introducing him[self] and recommending himself, his wife and little daughter eight years old to my attention and hospitality. As 'Acows' the only hotel for strangers which Canton boasts is no fit place for a lady, and they knew no one at Canton, I could not do less than place my cabin at their disposal. They very gladly accepted my offer and remained until Friday morning when they left for Hong Kong. It put me to considerable inconvenience but I was repaid by the pleas ure of their company. Mrs. O. being a very agreeable and ladylike person of about five and twenty years of age and the little girl a well behaved chatterbox.

They live when at home in 14th St. just out of Fifth Avenue New York, and judging by their manner of spending money are wealthy. He has told me of a ship which he owns besides his Brown stone front in 14th St., and mentioned making $86.000 in California where he has resided five years during two of which Mrs. O. was his companion. She has been a traveller too, and has visited Texas, Nebraska, several of the W[est] India Islds, has crossed the Isthmus of Panama three times, and came here from California via Callao and the Sandwich Islands, and are now bound home by the overland route. In the afternoon under the guidance of Mr. Bonney[193] the Am. Missionary I accompanied him to Honan to see its famous temple, and walked all over it. We drank tea with the Chief Abbot, and witnessed another priest soothing himself with a pipe of opium. Returning from our interesting visit, we had a call from Mr. and Mrs Kean both missionaries who live about a mile down the river near Dutch folly. Mrs. K. is now the only lady residing in Canton; she is a pretty quiet little woman of 23 or 4 years of age, deffident before strangers, and not accustomed enough to the ways of the great outside world to be at ease in Society. She arrived in China last May and must be weary of her solitary and isolated life down the stream.[194]

Wednesday our indefatigable Mr. Bonney came on board at daylight to invite Mr. Oliver and myself to go down stream about two miles in his boat and walk back with him through the suburbs, and under the walls of the city. He said regulating the direction up or down river according to the tide he took such a walk every morning distributing Testaments or portions of the same in the Chinese language to everyone he thought would or could read them. Before giving a full Testament he tested the applicant's scholarship, by caus-

[193] The Reverend S. W. Bonney, a missionary, was sent to China by the American Board of Commissioners in 1845. He worked in Canton and Whampoa. See Dean, *op. cit.*, 162.

[194] The names of Mr. and Mrs. Kean are not indicated in examined sources on China missions. They seem to be known to the Prebles and perhaps were from Portland.

ing him or her to read a few lines of the most compound and difficult of the hieroglyphics. Mr. B. is a fast walker, and I think from our pace, and number of corners we turned we must have walked six miles before returning at half past nine to the *Queen* for breakfast.

Mr. B. distributed about two hundred small portions of the New Testament of 'leaves of grace' and half a dozen complete Testaments with fifty or sixty Christian Almanacs all in Chinese. It was interesting to see how the Chinese crowded after him, catching at his coat to detain him and obtain the much coveted book. On our walk we examined a large Chinese House, now rented by a Missionary, and passed through the Execution square where this year over two thousand people have been beheaded. This execution ground is an open muddy space four hundred feet long by thirty broad, enclosed on one side by a high wall, and on all the others by shops and manufactories of earthen ware. During the last two months in consequence of the troubles all the executions have taken place within the walled city. This ground being outside. Next the high wall I have mentioned and near about the centre of the square there was a pile of dark hair and Chinese tails, which with the blood stains spattered on the wall was all to identify it as an execution place.

There was also three or four moveable wooden crosses to fasten criminals upon to be chopped to pieces when condemned for heinous crimes. The last person so executed was a woman, who had poisoned both her husband and father. She was cut up according to rule in twenty-five parts. The first and second cuts took off the eyebrows and this butchering was continued by cutting off the breasts, feet, legs, hands, arms, etc, until the vital parts were reached—and then the head was cut off from the mutilated trunk. The forenoon of Wednesday I assisted the Olivers with their shopping; and taking an early dinner at Mr. Bonney accompanying us, we all went up the river to Hawgua's garden, and beyond it to an artificial duck hatching establishment where the little girl was made perfectly happy with the present of a duckling hatched while we were looking on or as her father expressed it "made to order." It is now on board my sampan (the name by which the native boat attending the ship is called) and thriving finely.

It was a curious establishment, and I desired to go up again the next afternoon when we were told over thousand of these born orphans, were expected to break through their shells.

We wandered about Howquas extensive and curious gardens until almost Sundown and then returned tired to the ship with our pleasant experiences.

Thursday Mr. Bonney was again on hand at daylight and Mr. Oliver, and Mr. Stamm[195] our engineer, and myself went up stream, with him, and had another six mile walk back, seeing an entirely different quarter of the suburbs. We examined a large tea packing house, a Chinese tobacco manufactory, a glass blowing establishment, a grist mill and a Fort, and refreshed ourselves in a Chinese eating and tea house. We also examined the residence of Howqua the rich merchant, where it is usual for all the Foreign Ambassadors to be officially received. It would be impossible to describe in a letter all we saw in this walk throughout which Mr. B. was scattering his Gospel 'leaves' as before.

After breakfasting we did some shopping and Mr. Bonney took my guests to Pontinqua's gardens, while I went and dined with Mr. H. W. Hubbell on shore. In the evening a party of gentlemen came on board to call on Mrs. Oliver and all night long we had a lively time with the musquitos.

Friday morning Mr. B. was ready for another excursion but the Olivers were preparing for their departure and left by the Hong Kong boat at 8 AM. After seeing them off I went shopping and bought you a crimson crape shawl for which I paid twenty five dollars. I think it will suit your taste. Crimson shawls on age of the dye cost about four dollars more than white ones. The body of your shawl is 7/4 square and the fringe is sixteen inches long. It is richly worked in the four corners and has a small plain spot in the center, where it folds around the neck. The very best and heaviest shawl made here, if white is sold for forty eight dollars, and if crimson not over sixty. The most valuable I have seen was a crimson one for forty eight dollars. Your shawl weighs two and three quarter pounds, and will be as much weight as you will care to carry on your

[195] William S. Stamm was made third assistant engineer on February 26, 1851; second assistant engineer, May 21, 1853; first assistant engineer, May 9, 1857; chief engineer, July 29, 1861; retired list, December 1, 1887; died, June 27, 1897.

back. Last year one of our merchants informs me 260,000 shawls were imported into the U. S. from China, and the year before 380,-000. This year the import to the U. S. will exceed 300,000. The average cost of these shawls however is only five dollars. I have ordered a Mazarin blue camblet silk twilled[196] for which I pay 7.60 cts for 12 yds and four sarsanet[197] silk dresses two of 12 yds and two of 18 yds each at 33 cts a yard. The silk is 23 inches wide. The two last are made to order. A cargo of these silks has just been sent to N. Y. so I am sure they are of a style that will be worn. Counting up yesterday, I find I have already sent you 234 yards of silk and silk gauze, costing only about 41 dollars. You can open a dry goods establishment Returning from my shopping after dining, hearing a good many big guns fireing in the rear of the city, I went on shore again, and mounted one of the bamboo lookouts to see the fun and fighting, but could only see the smoke of the battle and fire balls and rockets. Finishing the day by teaing at Russell & Co's.

Saturday after a long sleep and late breakfast strolled through the back streets of Canton and purchased a beautiful stone card receiver for 2$, an astonishing amount of work for a very little money. The stone is a carved representation of a melon, surrounded by leaves and bugs, and is set in a wooden stand carved to represent the lotus and this again stands upon a little low table with a thin marble top.

In the evening tea'd with Mr. Purdon,[198] and finished the day by confining two riotous and drunken sailors who were glad enough on promise of better behavior to be released this morning.

Today we have had service from the Rev. Mr. Cox on board the *Kennedy* and this afternoon I dined on board the *Comus* with Capt. Fellowes. Glisson was also his guest, and we had a pleasant dinner.

Sunday Oct. 8, 1854

The mail leaves tomorrow for England and tomorrow I have to go to Whampoa to bring Captain Abbot up. The week until friday

196 Camblet, or camlet (or camelot, chamlot, etc.) is all silk or velvet, especially pily and plushy.

197 Sarsenet, or sarcenet, is a very fine and soft silk material made both plain and twilled in various colors.

198 He was James Purdon, co-owner of James Purdon and Company of Canton and Hong Kong. See *The China Mail*, Vol. X, No. 510 (November 23, 1854).

was uneventful. On Monday I dined at Purden at half past three.

Messr. Hubbell, Tuckerman and Glisson being of the party. On Tuesday Glisson dined with me on board the *Queen* and we took our tea at Russell & Co's. Wednesday the *Macedonian* arrived at Whampoa, took tea at Wetmore & Co.[199] Thursday at home completing my chart of Keelung Harbor. A walk among the shops or on the beautiful square fronting the Factories, helped vary the general monotonous routine.

On Friday got the steamer underway and went down to Whampoa to communicate with the *Macedonian*, and put on board her some men from the *Kennedy*. We had for passangers three missionaries, three merchants, four officers from H.B.M.S. *Comus*, their servants, the steward of a merchant man, and my old messmate Jones of the Marines. It rained nearly all the day, and all through saturday was 'spilling' weather, this morning opened bright and glorious. Capt Abbot informs me, the *Queen* has been rechartered for five months. I am therefore secure to command her until February. The Rev. Mr. Cox preached on board today from the text Luke 18, 'God be merciful to me a sinner.' As Capt I lead off in the responses. Mr. C.'s Christian name is Josiah. He is an Englishman. Mr. Bonney, the untiring missionary, who helped me so to see Canton will visit the U. S. soon in pursuit of a wife. I shall give him a letter to you and hope you may be able to help him to a good one. Mr. B. is not a clergy man. I believe he came out as a painter. How would Mary P[reble][200] or Lucy B[arbour][201] like to be a trinitarian missionary? I think it a little singular that the steward of the English ship *Java*, who was one of my passengers to Whampoa, should have known my

[199] Wetmore and Company was an American firm founded in 1833 in Canton, with branches at Shanghai, Foochow, and New York, by William Shephard Wetmore, nephew of a partner of Edward Corrington of Providence, and Joseph Archer of Philadelphia. During the Chinese hostilities of 1856, the company suffered losses but was able to reorganize its activities under new arrangements as Wetmore, Williams and Company. There were three partners, brothers, L. S. Wetmore, P. M. Wetmore, and W. S. Wetmore. Griffin, *op. cit.*, 243–44 and 244 n.11; *NCAB*, IX, 407.

[200] Mary Preble (b. December 14, 1835) was the daughter of Edward D. Preble and Sophia Wattles and a first cousin of G. H. Preble. *Sketch*, 197.

[201] Lucy E. Barbour was a daughter of Joseph Barbour and Sally Preble, second cousin of G. H. Preble. *Ibid.*

father, and hearing my name asked me if I knew Capt. Enoch Preble.[202] He was on board the Brig *Washington,*[203] Capt. Cooligan,[204] in which father took passage to Honduras in 1825. He was delighted to find in me, his son. Mr. Doolittle[205] one of the missionaries here gave me the other day some "Chinese paper money" which I shall send to you. It is the first I have ever seen and to me a great curiosity. The bill (value two dollars) having been redeemed at Foo Chow foo has been cancelled and is therefore valueless except as a curio. The writing on the back is the endorsement of those through whose hands it has passed, and the circular ink mark on its face cancels it. To secure against counterfeiting it is cut from a book in which certain figures along the edges are divided, so that it only will match them. Notice the blue Chinese characters surrounding it. The left-hand half of all these characters you will see is the same, but combined on the right with a different character.

Doct Williams told me today he procured for a wealthy lady in N. Y. the most expensive white crape shawl made to order. He could, and it cost just 85$ and 10$ for a lacquered box but when the lady received it, the expenses and duties, etc., made it cost 175$ or nearly double. Dr. W. added, it was a useless article for the work upon it made it too heavy to be bourn.

A shawl costing 700$ was sent to the 'Worlds Fair of 1851' but was worked in colors each flower and leaf being a copy from Nature —exsquisitely wrought and shaded. I shall send by the first oppor-

[202] Enoch Preble was the fourth son of Brigadier General Jedidiah Preble and Mehitable Bangs. *Sketch,* 184; see also the biographical sketch of G. H. Preble in this volume.

[203] In the "Memorandum of the different Voyages that I have been from my first going to sea," by Captain Enoch Preble, it is stated that in 1823 he sailed from Portland to the Bay of Honduras on the brig *Favorite* and back to Portland on the brig *Washington. Sketch,* 186.

[204] There is no brig *Washington,* Captain Cooligan, in lists of private American ships. She might have changed her name, as often happened with private ships, or the return voyage from South America might have been a tramp enterprise.

[205] The Reverend J. Doolittle was sent to Foochow in 1850 by the American Board of Commissioners. Mrs. Doolittle died at Foochow in 1856. Dean, *op. cit.,* 163, 166.

tunity a box of Chinese flower seeds to be divided with Doct. Wood[worth]. We have just heard of the arrival of the *Powhatan* at Shanghai after an eight days passage from Hong Kong, with Mr. McLane on board. I forgot to mention that Thursday of last week we had an earth quake; it was no great shakes however, though the newspapers call it a smart one. I was walking with Mr. Bonney and the Olivers at the time but none of our party noticed it. Yet, at Macao several ice built houses were shaken down.

Today has been delightful. I dined with Mekerman at Mr. Nyes, took tea at Russell & Cos and since tea have been enlivening my invalid friend Goodridge of the house of Wetmore and Co. Capt Abbot has ordered an acting Master to the *Queen*, but he is to remain on board the *Macedonian* as Flag Lieut. The appointment is only nominal to give him the pay.

Monday October 9, 1854

Got underway at 9 A.M. with Capt. Gardner[206] of the *Comet* my only passenger and at 10.15 anchored at Whampoa. At 1 P.M. got underway having Capt. Abbot, Purser Allison, Doct. Gilliam, and a dozen other passangers and anchored off the Factories at 2 P.M. Gilliam, Allison, Sproston, Waters and Mr. Adams all messing on board the *Queen*.

Tuesday October 10, 1854

On shore helping the Capt and Purser and Doctor shopping. Took tea with Mr. Habbell and passed the evening pleasantly at his house. Nineteen years in the Navy today.

Wednesday October 11, 1854

Shopping with Capt and others. Mr Oliver came up and took lodgings on board the *Queen*. Dr. Gilliam and I dined with Tuckerman and we passed the evening with Goodridge.

Thursday October 12, 1854

Dined at Mr. Hubbells, a pleasant dinner party.

Canton, Sunday Oct 22d, 1854

Friday 12th unexpectedly got underway and took Capt Abbot

[206] See note 186 above.

to Hong Kong, towing Mr. Sturgis'[207] yacht *Atlanta*[208] which had been fired on the day before by Chinese pirates on her passage up. One object of our trip was to look after the lawless chap and capture him if possible. The result was our violent chase of a couple of poor fruit boats and bringing them to, in great terror by firing through their sails. We anchored that night, and I went ashore at Hong Kong and read the newspapers by the overland at the Club Canton. On anchoring at Hong Kong 'Capt' Upham came on board to see me and enquire about Portland people and Portland news.

Saturday (14th) morning news came of the plunder of a ship the *Caldera*[209] by pirates down the coast, and that the crew and a lady passenger a French woman, were in the hands of, and at the mercy of the wretches. I therefore got underway as soon as practicable and crossed over to Macao, where I learned further particulars and the next morning Sunday (15th) at the solicitation of two American Merchants went out on a cruise among the Islands, and returned to Macao the same evening. The next morning (Monday 16th) I was underway again and anchored at Hong Kong about noon. I passed a very pleasant evening at Macao at Mr. Nyes in company with all the beauty and fashion of the place. I mean the foreign beauty and fashion. Tuesday 17th coaling at Hong Kong and taking stores on board, playing the agreeable to Mrs De Silver on shore and entertaining guest on board. Wednesday (18th) dined at De Silvers. Thursday 19th left Hong Kong with Capt Abbot, and a large party including Upham and anchored the same evening at Whampoa.

The next morning (Friday 20th) after doing a variety of buisness on board the *Macedonian*, took Capt. Abbot and our party on board and steamed up to our anchorage off the Factories at Canton. Yesterday I was shopping with Capt. Abbot and others and dined at Wet-

[207] R. S. Sturgis was appointed U. S. vice-consul at Canton on December 8, 1854, and served until September, 1855. He was a partner in the American firm Russell and Company from 1850 to 1857. Griffin, *op. cit.*, 306, 360.

[208] The *Atlanta* was a California clipper ship. She is little known. *Clipper*, 298–99.

[209] The *Caldera* must have been a local ship. Her name recalls the fact at that time there lived the Reverend John Calder, who was appointd U.S. vice-consul at Foochow in 1851. Griffin, *op. cit.*, 82, 360.

more & Co where Upham is. Today we have been arranging for a trip up the river. Rev. Josiah Cox performed divine service on board this morning and gave us a sermon on unclean spirits, argueing the actual existence of such beings. He took his text from the 1st of Mark.[210] Every day has its incident to mark it. I have scarcely at any time for the last ten days had less than eight or nine guests. I fear my increase of pay will not cover my increased expenses. 'Capt' Upham has chartered his ship the *Alferd*[211] to take Chinese passangers to California for 15.000$ the trip considered a paying charter. If I am not making money, I hope I am making reputation as an officer. I have had an ivory stamp made to mark my books and linens of which I send you an impression. It only cost with ink and china box and all but one dollar and seventy five cents.

I wrote in my last of an agreeable lady a Mrs. Oliver, who with her husband and two little children was my guest. Appearances are certainly at times deceitful for I must say I found her agreeable and intelligent and really enjoyed the few days she passed on board. I say nothing about Mr. O. It now appears she is proved to be the wife of another man, who is in hot pursuit to rescue his children from the hands of herself and paramour, and that Mr. Oliver is no less than a rogue and a swindler. I am thankful I did not feel authorized to introduce them about. They have managed to escape to Manila, but it is hoped the record of their guilt may precede them. The name of the lady's true husband is Wolfe and he is hurrying on from the Sandwich Islands whether he had chased them, and is expected in the next arrival from there. It is a mystery to me how she could be so correct agreeable and ladylike, and her two children, one of nine and the other five years old so affectionate to her and Mr. Oliver. Truth is often stronger than fiction.

Wednesday Oct. 28, 1854

I have been very busy since sunday and have now considerable official buisness to attend to. Yesterday Capt Abbot intended returning to the *Macedonian,* but was taken ill with cholera morbus, and I

[210] Mark 1:2: "Behold, I send my messenger before thy face . . . ."

[211] The *Alferd,* 1,291 tons, was a British frigate commanded by Captain Henning. *Clipper,* 36–37.

went down in the *Queen* and brought up Doct Woodworth, the Fleet Surgeon to attend him. He is better this morning, and hope my good old friend[212] may soon be well, such attacks (and he has had several lately) in this climate, on one of his years, tell seriously. Upham made the excursion down and up with me. It was a pleasant day and we were gone but four and a half hours on the round trip. Upham is quite encouraged about his buisness prospects, and hopes to realize something handsome from his adventure. I send a note I have received respecting the Olivers. I have an oil painting of his imaginary ship. *The Banner* mentioned in the note, and which he gave me. There will be a story to tell about it. I believe the only person he succeeded in swindling was the Captain who brought him to China. He was so pleased with the family after having them on board his ship forty days that he cashed his draft for one thousand dollars taking his passage money out of the amount. I saw the Capt. yesterday, and was still doubting his dishonesty and the stories in circulation, for he never had seen more correct well behaved people or had pleasanter passangers. The children he said were regularly taught sunday school lessons by their mother. Poor old man! he is sadly duped. We all were, but not in pocket as he is. I believe I write you that I thought Mr. O. a vulgar California nabob, and often wondered that she with her refined manners had mated with him. Such was my first impression and what I always said, when the gentleman on shore asked me about him.

Last Friday evening there was a capital theatrical performance on board the *Comus* which I forgot to mention. The Officers performing one of the plays and the crew the last. I will send you the bill printed on satin. Upham expects to sail in about thirty days for San Francisco, and will leave his ship there and return to Portland via the Isthmus. In four months I hope he may give you his personal assurance of my health and good looks. Our trip up river has been delayed by Capt. Abbot's illness; we hope when started to penetrate some thirty or forty miles further than any European or American

212 On p. 353 of the manuscript diary, which page ends here, is inserted a program of three plays, *The Irish Lion, The Ring Doves, and A - S.S.*, which were performed on the *Comus* in Canton.

has ever done, and give the name of American branch to the stream we explore.

Sunday October 29, 1854

The mail which ought to have left on the 25th was detained by the English Admiral, who just arrived from Japan, wished time to write up his dispatches. It did not leave Hong Kong until yesterday. Here after we are to have only monthly mails instead of semi-monthly, one of the steam packets between Point de Galle and Bombay having been withdrawn. Capt Abbot has been quite sick, I took him to Whampoa yesterday. He thought he would be more comfortable in his own cabin, than on shore. It was fortunate for me, that he went down, as I obtained a freight back of fifty two boxes of treasure for which I am to receive as many dollars as there was boxes, which will help pay my increased expenses.

After writing on Wednesday I went with the steamer on a search after some river thieves, who had stolen a boat. The whole expedition was under the command of Capt Abel Fellowes of the H.B.M.S. *Comus*. I took three of his boats in tow, and received on board from her an armed force. Then steamed down to the *Macedonian* where I took in tow three of her boats under command of Lt. Avery, and proceeded to the creek where the pirates were supposed to be lurking. When we had anchored as near it as was possible for the steamer to get, the boats shoved off and the united force landed, and searched the villiage of Forgua. No resistance was offered, and nothing discovered. After a search which lasted four or five hours the boats returned and we got underway. After dropping the *Macedonian*'s boats alongside at Whampoa, we steamed back to Canton bringing with us three prisoners, hostages for the recovery of stolen property. The men are now on board the *Comus*. The next day Capt Abbot was so ill it was thought best to send the ship for medical aid, and went down and brought Doct. Woodworth up.

Upham made the excursion with me. He has been living at his consigners Wetmore & Co. but returns to Hong Kong tomorrow. I breakfasted with him on shore this morning, and we had rice birds blue winged teal, and grilled pigeons, delicacies to make an epicure's mouth water. He has chartered both his ships, the *Alferd* for 15.000

and the *Leonore*[213] for 9.000$ He showed me today two beautiful silk dresses he had purchased for 15$ each which I suppose he intends for Mrs. L. He has also bought a 40$ crape shawl besides several of less value.

On Friday we had a regular New England Cod fish dinner at Wetmore & Co, got up by Goodridge. Today I dined at Mr. Hunters. The mail from the U. S. arrived on Wednesday but I did not get my letters (one from you Augt 12th) until yesterday. I received your letter with great joy for as I had missed hearing from you for two mails I feared you were prevented from writing by your own or Ellen's sickness. We are having delightfully cool and pleasant weather at this time, with proper care and precaution I think the climate here as healthy as any. I am allowing all my beard to grow again as I did in Japan, not wishing the ladies to fall in love with me. I am thankful that Our Lily was preserved in sickness, and fully restored to health again when you last wrote.

Wednesday November 1, 1854

Rec'd on board a light 12 pd. Boat Howitzer and at 6:30 A.M. got underway. At 8.15 anchored at Whampoa and rec'd from the *Macedonian* fourteen additional men, and Mr. Sproston. At 10 A.M. got underway for Hong Kong, passed the Chinese Imperial Fleet at anchor near the Bogue and at 5 45 P.M anchored at Hong Kong. Got underway again and anchored off the naval store house.

Hong Kong, Thursday Nov. 2^{d} 1854

At noon got underway for Macao Fleet Surgeon Woodworth and Passed Mid. J. G. Sproston[214] of the *Macedonian* on board, also Mr. Alvord and Mr. Moses of Macao[215] and Mr. Upham, passangers. At 330 P.M. while standing into the Bay of Tyho was fired upon by

213 The *Leonore* was a packet ship of about 350 tons built by John Currier, Jr., at Newbury Port, *ca.* 1835. *Clipper,* 52.

214 John G. Sproston was made midshipman on July 15, 1846; passed midshipman on the *Macedonian,* June 8, 1852; master, September 15, 1855; lieutenant, September 16, 1855. He was killed in the Civil War on June 8, 1862.

215 It is known that in Canton in 1850 there was an A. R. B. Moses, an American merchant, whose trading difficulties with the Chinese were administered by American consular jurisdiction. There is abundant evidence concerning his case in the National Archives; see also Griffin, *op. cit.,* 94 n. 22.

a Chinese Piratical Fleet of ten junks mounting heavy guns. There at anchor, released all prisoners from confinement and sent them to their duties at quarters. We immediately returned the Pirates fire from our brass howitzer and 4 Pd. broadside guns and had a smart engagement which lasted about twenty minutes, when finding that the water would not allow our nearer approach, and having no boat to take them by boarding, we being in point blank range of their heavier guns, stood off, and at 4.30 sent a dispatch by a Portuguese lorcha[216] to the British Admiral at Hong Kong requesting him to send assistance to bag the rascals. After dispatching the lorcha returned to the Bay of Tyho and fired again at the Piratical Fleet, the pirates briskly returning our fire.

Unable to bring our guns to bear effectively, left and steamed for Macao to consult with the Capt H.B.M. Ship *Encounter*, feeing a fisherman to watch the scoundrels during my absence. During the fireing carried away the axle and truck of the Port forward gun, spliced the main brace. The fireing called us away from a comfortable dinner in the cabin. At 7.30, anchored in Macao roads near H.B.M.S. *Encounter* boarded her and persuaded Capt O'Callaghan[217] to return with me to Tyho. Got underway and went in closer to the Proya[218] and collected on board several officers of the *Encounter* from on shore, and returned with them to her and put them on board. At 11 P.M. the *Encounter* got under way with us for Tyho.

Expended between twenty five and thirty five cartridges and two hundred rounds of musket cartridges; 2[d] attack on Chinese Pirates in Tyho.

Friday Nov. 3[d] 1854

At daylight stood into the Bay of Tyho, found the Pirates reenforced by seven more junks had left their anchorage under the left arm or Cape forming the bay and gone in nearer the town into very shallow water. On arriving off the place the pirates commenced

216 It was the *Amazon;* cf. Fox, *op. cit.*, 125.

217 British Captain O'Callaghan took part in the expedition organized by Sir James Stirling to stop Chinese piracy. He was successful in destroying the pirate stronghold at Kulang in November, 1854. *Ibid.*

218 Praya or Connaught Road is the main street in Hong Kong, Victoria.

waving flags, beating drums and other acts of derision. Went on board the *Encounter* to confer with Capt O'Callaghan and while he was preparing a dispatch to the Adml at Hong Kong, which I volunteered to take, I went in to try the range of my guns on the pirates in their new position. Stood in until nearly aground and opened fire. I was out of range of the 4 pounds but that the Howitzer was effective. The Pirates immediately returned our fire; at the 4th discharge of the Howitzer the carriage was disabled, and I backed out, returned to the *Encounter*, received Capt O'C's dispatch and steamed away to the Admiral at Hong Kong for instructions leaving the *Encounter* to blockade the rascals until my return. At 10 A.M. anchored at Hong Kong and waited upon Rear Admiral Sir James Stirling[219] who decided to send down an additional force consisting of the *Barracouta* and boats of the *Spartan*. Received on board from the latter five officers, twenty two men and took in tow two of her boats and got underway. Upham, Alvord, Moses, Woodworth and Spros-ton all on board. At 4 P.M. arrived at the Bay of Tyho and communicated with the *Encounter*. At 4.30 after Her Majestys ship had thrown several of her shells into the place, I took six of her boats in tow and stood in as far as the depth of water would permit, when the boats shoved off under cover of the fire of my howitzer, which I lashed down on its axle, the wheels being disabled. At 5 P.M. the boats effected a landing and set fire to the Junks lieing in the creek and to the pirates store houses on shore. Two of our boats went on shore, and I went in one of them, leaving the steamer at anchor in eight feet of water. At 9. P.M. returned with our boats hoisted them up and got underway, and went out near the *Encounter* and anchored in six fathoms of water. Just as we had finished the distruction of the piratical fleet and store houses the *Barracouta* arrived from Hong Kong.[220]

219 Sir James Stirling (1791–1865), admiral and first governor of Western Australia, was born the fifth son of Andrew Stirling of Drumpellier, in Lanarkshire, by Anne, daughter of Sir Walter Stirling. He entered the navy in August, 1803. His first duties took him to the West Indies, then to the mouth of the Mississippi, Hudson Bay, the Gulf of Mexico, and the Mediterranean, but his achievements were in the Pacific. He rose to the rank of commander-in-chief in China and the East Indies waters, 1854–56. *DNB*, XVIII, 1267–68.

220 The antipirate squadron organized by Sir James Stirling was composed of the

When we commenced the fight with the pirates yesterday Upham took off his coat to it—as we laughing said to save it. One of my trophys is a large cotton flag inscribed with Chinese characters written with blood which states it is the flag of Lue-ming-suy-ming of the Hong Shing-tong Company, Chief of the Sea Squadron,[221] and that he takes from the rich and not from the poor, and his flag can fly anywhere, another has the inscription opposite which are translated by Doct. S. Williams In the pirate chiefs junks which I burned we found a lamp burning and over thirty idols three of which I am preserving for parlor ornaments. They are curiously carved and gilded. I have also secured a double sword, and a set of Chinese weight and scales.

Saturday Nov. 4, 1854

No sooner had we destroyed the piratical vessels, than a large fleet of fishing junks came into the Bay rejoicing and anchored. During the night there was a great noise and to do among them which we could not understand, but this morning we learned that the pirates whom we had driven from their vessels to the hills, came down and attempted to board and capture some of the fishing craft to make off in, but were driven back. This morning a deputation of the chief men of the villiage came on board the *Queen,* with a present of chickens, pork, fish, etc and brought the card or note preserved on the opposite page. I sent a portion of their cumshaw on board the *Encounter.* Gave the crew an extra lot of grog, and at 9 A.M. after a visit to the shore to view the ruins we had made got underway for Hong Kong, where we arrived at 11.40 a.m. and anchored off the Naval Store house in 5 fathoms of water. I immediately went on board the *Winchester,* to give Sir James my dispatches, and narrate to him our doings. He seemed well pleased and invited me to dine with him

British ships *Encounter*, *Barracouta*, and *Styx;* the launch of the *Winchester* and the pinnace of the *Spartan;* the Portuguese lorcha *Amazon;* the American-chartered vessel *Queen,* under Preble; the two hired vessels of the Peninsular and Oriental Company; and the war junk under the command of Captain O'Callaghan, who was assisted by a higher Chinese official. Fox, *op. cit.,* 125.

[221] The flag is preserved in the Naval Museum, Annapolis, Maryland. However, I could not obtain a picture of it from the curator.

which I did. Gave liberty to several of the men for their meritorious conduct.

The pirates have become very daring of late and it is quite time energetic measures are taken to put a stop to their numerous piracies and destroy their means of annoy and plunder. The greatest difficulty is to discover seasonally their true character. In the disorganized states of the country, the dividing line between pirate and rebel is very finely drawn. In this instance their attack upon my vessel with my ensign and pennant flying left no doubt as to what they were—though it was difficult for me to persuade Capt. O'Callaghan of the *Encounter* at my first interview to assist in their destruction. His orders as he said being very positive from the Admiral "Not to attack a Chinese pirate unless they had first attacked a British vessel or British Officer." The attack on my vessel he did not think authorized him to pitch in, without the further instructions from the Admiral which I volunteered, and went to Hong Kong to get. When I arrived back with *Spartan* boats, he asked me what orders I brought. I said none, but a force which I supposed was sent with one object, viz to make an attack upon the rascals, and so thought Lieut. Palliser who commanded the *Spartan*'s boats. So the attack was commenced, when just as we had about completed the work, when along came the *Barrocouta*, with the Admiral's orders not to make the first attack which put poor Capt. O'Callaghan in a great funk. I will give however a Yankee guess that is all right and the Admiral well pleased though he was glad to shirk the responsibility. Nevertheless Sir James is a good old man and a true specimen, with his rosy cheeks and long silver hair of the fine old English gentleman all of the olden time.

Hong Kong, Sunday Nov. 5, 1854

Guy Fawkes day. Clear and pleasant, mustered the crew, read the articles of war, and gave a dozen men liberty until sundown. I find giving the men liberty as much as they want, when they deserve it, and their services can be spared the best means of enforcing discipline especially when it is with held from the unworthy. Wrote my official report of our affairs with the pirates. Our expedition is all in the Hong Kong papers.

Hong Kong, Nov. 6, 1854

Clear warm and pleasant. Repairing our paddle wheels. Rec'd on board a supply of provisions and stores for ourselves and for the *J. P. Kennedy*. The English Admiral told me today of his intention to organise an expedition against the Pirates at Kulor. Volunteered my own service and those of the *Queen*, and wrote Commodore Abbot at Whampoa.

Tuesday Nov. 7th 1854

Was afraid the Commodore would not receive my letter or answer it favorably, so got underway at 7.30 AM. for Whampoa. At 7 P.M. anchored near the *Macedonian* and went on board to see the Commodore and returned to the *M* the 13 extra men obtained from her for our expedition. Found Com. Abbot approved of my offer to the English Admiral and had written to me to that effect and he told me to go back with Carte blanche orders to do as I pleased satisfied I would act with judgement and do right—all very gratifying.

Wednesday Nov. 8th 1854

At 4.45 got underway for Canton, and at 6.10 anchored off the Factories, delivered her men to the *John P. Kennedy* and returned and was at anchor at Whampoa at 10.30. Having received on board a boat howitzer mounted on a field carriage, and two boxes of ammunition, Rec^{d} from the *Macedonian* four boxes of ammunition, one howitzer slide and thirteen men and took her pinnace in tow and started for Hong Kong quarter before two oclock. At 5. P.M. passed the Bogue Forts and at 11.15 anchored off the Naval Store House Hong Kong, and so finished an active days work, though I did not get turned in until tomorrow morning.

Thursday November 9th 1854

Pleasant weather, waited upon Rear Adml Sterling and renewed my offer of the services of the *Queen*. He said he had about given up the Expedition in consequence of the non appearance of the promised Chinese Admiral with his war junks, but now that I had renewed my offer he would see what could be done, etc. Finished the repairs on our paddle wheels, and gave a number of men liberty. One of the most interesting events of the past week has been the arrival of the *Enterprise* Capt. Collins on R W from the Artic Seas after having been frozen in since 1851 and been absent from Old England since 1849. The Purser committed suicide during the cruize and all the officers are at sixes and sevens. No two speaking with each other; pleasant that must have been in the solitude of the frozen regions. Capt C. told me when I called upon him, that on his passage up he visited San Francisco bay and found it almost a solitude and was quite bewildered on his return, sailing in at night and seeing the lights of a large city. It having grown up like new ground in his absence.

Friday November 10th 1854

Continues pleasant with Esty breezes. Capt Abbot on board the *Macedonian* is quite sick and I fear the climate is telling fatally upon his years. Where the *Macedonian* is anchored is a sickly place, and she has a large list of chills and fevers. The Sick list has increased so fast that Capt. Abbot has resolved to bring the ship down to Hong Kong, and Sir James has offered his Hospital Ship for the accommodation of her sick.

Saturday November 11th 1854

Clear cool and pleasant with light breezes from the Nth and Est. The *Macedonian* arrived from Whampoa. Carpenters employed in mounting an iron two pounder captured from the Tyho pirates on the bow of the Macedonian pinnace.

At 4.40 P.M. got underway for Kulan in company with H.B.M. Steamers *Encounter* and *Styx*[222] and the P & O Company's[223] Steamers *Canton* and *Forbes*. Off Macao was joined by H.B.M. Steamer *Barracouta*, the whole forming an Expedition against the pirates, under Command of Capt. O'Callaghan of the *Encounter*. We had on board the *Queen* as passangers and volunteers, Mr. Keenan U. S.

222 See note 220 above.

223 The Peninsular and Oriental Steam Navigation Company was established in Hong Kong by the British in 1843 for mail and passenger service in the Far East. It maintained many local steamers between Hong Kong and various Chinese ports. The *Canton* and the *Forbes* were two such steamers. See *Commercial and Industrial Hong Kong*, 168–73.

Consul at Hong Kong[224] and Messers Moses and Alvord. Two War Junks of H.J.M. *Hienfung* also accompanied the expedition in tow of the *Styx* and *Encounter*.

Sunday November 12, 1854

Clear and pleasant, with fresh breezes at day light the expeditionary force was off the Island of San Schian and stood for the Islands off Tyloo. At 10.30 A.M. anchored in three fathoms of water in Cow Cock Bay, and at 12 got underway and went closer in towing two boats from the *Styx* and *Barracouta* and anchored again in two fathoms where under cover from guns the two boats and our pinnace boarded and burnt three junks close in shore on board of which we found evidences of their piratical character, and articles belonging to the *Caldeira*. The pirates threw overboard their guns on our approach and made their escape to the shore.

During the afternoon the *Canton* reconnoitered Kulan and returned to report the pirates in force at that place and that the Portugese government lorcha *Amazonia* had been fired upon by them. At 2.30 P.M. got the *Queen* underway and anchored near the *Encounter*; at 5.20 underway again. At 6.20 came to anchor. At 8.30 underway in company with the Steamers *Forbes* and *Canton*, and lorcha *Amazonia* and at 9.40 P.M. anchored in the Bay of Kulan, where we received on board a deatchment of Marines from the *Styx*. Our force blockading the place in preparation for the attack tomorrow.

Kulan, Monday November 13, 1854

Clear and cool with fresh northerly breezes at 6.30 A.M. got underway and stood in towards the town in company with the Str. *Canton* and Portuguese Lorcha *Amazonia*. She anchored just beyond the range of the batteries and was soon fired at, but the shot fell short. The *Canton* and *Forbes* steamed back to bring the boats from

[224] James Keenan was appointed U.S. consul at Hong Kong on May 23, 1853, and served until January 26, 1859. He was known for defending American rights of adjudication on ships stationed in foreign ports as long as the peace of the community was not disturbed by them. He was an American merchant in Canton. Griffin, *op. cit.*, 157–58, 361.

the large ships and we and the *Amazonia* moved closer in. When the steamers returned with the boats we were ordered to open fire. At 9:30 A.M. we got underway and stood towards the town and opened on it with shell from our only effective gun the 12 Pd. Brass Howitzer. The batteries on shore returned our fire but oweing to the inaccuracy of their range all went over us, and none hit us. The *Amazonia* also opened on the rascals with her 32's. The whistling of the pirate shot was sharp and neighborly.

As we found our shell fell short after 14 or 15 rounds we ceased fireing, and the *Amazonia*, having frightened the rascals from their battery on the shore (mounting 100 gun) ceased hers, and the boats made landings on both sides of the bay and took possession of the pirates works. The *Macedonian*'s pinnace under command of Sproston, and conveying my volunteer passangers landed with the other boats and had two oars broken by the pirates shot. I also landed at the same time in my gig leaving the *Queen* in charge of Mr. Williams. The result of our operation was the destruction of forty seven piratical junks, with numerable boats. The capture of over 100 cannon, fifty or more of which were brought off, and the burning of three towns, with the capture of innumerable flags; and the complete breaking up of a piratical depot that had put the Chinese government at defiance for over five years, and whence had issued cruisers to rob and murder whenever opportunity offered. We also took some 15 or 20 prisoners, and killed between 45 and 50 of the pirates. The only casualty in effecting this victory was the death of one of my men John Morrison killed by a shot in the head. I heard of his death just as I was ordered by Capt. O'Callaghan to burn one of the villiages, and went over to where he was shot not one hundred yards dist. and sent his body on board ship. My impression is that he was shot by some of the John Bulls who were foraging and shooting chickens regardless of orders or discipline. Our men I am happy to say behaved better and were kept under control and at the time Morrison was shot he was marching in column with the pinnace crew. My gentlemen volunteers however disregarded instructions and Mr. Keenan was the first to enter the most distant rebel fort and haul down its colors. Just as he was in the act Lieut. Fellowes (Chas) of the *Winchester* rushed up, and with an eye to his own promotion said, look here, you don't want that let me have it. No by G–d says, you Keenan you can't, Stranger it's what I've been fighting for all day. Keenan cut the flag from its staff and intends sending it to the State Department. It is ornamented with very curious devices, and is undoubtedly the flag of the chief pirate. I have secured ten flags which I intend sending to the Navy Department.

At 4 P.M. the boats returned from shore when we got underway and at 5.30 came to anchor near the *Encounter*. Sent the remains of John Morrison in charge of his two messmates on board the *Barracouta* to be taken to Hong Kong for burial. Mr. Keenan also went back to Hong Kong with my dispatch to Com'dre Abbot.

Tuesday November 14, 1854

Clear and cool, with light northerly breezes. At 9.30 A.M. got underway and stood out to an anchorage near the *Canton*, as we were rather too near the bottom. Remained at anchor all day with banked fires. A party landed today on the South Side of the Island and marched across scouring the country in every direction without making any very great discoveries, and destroying the paddy fields. Several prisoners were brought in and consigned to the tender mercies of the Chinese Admiral who now that the fight is over is quite happy loading the H. Ch M. Junks with the captured cannon. I saw his highness yesterday afternoon after the rout, in his satin shoes with pipe clayed soles, picking his way fan in hand over the muddy flats. About sunset I sent the pinnace in shore to look at a suspicious junk at anchor but nothing was found on board to identify her with the pirates. I imagine this is the first expedition in which Englishmen, Americans, Portugese and Chinese have cooperated as allies. In the pirate Junks we found tea, matting, and other articles plundered from the *Caldeira*.

My cabin is carpeted with scraps of matting which was taken from her, and my table is ornamented with six gilded Josses. I have looted, as the English say, a fine pair of Chinese money scales, a grey fur Mandarin hood, a large gong, an English spy glass—evidently taken by the pirates from some unfortunate vessel—and several minor articles. The impressions on the foregoing page are made with stamps found in the cabin of the pirate chief which I have secured box ink and all so that I can issue decrees under his signet.

The P. O. Co's Strs. *Canton* and *Forbes* which formed part of our expedition were hired by a wealthy Chinese whose family and sixty thousand dollars have fallen into pirate hands. It is said he placed $15.000 at the disposal of the English Admiral to gratify his revenge. In one of the junks was found a womans flannel petticoat marked M. F. N. the garment of some poor woman whose fate can only be conjectured.

Wednesday November 15, 1854

Clear cool weather, with fresh breezes. At early daylight got underway in company with the other Steamers for the Ladrone Islands. Towing the pinnace astern; in consequence of the boat keepers not steering her properly, she was capsized, loosing 10 muskets, 2 pistols, and other articles, oweing to the heavy seas could not right her, though we stopped to do so, and continued towing her bottom up, until 11.30, when she righted herself. Immediately stopped the engine lowered our quarter boat bailed her out and proceeded on. Saw nothing piratical among the Ladrones, and at 3.20 anchored in the Broadway passage in two fathoms water. Sent a boat to the *Barracouta* on her rejoining the Expedition and received from her three men sent up from the *Macedonian*. Remained at anchor all night with banked fires. Capt O'Callaghan went up river in the *Canton* to reconnoitre.

Thursday November 16, 1854

Clear and cool with light breezes from the Nth & Est. Got underway before breakfast and anchored nearer the *Encounter*. Capt O'Callaghan returned with the *Canton* having learned that sixty piratical junks we were in pursuit of under command of Apping[225] had joined the Imperial forces, and so became Chinese fashion honest fellows and could not be touched, and the chief had been

[225] Apuk, or Apak (Aw-ung), a notorious Chinese pirate, was made captain in the imperial fleet. He united thirty junks with imperial forces near Macao. The rest of his fleet was destroyed. See Fox, *op. cit.*, 125, 128. His real name was P'u Hsing-yu. For the piratical operations of his brother, P'u, see Fairbank, *op. cit.*, I, 343–45.

made a high mandarin and retains command of his squadron. This unexpected union brings our Expedition to a sudden conclusion. We rec-d our mail by the *Barracouta* by which I got your letter of Augt 27. and notice in a newspaper the arrival of the *Saratoga* at Boston.

Friday November 17, 1854

Clear cool and pleasant Light breezes from the Nth & E^st^. Capt O'Callaghan informed me that the piratical having joined with the Imperial fleet he should have no further occasion for our services and that the Expedition was dissolved.[226] Accordingly got underway at 10 A.M. for Macao, and at 2.50 P.M. anchored in the Inner Roads. In passing through the Hymoon and Typa passage found the depth of water less by four feet than was given on our chart, and in consequence the Steamer grounded twice in the soft mud, but was forced through, and floated again without damage.

Saturday November 18, 1854

I had anticipated celebrating this the ninth anniversary of our wedding day by the destruction of a pirate town and fleet but instead have been writing my official account of our doings at Kulan. At 6 oclock this morning I got underway with a cool fresh breeze and at 9.20 anchored at Tyho where I took the pinnace and accompanied by Gene Kennan boarded a Mandarin war junk at anchor in the bay for information, but heard nothing of importance. Returned to the Steamer and got under way again for Hong Kong where we arrived about one P.M. and anchored off Spring Gardens. Returned the pinnace and her crew of 13 men in charge of Mr. Sproston to the *Macedonian*. Gave several of the men liberty. During our absence from Hong Kong we missed attending regetta ball and one given by the Admiral. Your health was duly honored and remembered today at our mess table. Capt. Abbot continues very ill and I fear he will never recover. He says he will die rather than abandon his command.

[226] According to the report Captain O'Callaghan sent to Admiral Stirling on November 17, 1854, fifty junks had been burned and two batteries of twenty-seven guns leveled. In addition, the Americans took six guns, the Chinese seventeen; the pirates had thrown fifteen guns overboard; twenty-seven guns were sunk because they were too heavy to embark. Between fifty and sixty pirates were killed; of the thirteen captured pirates, nine were released by th assisting mandarin. Fox, *op. cit.*, 125.

Hong Kong, Sunday November 19, 1854

Nothing particular, attended church at the Cathedral and heard a not remarkable sermon from Bishop Smith.

Monday November 20, 1854

Held a survey on our awnings. Sent a howitzer and slide to the *Macedonian*. Rec'd from her ten men, and Mr. Sproston and at halfpast three started for Canton. At 8.30 passed the Bogue Forts and at 12.30 P.M. anchored off Canton in our old berth near the *J. P. Kennedy*.

Tuesday November 21, 1854

Sent on shore two boat howitzers and field carriage with ammunition. Among my trophys I have a small brass cannon for Henry. It will make him the envy of all the boys around whether big or little. I came upon it concealed in a paddy field, where it had been thrown by the retreating pirates, and with assistance, lugged it a mile or more to the boat. Henry will scarcely appreciate the trouble I was at, but he will appreciate the cannon.

Canton, Saturday November 25, 1954

We have been enjoying a quiet week after our excitements. I have been sorry to learn from your letter of Lizzie Preble's voiceless condition, and Uncle Harrod's[227] failure in buisness. The country about Canton continues in a very disturbed state and the rebel and Mandarian forces[228] have almost daily encounters in sight of our anchorage. Last week the Mandarian had a signal defeat at Faitshan about twelve miles dist. losing nine hundred men and between 70 and 80 junks. The Canton Community were alarmed and expected an attack, and it was the news of this defeat, which hurried me up from Hong Kong. When I arrived the alarm had subsided.

Many of the Merchants have gone to Shanghai, among others Mr. D. N. Spooner and his family. Several of the missionary ladies

[227] Deacon Joseph Harrod was married to Eliza Cox (1788–1843), who was an aunt of Mrs. G. H. Preble through the Cox family, from which her mother came. Hence Harrod is called "Uncle Harrod." *Sketch*, 241, 247. See also note 192 above.

[228] The "Mandarian forces" were the Chinese governmental, or imperial, forces fighting against the Taiping rebels.

have returned in my absence—viz Mrs Williams[229] Brewster,[230] French[231] and Happer.[232] We have also Mrs. Hunter an American Merchants wife, Mrs. Tomslee the British Vice Consuls wife, and several other desirable additions to the Society of the place. While I write this a balmy breeze is blowing through the open windows of my cabin. Don't you envy me shivering as you must be with cold or breathing the gases of anthracite. I send you a Japanese drawing of Com. Perry and two of his officers done in a high style of art, which I procured at Simoda, and I think will make you laugh.

Canton, Sunday November 26, 1854

A pleasant day. Mr. Preston preached on board taking for his text Psalm 62 verse 11 "God hath spoken once; twice have I heard this; that power belongeth unto God."[233] A clever sermon but unadapted to his jacktar audience. Tiffined with young Spooner, our consul's brother. Dined at 6 P.M. on board the Comus with Captain Abel Fellowes. Walking through Old China Street, had my pocket dexterously lightened of a new silk handkerchief by some celestial pickpocket.

Canton, Thursday November 30, 1854

These are quiet times for our little *Queen*. She has not been underway for over eight days. Had quite a number of callers on board today and paid some visit myself. Sproston and I took tea at Mr. French's, a mile down the river, attended a prayer meeting and came back in Wetmores Hong boat with the missionary ladies.

[229] The wife of Dr. Samuel Wells Williams. See note 109 above.

[230] The Reverend and Mrs. F. H. Brewster were sent to Canton in 1853 by the American Baptist Board of Foreign Missions. He died in 1858. Dean, *op. cit.*, 163.

[231] The Reverend and Mrs. John B. French (1822–1858) were sent to Canton in 1846 by the American Presbyterian Board. Rev. French died on November 30, 1858, on the way from China to the United States. *Ibid.*, 162, 267–79.

[232] Elizabeth S. Ball was married to Andrew Patton Happer (1818–1894) on November 11, 1847; she died in 1864. Mr. Happer was a Presbyterian medical missionary in China; he stayed in Macao from 1844 until 1887. *NCAB*, XXII, 401.

[233] Ps. 63: "O God, thou art my God . . . ."

Canton, Friday December 1, 1854

Received the following complimentary letters[234] from Cmdre Abbot and Sir James Sterling which I read to the crew.

U. S. Ship *Macedonian*
Hong Kong, Nov. 28, 1854

Sir:

I have the honor and pleasing satisfaction to transmit to you a copy of a letter addressed to me from Rear Admiral Sir James Sterling, Knt., respectfully acknowledging in complimentary terms, the co-operation and the gallant conduct evinced by you and your companions against the piratical stronghold at Kulan.

I embrace this opportunity to express to you, and through you to the Officers and men and volunteers associated with you (sickness having prevented my doing so at an earlier day) my own grateful acknowledgements, not only in the affair at Koulan, but more especially for your and their good conduct and gallantry in your encounter with seventeen heavily armed piratical junks in the Harbor of Tyho and for your own prudence zeal and excellent judgement in obtaining assistance from the English Admiral Sir James Sterling by which combined force, the whole were captured or destroyed together with their depot on shore.

With high regard,
Your Obed't Servant
Joel Abbot
Capt. U.S.N., U. S. Sqdr in China Seas

Lt. Comdr G. H. Preble
U. S. Chartered Schr. *Queen*,
Off Canton

[234] The first letter was published by Preble in his *Sketch*, 206.

copy Her Brittanic Majesty's Ship *Winchester*,
At Hong Kong 22^{d} November 1854

Sir:

The joint expedition against the pirate stronghold at Coulan having successfully accomplished its object. I request you will accept and convey to Lieut Preble and his companions my respectful acknowledgements for their cooperation and for the gallant conduct they evinced.

I trust that a continued exercise of the repression thus applied will tend to put a stop to practice of piracy which for some time past has afflicted commerce on the neighboring coasts.

I have the honor to be, Sir,
Your most obedient Humble Servant,
Jas. Sterling, Rear Admiral and Comdr in Chief

Capt. J. Abbot
Comdr U. S. Naval Force
East India China and Japan Seas

The exploits of our little craft the past month have caused me to be envied by those who from seniority were better entitled to the command but who refused her to their now regret. My recent cruisings have thrown me into companion ship and acquaintance of the Commanders of H.B.M. Ships and I dined with Sir James at Hong Kong twice in one week, and was given the seat of honor at his right hand, his Captains and Commanders forming the circle that closed around his dinner table. He is a fine old gentleman, and was I think at one time the Lieut Governor of one of the Australian Colony. His wife is related to the Philadelphia family of Wills. The Colonel of the 59th Regt. called on board to see me, and we had invites to their mess. At Canton though many officers complain of the stiffness and inhospitality of the merchants I have always found a plate ready, and a welcome whenever I choose to drop in unceremoniously, and nearly every day have a particular invite to dinner.

A few days since with the undefatigable Mr. Bonney for our guide a party of us went to see the silk weavers and shawl embroiders and designers and had a pleasant and interesting excursion. Mr. Morse[235] Editor of the *New York Observer*, and now travelling for the recovery of his health was with us, and will I presume give a full account of our walk in his paper. It is singular in what muddy holes and hovels, the beautiful rich and glossy silks and exquisite embroidering have their origins. Few who wear them imagine the wretched squalid beings who weave and embroider these fabrics.

We have just received here news of the defeat of the English and French Squadrons at Petropaulski,[236] and the death of Admiral Price,[237] by the accidental discharge of his own pistol, or as some say suicide. Admiral P. is the friend of Capt. Grignon[238] the British Consul at Portland to whom he gave me letters when I went to England in the Steamer *Lawrence*. You may recollect his speaking of Mrs. Price as a most charming person. Congratulate Ellen Rogers on her engagement if that ring meant anything, and wish her much happiness.

Canton, Friday Dec. 8th, 1854

I have to steal time to write. Sunday being no exception to my busy time. We have been underway with our little steamer up and down

[235] Sidney Edwards Morse, American journalist and son of Jedidiah Morse, was born in Charlestown, Massachusetts, on February 7, 1794, and died in New York on December 24, 1871. He established the *Boston Recorder* in 1815 and the *New York Observer* in 1823. He was also successful in the field of mechanical inventions. He is noted for the *New System of Modern Geography,* of which a half-million copies were sold. *DAB* XIII, 251–52; *Encyclopedia Americana* (1956), XIX, 484.

[236] Petropavlovsk, of Petropavlovsk-Kamchatskij.

[237] David Price (1790–1854), British rear admiral, is known for his outstanding naval achievements. He was appointed commander-in-chief in the Pacific in August, 1853. In July, 1854, the British and French squadrons met at Honolulu; on August 29, they arrived at Petropavlovsk, where it was realized that defeat was imminent. Price shot himself. On September 4, the squadrons were repulsed by the Russians with an appearance of defeat. *DNB*, XVI, 326.

[238] James Grignon was appointed ensign on March 15, 1833; promoted to lieutenant, December 12, 1836; captain, August 27, 1841; sold out, June 17, 1842; vice-consul at Venice, January 21, 1847; consul at Portland, Maine, from August 7, 1849; transferred to the Canary Islands, March 3, 1860; transferred to Riga, November 15, 1860. Edward Hertslet (ed.), *The Foreign Office List, January 1867*, 97.

fromWhampoa nearly every day this week and go again tomorrow to take down the Hon. R. N. McLane who goes to Europe by the overland to meet his wife in Paris. It would be tedious to narrate all the exciting events connected with rebel movements which have kept me moveing about, or the numerous Chinese fights by land and sea, I have witnessed, This wretched country is in a sadly disturbed state and I can see no prospect for any improvement for years to come. Trade is now entirely cut off no tea or silk being allowed to come from the interior without a payment of so heavy a black mail as to amount to a prohibition. At Shanghai, on the contrary, trade has never been so active as now. It is thought the export from China this year will exceed that of any preceeding one.

The *Macedonian* will leave Hong Kong for Shanghai on the 1st of January and it is likely I will give up my commission on the *Queen* and go up in her. There has been some trouble on board her. Avery, the first lieut in consequence of his disgraceful frolics, has been forced to resign, in order to avoid the disgrace of a Court Martial and dismissal and has gone home in the *Nightingale*[239] via Shanghai. Walcutt, Actg Master and Actg Lt., has been drinking and is to be tried by a Court Martial and will probably be dismissed from the service. I am glad to have escaped these troubles. Both of these officers, when themselves, are real clever fellows and excellent officers.

Mr. Bonney whom I have so often mentioned for his kind attentions left this week for the United States. I gave him letters to you and other to Doctor Nichols, Mr. Pratt., Mr. Chickering and Neal Dow. He is an excellent and amiable man and after a nine year residence in China, goes home to find a wife. If Lucy B[arbour] would like to join the mission here's her chance. Perhaps Mary Oxnard would suit better, though he told me he liked the Unitarians. He is as amiable as Lucy B's father and as innocent and unsuspecting as a child. I send by him the Family Daguerrotype I have had copied on

[239] The *Nightingale*, 1,066 tons, was one of the most beautiful of the clipper ships. Launched in 1851, she sailed during the palmy days of the China trade. Her master was Captain John H. Fiske of Sampson and Tappan, Boston. She was abandoned at sea in 1893. *Clipper*, 164–65, 206–207; *Greyhounds*, 416ff.; see also the illustration in *Clipper* facing p. 164.

ivory. Let me know how you like it and what others say about it. It cost me frame and all just forty dollars.

Every Moment of my time has been occupied in completing my chart,[240] writing official reports, or makeing passages to and from Whampoa. Tomorrow the mail leaves. I am now writing after a hard days work and half dressed to attend a large dinner party at Mr. Nye's given in honor of Mr. McLane whom I take away tomorrow. The mail from the *U.S.* [*United States*] to our great disappointment has not arrived, and it is conjectured she has been dismasted, wrecked or taken by the Russians. If the latter, I hope those bearded northerners were amused by your letters. I have dined out every day this week; you may judge at what expenditure of small talk.

Dec 5th got under way at 10 A.M. passed Whampoa, met the *Powhatan* turned, and followed her up. At 1.15 P.M. anchored near her at Whampoa, took on board the Hon. R. M. McLane and suite, Capt. McCheney and others, and the *Powhatan* band, and started for Canton where we arrived at 4. P.M. Got rid of our passangers and sent the band on board the *J. P. Kennedy*. Dec. 6th got underway for Whampoa anchored near the *Powhatan* and returned the same evening to Canton. Went on board Capt. Drinker[241] vessel at Whampoa and warned the crew against violating the neutrality of the United States, and advised them to disperse and warned Capt. Drinker who had taken a commission as a Chinese Admiral to report to Mr. McLane and avoid trouble. Dec. 7th got underway again for Whampoa, anchored near the *Powhatan* about noon. At 2 P.M. got underway moored ship here between 2 and 3 P.M.

Canton, Sunday December 10, 1854

I was delighted and refreshed last evening on my return from down river at receiving your letter of the 3[d] to 13th of September, which informed me of the safe receipt of the package sent by the

240 This was the chaht of the port of Keelung, Formosa, which Commodore Perry included in his official report. See *Narrative*, II.

241 Captain Sandwich Drinker, an American, was hired by Chinese authorities, who bestowed upon him the rank of admiral, to lead the war against the Chinese pirates. Griffin, *op. cit.*, 188–89, 280.

Saratoga. I took Mr McLane down to the *Powhatan* yesterday, and tomorrow at 2 P.M. he leaves Hong Kong, to meet his wife and children in France and return at his leasure to the United States. Fortunate man to have a 3000 ton Gov't steamer at his disposal to come and go as he pleased, and see all he thought worth seeing and after a pleasant six months variety in China returned home with $27,000 in his pocket. Absence like his pays. I wrote I thought the *Macedonian* would go to Shanghai, but Mr. McLane thinks the Senior Naval Officer is needed here and it is doubtful if she goes. The troubles about Canton are thickening and I anticipate seeing a great deal of Chinese warfare in the coming six weeks. Mr. Bonney was to have sailed in the *Comet* Capt. Gardner from Hong Kong yesterday for Batavia and England. Look out for your package bye him. I am sorry the Japanese candy sent by the *Saratoga* was spoiled as it was good and tastefully gotten up. Tell Ellen[242] I have seen a boquet of rare flowers, which would last but a day sold for 100$ and not to have any conscientious scruples about teaching Grecian painting however ephemeral it may prove.

My command of the *Queen* I find profitable out of pocket, oweing to the hotel life I have to lead, giving free passage, and entertaining guests at my sole expense. I am now only the eighth in rank and seniority on this station which is quite remarkable considering the low no. I hold on the List of Lieuts and that there are three vessels in the squadron. The Revd. Mr. Culbertson[243] performed divine service on board. Mr. C. was formerly a Capt. in the U.S. Army. After service I read to the crew Mr. McLanes proclamations forbidding Americans entering the Chinese service.

Thursday December 14, 1854

The 11th 12th and 13th pleasant nothing particular happening. At 4 P.M. got underway and at 6 P.M. anchored near the *Macedonian* at Whampoa, she having come up from H. K. [Hong Kong].

[242] Ellen Bangs Preble. See note 180 above.

[243] The Reverend M. L. Culbertson, an American Protestant missionary in China, is known for his translation of the New Testament into Chinese. Dr. E. C. Bridgman, an American medical missionary, collaborated with him. Couling, *op. cit.*, 65.

Friday December 15, 1854

Received Capt Abbot on board and at 9.30 got underway for Canton via Macao passage. At 12.30 moored ship in our usual anchorage off the Factories. Rec[d] from the *Macedonian* a gun slide for our Howitzer.

Saturday December 16, 1854

Went to Whampoa communicated with the *Powhatan* and returned. Capt Abbot a guest of Mr. Nyes.

Sunday December 17, 1854

A Quiet day—gave the men liberty—that is all that could be spared from duty.

Monday December 18, 1954

Went to Whampoa, communicated with the *Powhatan* and returned.

Tuesday December 19, 1854

Went to Whampoa and alongside the *Powhatan* filled up my coal bunkers from here, and returned.

Wednesday December 20, 1854

Gave liberty to several men, as is my daily custom when there is nothing to do.

Thursday, December 21, 1854

Went to Whampoa, communicated with the *Powhatan,* and returned.

Friday December 22, 1854

Went to Whampoa and returned, towing down the pinnance of H.B.M. Str. *Barracouta* conveying the remains of one of her officers for interment at Whampoa, also towing the *Macedonian's* gig and put on board the *M* two sick men.

Saturday December 23, 1854

Got underway and conveyed Sir James Sterling to Whampoa, communicated with the *Macedonian* and returned to Canton.

Sunday December 24, 1854

Rainy. The Rev. Mr. Preston who was married this week to Mrs. Brewster, the lively widow of another missionary performed divine service in the *Queen*'s cabin. I was invited to the wedding which took place at Mr. Williams house, the ceremony being performed by Doctor Peter Parker, actg U. S. Commissioner in Mr. McLane's absence. After the ceremony was concluded little Matty Williams a young gentleman of our Henrys age, went up to the bride and asked her "what people got married for, and what they were going to do next." I have not learned her answer, but as she had been through the mill before the youngster could not have applied to a better person for an increase of his store of knowledge. I called upon the bride today to tender my congratulations when the blooming bride naively remarked that "marrying did not seem to agree with Mr. Preston as he had been sick ever since the ceremony."

Canton, Christmas evening, 1854

It is seasonable for me at this hour to wish all my friends in the new world 'A Merry Christmas' for while I am about to close my eyes to midnight slumbers, the day being past and gone they are just greeting the morning sun, and the little folks examining their stockings to see what generous old Santa Claus has left for them. With us the day has been raw and rainy, and after breakfast Capt. Abbot, Purser Allison, with a dozen other Officers and Doctor Peter Parker, Actg U. S. Commissioner, came on board, when we got the *Queen* underway and went down to Whampoa and anchored near the *Powhatan* and *Macedonian*. Doctor Parker held a court in my cabin for the trial of eight sailors charged with mutinous conduct on board an American Merchant Ship. It resulted in six of the men being permitted to ship on board the *Macedonian*, and the remaining being brought up here by me and confined on board the *J. P. Kennedy* for a final trial and judgement. While at Whampoa was kept busy calling on board our ships and on Sir James Sterling on board the *Winchester*. His ship having come up to Whampoa to go into the dry dock. Doct. Parker dined with us, but dinner was interrupted by a load of coal coming alongside, and was hastened to enable us to get underway and return to Canton. Capt. Abbot has written a strong letter to the Secretary of the Navy urging the return of our squadron next summer, but I have little hope as I cannot see that any vessels are being equipped as our relief.[244]

Canton, Tuesday December 26, 1854

Damp and cloudy with light breezes from the Nth. We have news by way of California to the 5th of October from New York, ten days later than the last 'overland' brought us. By this arrival we learn that Capt Adams left New York with the Japan Treaty on the 1st of October, and may be expected by the overland now due. Until his arrival our movements are uncertain. The *Macedonian* or *Powhatan*, and perhaps both will go up to Japan with the treaty, but whether now, or after the S. W. Monsoon commences in March is conjectural. The Court Martial on board the *Macedonian* has adjourned and Walcutt has been dismissed the service, but Capt. Abbot has mitigated the sentence and ordered him to the *Vandalia*. What a pity his habit of drinking to excess, should ruin an otherwise excellent officer. He has now an opportunity to reform, and I hope will do so. Lt. Avery's resigning has alone prevented his disgrace. I rejoice that I was not on board the *M* during these troubleous times, and now that these two disturbing elements have left, imagine the wardroom will be more harmonious.

Sunday December 31, 1854

27th, 28th, 29th, and 30th at anchor at Canton. This evening got underway for Whampoa to enquire into the plunder of four chop boats attached to the Am. ship *Staghound*, anchored near the *Macedonian* and banked fires at midnight. So ends the old year.[245]

244 Between pp. 386 and 387 of the diary is inserted an invitation to a Masonic ball held on December 13, 1854, at Hong Kong.

245 On p. 387 of the diary is pasted a lithograph entitled "Summer House and Pagoda, Island of Whampoa."

The Diary: 1855

The Diary: 1855

[Canton] Monday January 1, 1855

Commenced the New Year by anchoring at Whampoa and lunching on ham, cheese, bread, porter, and ale, and toasted absent friends with true feelings. I came down last night with the owner of some sugar that had been robbed from some boats attached to the stern of the *Staghound* and to communicate with Capt. Abbot and institute means for its recovery—as I had supposed, it has already been recovered and restored to its rightful owners.

Looking over some newspapers today my eye was caught by the following advertisement.

"Patent Baby Walker

The depot for the sale of this useful article is now open at No. 436 Broadway. Fathers, Mothers, Nurses, and all others interested in babies are invited to call, examine and purchase State rights for sale."

I suppose this invention is designed to make babies bless their dear little bodies, walk right off, and stop all future tending and creeping. What won't we Yankees invent next? I imagine some ingenious Brother Jonathan[1] fixing some machine to the dear little

[1] In 1828, James H. Hackett (1800–1871) gave the name *Jonathan in England* to a popular comedy entitled *Who Wants a Guinea?* The stage Yankee was developed in comedies, starting with Royall Tyler (1757–1826) as Brother Jonathan, a nickname for a typical New Englander. From a comic stage figure he became a symbol of simplicity, honesty, and common sense. W. P. Trent *et al.*, *The Cambridge History of American Literature*, I, 227–28; *The New Century Cyclopedia of Names*, II, 2211.

innocent mouths by which their crying will be rendered melodious and according to the taste of the parent, be converted into "Old Hundred" "Home Sweet Home," Auld Lang Syne," or some other standard tune.

I had written thus far when Capt. Abbot came on board and I got underway for Canton, where, after securing the ship, I dined at Mr. Hunter's by invitation of his agreeable and pleasant wife. My most acceptable New Years treat was your dear letter (No 38) of Sept. 28, which came by the Formosa last week, and ought to have been received sooner. It was put into my hands just after dinner and furnished an agreeable dessert. I ought to have received it sooner, but it was sent back to Hong Kong by mistake after having been forwarded here. Messr. Hubbell, Heard[2] and Sturgis were of our dinner party. Mrs. Hunter is the mother of five or six children, though no one to see her would believe it. Her sister Mrs. Myers of Richmond Virginia gained an unenviable notoriety a few years since eloping, and occasioning either his or her par-amours death, I forget which. Recently another of her sisters has been married a la Gretna Greene.[3] Mrs. H[unter] appears quite a different sort of person. She showed me last evening something I had never seen, a couple of daguerreotypes fitted or mounted with a stereoscopic attachment so that seen through it only one image was shown, and every part stood out with the fulness of a statue, and the perfection of life, or rather of life petrified. She has also a stereoscope and some two dozen slides, all of which are truly wonderful. I doubt whether you have ever seen the little instrument, though Cory Bartlett, I know, has one but hers did not compare with the one I saw this evening. I wish you could have seen the daguerreotypes. If they can be taken in the U. S. I must have one of you and our babies.

[2] Augustine Heard and Company wash an important American trading firm in Canton. Augustine Heard was at one time a partner in Russell and Company. His son, John, continued the Heard firm until 1862. Griffin, *op. cit.*, 189, 194; Dennett, *op. cit.*, 72. For biographical notes on Heard and his associates, see T. F. Waters, *Augustine Heard and His Friends.*

[3] Gretna Green was a farm near the village of Springfield, Scotland; the name was later applied to the village, which became notorious for irregular marriages contracted by runaway parties from England. *The New Century Cyclopedia of Names*, II, 1835.

Tuesday January 2d 1855

Clear cool and pleasant with northerly breezes, borrowed two tons of coal from H.B.M. Str. *Styx*, and at 3 P.M. got underway with Capt Abbot on board and at 4.30 anchored near the *Macedonian* at Whampoa.

We are all anxiously and impatiently expecting the next mail, the arrival of Capt. Adams, and his dispatches. It is thought Capt. Abbot will receive orders to hoist a broad pendant, an honor the old man very much craves.

Whampoa, January 3d 1855

Got underway at noon, and followed the English Squadron down to the 1st Bar, and conveyed back the 'Bar boats' placed to mark the best water. At 1 P.M. anchored again near the *Macedonian*. At 3.15 again underway and at 4.50 moored at Canton. At 6.30 once more underway, and at 8 P.M. anchored near the *Macedonian* at Whampoa. A busy day.

Thursday January 4th, 1855

Henry 8 years old. Cool and pleasant weather with a fresh northerly wind.

Friday January 5th 1855

Commander H. A. Adams, late Comdre Perry's flag Capt., arrived from the United States, bringing the ratified Treaty with Japan. He has taken up his quarters on board the *Macedonian*. He also brings authority for Capt. Abbot to hoist his broad pendant as Commodore. Rec'd your letter of Oct. 15th.

Whampoa, Saturday January 6th 1855

At 9 A.M. the *Macedonian* hoisted the broad pendant of Commodore Abbot and honored it with a salute of thirteen guns. I also had a salute of thirteen guns fired from the *Queen*, useing the guns captured from the pirates. Commodore Abbot immediately ordered it returned by the *Macedonian* with seven guns the salute for a Lieut.Com'dg. This is the first time I was ever honored with a salute.

Canton, Sunday January 7, 1855

Cool and pleasant with light northerly winds. The Rev. Mr.

Preston performed divine service on board. Capt. Adams brings little news from the U. S. He is to go to Simoda in the *Powhatan* as soon as she can be got ready and exchange the ratified treaties. I saw our document yesterday. It is beautifully engrossed on parchment, signed by the President, countersigned by the Secretary of State, and ornamented with a huge seal, which is put up in a solid gold box, as big a ship biscuit, and is embossed with the arms of the United States, the whole attached by a cord of blue and gold with heavy tassles of the same. Capt. Adams letter of credence is also on parchement, and has a similiar seal in a silver box, with silver and blue cord and tassels. The whole is in a richly polished walnut casket.

In the disturbed state of this country Comdre Abbot will remain in this neighborhood with the *Macedonian* until the return of the *Powhatan* from Japan and I shall retain command of the *Queen* for three months longer.

I was glad to learn by your last letter that you had a visit from Sue Gore before she became Mrs. Richard Warren; send her my congratulations, or rather congratulate him that he has secured so good a wife. Our wedding brought luck with it! All my grooms men John, Alex, Arthur, are married and two of your three bridesmaids; perhaps Mary O. is only waiting for Mr. Bonney, the missionary celebs who has just left.

The accounts of the loss of the steamship *Arctic*[4] are heart rendering. Capt. Luce's escape from death is one of the wonders of Providence. Everyone must rejoice at it since he so nobly prefered death to the abandonment of those under his charge. The conduct of the crew, and firemen particularly, appears to have been shameful. Had I been in Capt. Luce's place, I would have shot some of them. The news of the *Artic's* loss was conveyed to England two days before it reached N. York. I notice in Capt Luce's statement that the Mrs. Child and daughter you mentioned bade him good bye, as the ship went down.

[4] The *Arctic*, a steamer of the Collins Line, was under Captain Luce. The line competed successfully with the British Cunard Line in the North Atlantic. The *Arctic*, with about four hundred person on board, went down in a collision. *Greyhounds*, 141, 303.

A scene only less distressing than that on board of the *Arctic* occurred recently in these seas. The *Gazelle* a fine clipper ship of 1500 tons, on her passage from California to Hong Kong, was thrown suddenly on her beam ends in a furious hurricane and dismasted. The mast being snapped off like pipe stems close to the upper deck, and most of her beams and timbers were cracked and rent by the blow. She went over so far, that her masts were buried in the water before broken, and her Captain washed off its spindle. It is a wonder that she ever righted as she did, and full of water. Fifteen Chinese passangers were drowned between decks. The Captain was on deck, and all his thoughts and energies were at the moment requisite for the preservation of the ship. His wife and three little children were in the cabin on deck, and but [for] the energy of the steward would have been drowned. A huge sea broke in the sky light deluging the cabin tearing down bulk heads and floating everything about. It was some time (minutes seeming hours) before one little boy, who had been washed into an after berth could be found and got at. He was plaintively crying 'save me Mother save me!' The Capt.'s wife as she herself told me cut her feet, walking over the looking glass which was fastened to the side partition. You can judge that from the ship's position this disaster occurred in the middle of the Pacific, 1700 miles from Hong Kong. Yet with a maintops gallant mast, steering sail boom, and topsail yard lashed to the stump of the old mast for a jury rig—they made sail, and favored with a continuance of fair wind and good weather reached Hong Kong in fourteen days. I have visited the ship, and am astonished at the wreck she displayed. The provisions in the hole were broken up and turned under the ballast, and the stench arising from them and the dead Chinamen, was intolerable. The Capt's books charts and instruments were washed and knocked to pieces, and his own and his wife and children's clothing reduced to a pulp or torn to pieces. This was that lady's first sea experience, and she was tempted to take the voyage, by the strength size and beauty of the ship. To add to the whole she is happy. Wouldn't you like to go to sea?

I have written Dr. N. the New Year's note which you wished, and I believe remembered in that each one of the family.

Monday January 8, 1855

Anniversary of Genl Jackson's victory at New Orleans.[5] At 5 A.M. got underway for Whampoa. At 6.20 anchored there. At 9 A.M. underway for Canton with Com'dre Abbot and hoisted his broad pendant on board the *Queen*. At 10.40 anchored off the Factories. At 7.30 P.M. underway again with Comdre Abbot, and at 9 P.M. anchored near the *Macedonian* at Whampoa.

Tuesday January 9, 1855

Cool and cloudy with light Easterly breezes. At 9 P.M. Com'dre Abbot with his gigs crew came on board, took the gig in tow. Hoisted the broad pendant and at midnight got underway for Hong Kong with Capt. Adams and other passangers.

Wednesday January 10, 1855

Anchored off the Naval Store House at 'Gardens' Hong Kong at 9 30 A.M. The *Powhatan* and *Winchester* saluted the Commodore's pendant with thirteen guns each. Returned the *Powhatan's* salute from this Flag Ship, and the *Powhatan* returned the *Winchester's*. Sent seven small cannons which I took from the pirates, on shore to be sold by permission of the Commodore.

Thursday January 11, 1855

At Hong Kong, taking in stores for the *Queen* and the *Macedonian*.

Friday January 12, 1855

Received on [board] twenty one tons of coal. Expected to remain here several days, but this afternoon Commodore Abbot came on board, with numerous other passengers and we are hurried back to Canton, as it is rumored the rebels intend an attack. We left Hong Kong at 3.30 P.M. and are now on our way up river.

Saturday January 13, 1855

Soon after midnight this morning as we were passing the Bocca

[5] Preble refers to Andrew Jackson's (1767–1845) defense of New Orleans, 1815, and his victory over the British, in which he was the major hero and a national figure. For a short life and bibliography, see *DAB*, IX, 526–34.

Tigris,[6] the *Queen* came in collision with a Portuguese lorcha, coming down, and it is wonderful it did not result like the affair of the *Artic* in the loss of nearly every soul on board, and that the vessel was so little damaged.

If we had been struck like the *Artic* in the side we must with our heavy load of stores and machinery have sunk instantly. The side would have been crushed in like an eggshell, as the steamer is so light built.

I was quite unwell yesterday, and was sitting in the cabin feeling rather poorly at the time of the accident. Mr. Williams and the pilot in charge on deck. The first thing I heard was the pilot's order, "Hard o port! Stop her!" and at the same instant the crash. I rushed at once on deck, where I found our bowsprit gone, and the lorcha alongside with her sail up pressing us towards the shore. I ran forward and examined above and below with a lantern, and satisfied myself that the steamer was not leaking badly, and then returned to the deck to see what could be done to clear us of the stranger. After some delay, we got the lorcha's sails down cutting them from her yards, when a panic struck her people, and they all jumped on board us, first throwing on board their boxes and bundles. Our sailors as promptly threw the bundles and their owners back with the lorcha. At first thinking they might be pirates boarding us and then because they careened the *Queen* so by all crowding on one side their was danger of our boilers exploding. At last however seeing their fright I permitted them to come on board, though there was no danger of the lorcha's sinking as she was cotton loaded.

At last, after much excitement we got clear and proceeded to Whampoa. On a further examination at daylight we discovered we had been struck directly upon the cut water where best able to resist the blow, and it was stove completely to within a foot of the waters edge, and about eight feet abaft the cutwater, there was a hole in the side ten inches long by four wide, only six inches above the water line. Had the sea been at all rough we could not have kept her afloat.

[6] Bocca Tigris is the name given by the Portuguese to the mouth of Pearl, or Canton River. The name was derived from the resemblance of the hilltops on Tiger Island. Here were Chinese fortifications against foreign invasions.

At first we could not work the engine or steer the ship; the lorcha having swung her low deck directly under our paddle wheel which was all knocked as they say into a cocked hat. The Master, crew and forty of her Chinese passangers off the lorcha sought refuge on board of our vessel. From these we learned the lorcha was from Canton bound to Amoy, that they were on the lookout for pirates, and seeing the steamer got suddenly and needlessly alarmed, and put their helm the wrong way that is to starboard instead of to port and so cuffed into us. Had they kept directly on or put their help to port there would have been no collision. The Master said he took refuge on board of us because he was afraid of the pirates, and because the lorcha had a hole in, though she could not sink. In consequence of our crippled condition, having only one wheel, we did not reach Whampoa only 15 miles dist. until after daylight and were thirteen hours and a half from Hong Kong. We immediately discharged our freight and passangers, procured carpenters from the *Macedonian* and commenced repairs, at 2 P.M. took Commodore Abbot on board their being rumors of fresh disturbances, and an attack upon Canton and came on up. The rebels all around have been victorious of late, and are very much elated in consequence. Com'dre Abbot is at Mr. Nye's, but I have his flag flying on board the *Queen*. On our arrival H.B.M.S. *Comus* and the *J. P. Kennedy* saluted his pennant, and the *Kennedy* returned the salute of the *Comus* gun for gun. Thirty-nine guns waked all Canton from its slumbers to look at our crippled wheel and broken nose. Just like a drunken man who is always sure to do something calling attention to his condition.

Sunday January 14, 1855

We have kept the Armorers and Carpenters at work all day, as our repairs are a necessity. There is already a call for the *Queen* to go on some expedition for sugar which is said to have been stolen by the pirates, rebels or mandarins hereabout nearly synonomous.

Some of the ladies have again left Canton but more remain and I hope will not allow themselves to be frightened away. The Chinese are leaving in crowds, and the passenger steamers have raised the fare from \$2 to 5\$ to lessen the demand. The *Spark* went down two days ago loaded to her guards and towing two Junks just so crowded.

These are exciting and eventful times. My life for the last four months has been one continual turmoil.

The *Powhatan* leaves with Capt. Adams and the Treaty for Japan tomorrow. I do not envy them their cold and unpleasant cruise.

Sunday, January 21, 1855

The past week has not been eventful or exciting. The repairs upon our wheels have been going on and are still continued. They have kept four blacksmiths and eight carpenters hard at work. On Friday we were able to take the Commodore to Whampoa and return with him. Today the Rev. Mr. Preston performed Divine Service on board and fourteen of the crew took french leave and went on shore on a frolic; confined them in irons or otherwise punished them when they came on board. I learn the Lorcha that damaged us arrived at Macao. The rebels have had some successes down the river, and are closing up all the approaches to Canton and threaten to attack it. Tomorrow is said to be the appointed day and the foreign community is very generally alarmed as the rebels are by them thought no better and the same as pirates. As I write I see through my cabin windows the light from a villiage on Hanam, which they burnt today.

The most sanguinary warfare is carried on. No quarter is given or taken by either party, and prisoners if taken are beheaded or disemboweled. In some instances the livers of Mandarins have been torn out and eaten by rebs. [rebels] as they say, to make them brave. The Governor of Canton in retaliation has issued a proclamation that all friends and relations, male or female, old or young, of any person who may join the rebels shall suffer death. It is notorious that at the north a noted pirate chief Apak has been taken into the Imperial service with all his fleet, and that he has been rewarded with a 'Blue' button. It is also known that Awang[7] chief of the Kulan pirates is now in Command of an Imperial fleet in this neighborhood, and a large part of his fleet composed of the piratical junks that have been the pest and nuisance of this province. The rebels are a rowdy

[7] He is the same as Awang (or Aw-ung); see note 225 under the year 1854. Preble repeats the confused name, perhaps made so by foreign residents in Canton.

set, but evince great bravery and judgement, and are invariably the attacking party.

The *Powhatan* left Hong Kong on tuesday for Japan will probably be ten days on the passage, remain there two weeks, and then return to Shanghai, to relieve the *Vandalia*. The latter will reach Hong Kong about the 1st of March when the *Macedonian* received by her will go to Shanghai, and I shall then quit the *Queen* to go by her. At least such is the programme now and while if nothing occurs to defeat it will be carried out.

Walcutt who was dismissed by the Court Martial has been pardoned by the Commodore and ordered to the *J. P. Kennedy*. He came up with us last week and I had a long and serious talk with him. He has signed a temperance pledge and I hope he will keep it. I have been reading Mrs. Stowes' 'Sunny Memories'[8] It is a gossiping book, she sees everything through rose-colored glasses, and lords and ladies are are plentifully besprinkled through its pages as butter cups in a clover field. I have also been reading 'Potiphar Papers."[9] English reviewers call it dull and stupid but I think it a Capital caracature of new world society. The Canton Library is a great addition to my comforts now that I am having a little leisure. It is furnished with the chief English and American periodicals and newspapers, and has a thousand and more of excellent Modern books collected with the year.

Imagine me with my usual beard and a heavy mustache and imperial. Several have told me I ought to shave all else, and so perfect my extraordinary likeness to Louis Napoleon.[10] Did you ever notice any such resemblance? Frenchmen always tell me of it.

[8] Harriet Elizabeth Beecher Stowe (1811–1896), *Sunny Memories of Foreign Lands* (New York, J. C. Derby, *ca.* 1853). Preble apparently read this book during his cruise in the Far East. W. J. Burke, *American Authors and Books* (New York, 1943), 729, but here the title is given incorrectly as "Memories in Foreign Lands (1854)."

[9] The *Potiphar Papers* (New York, 1853), published anonymously, were written by George William Curtis (1824–1892). He also contributed part of the essay under the same title to the first issue of *Putnam's Monthly Magazine* (January, 1853). Trent, *op. cit.*, III, 114–15, 313.

[10] Louis Napoleon (1808–1873), or Napoleon III, was the third son of Louis Bonaparte, brother of Napoleon I, and Hortense de Beauharnais.

Tuesday January 23d, 1855

Got underway at 10 A.M. for Whampoa arrived at 11:30. Commodore Abbot communicated with the *Macedonian* and at 2 P.M. returned, when we got underway and anchored at Canton at 3.40 P.M. Passed the rebel fleet near the Barrier, preparing to attack the forts.

Wednesday January 24, 1855

A fire broke out in the rear of the British Consulate in the suburbs of the city and burnt until midnight.

Thursday, January 25, 1855

At 2.30 P.M. the rebels attacked the Barrier Forts and were repulsed.

Friday January 26, 1855

At 10 A.M. got underway for Whampoa with Com'dre Abbot and Mr. Roberts on H.B.M. Consul[11] for Canton on board. At 11.40 anchored near the *Macedonian* when our passangers went on board, and Mr. R. received a salute of nine guns. At 4.15 our passangers returned and we got underway for Canton, where we arrived at 5.30 P.M.

Saturday January 27, 1855

Continued our repairs, interrupted of late by our getting underway.

Sunday January 28, 1855

Rev. Josiah Cox performed Divine Service on board. The overland mail has not arrived, and I have comforted myself by reading over the letters brought by the last mail. I see I have been made an Honorary Member of the Portland Rifle Corps. I fear I shall sink under the weight of my responsibilities. I have been to Whampoa twice the past week convoying American property through and

[11] D. B. Robertson was acting British consul at Canton from May 1, 1853, with interruptions, until December 21, 1858. He was consul at Amoy from April 29, 1853, to January, 1854. He was also in charge of the consulate in Shanghai, with interruptions, in 1854–55. See Fairbank, *op. cit.*, II, 51–53.

beyond the rebel and Mandarin fleets which have made a great show of fighting on the river. The *Potomac*[12] an Am. ship commanded by Capt. Stone[13] will sail for New York tomorrow or in a day or two, and will probably arrive sometime in May or early in June. I shall send by her two boxes, one a box of 35 lbs of fine oolong tea from Mr. Nye for Mrs. Preble. The other containing three idols captured from the pirates. They will be forwarded from N. York by Adams & Co. Express. The rebels have advanced to the Barrier with over 200 boats and from 10 to 20,000 men, and there has been some hard fighting there abouts.

One of the principal chiefs of the rebels has been captured by the Mandarins. The rebels retired after his capture and it is reported will attempt the other channel. On one of our trips we passed the rival belligerents engaging each other and some of their balls skipped along rather more neighborly to us than agreeable. A pretty little villiag near the Barrier, embosomed in trees was burnt by the rebels while they held it, and when they retreated, what had been spared was burned by the Imperialists when they took possession. The attrocities of both parties upon inoffensive people are too horrible for narration. Those not decidedly for them, are punished for being against them.

Com'dre Abbot remains here. Sir James has removed his whole squadron to Whampoa to be at hand in case of emergency. Another ship will leave for N. Y. ere long and I shall send you by her a box of Chinese paintings. The *Potomac* is an old ship and her Capt a poor navigator, and she is certain to make a long passage and may be lost. Her cargo is valued at 200,000$. Stowed down to her a chop boat loaded with $60,000 worth of silk.

Capt. Stone lost father, mother and sister in the *Arctic*. He had been disinherited in consequence of his irregularities and because of his marrying a public singer in California. He now is hoping his

12 The frigate *Potomac*, 1,457 tons, 20 guns, was built in 1819 and launched in 1821. She became a receiving ship at Philadelphia in 1874 and was sold in 1877.

13 Edward E. Stone was made midshipman on October 19, 1841; passed midshipman, August 10, 1847; master, September 14, 1855; lieutenant, September 15, 1855; lieutenant commander, July 16, 1862; commander, July 25, 1866; retired list, January 5, 1874; died, June 18, 1892. See also *Records*, 158.

father died without making his will. His wife is a pretty modest and intelligent little woman decidedly his better half whatever his friends may think. They have a noble blue-eyed baby seven months old.

Time drags on with slow but unfettering tread and two years of exile will soon be finished, and if grey hairs and wrinkled brows follow in its footsteps, we are also brought daily and hourly nearer each other. Thank heaven I am in the enjoyment of good health.

Canton, Wednesday January 31, 1855

At anchor all this week painting ship and completing repairs.

Friday February 2d, 1855

Hauled down Com'dre Abbot's broad pendant and sent it to the *J. P. Kennedy*, and at 6 A.M. got underway and went to Whampoa, and anchored near H.B.M. Frigate *Winchester*. Reported myself and vessel to Admiral Sir. Jas. Stirling as at his command, and breakfasted with him on board the *Winchester*. After noon he came on board the *Queen* with his suite and we got underway at 1:15 for Canton, and anchored there about a quarter before three, and moored ship as usual.

Saturday February 3, 1855

Accompanied Sir James to the picture shops and at his request assisted him in the selection of four landscapes. One of them like one I have hanging in my cabin. In the afternoon got underway and took him and his suite to Whampoa, where I dined with him on board the *Winchester* at six oclock. He is truly a fine, a very fine specimen of the Old English gentleman, all of the olden time. He is 76 years old, has been a member of Parliament from London, the Govr of a Colony and filled various other responsible offices.

Sunday February 4, 1855

Got underway and anchored near the *Macedonian* and at 10.15 got underway again and at noon moored in the old place at Canton. The varnish on good Doct. N's [Nye's] picture which Ellen sent me is a little cracked but can be easily restored. I shall get it framed. Her Grecia coloring of it is a great improvement on the black engraving.

I saw a letter this week from Mr. Bonney, dated in the Crater of Mount Gede thirty eight miles south of Batavia, Isld of Java. He writes the *Comet* is to go to Samarang to take Cays, return to Batavia to complete her load, and then go to Bremen and thence to Liverpool, where Mr. Bonney will leave her and take a steamship to New York. Our Family portraits will have traveled about a good deal before reaching you.

There is no telling the barbarities that are committed daily in this neighborhood by both parties. The bodies of dead Chinamen are constantly floating down the river and the light of burning villiages, and dwellings nightly illuminate the horizon. A few nights since a fire in the heart of the outside city of Canton destroyed over a hundred shops and houses. Commodore Abbot is again quite sick, from imprudence in his diet and I fear with his feeble constitution the coming summer will prove fatal to my friend, but he is determined to die in harness or go home in the ship. I was surprised to learn by my letters this week that John Cox had established himself as a Grocer, but wish him success.

Tell Ellen that when I get her head of Doct. N[ye] framed I think I shall give it to Sir John Bowring[14] the Govr. of Hong Kong who is an out and out Unitarian. It is very singular, but until I told him he was not aware that his beautiful colloquy, "Watchmen tell us of the Night," etc., had been set to music. Did I tell you that I have

[14] Sir John Bowring (1792–1872) was a linguist, writer, traveler, and statesman. He was born into an old Devonshire family and started his career as a clerk but showed a vital interest in linguistic studies, including a good command of Polish. Bowring maintained cordial relations with such well-known contemporaries as Jeremy Bentham, James Mill, and others. He performed several governmental missions in Italy, Prussia, and China and was a member of Parliament. His representation of English commerce met with Chinese contumely, 1847–52, and he became plenipotentiary to China, 1854, and governor, commander-in-chief, and vice-admiral of Hong Kong, as well as chief superintendent of trade in China with accreditation to the courts of the Far East. In October, 1856, he was responsible for the outrages of the lorcha *Arrow* with the Chinese, acting on his own authority, but was exonerated by parliamentary decision. He was awarded many foreign and distinguished knightly insignia. His first wife was the daughter of Samuel Lewin of Hackney, who died in 1858. Preble had many graces from her, as is evident from his diary. *DNB*, II, 984–88; *Sketch*, 206–207; see also Lammer Moor (Bowring's pseudonym), *Bowring, Cobden and China, a Memoir* (London, 1857).

made a clean shave of all but my mustache and imperial and appear à la Emperor to the delight of all the Frenchmen here?[15]

Monday February 5, 1855

There was a continual fireing all night down the Macao passage between the rebels and imperialists. I suppose we will learn tomorrow what it amounted to.

I think I wrote last summer that it was intended to give me the command of the *Porpoise*,[16] one of the Explorers. That I did not arrive in season to get her, is shown to be in my case that 'alls for the best.' Here I have been able to gain some little reputation, and there is but little doubt the *Porpoise* has foundered with all on board. The *Vincennes*[17] after a prolonged search for her has returned to Hong Kong.

Tuesday February 6, 1855

Last night Mr. Seare, an English gentleman, an admirer and friend of Dickens, gave us a lecture and some readings which was agreeable and amuseing. He brought out all the foreign residents.

Wednesday February 7, 1855

Wm. Dougherty one of my sailors when ordered into confinement for neglect of duty and being made an assult upon me and bruized my forehead, but was quickly and easily secured. His usual conduct has been good, and I can only account for his insubordination, that cornered in an untruth it irritated him so he did not know what he was doing.

Thursday February 8, 1855

Got underway at 9.30 A.M. to the assistance of the American bark *Science* aground with the Macao pass. Wore our colors at Half Mast all day on receipt of the official news of the decease of Commodore John Downes.[18] At 10.15 A.M. anchored near the *Science*, and found she was afloat and did not need assistance. Ret'd to Canton.

[15] Between pp. 405 and 406 of the diary is inserted the program of a lecture (delivered on February 5, 1855, at Canton Public Room) by Benjamin Seare on the early writings of Charles Dickens.

[16] The second *Porpoise*, 224 tons, ten guns, was built in 1836.

[17] The *Vincennes*, 700 tons, 18 guns, was built in 1825 and sold in 1867.

[18] Commodore John Downes (1784–1854) was acting midshipman in September,

Got underway during the forenoon with Comdre Abbot and at noon anchored near the Flag Ship. Comdre went on board the *M*[*acedonian*] and hauled down his broad pennant and hoisted my own narrow one.

Whampoa, Sunday February 11, 1855

Received and read to the crew a general order increasing the pay of seamen and others.

The rebels have been quiet the past week and say they are waiting for the rainy season, and more water in the river to allow their largest junks to come up. I visited the rebel village of Sunchow yesterday with Purser Allison and Doct. Gilliam. We were civilley treated by its motley populace, and saw the forging of swords, and cultivation of turnips going on side by side. The rebels are no doubt a vagabond set—little better than pirates—but scarcely worse than the Mandarin soldiers. The devil is never so bad as he is painted. Today the rebel chief Chin-bing-leong visited the *Macedonian*. I had just a sight of him and that's all, as he was leaving—a good looking Chinaman.

Commodore Abbot has advice which have decided him to go in the *Macedonian* to Guam on the arrival of the *Vandalia* from Shanghai. It is not settled whether the *Queen* is to be rechartered for another five months or I am to return to the *M*. I have purchased a tea and desert set of green china like the plates we now have at home; altogether costing me 23$, and have a punch bowl and various ornamented articles of china ware vases, etc., for mantil ornaments besides.

Monday February 12, 1855

Com'dre Abbott came on board today noon, when I hoisted his pennant and took him to Canton. Purser A. came with him. Rec'd a long expected package by the Ship *N. B. Palmer*. The Papers and Magazines were a real treat.

1800; midshipman, June, 1802; participated in the war with Tripoli, 1803; lieutenant, 1807; took part in the memorable cruise on the *Essex* from the Delaware Capes, October 28, 1812. In April, 1813, Downes captured two British vessels in the Pacific; made commodore, 1815; ordered to the *Macedonian* in the Pacific, 1818; served on various vessels, 1818–32; spent the rest of his life on shore duty. *DAB*, V, 416–17 and bibliography.

Canton, Friday February 16, 1855

The U.S. Str. *John Hancock* arrived at Canton. The Chinese think her a beauty because "she lookee allo the same as one Chinese junk."

Canton, Sunday February 18, 1855

Rev. J. F. Preston performed divine service on board the *Queen*. While you are wrapt in furs, or enjoying the warmth of a winter fire, your more comfortable half is writing you with doors and windows wide open and the balmiest of spring like airs breathing upon him.

Yesterday was the commencement of the Chinese New Year, being the 1st day of the 1st moon and called Yuen-tan, the celebration is continued for a week or longer according to the taste or wealth of the individual.

Just before Yuen-tan, there is a great cleansing and scouring of all the shops and houses. An annual washing day. On the evening preceeding New Years day all tradesmens bills and small debts are paid. Inability to 'settle up' causes a man to "lose facee," in other words destroy his credit. Yesterday all the shops were closed. Today all the Chinamen are going about dressed in their best exchanging calls, and carrying immence sized visiting cards of red paper. They also have the custom of 'cumshawing' that is exchanging presents.

The Foreign merchants at this season generally receive handsome 'comshaws' from those they have dealings with. The first ten days of the Chinese New Year are named after birds animals, etc., as Fowl-day, Dogday, etc. The seventh being considered the greatest and named manday. This seems something like a tradition of the order of the mosaical creation. You can form no idea of the din that is kept up on this river by its floating population by the beating of gongs, explosion of fire crackers, bursting of squibs, banging of guns and the like. Chin-Chining Joss, as they call it, that is propitiating their deities for the ensueing year. All Chinese enjoyment seems to center in makeing a noise, and the more noise, the more happiness.

I have been looking at a cheap set of blue china of the willow pattern with a view to purchase. Did you know that that pattern illustrates a Chinese love story? I will tell it as it has been told to me. The house on the right surrounded by orange and other trees represents the dwelling of a Mandarin whose daughter had formed an attachment to a man of lowly birth and station, whom her father forbade her seeing. With the aid of a fisherman, the loving couple escaped to an adjoining island, and the father with his men is pursuing them over a bridge. The two doves are the souls of the lovers, and emblematical of their happiness.

Think of me as quite well, and looking like Louis Napoleon for everybody here remarks the resemblance. I hope the resemblance is only in face and feature, for I am not an admirer of the man, yet should not have objection to his talents.

Canton, Monday February 19, 1855

Hauled down the Commodore's pennant at sundown and sent it to the *Kennedy*. Today the Chinese festivities of New Year have been continued; amused myself by calling upon my 'celestial' friends and viewing their arrangements. Every shop was shut to trade and converted into a temporary temple for the household 'Joss.' The counter at the lower end converted into an altar and loaded with fruit, flowers and confectionary. The shelves behind the counter draped with clothes and covered with pictures and inscriptions. This evening all Canton is feasting and reveling. Dined at Mr. Nyes.

Tuesday February 20, 1855

At 8. A.M. got underway with Mrs. Nyes and several gentlemen passangers and at 5.40 anchored at Hong Kong and landed my passangers. The long expected *Calcutta* mail Str. has arrived. She got out of coal and had to put in at Manila, hence her delay. The owner of the Queen is disposed to make trouble about her recharter, wishing to sell her, and if the *Vandalia* can be lightened when she comes from Shanghai so as lie off Canton, she will be given up and I return on board the *M*[*acedonian*] biding a long farewell to all my (present) greatness.

Hong Kong, Wednesday February 21, 1855

Coaling and taking in provisions; received my missing letter and some newspapers. Called on Mrs. Nye,[19] and on the Govr. Sir John Bowring, who invited me to dine with him at 7 o'clock. Dressed in

[19] See note 184 under the year 1854.

full uniform I attended at the appointed hour. Capt. John Rodgers[20] with several officers of the Explorer Expedition made up the dinner party. It was a pleasant dinner and in the evening I had a pleasant conversation with Lady Bowring on Unitarians and Unitarianism in England and America. On leaving she gave me a file of the English Unitarian Inquirer,[21] which Miss Bowring said was always cordially greeted by them, as the exponent of their party. I told Miss Bowring I thought ours, the Unitarian, pre emenently the ladies party as it is founded in love. Learning I was from Portland Sir John asked me if I was acquainted with John Neal,[22] and inquired if he was living. Sir John said that they were fellow residents with Jeremy Bentham[23] in England, and gave an amusing and characteristic anecdote of J. N.'s impudence. He said J. N. forced himself into Bentham's house called the old philosopher 'Jere,' and kicked his cook out of doors, when he himself was only a guest on sufferance and was so outrageously impertinent that he, Sir John, was directed by Bentham to inform Neal that he must leave his house. Neal swore he wouldn't go, and wouldn't be turned out as he had no money and didn't know where to go. At last he was forced out. Sir John said Neal accused him of being the cause of his dismissal and abused him in one of his books for it.

[20] See note 163 under the year 1854. For the correspondence of the American Exploring Expedition, see Cole, *op. cit.*

[21] Neither the *British Union-Catalogue of Periodicals* nor other indexes of periodicals list the *English Unitarian Inquirer*. Preble gave his own title to a periodical difficult to identify. There were several Unitarian periodical publications in his day.

[22] John Neal (1793–1876), a native of Portland, distinguished himself as a writer. He contributed articles on American subjects to *Blackwood's Magazine* and other British periodicals. He also published short stories, novels, and poems and was perhaps the first advocate of women's rights. *NCAB*, XI, 346; for a short bibliography, see *DAB*, XIII, 398–99; see also an interesting book by H. E. Dickson, *Observations on American art: Selections from the Writings of John Neal (1793–1876)* (State College, Pa., 1943), with notes.

[23] Jeremy Bentham (1748–1832), a prominent English philosopher and jurist, lived in London. He was described by Richard Rush (1780–1859), American minister to the Court of St. James, in *Memoranda of a Residence at the Court of London* (London, 1833 and 1845). *DAB*, XVI, 235–36; for a substantial bibliography on Bentham, see Encyclopaedia Britannica (1956), III, 416–18.

Thursday February 22, 1855

Washington's birthday: rainy. Got underway early in the morning and anchored at Canton about 4 P.M. and went alongside the *Kennedy* and gave her her provisions. Dined at Mr. Nye's at 7 P.M. who gave a dinner party in honor of the day.

Friday February 23d 1855

At 7.30 A.M. got underway from Canton for Macao having on board Doct. Peter Parker, Actg. U. S. Commissioner. At 9 A.M. anchored and boarded a sloop boat belonging to Mr. Cook, which had a signal of distress flying. She had been taken by a rebel boat still alongside and plundered. Fired again to attract attention and made signal to the *Macedonian* for a boat; one arriving from her, and another from H.B.M.S. *Spartan*. I left the matter in their hands and got underway again and at 5:30 P.M. anchored at Macao. The day was very rainy; put our Doctor Commissioner on shore in my gig at the expense of a heavy wetting to him because he thought it would look better; after he had landed called a Sampan alongside and Tuckerman (who was also a passanger), and I went on shore comfortably though without dignity. Remained all night with Tuckerman at Mr. Nye's place as it was too rainy to go out, or think of returning on board. Occupied myself with a book or in pleasant chat until bedtime.

Macao, Saturday February 24, 1855

Got underway at 11.15 A.M. for Hong Kong with Doct Parker and at 1.15 anchored off the Naval Store House. Mr. Hitchcock also a passenger. Called on my senior officer Capt. Rodgers on board the *Vincennes* and went on shore and dined with Mr. Hitchcock at the Club. We sat late over our wine and segars and returned to the Str. abt. midnight and tumbled into bed.

Sunday February 25, 1855

Clear warm and pleasant. My birthday. Released Wm. Doherty whose offence was personal to myself from confinement and pardoned him. Called upon the officers of the Exploring Squadron and upon the Admiral and officers of H.B.M. vessels in Harbor. Sir James invited me to dine with him, but I had to decline, as Rodgers had engaged me to take my birthday dinner with him on board the *Vincennes*. The Admiral then invited me to dine with him tomorrow. The wardroom officers of the *Winchester* understanding it was my birthday, broached a bottle of champagne and drank to my health and long life. In the P.M. sent Sir John Bowring the picture of Doct. Nichols and two Unitarian reports. After our dinner on board the *Vincennes* went on shore with Capt. Rodgers and passed the evening at our Storekeepers Mr. Robt De Silver both the De Silver and Mrs. 'Emily Bob' and Mrs. Emily Hal were there, also Mrs. Endicott and her sister Miss Russell, the latter has just arrived from England after a passage of 160 days. It is said she comes out to get married, just as her sister did 'to order,' but notwithstanding that Mrs. Endicott is amiable and charming and a truly domestic woman, and Capt. E[ndicott] rolling in fat drew a prize when he got her. The sisters have been seperated three years and a half and Mrs. E. has a husband and two children to show. Her eldest she calls Lily, though named Cordelia.

Hong Kong, Monday February 26, 1855

Clear and pleasant breezes from N^th^ and E^st^. Visited the observatory of our Exploring Exped. which is at the Morrison Hospital. Mr. Kern took my daguerreotype not a very good or clear one, but it will do to send and show you how I am looking. Returning to the vessel found an invitation from Sir John to take a family dinner with him which I was obliged to decline, as I was already engaged to Sir James. The dinner on board the *Winchester* was very pleasant, and I remained until quite late. I like the old admiral very much, perhaps it is because he seems to like me, for likeing begets likeing.

Tuesday February 27, 1855

Plenty of business to attend to, and made a great many calls so that I was quite fagged out, but felt it a duty to attend the Governor's reception at 10 P.M. and went in full dress accordingly, first passing a pleasant evening at our storekeepers, whose house is next door to Sir John's.

As it is Lent, there was but a few ladies present at the reception, and the company consisted chiefly of the Admiral and his staff. Capt. Rodgers and his officers and Sir John's Staff and his family. Mrs.

Nye and Mrs. C. D. Williams and Doct. and Mrs. Parker, who are stopping at Sir Johns were also present. With so great a disparity of sexes, the evening was as stiff and unbending as the gentlemens uniforms. I had a pleasant talk with Lady Bowring who is lame, and uses crutches. Fatigued as I was I was glad to get back to the little *Queen*.

Wednesday February 28, 1855

At 10 A.M. left Hong Kong for Macao. Having on board Doct. and Mrs. Parker, Miss Bowring, Capt. and Mrs. Endicott and their children. Miss Russell, and a dozen others with no end of Chinese servants. The passage across was rough, and the steamer being light rolled about considerably, but we made a quick run over anchoring at Macao four hours after leaving Hong Kong. The ladies were all of them more or less sick even Miss Russell who had just arrived from a sea voyage of 160 days. The Chinese nurses were sicker than their mistresses, and I had in a measure to supply their places. You should have seen me mixing and serving out Browns Essence of Jamaica Ginger.

Poor Mrs. Endicott alarmed by her sea sickness and distressed by the crying of her children, seized my arm and asked me if there was any danger, declaring she had confidence in me but none in Capt Endicott which of course was flattering to me. Miss Bowring went over to stay a few days with Mrs. Parker. She is a plain sensible girl and wears spectacles. I was sorry her seasickness prevented my getting better acquainted with her.

Thursday March 1, 1855

The weather was still rough and breezy but at 8 A.M. I got underway for Canton with Doct. Parker, the Lord Bishop of Victoria and Messr. Tuckerman Parker, Lt. Maynard and other passangers. At 6 P.M. anchored near the *Macedonian* at Whampoa. Communicated with her and at 6.40 got underway and at 8 P.M. moored off the factories in our old place. Sent a man named Phillips to the *Kennedy* and had a row at his reception, oweing to the foolishness of her commander. The Lord Bishop of Victoria of today is the young missionary Mr. Smith, who ten years ago in a walk to Honam with Doct. Parker, Capt. McKeever and other and myself said he did not consider Unitarians Christians. Introduced to him today by Doct. Parker. I reminded him of our previous acquaintance, when he said in an aside to Doctor P. "that was the time I was so uncharitable." He said today, he had never heard the name of Doct. Dewey and that a few years ago, if he had known he was talking to a Unitarian he would have shuddered. He told Tuckerman not long since, when a guest of his at Mr. Nyes house, that he was so uncharitable at one time he could not have broken bread or eaten with a Unitarian. It is very well you have gotten over it said Tuckerman for I am a Unitarian.

Friday March 2d, 1855

At Canton clear and cool with pleasant northerly breezes. Called upon old friends and executed various shopping commissions from my friends on board the *Macedonian*. Dined at Mr. Nye's.

Saturday March 3d 1855

Shopping for the Commodore. Soon after noon he came on board hoisted his broad pendant, got underway and at 2 P.M. anchored at Whampoa and put him on board the *Macedonian*.

Sunday March 4, 1855

Clear warm and pleasant weather with light breezes. As we left Canton yesterday the English mail arrived and all have their letters but myself. Mine are somewhere and I am impatient to get them.

Monday March 5, 1855

By order of Com'dre Abbot detained the lorcha *Rapid* and forbid her flying the U.S. flag until it could be ascertained what right she has to it, or had when boarded and plundered by Chinese pirates.

Tuesday March 6th, 1855

Allowed the lorcha to proceed to Canton on receiving a pledge she would not wear 'our flag.'

Wednesday March 7, 1855

Damp and foggy, went down to *Macedonian* at the 1st Bar and took her in tow, and at 5 P.M. cast her off near 2d Bar, and continued on to Hong Kong.

Hong Kong, Thursday March 8, 1855

At thirty minutes after midnight anchored off the Naval Store houses at Hong Kong and during the day rec'd 18½ tons of coal from the Bark *Nile*,[24] breakfasted, dined and tea'd at R. P. De Silvers, and met a crowd of the Explorers at his house in the evening.

Friday March 9, 1855

Got underway from Hong Hong at 7 A.M. with Mrs. Nyes on board. Communicated with the ship *Science* aground, and at 2 P.M. with the *Macedonian* above the 2d Bar and also at Whampoa and at 5 P.M. moored off Canton.

Saturday March 10, 1855

Got underway at 8 A.M. and went down to the *Macedonian* intending to tow her to below the 2d Bar, but wind and tide proving too strong for our steam power, had to give up and returned to Whampoa where I anchored at half past five this evening.

Sunday March 11, 1855

At Whampoa warm rainy weather with wind light from the East. During the past week a great change has taken place in affairs in this vicinity. The Imperialists have driven the rebels from their strongholds and captured the best of their junks and boats. The butcheries have been heart-sickening.

The *Vandalia* is expected from Shanghai and on her arrival the *Queen* will be given up and I shall return to the *Macedonian* as her 2d or if wish Flag Lt. You thought when you wrote Josiah would be married last month. I must therefore wish him and his Mrs. Cox the happiness and success a young couple always hope for. Who would want to be married and childless? Neither of the Mrs. De Silvers, or Mrs. Parker have children and they waste a precious lot of affection, upon whining, yelping snarling little puppy dogs, which a dog eating Chinese would view with contempt. Mrs. Emily Bob (R.P. De.S.) about a year ago had a small dog named 'Preb' (because presented her by officers belong to the Ship *Preble*) which some

[24] It seems that the *Nile* was a local bark operating between Canton and Hong Kong. She is not indicated in lists of American and British ships of the nineteenth century.

idle fellow shot with an airgun. She mourned the loss of the red and white cur and had its skin stuffed and preserved in a glass case, which ornaments the side board of her dining room. She has now Preble No. 2 equal to No. 1 in uglyness and a frolicsome puppy whose great feat is to stand on the dinner table and take his desert of nuts and wine from a wine glass. I have had to stand godfather to the brute because of its name and furnish it with a silver collar.

I am interested in the forthcoming memoirs of Harriet Preble[25] but have not written to Mrs. Barlow[26] to condole with her on her sisters death, because I do not know how. I am discouraged writing to Henry Oxnard[27] since I get no answer from him.

My command of the *Queen* has enabled me to get better acquainted with the Am. and foreign residents of Canton, than I could otherwise have done: Mr. and Mrs. Nye, and Mr. and Mrs. Hunter, Mr. and Mrs. Elmslie,[28] Sir John Bowring and family, the Rowles, Drinkers, Nyes, Williamsons and many others. Mr. and Mrs. Nye I particularly like. He so kind and considerate, she so intelligent and amiable and each loveing the other, as you and I love. At the first Mrs. N. seemed formal and Mr. N. unpleasantly attentive and considerate, a closer intimacy has caused me to esteem them very much. I fear Mr. Nye has met great business losses this year which it will be hard for him to recever from. Such is the prevailing impression. He has tried to control the tea trade, and the attempt has been too great for him and teas are falling. He is living in princely style here and has quite a palace at Macao, and a gallery of painting in New York which has cost him $75,000.

[25] Preble refers to R. H. Lee's *Memoir of the Life of Harriet Preble.*

[26] Frances Anica Preble, daughter of Henry and Frances Preble, was born in Paris on November 25, 1797. She was married to Thomas Barlow (1792–1859). She lived (1870) at Washington, Pennsylvania. She was a very dear aunt of G. H. Preble. *Sketch,* 287–96.

[27] Henry Preble Oxnard (1822–1856), a relative of G. H. Preble, was the son of Henry Oxnard and Charlotte Farnham. He died unmarried in Portland. *Sketch,* 149–150.

[28] A. W. Elmslie was British vice-consul in Canton from April 23, 1847, and acting consul from March 25, 1848, to April 20, 1849. He served in this office for short periods until July, 1855. See "British Personnel in China," in Fairbank, *op. cit.,* II, 48–52.

Mrs. Hunter is at Hong Kong now having an operation performed on the feet of her little daughter. The feet were so turned over that the child walked upon the instep. By cutting the chords which held them so they have been placed in a natural position and there is hope that the deformity is permanently cured. One foot has been operated upon three times, twice under the influence of chloroform. The child would allow no one but her mother to be present, a great trial of her nerves. Mrs. Elmslie is a Guernsey woman, French and free in her manners and chatty and agreeable for an evening party; she is the wife of H.B.M's Vice Consul. Mrs. Hunter's name is Rosalie, but her husband calls her Rosa. Mrs. Robt. De Silver (Emily Bob) is a more masculine woman and has the misfortune of being unpopular with her own sex. I do not undertake to say right. I must say I like her and she and her husband are an attached couple. She is a Unitarian, and the daughter of Mr. Bates, the advocate of Cheap postage. Mrs. Hal De Silver is a silly little woman who bothers her husband, and often puts me out of all patience with her. Mr. De Silver saw her in England, and wanting a wife, wrote and offered himself was accepted and she came out about two years ago in charge of Capt. Buchanan and was married. She has I believe a kind heart, but I should be sorry to be tied to such a wife. Mrs. Endicott on the contrary makes a good wife to that jolly lump of flesh her husband. Capt. Endicott is now in the full tide of success and everything he touches seems to turn to gold.

The books by the Palmer's[29] still lie on my shelves unread I am reserving them for my sea voyage as I can obtain abundance of reading from the Canton Club Library. The death of Aunt Susan Gore just at the time it occurred must have been a severe affliction. I hope it did not delay Sue Gore's marriage. She can better mourn for her mother with a husbands sympathy than alone. It is feared the U. S. Sloop of War *Albany*[30] has foundered in the West Indies

29 There were three Palmers, all authors of books. I would think that Preble refers to Ray Palmer (1808–1887), Congregational clergyman, and his three books on spiritual subjects. Preble was interested in reading this type of literature. See *DAB*, XIV, 191–92.

30 The *Albany*, 1,064 tons, 15 guns, was built in 1818 and belonged to the New York Naval Militia.

with all on board, not one left to tell the tale, dreadful to think of. John Quincy Adams[31] was on board, the 2d of my class that has met such a death. The other, Issac S. Keith was lost in the Grampas. Capt. Rodgers who has just reported the probable loss of the *Porpoise* with all on board, to the Navy Department had a brother on board the *Albany*. The *Porpoise* has not been heard of since last Sept. How fortunate for me that I was not given the command of the *Porpoise*, but then again with me her fate might have been different. Lieut Palliser of the *Spartan* has just received his promotion to a Commander for his services against the pirates, and Com'dr Parker who is only 27 years of age has been made a Captain for aiding a French Frigate when aground. Of course without influence this would never have occurred and they might have remained Lieuts in H.B.M. Navy to the end of time. If Edwin were here instead of on board the *Fleetwood*,[32] I could get him a position of Masters Mate on board one of the Exploring vessels.

Whampoa, Thursday March 13, 1855

Cool cloudy rainy unpleasant weather for two days past. Everything quiet, the rebels seem to have vanished. Letters have been rec'd here from Mr. Bonney, dated Batavia Feb. 13. The *Shooting Star* and *Winged Racer* by which I sent packages passed the Straits of Sunda last Nov. The *Potomac* Capt. Stone[33] by whom I sent the tea sailed Jan. 31, and I have put three boxes on board the *N. B. Palmer*,[34] which will arrive at New York in July or August. I also send by her a small box for Doctor Wood.

[31] John Quincy Adams was made midshipman on July 3, 1835; passed midshipman, June 22, 1841; master, March 22, 1848; lieutenant, February 21, 1849; lost, September 28, 1854.

[32] The *Fleetwood*, 663 tons, was built in 1852. A little California clipper commanded by Frank Dale, she was lost in sea ice on May 3, 1859. *Greyhounds*, 225, 356, 420. *Clipper*, 356.

[33] See note 13 above.

[34] The *N. B. Palmer* was a California clipper ship of 1,490 tons, built in 1851, and owned by A. A. Low and Brothers, New York. She is known for her record voyages, especially in racing with the *Flying Cloud*, between the China ports and New York under Captain Charles P. Low. *Clipper*, 214–15, 365; *Greyhounds*, 207–208, 220–22, 417. She was named in honor of Nathaniel Brown Palmer

Macao, Sunday March 18, 1855

Got underway from Whampoa yesterday morning and went up to Canton and anchored. Rec'd on board from Russell & Co 25 boxes of treasure to put on board the *Resolute*[35] at Hong Kong, and 21 men from the *Kennedy* to put on board the *Macedonian*, and at 1 A.M. this morning got under way for Macao where we anchored to night at 10:15 P.M. The rebels have been whipped out of the river, and there is no longer necessity for an armed force to protect our country men at Canton. Four Thousand unfortunates have been beheaded at the Execution grounds Canton within a week and Mr. Stamms our engineer told me, he saw at Sunchow in Blenheim Reach near Whampoa a pile of human heads which would be a good load for the *Macedonian* launch.

At Canton four of the rebel leaders were cut to pieces alive, and a woman was flayed alive for having committed adultery. I have had no curiosity to witness these executions, though many Europenas have had. Lt. Jones, the Marine officer, saw in five minutes 150 decapitated and the four above mentioned chopped to pieces. Such wholesale slaughter exceeds the worst of the French reign of Terror. Before decapitation the poor wretches were tortured to exhort confession. This is how they were tortured. They were made to turn out their foot, and one man stands on the instep, another on the calf of the leg while a third hammers at the ancle bone with a heavy piece of wood until the bone is forced through the skin.

All the week until yesterday we have been being at Whampoa and having a quiet time, but very rainy disagreeable weather. On Thursday I dined with Capt. Sir Wm. Hoste, Bart.,[36] on board H.M. Ship *Spartan*. Today I settled bills and made P.P.C. calls not expecting to return to Canton. All the gentlemen came off to "chin chin" me. The *N. B. Palmer* sailed today from Hong Kong with

---

(1799–1877), a famous New York clipper captain. *DAB*, XIV, 189–90; *Clipper*, 77–87 and the photograph facing p. 128.

[35] The *Resolute* was a California slipper ship of 786 tons under the command of John W. Perry. She was built in 1853 and sold to the British in 1862. *Greyhounds*, 431; *Clipper*, 291.

[36] He was the son of Sir William Hoste (1780–1828), the first baronet and captain in the British navy. *DNB*, XXVII, 401.

my boxes. I had for passanger today Capt. Beard of the *Gundreda* which brought out Miss Russell. He has promised me some books, of which he has a great variety furnished him by his brother who is a London Editor.

Canton, Sunday March 25, 1855

I thought last Sunday was the last time I should write from Canton, or from on board the *Queen,* but best laid plans of mice and men sometimes gang apes. On Monday night on our arrival at Hong Kong the Commodore directed me to leave the next morning with Doct. and Mrs. Parker, Mrs. R.P. De Silver, and the two Emilys and others. We arrived at Macao in the afternoon, and remained there until Thursday morning when we left for this place where arrived in the afternoon, and where have remained. We brought with passangers Doct. and Mrs. Peter Parker, the two Mrs. De Silvers, Doct. and Mrs. MacGowan[37] of Ningpo, and their two children. Tomorrow morning we leave here for the last time, and take back the two Mrs. De Silvers to their impatient spouses at Hong Kong, and expect to have as passangers Capt. Elliott and Fellows of the R.N. [Royal Navy] a chaplain, three or four Midshipmen R.N., Capt Ayres, Mr. Tuckerman and others; all to subsist on my hospitality.

The *Vandalia* arrived from Shanghai Tuesday and the *Macedonian* is to sail the day after the next mail arrives from England and I go in her. Mr. and Mrs. Hal De Silver are to go to England by the next steamer. He is said to have made $30,000 the past year at his business. If it were not for my connection with the Navy, I could

[37] Dr. Daniel Jerome MacGowan (1814–1893) came to Ningpo in 1843 as a medical missionary of the American Baptist Board of Foreign Missions and opened a hospital for Chinese which was soon closed. He resided in several Chinese ports and studied Chinese culture and language; he later joined the China Custom Service. He was also U.S. vice-consul at Ningpo, appointed in June, 1855. Griffin, *op. cit.*, 362, apparently made a mistake in noting that MacGowan resigned in June, 1855. Griffin also says, contrary to Preble's diary, that MacGowan "never appeared in Ningpo. MacGowan succeeded Consul McCartee, another American in China, who was appointed by Townsend Harris. *Ibid.*, 298–99. He translated Taiping documents (1851–64) in a serial, "Dr. MacGowan's Notebook," in the *North China Herald*, Shanghai. Couling, *op. cit.*, 321; Alexander Wylie, *Memorials of Protestant Missionaries to the Chinese.*

obtain command of a steamboat on the river, which would give me $8,000 a year at least. Mr. Williams who has been with me as a Masters Mate on board the *Queen,* has resigned and is to have a steamer on the river, that will bring him very near that sum. I certainly was born with a wooden spoon. Golden visions of a fortune are all I get, but never the reality.

The *Queen* has been purchased from Mr. Bowra[38] by a Chinese company who pay $34,000 for her. Mr. Stamm who has been my Engineer and whose pay is only 50$ a month, has been offered $200 a month by Capt. Endicott, until the *Powhatan* comes down and will if allowed, probably resign. Capt. Endicott seems to have got hold of the golden spoon at last. He had been here many years without making anything more than a respectable livelihood but the last year his little steamer *Spark* has been making him 2,000$ daily, and every speculation he has attempted has been transmitted into the precious metal. Poor Mr. Nye during the same time has suffered sad losses and is probably 300,000$ poorer than he was twelve months ago. His teas have depreciated in price. His vessels been wrecked, his insurances contested.

He is one I most esteem, and Mrs. Nye is truly loveable. I dine with them today, for he has not yet given up his princely hospitality. Today Mrs. Nye sent me a Jade Stone dragon as a present for you. It is worth here from 30 to 50$, but no one unacquainted with its value would give 2$ for it. It is something I should never think of buying, but it is a rare and curious present. It was a cumshaw to Mr. Nye from a wealthy Chinese tea merchant at New Year. An arrival from California brings us dates from New York to Jan. 12 by which I see Com'dre Perry has arrived there. Our papers will inform you of a terrible earthquake last December at Simoda which nearly destroyed the place, only six homes remain standing. The rest were washed away by a remarkable ebb and flow of the sea.

Hong Kong, April 1, 1855

I still write from on board the *Queen* but for the last time as I have restored her to her owner, paid off my Chinese crew sent the

[38] Charles W. Bowra, a British merchant in Hong Kong, was the owner of the *Queen*. Orange, *op. cit.*, 137, 327.

Americans back to the *Macedonian* and hauled down my pennant. In fact the *Queen* is out of commission and I am only remaining on board to settle the bills. Tomorrow forenoon I go on board the *Macedonian* to resume my duties as a watch officer. Last Monday on my arrival here from Canton I was ordered to return the next day with Capts. Adams and Pope, left the next morning at 7. Arrived there the same evening and remained until Friday when I brought both the Capts. Mr. and Mrs. Nye, Mrs. Rawle and others down to Hong Kong. Capt. Pope has had a silver tea service presented to him for services at Shanghai. It was manufactured at Canton, cost 500$ and is marked Presented to Capt. Pope by his countrymen in China. The English Squadron is going to Japan to make a Treaty. Two of our Exploring Squadron have gone there, and Capt. Rodgers is holding on with the *Vincennes* to learn by the next mail the fate of the *Albany*. His brother being one of the Lieuts of that missing ship. It is now the rainy season and we have heavy showers daily besides the air is damp and chilly. I would much rather have you my Queen in my arms, than to be surrounded by the arms of my *Queen* here tonight.

The following is my report of the abandoning of the *Queen* to her owner.

U.S. Chartered Str. *Queen*, March 31, 1855

Sir—I have the honor to inform you that agreeably to your order of this day and date, I have delivered up the Steamer *Queen* to W.A. Bowra, Esqu., and have received from him the receipt herewith enclosed. All the seamen belonging to the *Macedonian* and *Powhatan* have been sent with their bags and hammocks on board the *Macedonian*. I shall pay off the Chinese firemen and servants tomorrow having notified them of their discharge.

I am very respectfully
Your obedt Servant
Geo Henry Preble
Lt. Comdg. U. S. Str. *Queen*

Commodore
Joel Abbot
Comdr in Chief
U. S. Naval Forces
East India China and Japan Seas, Etc.

U. S. Flag Ship *Macedonian,* Hong Kong, April 4, 1855

I am again back to the old ship, having returned to her on Monday. I have not yet commenced my duties on board having been busily engaged settling the affairs of the *Queen* and troubled with a heavy cold. Weather permitting we sail tomorrow for Shanghai, and have on board the pilot brought down by the *Vandalia.* Night before last the overland mail arrived, and I was on shore until 2 A.M. yesterday walking the streets, in waiting for its distribution and my letters. The mail brought the good news to Lt. Charles Fellows of the *Winchester* of his promotion to a Commander for his service at Kulan. Tyho and Kulan, which was almost altogether my 'pidgeon' and brought about by me, has brought promotion to my English friends but I suppose mine is as far off as ever. I was glad to learn by my letters that Doct. Nichols had a colleague associated with him. I hope Mr. Stebbins may be approved, and the uninterrupted succession of the old Parish continued by him.

At Anchor Coast of China, April 6, 1855

We weighed anchor today noon, and drifted out of Hong Kong harbor by the Ly-mun pass. When the tide turned adverse, we came to anchor, with the pilot still on board. We have quite a concert, two guitars and a violin[39] playing in the wardroom.

Saturday April 7th, 1855

The ship got underway at daylight, and soon after the pilot left us. Spoke the American ship *Waverly*[40] 145 days out from Liverpool,

[39] Between pp. 431 and 432 of the diary is inserted the following letter from Preble to his wife:

U. S. Flag Ship *Macedonian*
Hong Kong, Good Friday, April 6, 1855

My dear Wife,

The gale is over, the tears of heaven are dried up and the sun smiles upon our departure for Shanghai. The *Vincennes* is under way, and we sail in a few hours. I hope we may have a safe pleasant and speedy passage. God bless you, good bye with all love

In haste
Your ever affectionate
George

[40] The *Waverly,* a California clipper of 749 tons, was built in Charlestown,

nearly half a year at sea, how they must rejoice at approaching port.

April 8th to 22d, 1855

Date		*Lat.*	*Long.*
April	8	—	—
	9	22.39N	115.44
	10	22.57 "	116.46
	11	23.15 "	117.25
	12	23.02 "	117.50
	13	23.43 "	118.22
	14	24.25 "	118.55
	15	24.56 "	119.53
	16	27.40 "	121.34
	17	29.59 "	123.07

On the passage from Hong Kong to Woosung at the mouth of the Yangtse Kiang. We run the *Vincennes* out of sight on the 8th and caught up with the American Clipper Ship *Mandarin*[41] which sailed from Hong Kong two days before us. The 8th completed my two years of absence. The 9th we had the Coast of China and thousands of fishing boats in sight. The 10th was employed attending to the serving out of flannel to the crew and we passed the Am. Ship *Race Hound*[42] which sailed from Hong Kong a week before us. She is better known as the *Lady Pierce*[43] having under that unauthorized

Massachusetts, in 1853. She was under the command of Captain William F. Clark. She sailed in the China trade and was lost on a voyage to Calcutta in 1862 under Captain Reed. *Greyhounds*, 433, 515.

[41] The *Mandarin*, a noted California clipper ship of 776 tons, was built in 1851 for China voyages. She started under Captain Thomas C. Stoddard but was later under J. W. C. Perit. *Greyhounds*, 155–57, 413, 448; *Clipper*, 145–46, 349.

[42] The *Race Hound*, an American bark under Captain Copeland, was built in 1852. *Greyhounds*, 482.

[43] The *Lady Pierce* was named for a short time to honor President and Mrs. Franklin Pierce. Her register name was the *Race Hound*. The *Lady Pierce* was the first American ship to visit Japan after the Perry treaty. She arrived in July, 1854, and was well received in the port of Edo. Griffin, *op. cit.*, 320–21, did not realize that her registered name was the *Race Hound*. She was owned by Silas E. Burrows, who intended to establish commerce with newly opened Japan. See also Richard Hildreth, *Japan as It Was and Is*, 534.

name followed our squadron to Japan as the yacht of Silas Burrows. We had the coast of China between Breaker pt [port] and Cape of Good Hope in sight, and came very nigh running over one of the innumerable fish boats which stud this coast carrying away one of her masts. Wednesday the 11th wind became light and weather pleasant but the rolling seas continued. We had the Lamock Islds in sight, crossing Formosa channel, a singular accident happened to me. Mr. Ayres and myself were useing a measuring line he holding one end near my feet, and I had the other end over my head, and bringing it down as he raised his up, our hands met, and in his was an open penknife which struck into the lower joint of my second finger bringing up against the bone. It was a painful wound and temporarily disabled me from writing. The next day I had to call a servant to help me dress. The 12th was calm and in the afternoon we saw a Naval engagement between two whales and three threshers. The combat lasted an hour or more, and they moved all around the ship without seeming to notice us. I thought the threshers had the best of it. The water resounded with their blows, and the poor whales bellowed outright. April 13. Had a fair wind, and at sundown were up with Amoy and saw a fleet of fishing boats returning into its harbor. Our 713th dinner consisted of Fresh Clam Soup, Fresh Salmon, roast capons, oranges, sponge cake, custards and nuts and raisins, with port and sherry, not bad considering. Puzzled through Lizzie Preble's letter which with its pale ink was as faint as her voice is said to be. Apl. 14, Sunday. Spoke an English Ship bound for Shanghai to Amoy and were enveloped in fog all day. Were startled during the night by discovering the little Isld of Ocksen close abroad when we thought we had left it five miles away; the currants had set us out of the way. We soon lost sight of the Island in the fog. Apl. 15. Making good speed towards Shanghai and leaving Formosa Channel behind. April 16. In the thick fog came near running over a Chinese junk which emerged from it directly on our course and was lost sight of the next moment in the mist. I could not but admire the nonchalance with which the celestials saw our huge hull brush their pigmy craft at the rate of ten miles an hour.

General Quarters visited us and exercised us all for a couple of hours in a bloodless, though not a noisiless battle. Our big guns opened their throats, and proclaimed to the world that we were about.

Tuesday April 17. Dropped anchor to wait for tide and daylight. The Yangtse being only 40 miles dist. Last night was wildly dark and terrific. There was little wind but the dense fog made the sea so dark that we could only see the sails by the flashes of lightening which was very vivid and accompanied by deep rolling thunder, which with rain continued all night. This afternoon as we were sailing smoothly along Mr. Hayden[44] the Boatswain fell overboard and there was great excitement and a rush of all hands upon deck. Fortunately he caught the trailing lines from our stern ladder and the ship's way being checked he was hauled on board. An hour later a large shark was cruising about the ship looking out for his dinner. Fortunate Mr. Hayden, that he came late to it. Mr. Hayden scraped along the ships bottom, or rather she sailed over him and when he got on board he naively remarked he had no idea the copper was so rough. At anchor Thursday evening, April 19. Little by little in spite of tides rain and fog we are approaching Shanghai. We are tonight close to the entrance of the Yangtse and several ships in sight at sundown showed we were approaching a commercial centre. April 20th at anchor all day. The thermometer has been as low as 50° and the cold raw cheerless weather has set the rheumatism skirmishing all through my poor limbs and up and down my back so that I have been tortured not a little. A number of sparrows, swallows and other small birds and one curlew have made our ship an ark of refuge today, and I have been feeding the poor forlorn little creatures and preserving them from the longings of pussy. They became quite tame, smoothed their wet and ruffled plumage and pecked the broken grains of rice fearlessly at our feet. The Commodore remarked today that many a prisoner in a Mass[achusetts] jail had been more comfortable than we have been, which is quite true though I can't say I wished to be there.

Saturday April 21st. The weather cleared up bright and pleasant this morning and enabled us to make another jog towards Shanghai.

[44] John C. Hayden was made boatswain September 20, 1852; dismissed from the U.S. Navy, November 2, 1857. According to Preble's note in the diary, he died on May 31, 1853.

We are now about fifteen miles distant and will cross the bar when the tide makes tomorrow. All around us is a muddy waste of water with a low slip of land and trees on our left. A few ships and countless junks are in sight. Certainly not a picturesque panorama.

Sunday evening, April 22d. A rainy day; we have made another hitch and are at anchor off Woosung where we have to remain until Friday for a high tide to take us over the bar. The pilot left us this P.M. We got aground once but the tide rose and floated us, and we gained this anchorage. It has been a busy working day but work of necessity.

Looking over your letters I found a whole page I had left unread. Your "help" troubles amuse me. I must examine my letters and count up how many 'real treasures' you have had since I left. I shall be curious to know how long the last described from 'New Gloucester' age about 35 "nice respectable looking," "seven years in one family," who prefers living alone to have a 2d girl and is willing to be called upon and is "a quiet and sensible woman" will hold out. Experience is against her making any lengthy residence with you. I think you were a little hard hearted in driving out both of Marys lovers.

At Anchor off Woosung, April 25, 1855

The Boat'n of the *Powhatan* was killed a few days since while arresting some sailors. He gave orders to a Marine to beat in a door with his musket, the concussion discharged the piece and the load took effect in his body, and he died instantly. We hear also that Am. Clipper *Young America*[45] has sailed from Shanghai for Japan to take thence the crew of the Russian Frigate *Diana*[46] wrecked at Simoda by

[45] The *Young America*, a celebrated California clipper ship of 1,961 tons, was built in 1853. Captain David S. Babcock was her master and George Daniels of New York her owner. Subsequently, Babcock became a president of the Pacific Mail Steamship Company. His sister was married to the widely known Captain N. B. Palmer. The *Young America* voyaged between Canton and San Francisco. Captain Babcock negotiated with Admiral Putiatin to take the crew of the sunken *Diana* to Petropavlovsk. Babcock's American crew revolted against going to the Russian port. Lensen, *Russia's Japan Expedition*, 105–107; *Clipper*, 84, 232–34, 297–300, with a picture of the *Young America; Greyhounds*, 354–55, 434.

[46] The *Diana* was a new Russian frigate from the Baltic fleet assigned to Admiral

the earthquake, and that the French ship of war *Constantine*[47] sailed in hot pursuit to prevent her. Went on shore today and walked through the muddy streets of Woosung which of dirty Chinese towns seems the dirtiest. I had quite a pleasant walk through the country. The fields of barley, wheat and rye look very refreshing. Scattered over the fields, generally under the shade of a tree are massive wooden coffins, thatched over with straw. The country is very level and wet, and this is probably the reason of the custom of burying above ground. When the coffin decays, a mound of earth is heaped over it, and finally the bones are collected in an earthen vessel, large enough to receive the head, and very like a colossal yankee bean pot, and these pots are collected in clusters and mark a family burial place. When land is disposed of these burial places are invariably reserved and it is extremely difficult to purchase the right of removing them. The river banks are leveled similar to the banks of the Mississippi. Opposite our ship there are embresures for 170 guns though nothing like that number of guns, and nearly all have one or both trunnions knocked off by the English and have been fixed upon their carriage by means of straps.

It is now the kite season here and I have been amused at some that I have seen: one set represented a flock of several geese, and another a hawk. The flight of these birds was so well counterfieted that we at first thought them real birds. These northern Chinese are fairer than their brethren to the South, and I think more akin to the Japanese. I saw some very pretty children today. I had for companions the Purser, and Doctor Gilliam and we had a spring like day for our walk. We saw the preparation and spinning of cotton after all their

E. V. Putiatin to replace the old *Pallada* in his Japan expedition in 1854. She had 484 men on board. Putiatin left the De-Kastri Bay on August 16, 1854, and arrived at Shimoda to negotiate the Russo-Japanese treaty on December 20–21, 1854. On December 23, an earthquake shook the vicinity of Shimoda, and the *Diana* suffered irreparable damage. At the end of January, 1855, she sank near the port of Heda, Japan. On Russo-Japanese relations during the middle to the nineteenth century, see two books by G. A. Lensen, *Russia's Japan Expedition*, especially concerning the *Diana*, 72–103, and *The Russian Push Toward Japan*, 330–35.

[47] The *Constantine*, a French corvette, was sent to observe the Russian opening of Japan and tried to capture the Russian ship *Diana* after her disaster in January, 1855. See Lensen, *Russia's Japan Expedition*, 106–107.

methods in all its stages. A ship sailed today for New York and passed us in tow of a steamer.

Friday April 27, 1855

We were to have moved today, but there is not water enough on the bar and we must wait. The Purser heard today from Hong Kong of the arrival of the *Indiaman*[48] and I shall look for my package.

Saturday April 28, 1855

Not able to move yet enjoyed a long walk with the Purser. The heat was oppressive, and we found no shade yet the exercise was refreshing. We stopped many times to watch the dirty inhabitants weave and spin. Our curiosity drew a large crowd of idle ones around us, when we "chin chinned" and walked on.

Sunday April 29th, 1855

A rainy morning but the sun cleared the clouds and dried up the rain drops, and we had a delicious day. We are to be towed up to Shanghai tomorrow.

At Anchor at Shanghai, Monday April 30, 1855

We anchored here at noon having been towed up by the *Confucius*.[49] In coming up got afoul of a Chinese junk damaged her sails crushed one of our boats and wounded one of her crew, whom our Doctor attended to.

Tuesday May 1, 1855

A pleasant May day. On shore with the Purser, Doct. Gilliam and

[48] The *Indiaman*, an American clipper of 1,165 tons, was built in 1854 by Hugh McKay, Boston, and in the beginning was under the command of Captain D. S. McCallum. *Greyhounds*, 436, 509, 512.

[49] The American steamer *Confucius*, manned by three officers and fifty men and marines from the *Macedonian*, was sent to aid the U.S. consul in Shanghai during the Taiping Rebellion. Preble was assigned to the Confucius on June 28, 1855, by Commodore Abbott. He returned to the *Macedonian* on July 17, 1855 (*Sketch*, 207), but again joined the *Confucius* on August 3, 1855, serving on her in expeditions again the Chinese pirates or sounding at Woosung, near Shanghai, and preparing sailing directions (later published in Hong Kong for use in navigation) for that port. (He also recommended certain improvements in the port of Shanghai which were adopted by the Chinese.) Preble returned to the *Macedonian* at Hong Kong on November 11, 1855. *A Naval Encyclopaedia*, 662.

Mr. Watters, and made the grand rounds, calling upon all the American ladies of the place. At the English Consulate my friend Mr. Robertson, who was promoated from the Canton Consulate invited us to tiffin and showed us his acre of garden.

At the Am. Missions grounds we systematically called at every house beginning at Doct. Bridgeman's,[50] next to the Nelson's,[51] then to Mr. Culbertsons, then on the Misses Jones, and lastly upon Bishop Boone.[52] The Misses Jones invited us to tea with them, which we accepted. Our last call today was upon our consul Mr. Murphy[53] whose wife we found pleasant and chatty. I never have heard a little body talk faster, or when I have laughed more than I did at her description of her first experience in housekeeping in China. And of her adventures crossing the Isthmus of Panama. Mr. Amory late Naval Storekeeper here I believe a nephew of my cousin Mrs. A[mory]

[50] Dr. Elijah Coleman Bridgman (1801–1861) was perhaps the first American Protestant missionary in China, having been sent to Canton in 1829 by the American Board of Commissioners. He founded *The Chinese Repository*, directing it until 1847, and was the first president of the North China Branch, Royal Asiatic Society, 1857–59. He was the author of a Chinese work on foreign countries (1838) and collaborated with Rev. M. L. Culbertson in translating the New Testament into Chinese. Couling, *op. cit.*, 65; Latourette, *The Great Century in Northern Africa and Asia*, 300–301; Hummel, *op. cit.*, I, 504–505. S. W. Williams, a contemporary missionary, supplied valuable data concerning Bridgman's early work in China, in *The Middle Kingdom*, II, 327–46.

[51] The Reverend R. Nelson was sent to Shanghai in 1851 by the American Episcopal Board. Dean, *op. cit.*, 163.

[52] William Jones Boone, M.D. (1811–1864), known also under Chinese name Wên, was one of the first American missionaries in China. He belonged to the Protestant Episcopal church. He went to Batavia in 1837 and worked among the Chinese there. In 1840, he resided in Macao; in 1842 lived in Amoy; returned to the United States in 1843; consecrated bishop in 1844. He went back to China in 1845, having been married for the second time, and settled in Shanghai. His first wife died in Amoy in 1842. He visited the United States in 1852 and 1857. In 1863, the second Mrs. Boone died at Suez, and Bishop Boone himself died in Shanghai on July 17, 1864. He is credited for his work on the Chinese translation of the Bible. Couling, *op. cit.*, 54; *NCAB*, V, 16.

[53] Robert C. Murphy, who arrived in 1854, was the first U.S. consul in Shanghai; see H. B. Morse and H. F. MacNair, *Far Eastern International Relations*, 139; T. Dennett, *op. cit.*, 226, 229.

leaves tomorrow a bearer of dispatches to Washington and I sha send some packages by him.

Wednesday May 2, 1855

Sent of my letters by the mail and my daguerreotype by M Amory this morning, and put a box on board the *Wild Duck*[54] Ca Hamilton, to sail tomorrow for New York.

Thursday May 3d 1855

By the arrival of the Clipper ship from California we have nev from Boston to the 20th of Feb. and hear that Upham has arrive at San Francisco, 63 days from Hong Kong. Among our other iten of news, is the arrival of the *Lexington* and *Supply* home. The bur ing of the Portland Museum building, the promotion of Genl Scott and the passage of a new Navy bill. I was elected Caterer of th Mess. I believe because none else would accept that thankless offic and inaugurated myself by giving tiffin to Mrs. Consul Jones[56] an Mrs. Nelson, and by dining Commodore Abbot, H.B.M. Consu Mr. Robertson, and Mr. Caleb Jones, U.S. Consul at Foo Chov It began to rain hard as we sat down to dinner and continued so w put our guests on shore under quite a temperance sprinkling. M Murphy our Consul here, the boys have nicknamed the "Irish po tato," and Mrs. M. "The Sweet Potato." Telling us some of he housekeeping experiences she said the day she commenced she unde took to give a dinner to Capt. Stevens of the *Hancock*, and anothe gentleman who came expressly to laugh at her trials. Dinner wa delayed, and she saw the gentlemen getting hungry when in rushe 'a celestial' with eyes sparkling who exclaimed "Missus, the coo have lost the soup." A queer thing to lose thought she, but said neve mind, bring up dinner, and exit the boy who quickly came back say

[54] The *Wild Duck*, a California clipper ship of 860 tons, was under the comman of Captain A. G. Hamilton and belonged to Olyphant and Company of New York *Greyhounds*, 324, 433.

[55] Winfield Scott (1786–1866) was a prominent soldier, statesman, and "pacifi cator." *DAB*, XVI, 505–11, with helpful bibliography.

[56] Caleb Jones was appointed U.S. consul at Foochow on August 11, 1853, an had arrived at his post by November 5, 1854. He met complex problems connecte with consular judiciary cases. However, he performed his duties at this port o busy American-Chinese tea commerce with distinction. Griffin, *op. cit.*, 293–94, 360

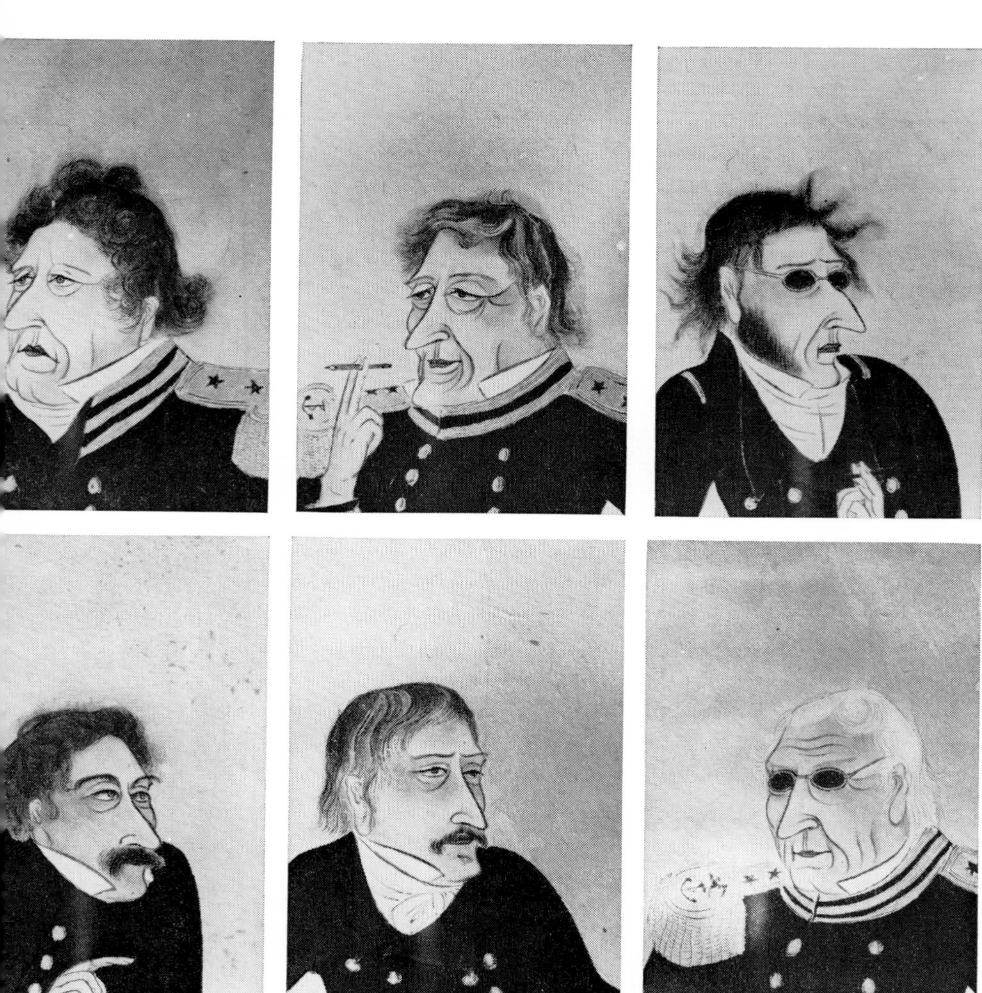

Courtesy Norfolk Museum

The Americans as Seen by the Japanese. Top, *left to right*: Commodore Matthew C. Perry; Commander Henry A. Adams; Samuel W. Williams. Bottom, *left to right*: H. A. L. Portman; Lieutenant Oliver H. Perry; Captain Joel Abbot.

The Japanese as Seen by the Americans. *Left to right*:
A Farmer Dressed for Winter; A City Dweller in Winter Clothing;
A "Soldier of the Tycoon."

ing "Missus the cook have found the soup." It had in the confusion downstairs been mislaid.

Friday May 4, 1855

Frank Foster called on me today. He is with Heard & Co. The *Wild Duck* sailed this afternoon. I was kept busy all day attending to a survey on the furniture of the *Powhatan's* cabin and wardroom.

Sunday May 7, 1855

The overland mail arrived last night and I got my letters up to Feb. 19. this morning. Three newspapers cost me five dollars postage, from their being put up in one bundle at Hong Kong and charged with letter postage. Purser Allison has a letter from his father in law, Judge Taney, in which there is a letter from the Secy of the Navy to him saying The *Macedonian* will return home in the spring of 1856 and will be relieved sooner if men can be shipped. I notice your 'treasure aged 35' was about to be succeeded by another and was a treasure no longer. I was quite surprised to hear of the marriage of Edwd Thomas.

Wednesday May 10, 1855

A rainy day and we are free of visitors which allows me time to write. I sent some packages by the *Mandarin* Capt. Perit,[57] which sailed this morning for Foo Chow and New York. He does not expect to reach New York before Oct. Our Purser went down and came back to the steamer that towed her over the bar to accompany Mrs. Caleb Jones who goes in her to Foo Chow who was very sad at parting from her friends here, as she has a disease of the heart and there are few if any foreign ladies at Foo Chow. Last evening I was at a prayer meeting at Bishop Boone's, where several of the missionaries with their families assembled. It was a pleasant service and we found the black coated gentlemen and the ladies very agreeable. The ladies of the mission are not beautiful or fashionable but good and solid, and associating with them revives homely feelings. They feel flattered by our attention. Mrs. Nelson is lively and chatty and has a

[57] Captain John W. C. Perit of the *Mandarin* is noted for his record of sailing from New York on December 21, 1855, and arriving at Melbourne on March 1, 1856—seventy days. *Greyhounds,* 262, 448.

sweet voice for song or hymn. The Bishop is a very pleasant man, and enjoyes a fat laugh, as well as anyone. Mrs. Perit, with whom I tiffined yesterday at Heard & Co has promised to take special charge of my package by the *Mandarin.*

John Lewis,[58] the last of our steerage officers has been invalided and has gone in the *Mandarin,* his brother Laurence has been appointed by Capt. McCluney as his clerk. They are grandnephews of Genl Washington and twins. Mr. Adams has been made Commodore's Sec'y and takes his place in the wardroom as the steerages are empty. Doct. Parker Commissioner ad interim, etc., leaves Hong Kong today for the U.S. to recruit his health, and Com'dre Abbot has his duties until Mr. McLane returns or a new commissioner comes out, though I believe the Commodore is the sickest man of the two. The rain has prevented the races which were to have commenced today.

Shanghai, Thursday May 11, 1855

The rain holding up I went on shore last evening at the Consuls. His house is only a stone's throw from our anchorage. We had music vocal and instrumental. Mrs. Murphy is an affectionate little woman, full of her loves, courtships and marriage and last but not least 'the baby.' She is artless as a child and allows the tongue to betray every thought.

Saturday May 12, 1855

"Here's to Sweethearts and wives God bless them!" What a changeable climate is this: yesterday an overcoat comfortable and last night sleeping under a quilt and two blankets, and today the ther. has ranged between 80° and 87° in the shade. As I write the lightening flashes through my air port, I hear the growling of the thunder, and here comes the cooling and delicious rain.

Sunday May 13, 1855

Mr. Nelson performed divine services on board. Mrs. N. and her beautiful boy, and Bishop Boone's two sons came with him. He took for his text "This man receiveth sinners"[59] with a good manner and

[58] John Lewis, rated as acting master's mate, together with his brother, Lawrence, of the same rank, served on the *Vandalia. Narrative,* II, 414.

[59] Luke 15:2: "This man receiveth sinners, and eateth with them."

voice he gave us a very plain sensible sermon. After dinner I went on board the *Sweepstake*[60] and took tea with Capt. Lane, who is from Cape Ann.

Shanghai, Wednesday May 16, 1855

Monday was pleasant and I improved it to walk on shore and came on board seasonably to escape a heavy rain which continued all evening. Yesterday I dined on board the British Bark *Gundreda*. Capt. Beard to whom I was able to show some attentions at Hong Kong. Today I have had the days duty on deck. What a lot of letters we have exchanged though I believe mine have not been so prolific as the Irishman's whose wife presented him with a sweet pledge—when he had been absent over fourteen months. When Patrick heard of it and was rejoicing at his having a son and heir some envious friend suggested it was a long time in coming. "Shure that makes no difference," said Patrick, "Hasn't she writ' me often since?"

Yesterday the Tau toe, or as it is pronounced Tou-tu,[61] a Governor of the Province, visited the ship and was received with all the honors due to his rank. We also exercised at Quarters, and fired a broadside from our big guns. He is a fine looking Chinaman, and holds the power of life or death over the thirty millions who inhabit the Province of Kiangsi.

Friday May 18, 1855

Last evening I passed socially at Bishop Boones—most of the mission ladies were present and the evening was closed with a prayer for Mr. Nelson and Mrs. N. played while the rest sung the 170th Hymn.[62] With all my grumblings I felt echoed in my heart the second verse

[60] The *Sweepstake*, 1,735 tons, one of the finest California clippers, was under the command of Captain George E. Lane. She belonged to Chambers and Heiser, New York, and was condemned at Batavia in May, 1862. *Greyhounds*, 290, 432, *et seq.*; *Clipper*, 280–90 *et sqq*.

[61] Taot'ai—the supervisor of a circuit, or tao, to which belonged several prefectures. The republican (after 1912) equivalent to taot'ai was taoin.

[62] "O Come All Ye Faithful," translated from the Latin *Adeste fideles*.

Minutes and mercies multiplied,
Have made up all this day;
Minutes came quick but mercies were,
More swift more free than they.

The Bishop is fat and jolly and was troubled last evening with that gentlemanly complaint the gout. Mrs. B. is fat and awkward in figure but gentle in her manner and pleasant in her conversation. Mrs. Nelson is bright and lively. Mrs. Keith[63] who reminds me of Agnes is sensible in her talk and full of missionary zeal. She has an awkward habit of dry washing her hands. Miss Jones,[64] the daughter of Genl Walter Jones of Washington is a very plain old maid. Miss Conover, a relation of the Bishop and living in his family is another, with very round black eyes, and sits prim and tight waisted. She and Mrs. Keith teach in the schools. Mrs. Nelson and Mrs. Boone find enough to do in careing for their families. It was the 9th birthday anniversary yesterday of the Bishop's son.

Today has been rainy and I have been quiet on board ship. Tonight half our mess is on shore at a service dansante given by the officers of the *Powhatan*. Yesterday forenoon I took a walk on shore, but after getting wet through and loseing my shoes in the mud, was glad to get back to the ship. I expect to have to survey the mouth of the river for the purpose of putting up bouys and beacons for the safety of navigation. The Chinese authorities are willing to pay the expense if the foreigners will point out what is desireable. It will give me some hard and disagreeable work, but no matter.

Sunday May 20, 1855

Today and yesterday have been rainy. It held up for a little while yesterday noon and allowed the Commodore to make his grand visit to the Tautoe, escorted by the band of the *Powhatan* a guard of the Marines of both ships, and a dozen officers in his suite. I remained on board ship and lost nothing but a cup of tea. Today the *Pow-*

[63] Mr. and Mrs. Keith were missionaries in Shanghai; they were sent there in 1851 by the American Episcopal Board. Dean, *op. cit.*, 163.

[64] Miss Agnes Jones was a daughter of General Walter Jones (1776–1861) of Washington, D.C. She was one of eleven sisters. On Walter Jones, see *DAB*, X, 203–204.

hatan left for Hong Kong and Dr. Bridgmen preached on board. Half a dozen merchants and merchants clerks tiffined on board with our mess. A sultry day.

Tuesday May 22[d], 1855

A fiery hot day, ther. on board 92° and on shore 95° in the shade. On shore this A.M. and only saved from melting down by a few reviving drinks of iced water. This evening I was on shore and watched from the Grand Stand of the Race Course a grand shower which poured down like bullits in big drops and passed onward to refresh the burning earth elsewhere. Several ladies and gentlemen less fortunate in gaining shelter galloped by us, completely drenched and looking draggled and miserable from their impromptu shower bath. One young man's pony threw him, and then eyed him ascance during the shower, a little distance off, and when he attempted to catch him galloped off, leaving the young man to plod home through the mud for in fifteen minutes the dry road was turned into a muddy one ancle deep, with lakes and rivers of liquid mud cruising over it. After the shower I picked my way to "Keetch hong No 2" and took dinner with the young men of the House. An accident occured on board in the fire room which fortunately was not so serious as it might have been. It was young Tommy Boone's birthday, so the Purser invited him and his brother Willie, and little Jimmy Nelson, all three near our Henry's age on board—to run about the ship and have a nice time, and in the afternoon there was to be a grand juvenile party at the Bishop's. The youngsters came and were romping about with our little drummer and fifer, who though a few years older are but little larger, when the fifer and Jimmy Nelson slipped on the gun deck ladder, and fell through the berth desk into the main hold at least sixteen feet. Strange to say neither were hurt, though both hugely frightened. Jimmy fell on the fifer and so escaped, but what saved the fifer from broken bones and loss of life is hard to imagine. The Purser says he will never take the responsibilities of other people babies on board ship again.

Sunday May 27th, 1855

The 24th was Queen Victoria's birthday, and H.B.M.S. *Styx* having arrived the night before from Nangasaki, we dressed our ship with flags and at sundown fired a salute of twenty-one guns leaving the English flag at our mastheads while we fired the salute, and hauling down all others excepting our own ensign at the peak. We ought to have fired the salute at noon, but through omission of the 1st Lt.[65] did not, and there was considerable feeling among the English residents on shore that we did not, so I went to the Com'dre who is living at Mr. Murphy's and explained matters. He was sorry and thought it could not be helped. When I suggested, that if we had fired at noon with all the flags flying and the *Styx* did not, not being a saluting ship the Chinese would think it was in our own honor and not the Queen of England, but we might turn the slight into a marked compliment, by hauling down all flags with the English at sundown and then saluting, which was done. On board the *Styx*, determined to have some noise on the occasion, as their colors came down, they commenced fireing vollies of muskets. When we surprised them with our salute, they then rehoisted their Ensign, as also the colors at the consulate and dipped them in acknowledgement when we had finished.

In the evening Allison Gwathmey and I with the Governor of Macao, all the foreign consuls of Shanghai, and the officers of the *Styx* dined with Mr. Robertson at the British Consulate. The only toast drank was "the Queen." Some of the shore know nothings thought we ought to have fired one gun for every year of the Queens age but I told them she was a woman and did not care to have it proclaimed so loudly. Mrs. Murphy was the only lady at the consuls dinner and was quite overpowered with the civilities and politiness of twenty gentlemen. Friday I exhausted myself seeking for a cool place. In the P.M. called on Doctor Hall, the American Physician, and took tea and passed the evening with the Spooners at Keetch Hong. Frank Foster very sick; yesterday Dr. Woodworth and Dr. Hall were in attendance on him all day and all night. He slept this morning 4 hours, his first sleep in many days. Today the Rev. Mr. Blodget[66] preached on board from the text "Behold I stand at the door and knock; if any man hear my voice, and open the door I will

[65] L. B. Avery. See note 32 under the year 1853.

[66] The Reverend H. Blodget was sent to Shanghai in 1854 by the American Baptist Board of Foreign Missions. Dean, *op. cit.*, 163.

come in to him, and soup with him, and he with me."[67] We learn from Hong Kong that the *Vandalia's* boats have had an encounter with the pirates, and one of her sailors was accidentally killed by his own musket.

Thursday May 31st 1855

On Monday two thirds of our mess dined at the Consuls and met the Nyes. My duties on board prevented my going on shore. Late in the evening our real, or as someone would say our 'truly' negro minstrels were sent for to entertain the party. Tuesday I passed among the silken shops, and called upon Doct. and Mrs. MacGowan of Ningpo and Miss Bowring[68] who came up in the last steamer from Hong Kong. Finished the day by teaing at Wetmore & Co. Yesterday was cool and windy. With Mr. Culbertson and Gwathmey our 1st Lt. I went to the outskirts of Shanghai, and called upon two Chinese women who have become Christians, and whose life has been a romance. Born and bred at Sourayabaya Isld of Java, after many adventures and providential escapes they are settled here as wives and mothers. It was an interesting visit and I was struck with their gentle and lady like manners, especially by their children addressing them by the endearing name of mama, and speaking in English. One of the little ones had an unpronounceable Chinese name meaning "Precious Gem," another was called "Great Happiness," and a third "Beautiful Angel," though its mother truthfully said it was not beautiful but mothers always thought their children beautiful and good if no one else did. In the evening attended a prayer meeting at Bishop Boone's and 'tiffined' at 2. P.M. at Mr. Nyes, and had a gay discourse with Mrs. Clem Nye and the widow.

My hair is greyer than when I left home, and there is a dollar spot on my crown which promises baldness ere long. What I have lost on top, however, I am making up below, wearing my beard and mustache after the manner of the apostles unshaven. No razor has touched my face since I left Hong Kong and a friend says my mus-

[67] Rev. 3:20: "Behold, I stand at the door, and knock . . . .

[68] Most probably the daughter of Sir John and Lady Bowring of Hong Kong. See note 14 above.

tache is terrific. Would you like to kiss me as the sailors say "over all"? I am ordered to hold myself in readiness to go on an expedition against pirates.

Shanghai, Sunday June 3[d], 1855

The *Lady Mary Wood*[69] took our letters to Hong Kong Yesterday. Sent a draft to N. G. Jewett at N. York for 150$ to pay my note held by Jas Bagley. After wandering about the country all day dined in the evening with D. C. King[70] of the firm of King & Co. D. C. K. when the St. Nicholas was opened at New York gained considerable notoriety by being the 1st to occupy its famous bridal chamber. His engaging it was a mistake. He arrived late at night, asked for the best room of the house, and was shown to the bridal apartment unconscious of the Heralding that had advertised it—and that was likely to follow its occupancy. His wife was a Miss Briggs of Roxbury. We had a pleasant social dinner of seven gentlemen, and the only toast was from our host to sweethearts and wives.

Today after the usual muster and inspection Mr. Nelson gave us a sermon on the three persons of the Godhead, it being Trinity Sunday. He failed to convince me of the personality of the Holy Ghost or of the equality of the Father and Son. I like to hear Mr. N. preach he has so much earnestness, force and dignity of manner and his voice is as clear and sonorous as a bell. He reads without effort and his voice naturally modulates itself to the subject. Mrs. Nelson assisted at the singing; she is a charming woman. This afternoon I took a walk into and through the old walled city. It bears the mark of warfare, and is in many places a heap of rubbish from the cannonading it has suffered. Carpenters and masons are now however restoring things. There is a curious and extensive tea garden within the walls sadly delapidated by shot, which has the usual stagnant

69 The *Lady Mary Wood*, a steamer of 650 tons, belonged to the P. and O. Company in Hong Kong. She plied between Shanghai and Hong Kong until 1857. Orange, *op. cit.*, 428. For the well-known case of her captain's evading Chinese customs duties in 1850, see Morse, *The International Relations of the Chinese Empire*, II, 8–9.

70 In Shanghai there was a David O. King, a Prussian consul, who was a partner of King and Company. Possibly Preble mistook the middle name. Fairbank, *op. cit.*, I, 433; Griffin, *op. cit.*, 143 n., 244.

pools of water, grotesque architecture, and artificial rock work and islands. It has also within it several handsome shops, and numerous tea houses where thousands were partaking of that beverage and little cakes. In the open spaces several improvisatores were telling their storys to an admiring crowd. I noticed one particularly, a Chinese Dick Swiviller wearing his cap jauntily on one side who—to judge by his gestures and expression and the laughing humor of his audience—was a fellow of infinite mirth and humor. In one part of these gardens I saw a Punch and Judy show.[71] The action, management, cries, etc., a perfect counterpart of European and Am. Exhibitions, though the figures were all Chinese. Punch I knew, as an extensive traveller, but never before heard of his being at home among the celestials. I am curious to find out whether he is a naturalized citizen of China, or a true know nothing. Leaving the gardens I strolled through narrow filthy and stinky streets elbowing my way through crowds of ragged and dirty inhabitants occasionally stopping to shop, which invariably drew a crowd around. Outside the gardens but within the city walls we visited a large Buddist Temple kept very dirty and its courts crowded with trafficers. In the middle of one of its courts there is a large bronze tripod fifteen feet high and four feet in diameter. Its uses and objects are probably told in the inscriptions which cover it. On each side of the door way of the temple are four cross seated figures as large or larger than life, and over their heads hang models of junks grateful offerings no doubt for some providential preservation from the dangers of the sea. The Baptist missionaries reside within the old Chinese city, and the Baptists, Episcopalians, and Roman Catholics, have each a church within the walls. The Baptist Church has a square tower, which rears its head above the roofs of the Heathen temples. Besides the three Christian churches within the walls there are four outside among the foreign residents all handsomely stuccoed. After leaving the city I walked partly around the walls. They are surrounded by a shallow moat, along the edges of which are numerous coffins above the ground, some handsomely carved and gilded. Several had their tops

[71] Punch and Judy—an English puppet show, with two main characters: Punch, violent humpback, and his victimized wife, Judy.

knocked off exposing the mouldering tenant. Mr. Nelson told me, that a person selling land takes the coffin and its remains away. If too much decayed to remove entire, the bones are carefully collected and put in an earthen pot which is cemented over, and carried with him to the field he removes to. Hundreds of groups of these potted bones, are to be seen all around this neighborhood. H.B.M. Str. *Styx* sailed yesterday for Japan.

Monday June 4th 1855

Rev. Mr. Rankin[72] of the Ningpo mission dined with our mess. The papers inform me that Congress has given me 160 acres of land for services in the Mexican and Florida Wars.

Tuesday June 5, 1855

Bishop Boone, with all the mission people men women and children came on board to tiffin, and passed the greater part of the day. We amused them with our 'real' Ethiopian minstrels. When they had left, Mr. Spooner, Capt White of the *Flying Childers*[73] and Mr. D. H. Green of Manila called on us.

Wednesday June 6, 1855

Dined at Wetmore & Co., and passed the evening with Capt. White[74] on board his ship.

Thursday June 7, 1855

Doctor Woodworth and I called on the Nyes and Kings—bought a purple silk for Susie to send by the *Flying Childers*, 14 yds $8.00. Returned to the ship entertained a dinner party on board and then went on shore and dined with Russell & Co. Walked around the Race Course after dinner, returned to Russell & Co. and took a water and back to the ship at 11 P.M. with the mid watch in prospect. Shall we go to Kansas and settle on the acres Congress has so liberally (?) granted, or shall we tramp to Oregon and locate them there? I am

72 The Reverend H. V. Rankin was a missionary in Ningpo; he was sent there in 1849 by the American Presbyterian Board. Dean, *op. cit.*, 162.

73 The *Flying Childers*, a California clipper ship of 1,125 tons, was built in 1852 and competed with the British tea trade. Captain Jeremiah D. D. White was her master. *Greyhounds*, 225, 263, 420.

74 Master of the *Flying Childers*. See note 73 above.

afraid when found, they will prove "Bob Acres"[75] and as we near the chosen spot, find all their value oozed out of them.

Friday June 8, 1855

Today is the anniversary of Mr. and Mrs. Clem. Nyes wedding celebrated by a large party at dinner, which duty on board prevented my attending. Mr. Green of Manila and Dr. Barnet of the Str. *Shanghai* dined with our mess.

Saturday June 9, 1855

The first anniversary of Miss Anna 'Vandalia' Murphy's birth, and celebrated at the Consulate by a party of juveniles, whose happy movements I watched from our deck duty confining me on board.

Sunday June 10, 1855

Nobody on board to preach; read the *Inquires* and *Registers*[76] you sent me and towards sundown strolled over the fields with Woodworth and Gwathmey. The whole country is gardened and attests a superabundant population. The climate has been and is now charming but I have had to surrender at discretion to the musquitos, and retreat to the security of my bar.

Monday June 11, 1855

On shore and bought a silk dress for Ellen to send by the *Flying Childers*. Returned on board to dinner and after dinner on shore again with young Adams, and walked around the race course. Took tea at Wetmores, bought some curios and a curious mosaic plate for 3$. Kept the midwatch.

Tuesday June 12, 1855

Warm and pleasant. James Purden dined with the mess.

Thursday June 14, 1855

Yesterday Bishop Boone called on board. Today, Woodworth, Sproston and I dined at Clem. Nye's at the fashionable hour of 8

[75] Bob Acres, a character in R. B. Sheridan's (1751–1816) comedy *The Rivals* (1775) representing a boasting coward and ludicrous vanity of a country gentleman in England. *The New Century Cyclopedia of Names,* III, 3584.

[76] "*Inquires and Registers*" is a reference to the weekly *Portland Inquirer* (1848–55) and the weekly *Portland Register*. Gregory, *op. cit.*, 254.

P.M. We took the Negro Minstrels on shore and after dinner they amused the company. The French Steamer of War *Colbert*[77] arrived from Nangasaki, where she had been on shore, leaking badly. Put a package containing two silk dresses on board the *F. Childers*.

Friday June 15, 1855

Spent the forenoon catering for the mess. The Commodore, Consul, and Doct. Hall dined with us. We expected Mrs. Murphy but she was sick and could not come, and Gwathmey in his absent mindedness forgot to invite her.

Saturday June 16, 1855

Wrote Doct. MacGowan of Ningpo, and bought 20 yds. of a figured slate colored pongee silk for 5$.

Sunday June 17, 1855

The anniversary Battle of Bunker Hill.[78] Doct. Bridgman preached on Salvation. Frank Foster and Mr. Wheelock dined on board and Miss Boyd and Dunn[79] came to nuts and wine.

Monday June 18, 1855

This being the 5th day of the 5th month of the 5th year of the Emperor Hein-fung[80] has been a grand holiday. I went with a missionary picnic, to a villiage about five miles distant to see a dragon festival; our party consisted of Mrs. Boone, Mrs Fay, Miss Conover, Mrs Dearborn,[81] Sproston, Gilliam, Watters and myself, with any

[77] The *Colbert*, a French war steamer, arrived in Japan during the expedition of Admiral Putiatin. Russia was an enemy of France during the Crimean War (1854–56). The *Colbert* visited Shimoda on May 2, 1855, apparently trying to capture the Russian ship *Diana*, which left Shimoda on May 12, 1855. Lensen, *Russia's Japan Expedition*, 69, 136. See also note 129 under the year 1853.

[78] The Battle of Bunker Hill was fought on June 17, 1775, in the Charlestown district.

[79] It is very difficult to establish who Miss Dunn was. Possibly she was related to Thomas Dunn, U.S. vice-consul in 1857, or to Nathan Dunn, the owner of a trading firm in Canton. Griffin, *op. cit.*, 182, 244, 360.

[80] Emperor Wên Tsong Hien reigned from 1851 to 1861.

[81] Mrs. Dearborn was most probably the wife of Captain Dearborn, who in 1854–55 served Russell and Company in Canton. *Greyhounds*, 236; Griffin, *op. cit.*, 393.

amount of nurses and children. I walked both ways—from which you can judge my health and strength especially when I tell you that after my return in the evening I strolled around the Race Course. Most of our party were carried in chairs, or rode on wheel barrows which are in common use for conveyance from villiage to villiage over the narrow dykes which enclose the paddy fields. These barrows are like ours, and carry two passengers one each side of the wheel facing outward. I tried riding on one, and did not find it unpleasant, but prefered walking.

We were accompanied by one of the mission schools of Chinese and our train as it wound along the narrow roads across the cultivated fields, with its palanquins, mountain chairs, horsemen and horsewomen, wheelbarrows, footmen, and the attendant crowd, would have furnished a subject for a painter. Arrived at the villiage we made our way through its long and winding streets lined with a sea of human faces to the house of a Chinese teacher, where we refreshed ourselves from our picnic stores, distributing largely to the Chinese scholars. The house was soon surrounded by a dense and curious crowd—almost dense enough to crush in the walls bounding it. With the cry '*She bar*,' the Chinese for clear out, away from you sharply uttered, we managed to make our way from the house into a boat in which we floated down a stream, running through the villiages in the wake of the procession of Dragon boats. Yell it not in faith, that the Bishop's lady,[82] with ourselves formed part of an idolatrous procession in China. Several young girls in the crowd were really beautiful, but such beauty was thinly scattered and many were disgustingly ugly. I noticed one pretty and lady like girl, looking upon our lunch, and offered her fruit and crackers, but she refused everything from me, but accepted the same thing from Mrs. Boone. As we were leaving I gave her the gospel of Matthew in Chinese, which she accepted. Her smile and expression was very sweet.

Tuesday June 19, 1855

You may be sure I slept sound last night. Today has been a wet storm. I was invited to tea at Doct. Bridgman's but the weather pre-

[82] Mrs. William Jones Boone, wife of the American Episcopal bishop in Shanghai. See also note 52 above.

vented my going. Frank Foster and Mr. Wheelock, the latter the widowed son in law of Mr. Balkan, and the Deputy Collier of Portland, dined with us. Frank Foster has recovered his health.

Wednesday June 20, 1855

A rainy morning, but cleared up pleasant. Exercised my wrists at small arms. Bought me some pongee silk coats.

Thursday June 21, 1855

Cloudy and rainy. Clipper *Golden City*[83] sailed for New York. I have found among the missionaries here an acquaintance of our good Doctor Nichols. His name is Kieth, and he tells me John Nichols was his tutor. His wife is related to Mrs. Nichols and is a pleasant sensible awkward person, very fond of dry washing her hands. Both she and her husband are in ill health.

Friday June 22[d] 1855

Pleasant weather: The Hamburg Ship *Sincapore* sailed for Hakodadi. All the world will go to Japan; now we have opened the oyster.

Saturday June 23, 1855

Bot a beautiful carved lacquered box for 5$. Attended a book auction. Dined and tea'd at Wetmore & Cos.

Sunday June 24, 1855

Doctor Bridgman preached. Frank Foster and Wheelock dined on board. At the Consuls the other night Mrs. Murphy was beseiching him to tell a story to which he rather objected. Came out with "Do now I am sure you won't refuse your dear little wife," which had the desired effect. How could he resist it? The *Portland Transcript* says grey beards are all the fashion. I shall be in the fashion for once if that is so, when I return.

Shanghai, Monday June 25, 1855

The *Flying Childers* sailed and we had heavy thunder squalls in the evening and throughout the night.

[83] The *Golden City*, a California tea clipper, was built in Boston in 1852 and was known for her beauty. She was first commanded by Richard Canfield and later by Samuel F. Dewing. She sailed between San Francisco and China. *Greyhounds* 285, 290, 357, 421; *Clipper*, 216, 354.

Shanghai, June 26, 1855

Called on the Myers with Doctor Woodworth but did not find them at home.

Steamer *Confucius*. At Sea, Monday, July 9, 1855

On the 29-th ult. under order from the Commodore I prepared to embark on board this steamer, and on the 30-th did embark with fifty two men and marines—Sproston, Doct. Gilliam and Adams, the Consular Secretary, as my staff and assistants, and left the same day in her for Loo Choo on an Expedition, the objects of which are set forth in my orders. I was to communicate with the Consul, Mr. Jones, and have a lookout for a large fleet of pirates infesting the coast. The steamer in command of Capt. Dearborn was under a charter from Russel and Co. to convoy 250 junks loaded with wood to Ningpo, and Messers R. and Co. were desirous of having a force on board, as there was a probability of the pirates showing themselves to cut off the convoy. The Commodore readily granted one, and gave me the command of it. I was sorry to leave before the arrival of the mail due the next morning, but as I have said the 30-th found me and my party on board the steamer going down the river. We had a rough passage down the coast, and nearly everybody including your humble servant was sea sick. On the evening of the 2-nd inst we anchored under Matson an island near the entrance of the river Min, hoping to find a pirate fleet there to destroy, but none was seen. The following morning we got underway and passed up the beautiful river to the Pagoda where we anchored about 10 oclock.

Jumping into a Chinese boat, with Capt. Dearborn, I went at once to Foo Chow which was twelve miles farther up the river to communicate with our Consul. We remained there all night and in the morning (our glorious fourth) returned to the *Confucius* to celebrate the day by fireing the usual salutes, and a display of rockets, blue lights and the like, in all of which we were joined and aided by the American and English Merchants and opium depot ships at the anchorage. It was the first time the day was ever so celebrated or that an American salute had been fired there. The Chinese wondered what great pidgeon it was and why we 'chin chinned joss' so. Consul Jones gave a dinner at Foo Chow which I could not attend but he has since informed me twenty eight Americans were invited, and twenty came and partook of his hospitality. Thus you see the Eagle spreads himself here as elsewhere. The Am. Missionaries who were not invited number as many more.

The scenery of this river is of the boldest description and the most interesting I have seen in China. The highest mountains are terraced and cultivated to their very tops, and battaries and forts frown on you from every turn of the river.

On the 5th at the Consuls request I went up to Foo Chow accompanied by the officers of my staff to aid at his reception of the Prefect of the District. For some reason or other he failed to come, so we returned in the evening as wise as we went up.

On the 6th we dropped down to the entrance of the river where our convoy of junks had assembled and the day was employed in arranging for our departure with the convoy.

On the 7th we got underway and have since been proceeding slowly up the coast. Our convoying force besides the *Confucius* consists of an armed ship, two schooners, and three lorchas. The rogues are not likely to attack our convoy unless at night. Nothing happening to prevent we will be at Ningpo in two days. These wood junks have been loaded over a year, and are afraid to come out on account of the pirates. Some detachments of 20 to 50 each which made the attempt were captured, and made to pay a ransom of four hundred dollars each.

They have been waiting so long that the fastenings of their loads decayed, and had to be renewed. The wood is piled up and projects over the side of the junks so that but little of the hull is seen, and they look like an ass between two panniers. Our fleet of junks, as it stretches around us ten miles or more, reminds me of the pictures of the Spanish Armada, which was scarcely more formidable in point of numbers, and I had almost said in tonnage and class of vessels.

I was glad to escape from the hot weather at Shanghai and think the sea air, change and seasickness have done me good. At Foo Chow I could not go about much on account of the extreme heat. Shut in between high mountains the sun seemed to pour down between them a brazen heat. Musquitos and Flies were so annoying that we had to desert the cabin and live and eat up on deck.

On board the *Macedonian*, At Shanghai, Friday July 20, 1855

The day after writing as above (July 10) in the afternoon while passing through the group of Chusan Islands we fell in with, and set fire to five piratical junks which had attempted to plunder some of our convoy. They offered no resistance but were floating arsenals of all sorts of deadly weapons and missles. The next night we anchored with our convoy at the mouth of the Jung river and the following morning the 12th anchored off the ancient city of Ningpo, where we remained until we got under way on the 16th to return to Shanghai, where we anchored in the afternoon of the 17th, when I retransfered myself and force to the *Macedonian* and resumed my duties on board. While at Ningpo I was very much annoyed by the bad behavior of some of my men, which prevented my going on shore as much as I otherwise would. I had on the whole however, a pleasant visit and shall ever retain a grateful remembrance of the kind hospitality of the American Missionaries—Mr and Mrs. Rankin, Doct. and Mrs. McCartee,[84] Mr and Mrs Nevius,[85] Mr and Mrs. Wayand, and the two Mr. Martins,[86] Mrs. Martin, and Mr

[84] In 1853, Mrs. Joanna M. Knight was married to Divie Bethune McCartee (1820–1900), a Presbyterian medical missionary. He was sent to China in 1843, learned the Chinese language proficiently, and acquired much influence. He was frequently employed as U.S. consul in Shanghai and also worked as a scholar and diplomat in China and Japan. *NCAB*, XXIV, 159; R. E. Speer, *A Missionary Pioneer in the Far East.*

[85] John Livingston Nevius (1829–93), after his graduation from Princeton Theological Seminary, went to China with his wife, Helen Coan, in September, 1854. They labored in Ningpo, Hangchow, and Chefoo. In 1860, Dr. Nevius visited Japan, with the intention of establishing a Presbyterian mission there. He was unsuccessful, however, and returned to China and continued his missionary work. He is the author of several works on missions and China. *NCB*, X, 293; Couling, *op. cit.*, 396; Latourette, *The Great Century in Northern Africa and Asia*, 308, and *A History of Christian Missions in China*, 249, 367ff. See also Helen Nevius, *Life of Dr. J. L. Nevius.*

[86] Two Martin brothers arrived in Ningpo from the United States in 1850. William A. P. Martin (1827–1916) was more noted among the Protestant missionaries. He taught international law at T'ungivên Kuan, a college in Peking, becoming its president in 1869; he was also president of newly founded Imperial University at Peking in 1898. Latourette, *The Great Century in Northern Africa and Asia*, 307–308; Hummel, *op. cit.*, 429, 480, 674, 790, with information about Martin's Chinese friends; Couling, *op. cit.*, 335.

Quarterman.[87] Nothing[88] could exceed the kindness with which they received and entertained myself and the officers who accompanied me. While at Ningpo I called officially upon the Prefect a Mandarin of the 3d rank who is the military and civil governor over three cities and holds the power of life and death over three millions of inhabitants. He received me with a salute of three guns and the usual Chinese honors and gave an entertainment of what children would call goodies, i.e. sweet meat candy and the like. Two days after my visit he returned it, calling upon me onboard the *Confucius*, when I received and treated him just as he had treated me, with this exception that I served to him and his suite Champagne and Constantia, which they swiggled with great gusto. My object in visiting him was to correct some abuses of the Am. flag by Chinese boats in his district. Doct. McCartee was our interpreter. The cards we exchanged somewhat shorn of their dimensions to fit the book are on the proceeding page. The literal translation attached is by Doct. McCartee and my card was devised by him.

Mrs. McCartee and Mrs. Rankin are sisters and both were born in Portland. Old Mr. Knight,[89] the shipbuilder, was their grand-

[87] The Reverend J. W. Quarterman was sent to Ningpo in 1846 by the American Presbyterian Board. Dean, *op. cit.*, 162.

[88] On p. 464 of the diary, which page ends here, is pasted a name card of the Chinese prefect of Ningpo, and between pp. 459 and 460 is inserted the following letter:

U.S.S. *Macedonian*, June 28, 1855

Gentlemen

You are respectfully solicited to partake of a dinner which is to be served up on board of the above ship on the 4th day of July next.

In behalf of the Ship's Company

Charles Brookfield
Robert Lewis
Ephriam Taff
Joseph McCarty
Adrian C. Sterritt
Francis McNally

Committee of Arrangements

To Ward Room Officers of U.S.S. *Macedonian.*

N B. Dinner served at 2 P.M.

[89] The Knight family of Portland was well known for its civic position and

father. Another sister, the wife of a missionary, has recently died in India. Mrs. Nevius recently married is a sweet little woman, and is acquainted with the Rev. Mr. Brown of Graham and Miss Jamison. She gave us all a dinner and evidently worried her own appetite away in preparing for our's. I do not remember when I have met with pleasanter people than this missionary circle. Ningpo is the finest though by no means the largest Chinese city I have seen. The streets are wider and cleaner and the shops are larger and better kept. The Shuntong or Guild hall or Exchange is the finest building I have ever seen in China, containing within its walls a splendid Joss house and three theatres. It is full of quaint carvings in wood and stone and resplendant with crimson and gold. It cost over fifty thousand dollars, a large sum in this land of cheap labor. Not long previous to the time of our visit the walls of a large Roman Catholic church, not being strong enough to support its heavy roof, or else badly founded, fell in with a tremendous crash, much to the joy of the Chinese, who were jealous because its high towers vied with that of their ancient and lofty pagoda. Doct. McCartee told me a funny story of their superstition in this connection. The next loftiest Chinese building was surmounted by a grasshopper while the tower of the cathedral was surmounted with a cock, to the displeasure of the Chinese who said "that cock eat the grass hopper." And as if there was something in the idea, the Chinese building not long ago was burnt to the ground, when it was rebuilt, they put a tiger cat on top of it instead of the grasshopper because as they said, the tiger could kill the cock. Strangely in accordance with the superstition a few days after the tiger cat was hoisted to its place, the cathedral fell by its own weight a mass of ruin.

The salary of the Presbyterian Missionarys at Ningpo is 750$ for man and wife and fifty dollars for each child additional if under 8 years, and 180$ for older children. House rent free, and 'cumshaws' added. Mr. Quarterman the only unmarried one receives 450$ per annum. The Ningpo Mission contains two brothers, two sisters, and a brother and sister, quite a family party met to christianize the Chi-

wealth. Thomas E. Knight was a shipbuilder in Cape Elizabeth, Maine. He built the *Phoenix*, 1,458 tons, which remained under the command of Captain Crabtree. *Greyhounds*, 430; Willis, *op. cit.*, 154, 181, 420.

nese at the antipodes of their own home. One of the little girls celebrated her fifth birthday with a childrens party, at which there was assembled as many children as grown people. It was quite a bond of sympathy between the good people of the mission and myself that I had a wife and children. While at Ningpo I bought some of the Buddast shells which are very curious. It is the shell of the pearl oyster in which are numerous figures of that heathen deity apparently carved in the shell, but the manner in which they are produced there is this, thin disks of metal stamped with Buddas image are inserted into the shell while the animal is alive, and naturally the muscular action keeps them close to the interior side of the shell, until they are coated with the pearly matter of which it is composed, and form apparently a part of the shell itself. It is said the figures are inserted by means of a forked bamboo stick, and the process is completed in about a year. The animal being fed and cared for meanwhile leaden shot are put in at times and covered in the same way.

The 17th, the day of my return to the *Macedonian*, I was made happy with lots of letters from home and photographs. Chas. Brown a seaman in attempting to desert probably for a frolic on shore was drowned. On the 18th in company with the Commodore, Purser and Surgeon dined with Mr. and Mrs. Spooner. Yesterday I trimmed my beard and whiskers for the first time since April, and kept the day's duty, also assisted at the Burial of Chas. Foster, a Manila man, who died of congestion of the lungs. Rev. Mr. Nelson performed the divine service. Weather extremely hot, thermometer 91° in the shade. This evening after taking tea there I passed at Wetmore & Cos. Sent a box of china ware on board the American Ship *Channing*,[90] and had the plate of my false teeth repaired.

Saturday July 21st 1855

Another hot day, thermometer 96° in the shade, and no wind stirring to fan the air. By the kindness of the Commodore, permitted to write my letters in the cabin. Invited to dine with D. King, but declined because it was too hot; took tea with Keetchong mess. Heard

[90] The *Channing* is neither in the *List*, 725–50, nor in the published lists of private ships. The name must have been given inexactly by Preble.

of the death of Capt. Beard of the *Gundreda* with whom I dined not long since; probable cause, too much brandy for the climate.

Shanghai, Sunday July 22^{d}, 1855

Very hot. Ther 92° in the shade. Rev. Mr. Culbertson preached on board, and Mr. and Mrs. Spooner attended the service. A man died on board the British ship *Mirage* of Asiatic Cholera.

Monday July 23^{d}, 1855

The Chinese received the duties due the custom House in Mexican dollars, after considerable diplomacy and pen talking. The money has been deposited with us by our consul for some days.

Monday July 30, 1855

Went down the river yesterday in the *Confucius* as far as the North Bank to ascertain about some ships said to be on shore. Found an English Schn. the *Matilda* high and dry and deserted, a complete wreck stripped by the Chinese even to her deck beams her deck all cut up. The crew had fortunately escaped and arrived at Woosung though they had to obtain a boat by force to save their lives in. We also found the Am Ship *Metropolitan* in a dangerous position among the shoals though afloat, and she declined Capt. Dearborn's assistance. The Steamer *Lady Mary Wood* arrived from Hong Kong yesterday without a mail, which is to come up in another steamer hourly expected. She brings account of a fearful gale at Hong Kong which unroofed houses and swept wharves besides doing other damage. The *Lady Mary* will leave on Thursday taking the mail, which has started everybody letter writing. I shall send by it the most valuable enclosure I have yet sent, via a draft on England for one hundred pounds sterling. How do you think I became possessed of such a treasure? Not from any provident forethought of mine, but it came as a present from the agents of the *Confucius* for my recent services on board her. Each of the three officers who accompanied me received a draft for seventy-five pounds, and the well behaved of my crew had three hundred Shanghai dollars divided among them, while those who misbehaved had their reward in not being considered in the division. As the owners of the *Confucius* cleared $15,000 by the trip, and have since sold it to the Tauti[91] for $90,000 more they could well afford to be generous. At first, because I had prevented a portion, the undeserving portion of my crew from receiving anything and to prevent hard thoughts, I refused to accept my share and returned the draft with the following letter which I am sure you must approve.

U. S. Flag Ship *Macedonian*,
Shanghai July 26, 1855

Messr. Russell & Co
Gentlemen:

I have the honor to acknowledge the receipt through Commodore Abbot of your draft for one hundred pounds sterling on London intended as a remuneration for services rendered by me on board the American steamer *Confucius*.

With many thanks for your kind and liberal offer I beg leave to return the draft, feeling as I do that in the simple performance of my duty under the orders and instructions of my Commodore I have done nothing to deserve or entitle me to such a reward.

I take this opportunity to gratefully acknowledge the receipt of three hundred and four Shanghai (carolus) dollars for distribution among the deserving portion of the men who composed the detachment under my command on board the *Confucius*, and which I have distributed agreeably to your request.

Beleive me, with a full appreciation of your liberality I remain Gentlemen

Messr Russell & Co
Shanghai, China

Your obliged and humble servant
Geo Hny Preble
Lt. USN

It seemed like throwing away a very much needed five hundred dollars, but I thought it was only doing right, and that my letter ended the matter, but not so. The next day Capt Dearborn of the *Confucius*, met me and said he wished me to promise to do him a favor. Of course I said yes if it is anything within reason. He then produced the draft and said it had been given to him to do with as he pleased and he wished me to accept as a personal favor from him-

[91] Taot'ai. See note 61 above.

self, and on my again refuseing threatened to send it to you direct. Then I said make it payable to her and I will send it myself, as I cannot permit any other man to make such a present to my wife, and so you have it, and the history of it. I shall send the 2^{d} and 3^{d} of the set by the next mail.

I am now under orders to attend to the placeing of a beacon ship, and bouys to assist the safe navigation of the entrance of this river, a very important and responsible duty. I am promised a handsome cumshaw, when it is all done. The Chinese authorities having agreed to pay all the expenses. Thus there is another gleam of sunshine over the ocean of my debts. If ever a man prayed fervently and sincerely I have for the ways and means to extinguish all I owe.

We came back from the North Bank in the *Confucius* today noon, and Capt Dearborn dined with me on board the *Macedonian*. Last night we were at anchor at Woosung. The ship *Eagle Wing* arrived from Hong Kong today.

Wednesday August 1, 1855

A beautiful bright summer's day for the celebration of my dear wifes birth. At dinner our mess joined me in a glass of champagne to the toast 'The day we celebrate,' without being informed of the particular occasion. Wrote Susie two letters, one to be forwarded via Marseilles, the other via Southampton enclosing the 1st and 2^{d} of the 100£ Bill of Exchange. I also sent two newspaper reports of our trip in the *Confucius*.

Our mail has not yet come up from Hong Kong and is probably delayed by the severe gales which have prevailed to the Southward. Mrs. Clem. Nye broke the Sabbath last week and presented her dapper little husband with a fine boy which it is proposed to christen 'under the flag' on board this ship, and our ways suggest he should be called 'Macedonian Phalanx Nye.' Mother and child the happy father last evening told me between two puffs of his invariable cigar are doing well. Mrs. Nelson is quite sick. It is now expected our ship will remain here one or two months longer. The *Powhatan* machinery is injured to such an extent that it will take two or three months to repair. The *Vandalia* is away on her cruise to Guam and on her return is to be sent to Foo Chow. Wrote for my friends to send me their photographs bound in a book as a New Years present, the most acceptable that could be made.

Steamer *Confucius*, Sunday August 5, 1855

I am again in command of a party of officers and men on board of this steamer and in company and cooperation with H.B.M. Brig *Bittern* Com'dr Edw[d] W. Vansittart,[92] we are going to root out a piratical nest at a place called Shantung, the cape which forms the southern point of the Gulf of Pechili. That accomplished we propose to go into the Gulf of Leo tong to convoy a large fleet of junks detained by fear of these pirates to Shanghai when I am to attend to the bouying of this river as ordered. I anticipate seeing a great deal and expect to visit places where no American or European vessels have ever been. The steamer *Paushan*,[93] and Brig *Clown*,[94] both armed, and owned by Chinese are to accompany us. They are manned by rascals and we do not rely much upon their fighting. The *Clown* is so heavily loaded with coals that being an old rotten thing we fear she will founder if any bad weather is encountered. The Chinese assert coals are plenty where we are going but we have no confidence such is the case. The *Bittern* is a stout Brig mounting 12 thirty two pounders with a picked crew of one hundred and thirty men. We have on board the *Confucius* 5 twelve pounders and two nine pounders with a picked crew of thirty men, and the officers I had before. The pirate fleet is reported to consist of 30 or 40 heavily armed junks. The terror of the coast. We expect to release a large fleet they are holding for ransom; one of the reports is that every day they burn a junk, with its people and cargo on board to hasten the ransom of the rest—probably an exaggeration. The Tautai of Shanghai pays

[92] E. W. Vansittart commanded the British sloop *Bittern* and encountered the pirates on the China coast between San Pwan and Tong-whang islands. Fox, *op. cit.*, 130–31.

[93] The *Paushan*, an English screw steamer attached to the expedition against the Chinese pirates, performed her duty in supplementary service. See also *Sketch*, 209.

[94] The fate of the collier brig *Clown* is mentioned by Preble in *Sketch*, 209: ". . . but from having been overloaded by the Chinese, and being a weak and crazy old vessel, foundered at sea before reaching the appointed rendezvous at Shantung promontory."

two hundred thousand dollars so it is said for the aid of the *Confucius*. She still flies the American flag, though she has been purchased by the Chinese and we carry with us a Chinese flag in order that the northern officials may recognize and aid us if necessary. We embarked on board the *Confucius* and came down from Shanghai yesterday morning (4th) and took on board an additional armament of 4.12 pds from the *Ann Welsh*. The *Paushan* came down in the afternoon, and I took tea with Vansittart on board the *Bittern*, when it was arranged for us to start on Monday morning. I dined today with Capt Vansittart who is a go-ahead driving officer with whom it will be a pleasure to be associated. "A kindred feeling makes us wondrous kind." He has recently come down from Japan where he has been watching the Russians and is eager to obtain his promotion to a captaincy. He is probably my junior in age, though a commander of several years standing in the R[oyal] N[avy]. The day has been cloudy and threatening. The mail arrived in the morning and Capt. Vansittart went up in the steamer, and on his return brought me a note from Gwathmey telling me that "no letters came to the *Macedonian*."

Woosung, Monday August 6, 1855

Employed putting the *Confucius* in fighting order, overhauled the gun gear, cleaned muskets, made up cartridges for the 10 and 9 pdrs. Dined on board the *Bittern* with Capt. Dearborn and went on shore for a walk. Arranged to tow the *Bittern* out in the morning at 8, the *Paushan* to follow with the leaky and overloaded *Clown*. H.B.M. Str. *Styx* went to sea.

Tuesday August 7, 1855

At 8 a.m. took the *Bittern* in tow and went to sea wind light from the Nth. In the afternoon after passing Amherst Rocks cast off our tow and Capt. Vansittart came on board to see me. When it was agreed I should push on to save coals, and wait for him thirty miles south of Stanton Island, Capt. Vansittart was very much afraid I would rush on and bag the pirates before he came up and wrote me begging I would not do so and saying he "would not risk a sheet of copper off the bottom of Her Majesty's ship for all the pirates in China." After casting off, we soon lost sight of the Brig standing to the Nth and E[st], we going to the North[th] as fast as our steam would take us. At sunset the Island Sheenweshan bore W. by N. 10 miles wind fresh from N.N.W.

Wednesday August 8, 1855

We have no wind today which makes it bad for the Brig but with our steamer we have paddled along famously. Exercised the crew at quarters and scaled the guns fireing several rounds of shot and shell. Averaged nine knots an hour steering N. and E. and North.

Thursday August 9, 1855

At daylight saw high land ahead; sea calm and smooth. Steered directly for the land. The Island of Stanton on our port bow, and several small islands west of it. An island not on our charts forward of the Starb[d] beam. Several large coasting junks in sight, and numerous fishing boats watching nets which appeared to be laid out in every direction several miles from shore. At 9 A.M. we were close in with the mainland which was high and rugged and showed numerous small towns and clustered houses scattered along the coast. Sounded frequently in eight fathoms about two miles from the shore. Noticed a harbor which appeared to be the mouth of a river to the West of Hai yong so. The entrance was from the Sth with a small island off it. At 9.30 A.M. abreast of the little town of Hai yong so, the harbor of which is simply an open roadstead. At 10 A.M. steamed through a passage between the mainland and island not named on the chart abreast of the harbor of [Hai yong so] and obtained soundings in 6 fathoms two miles off shore. At 10.15 keeping in mid channel steamed into the spacious harbor Ta-Shit-taou with the town in full view on our port bow, and came to anchor. Contrary to our expectations we found only trading junks. The Str. *Paushan* reported having seen here two weeks ago a large fleet of the pirates. The whole of the water front of the town of Shatau was crowded with the gaping inhabitants and as soon as we had anchored we were surrounded by boats crowded with the Chinese inquiring who we were and what we wanted; chickens, ducks, eggs, fruit, etc., were offered for sale, but the noise of the escaping steam from our safety valve drove them all off in fear and astonishment. They soon returned to satisfy their curiosity and sell their provisions. At 11 A.M. three

Mandarins came on board who expressed themselves right pleased with the object of our visit, and were suitably entertained. We showed them an American Flag and obtained from them a promise to treat as friends those sailing under it. We also showed them our Chinese flag to show what we proposed to do, was under the sanction of their own government. We then exercised at quarters fired vollies of musketry and set them on shore under a salute of three guns. At 1 P.M. went on shore in the pennace with Sproston and Capt. Dearborn, and returned the official call. We were received in a most polite and friendly manner and saluted on leaving. We learned that the Pirate Fleet consisting of forty junks and two lorchas left for the north twenty days ago, and is supposed for New Chong. Before leaving they fired a number of houses and took away all the guns besides carrying off nine of the inhabitants. While here most of the inhabitants fled to the hills. The Mandarins told us our arrival was not unexpected as four days previous a letter had been received from the Tautai of Shanghai informing them of our expedition. The Tautai's letter could have been only four days on the way, and shows how rapidly messages are sent in China. The Mandarins also inform us that after leaving this harbor and while in sight the Pirate Fleet had an engagement with a fleet of fourteen junks which lasted several hours and resulted in the burning of nine of the smaller fleet and the escape of the remaining five to the South. The small fleet was said or thought to be from Ningpo.

Shatou, Friday August 10, 1855

Rec'd a supply of fresh provisions and fruit from the person appointed by the Mandarins. Took sights for and ascertained the Longitude to be 122° 24′ 45″ East of Greenwich. At noon the Chief Mandarin of the town accompanied by three others visited the steamer, and I received him with the officers and marines under arms. I plied them with questions as to the Pirates and their movements, and the towns, etc., along the coast facilities for obtaining coal, etc., all of which they answered freely. They pointed out on a Chinese chart: Fou Chan, on the north side of Shantung about a day steaming distant, and Fou Shan on the East coast of Leotung as places where coal could be obtained. In the afternoon landed with Sproston on the S.W. side of the Harbor, and took angles and compas bearings and mounting a deserted stone fort, made a sketch and out line of the Harbor. Then walked over the country, found the soi sandy but productive. The fruits and vegetables of the temperat zone growing to perfection. The inhabitants though curious, civil an obligeing. Quite a lively trade has been so established between ou tars and the shore people. Saw among those on board a red haire Chinese boy, the first I have ever seen. The prices asked were reason able, and Chinese copper cash in demand. They did not know th value of the 'almighty dollar' however and would not take it whe offered. Everything was passed on board for examination withou hesitation, and with a confiding trust in the honesty of our tars whic I am happy to say was not abused.

The town of Shilau is built entirely of red sandstone well pu together with lime and cement, and nicely cut, altogether the strong est and best built Chinese town I have seen. The inhabitants seen better looking and more stalwart than the southern Chinese. W have been reveling in peaches, apples, plums and the cool and invig orating air. The fruits are beautiful to the eye, but they are not s high flavored and juicy as those of New England, still they are good apology for them and as such to be enjoyed. The flies are ver troublesome and so infest the cabin that they are a very Egyptia plague, and I can only write by having a boy to wave a duster ove my head, while another boy is thrapping them about with a towel t clear the apartment.

Saturday August 11, 1855

Light and pleasant breezes at daylight took the Pinnace and ac companied by Sproston and Capt. Dearborn went up the Bay, sound ing as we went, and keeping the side of the Harbor on which the town is situated close aboard. The soundings from the steamer to the Point of Sand off the town were from 4½ to 3½ fathoms, the tide a quarter ebb. From the point to a bar which appeared to extend across the Harbor three quarters of a mile above the soundings were from 3½ to 2 fathoms muddy bottom. At the bar the width of the Harbor decreases but widens again beyond and extends about five miles farther inland. At its head a small river pours its tribute into the bay. Landing a short distance from a stranded and deserted Chin Chow junk near an unarmed earthworks we took a long walk through the country. Close to our landing were several large and half burnt masts that had belonged to the junks. We first directed our steps to and through a villiage where were kindly stared at we wandered into the country which was found well cultivated with Indian corn, beans, millet, etc., etc. On our return we followed a broad and well constructed road which the Chinese said led to Pekin. At regular intervals slabs of limestone ten feet high with carved inscriptions were erected at the side of the road, and near to them white marble slabs of a smaller size.

Purchased fruits and vegetables for Chinese money, but could not pursuade the people to take our dollars, as they were ignorant of their value. The evening proved rainy and stormy and we were forced to let go a second anchor. The sea outside being rough noticed breakers extending about a mile from the southern point of the Island off the entrance of the Harbor.

Sunday August 12, 1855

Morning squally with rain and some lightening to the Nth and W[st]. In the afternoon the weather moderated. Sent Mr. Sproston in the Pinnace to look after the *Bittern* outside but the day closed without any signs of our consorts.

Shatou, Monday August 13, 1855

Soon after midnight heard two guns in the offing and supposing they might be signal guns from one of our consorts sent a boat on shore at daylight and placed a lookout on the hills, who soon discovered the *Paushan* and *Bittern* in the offing. The *Paushan* came in ordered her not to anchor, and got underway and stood out to the *Bittern*. Learned from the *Paushan* that the day after our departure from Woosung, the *Paushan* towing the *Clown* came up with the *Bittern* and took her in tow also, that on the fourth day out when some forty miles to the Southard of Stauton Island, they encountered a S.E. gale, and after dark the *Bittern* cast off, and necessity soon obliged them to cut the towlines of the *Clown* a heavy sea on at the time; burning a blue light the *P.* went within hail of the *Bittern* and informed her Captain of his having cast off the *Clown,* and that she had four feet of water in her hold and was leaking badly. The *Bittern* on a lee shore could not render any aid. The next day was spent by the two vessels in a fruitless search for the *Clown*.

The Paushan preceding us out of the Harbor after this communication fortunately fell in with the long boat of the *Clown*, and rescued her officers and crew twenty in number, much reduced by their exposure in an open boat with nothing to eat. They reported that soon after the *Clown* was cast off, the wind changed to the N.W. and the Brig was hove to under a close reefed Main Topsail, but the water in her hold increased rapidly, and the Brig labored heavily the seas washing over her fore and aft. The officers and crew were forced to lash themselves to prevent their being swept overboard, When the water in the hold was awash with the deck, and the vessel was about to founder they took to the long boat, soon after which the gale moderated and they were saved.

At a little after noon the *Bittern* signalized to us she would send a boat and soon Capt. Vansittart came on board, together we went on board the *Paushan* and arranged for our future operations, and continued on with our little squadron steering N.E. Keeping the land about ten miles distant the wind light from the South and weather pleasant. At 4.30 P.M. we were abreast of Shantung promontory and distant from it about three miles. At 4.45 Alcesta Rock bore west about a mile—steered W. by N. the land tending nearly due West and dist from 8 to 10 miles. The hills appeared rugged but the vallies fertile; sea smooth. The *Confucius* averaging fourteen miles an hour. At 5.50 made out the Harbor of Wei-hai-wee, ahead, and at 7 P.M. anchored in that spacious anchorage in 4½ fathoms near to the small town Wee-hai-wee, where were a number of coasting junks, but saw none of the inhabitants. We have arranged to meet the other vessels at Che fow. Our object in steaming ahead being to save coals. Our dependance the *Clown* having foundered. During the day determined the position of several points and Alcesta Rocks. The latter we found to be 37°30′ N. and Long 122° 40′ E.

Tuesday August 14, 1855

Left Wee hai wee Harbor soon after daylight without communicating with the people, noticed it was a fine walled town, though small. The Harbor open and spacious. From our anchorage well inside of Leu Cung Island the town bore N.W. and W. and the harbor was land locked except to the Sst and Est and in the event of a gale from that quarter a vessel might shift her anchorage to the S.E. side of the Harbor, where our pilot assured us there is four fathoms of water, and ride in safety. Noticed another walled town but could see no guns mounted. Walls about thirty feet high. As we steamed out of the Harbor the inhabitants congregated on the hills in great numbers. When clear of the Northern point steered to the West. The appearance of the coast much the same as yesterday: large open bays with wide sand heap beaches extending for miles lined the shores with fertile vallies between rugged hills forming the background. Coasting along passed between some Islands and the Main. Counted ten pretty towns which we passed each surrounded by cultivated fields. At 8 A.M. discovered the *Bittern* in tow of the *Paushan,* and at 10 A.M. we all anchored in the Harbor of Chefow. The *Bittern* and *Paushan* near the town of Chefow. Ourselves in the Southern light near the town of Fuh Shan, anchoring near a fleet of coasting junks in ¼ less 4 fathoms high water. The junks Chin Chinned us with their gongs and we sounded our bell in acknowledgment. Along the water front of the town are numerous wooden and stone breastworks mounted with Cannon, which a Mandarin who came off to enquire the object of our visit said were erected to frighten off the pirate fleet, which appeared off the Harbor five days ago, but seeing the preparations did not come in. Went on shore with Capt. Vansittart and called upon the chief Mandarin and informed him of our want of coals, and that we could not continue our cruise without a supply. Messages were immediately dispatched to the principal town of the Province, Chefow, about sixty miles to the West and about five miles inland, requesting a supply sent down to us. In the afternoon the Chief Mandarin of Fou Shan visited us, and was shown the steamer, and treated in an appropriate manner and saluted with three guns on leaving, obtained three tons of coal from the shore.

Chefow, Wednesday August 15, 1855

Continued at anchor all day endeavoring to obtain a sufficient supply of coal to continue our search for the pirates, but have been able to obtain ten tons of suitable size and quality. There are huge heaps of coal dust on shore, which cannot be kept in our grates, but none in lump that we can burn.

The Chinese on board the *Paushan* are very anxious for us to go on, but Capt. Dearborn thinks it will be imprudent to make the attempt without a further supply of sixty tons, as the steamer has no sails and we have only enough on board to take us back to Shanghai.

We learned today that the coal mines are sixty miles inland, and that the coal is brought down in panniers on mules, or in small carts or boxes suspended between two horses. It would require some time to bring us down the required sixty tons in that manner, so I fear we have to give up our chase and can only return.

During the afternoon the *Bittern* stood out to sea about three miles and came back again. The men have loaded our decks with apples, peaches, ducks, chickens which they bought very cheap. Capt. Vansittart and I went on shore and walked to the Joss House Hill west of Fushan where we had a panoramic view which was very beautiful. The inhabitants appeared an inoffensive people and were very civil to us.

In the forenoon it rained hard, but the afternoon was all the pleasant.

Thursday August 16, 1855

Soon after daylight the *Bittern* left us in tow of the *Paushan* to continue the cruise; we being obliged for want of coals to return to Shanghai. Oh that the Chinese had accepted my caution and not overloaded the *Clown*.

All the lump coal we have been able to procure falls short of ten tons, and it would take ten days to get what we require from the mountains. It is said there is coal at Leotong but we would have to fight our way through the Pirate Fleet to get at it (not much matter if we had coal enough to manuevere with) and then probably find the same state of things as here.

At 9 A.M. we fired a gun and steamed out of the harbor. The battery on shore saluting our departure with three guns. Having obtained an offing shaped our course due East. At 2 P.M. we were abreast of Wei-hai-wee. At 5 P.M. Alcesta Rocks bore south two

Courtesy U.S. Naval Academy Museum

Rear Admiral George Henry Preble, U.S.N., in 1882

Courtesy U.S. Naval Academy Museum

The U.S.S. *Macedonian*, Aboard Which Preble Served, as Painted by C. Drew about 1784

miles. At 5.40 Shantung Promontory abeam and we kept away south. This Cape has a light house on it which is only lighted when a fleet of junks is expected. At 8 P.M. we were up with Tai-shi-tou Harbor where we first anchored. Rice has been so associated in my mind with the Chinese as their principle food that I have been surprised to find it so little eaten in Shantung. Beans and Indian corn are the principle products and of course the chief food of the people. Indeed on leaving today we wished to obtain some rice for the few Chinese on board, and could not obtain any.

Friday August 17, 1855

A pleasant day; steaming along bravely to the Sth passed numerous junks bound to the Nth. Find the coal procured at Fushan burns very well. During the night some heavy rains and squally which raised a rough and disagreeable sea.

Saturday August 18, 1855

Commences with squalls from the S.E. and rain. At 9 A.M. made the Island of Shaw-we-shan. At 10 A.M. had passed Amherst Rocks and had Gutzlaff Isld in sight south of us. Passed the Am. Ship *John Wade*[95] standing out. The English Ship *Ann Welsh* saluted us with her colors. At 6.30 P.M. anchored off the Mission at Shanghai near the *Macedonian* and transfered myself, and the officers and expedition crew, and pinnace to her. Hauled down the Am. Ensign and pennant on board the *Confucius* and ended our expdn after the pirates of the North.

Shanghai, U.S.S. *Macedonian,* Sunday, Augt. 19, 1855

Mr. Nelson performed service on board; wrote to Susie. Received a letter and box of carved frames from Doct. McCartee of Ningpo, also files of papers from the South. We hear from Hong Kong that the boats of the *Powhatan* have had a fight with the pirate junks, which resulted in the capture and destruction of the latter. Several of the *Powhatan's* men were wounded and five killed or have since

[95] The *John Wade,* a California clipper ship of 639 tons, was built in Williamsburg, New York, in 1851 and was first commanded by Captain George H. Willis, who, since 1854, was on the *Ocean Telegraph. Greyhounds,* 289, 416, 438; *Clipper,* 299, 351.

died of their wounds. It is estimated 5 to 600 of the pirates were either killed or drowned. It was a joint affair of English and Americans, the whole commanded by my friend Capt. Abel Fellows of the *Comus*. The Piracies of the coast are increasing and will require a constant exertion on the part of the European forces to put them down.

During our absence in the North, two sailors have died on board the *Macedonian*. The Commodore's health is feeble and he is contemplating a cruise to the ports we have just left to recruit himself and invigorate the crew. We have already hoisted in the boats.

Monday August 20, 1855

On shore and examined the brig *Ferdinand VII* which has been purchased in my absence for the Light Ship, I recommended. I think her a poor model for the purpose, and it will cost all of $3,000 to strengthen her sufficiently. Dined at the Keetch hong by invitation of Mr. Spooner. Took tea and passed the evening there and returned to the ship at 10 P.M. The Commodore inspired by the accounts we brought of the Northern country, has determined to make a cruise in that direction, but the pilot says the ship cannot cross the bar before Friday. The Com'd has a letter from Com'd Smith[96] saying Com'd Jas. Armstrong[97] will relieve him but it has not been decided whether he is to come out overland, or in a ship. The *Powhatan* and *Vandalia* are to be relieved by the *St. Mary*[98] and *Massachusetts*[99] both now in the Pacific. At last we have a glimmering prospect of returning.

[96] William Smith was made midshipman on March 4, 1823; passed midshipman March 23, 1829; lieutenant, March 3, 1831; commander, September 12, 185[…]; commodore, July 16, 1862; retired list, January 9, 1865; died April 29, 1873. See also *Records*, 71–73.

[97] James Armstrong was made midshipman on November 15, 1809; lieutenant April 27, 1816; commander, March 3, 1825; captain, September 8, 1841; commodore, retired list, April 4, 1867; died August 25, 1868.

[98] The *St. Mary* was a navy sailing vessel, 1,025 tons, 20 guns, built in 184[…] In 1874, she became the state school ship of New York.

[99] The *Massachusetts*, a tea clipper of 615 tons built in 1799, remained under the command of Captain William Hutchins. She was owned by T. H. Perkins, Stephen Higginson, Thos. C. Amory *et al.*, Boston. *Greyhounds*, 399.

Tuesday August 21, 1855

Rainy squally and every way disagreeable. My day's duty on board.

Wednesday August 22d 1855

Blowing a gale from E. to S.E. which kept everybody on board ship.

Thursday August 23, 1855

Weather warm and pleasant. Ship ready for sea; many gentlemen called on board to say good bye to the Commodore and Officers.

Friday August 24, 1855

Pleasant weather. The pilot reports only eighteen feet of water on the bar and as the ship draws twenty two, we cannot sail before Monday, when their highest tides are looked for.

Shanghai, Saturday August 25, 1855

Our happy anniversary which I am happy to be here to commemorate by writing to my dear little wife. Such a shivering and a shaking as I underwent before I said 'yes' thirteen years ago today. The agony did not last long but seemed ages. I tiffined at Wetmores and brought Mr. Rockwell their tea taster off to dinner with me. In the evening dined at the Consuls, it being their wedding anniversary. The dinner party comprised Dr. and Mrs. Bridgman, Rev. Mr. and Mrs. Culbertson, Mr. Poins Gwathmey and myself. Woodworth, Gilliam and Walters dropped in during the evening. Mrs. M[urphy] rallied from a sick bed to grace the occasion, and wore her wedding dress and looked as charming as a bride is bound to look. It is pleasant to see how devoted and loving Mrs. M. is. She looks upon her husband as a phenix of talent and worthy of any office from that of President of the U.S. down. She is a trusting loveing confiding little woman artless as a child. Her tongue exposing what her heart look and manners combine to speak. We had a very pleasant dinner, and left early for China, that is to say at eleven oclock, on account of Mrs. M's health.

Sunday August 26, 1855

The Rev. Mr. Culbertson preached on board. He was formerly a

Lieut. in the U.S. Army, and at one time stationed at Portland. He resigned to become a missionary and is soon to return to the U.S. tc recruit his health. We expect to get underway tomorrow. The Commodore is quite impatient to be off. The poor old man is quite feeble, and ought to be at home with his family, for this is his last earthly cruise.

One of my messmates (Boudinot) yesterday asked me how much I had saved from my salary since I entered the service, at the same time stating that he had saved $12,000. I told him my savings, were a wife and two children, and I would not exchange with him.

Monday August 27, 1855

Unmoored ship and got ready for sea, and prepared to be taken in tow by the *Confucius*, when the order was countermanded. The managing agent of the steamer came on board, and said he could no tow our ship as he had orders to go immediately to the rescue o some shipwrecked people which had been seen on a barren rock called Tong-ting, lieing to the East of the Chusan group, and supposed a part of the crew of the *John Jay*[100] whose non arrival ha caused apprehension as to her safety. They were seen on Friday, by a vessel just arrived, and which oweing to the weather was unable to communicate and are supposed to be in a starving condition. As th ship is not going to sea, I volunteered with Sproston to accompan the steamer on this humane search, and having attained the Commodore's permission to do so, went on board the *Confucius* and a 10 A.M. we steamed down the river. At Woosung we took on board Mr. Matheson[101] and Capt. Batting, and at Sunset anchored of

[100] The *John Jay* was an old packet ship built in New York in 1827. In 1855, sh was commanded by James Goodday. *Clipper*, 47; *Greyhounds*, 408. See also no 97 under the year 1854.

[101] Jardine, Matheson and Company was founded in England in 1782 by the Cc and Reid Company. Daniel Beale and his brother, Thomas, continued the compar after the death of Cox in 1791. Beale became Prussian consul in Macao in 178 Until 1825, the company had a virtual trade monopoly in China on clocks, watche musical snuffboxes, and mechanical toys. However, it was primarily engaged in tl export of tea from 1802 until 1835. The company, in conjunction with Davidsc and Company, the precursors of Dent and Company, was reorganized in 1834 Canton and Macao by Dr. William Jardine, who was a ship's surgeon. James Math son came to China in 1819 and joined Jardine in 1842; they established branches

Kafflis Isld one of the Rugged Islands the weather being cloudy and rainy.

Steamer *Confucius*, Tuesday Aug. 28, 1855

Got underway at midnight and at 7 A.M. came up with Tong-ting and steamed all around it. Nearing it we discovered people moving about on it, and thought it strange they made no signal for assistance.

A close inspection satisfied us that they were Chinese, and regular inhabitants to the rock. As we saw their rudely constructed dwellings, and their little skiff hauled up about twenty feet perpendicularly above the water, and lodged in one of the crevices of their rocky abode. We counted eight persons on the rock, which was scarcely larger than our ships hull, and had not fifty feet square of any green thing even on its summit. Their hut was built in the rock near the top of it, and we were near enough to see one of the men enjoying the luxury of a pipe. Our movements in the steamer must have been a puzzle to them. After fully satisfying ourselves with the character of the people we steamed away and through the Chusan group of Islands, threading its intricate channels and passing Tinghai, which I visited in the *St. Louis* ten years ago. The Chusans as far as scenery can make it are certainly the Paradise of China. A paradise however at this time infested with pirates which the indented shores, and winding channels are admirably adapted to shelter. After leaving Tinghai and in passing through Blackwall Channel we saw piratical junks engaged in the pleasant occupation of robbing some fishing and merchant junks, and steered for them when they made haste to escape from us with sails and oars. We soon overtook the largest, and fired at her several times to stop, but as she would not run her down, cutting her in two amidships. As she sunk under our bow twelve of the rascals climbed on board and were made prisoners, the remainder escaped by swimming to the shore. Having finished one we went after her consort which had been run on shore her crew escaping to the hills. After a heavy shower had passed, we amused ourselves with

Shanghai, 1843, and Yokohama, 1859. Cf. *Commercial and Industrial Hong Kong*, 132–35; Orange, *op. cit.*, 201, 325, 356; Griffin, *op. cit.*, 322; Couling, *op. cit.*, 258. For an exact list of partners in Jardine, Matheson and Company, see Fairbank, *op. cit.*, II, 56–57.

a little target practice at her hull, and then boarded and burnt her as she lay first spiking her cannons and throwing them overboard.

One of our prisoners, evidently the leader on board the larger junk, was wounded by Capt. Dearborn in the arm by a rifle shot, and appeared a perfect stoic. He did not come out of the vessel until she was sinking under him. Nothing could exceed the fury of our Chinese crew against the wretches we captured. They would have pulled them to pieces if we had not prevented.

Wednesday August 29, 1855

This morning the pirate Chief who had somehow got rid of his irons deliberately walked overboard and was drowned. He thought no doubt it was better to die so, than suffer the tortures he would certainly be subjected to on our arrival at Shanghai. I was standing talking with Capt. Dearborn at the time when he mounted the guards forward of the wheel close to us, and jumped overboard and was seen no more. At 6 A.M. anchored at Shanghai and returned to the *Macedonian.*

Macedonian, August 30, 1855

Dined on board and tea'd at Keetchong and passed the evening with Gwathmey at the new Keetchong.

Friday August 31, 1855

On board ship. Afternoon and evening rainy.

Saturday September 1, 1855

Dear little Lily's birthday, and my day's duty. Our wardroom mess dined our friends of the Old Keetchong mess. We have been forcibly reminded today that in the midst of life we are in death by the sudden decease of Robt. Gaskin, the ship's painter of Cholera. Yesterday he was in health but complained at noon of not being well. In the evening he called upon the surgeon, and at half past ten this morning died.

The Commodore has taken up lodgings on shore and abandoned the northern cruise. He is very feeble but I hope may be spared to return home in the ship with his flag flying, though I fear not.

Sunday September 2d 1855

Rev. Mr. Aitchison[102] preached on board from the text "Come unto me all ye that labor and are heavy laden and I will give you rest."[103] In the afternoon called on the Commodore at the Consuls and in the evening on Capt. and Mrs. Dearborn at the Hotel. The Brig *Bittern* and *Paushan* returned from a most successful cruise having destroyed twenty one pirate junks on the 18th and 19th ult., two and three days after they left us. How I envy their luck, and my misfortune [is] in having no coal to enable me to share with them.

Monday September 3d 1855

Took a look at the Beacon[104] brig and attended an Auction. Tea and evening at Russell & Cos. Introduced to Mr. Beale[105] and invited to dine with him tomorrow. Called on my friend H.B.M. Consul who read to me Capt. Vansittart's report of his encounter with the pirates, who it appears attacked him with forty junks.

Tuesday September 4, 1855

Rec'd by the mail Susie's letter via Marseilles dated Boston June 6. The *Bittern* in her engagement with the pirates was struck by shot several times but had no one killed or injured. A sounding line in the hands of one of her crew was cut in two by a shot but the man himself untouched. I was glad to hear by my letter of Josiah's and Ben Smith's[106] wedding.

The Commodore talks of a cruise to the South in the *Confucius* for his health. The 1st Lt Surgeon and Purser to accompany him which would leave me in command during his absence. The *Con-*

102 The Reverend W. Aitchison was sent to Shanghai in 1854 by the American Board of Commissioners. Dean, *op. cit.*, 152.

103 Matt. 11:28.

104 The *Beacon Light*, a California tea clipper of 1,376 tons, was built in 1855. She was apparently new in Chinese waters at the time of Preble's visit. *Greyhounds*, 440; *Clipper*, 362.

105 T. C. Beale was consul for Portugal in Shanghai. Griffin, *op. cit.*, 182.

106 It is evident from Preble's *Sketch* that some of the Smiths were connected with his maternal line. However, neither of them could be related to Ben Smith. The Smiths seem to be from Boston.

fucius is going out to search for the wreck of the Bark *Range* on board of which Mr. Fred King of Foo Chow[107] was a passanger. She is reported lost with all on board. Mr. King was on his way to Shanghai to arrange his business and bid farewell to China. His brother the head of the House here is very anxious, and has gone down the coast in the *John Dewan* to search for the wreck, and hoping to find his brother yet alive. What information we have is derived from two Chinese, who report themselves the sole survivers.

Saturday September 7, 1855

We have had three cases of Cholera on board but only one proved fatal. This and the dysentry which has prevailed has decided the Commodore to have the ship moved to an anchorage outside the river when after seeing her moored he proposes to take a cruise in the *Confucius*. Rec'd today a pleasant little note from Mrs. Nye acknowledging the receipt of a book of autumn leaves. A friend writes me from Canton that thirty thousand persons have been beheaded in that city since the 1st of March, an average of over a hundred a day.

Saturday September 8, 1855

Went on shore bought a bronze bowl and vase and on my return on board found the missing letter from Susie which enclosed one from Doct. Nichols. The mail steamer left for Hong Kong at daylight and Mr. and Mrs. Spooner went in her.

Sunday September 9, 1855

On shore all day by order of the Commodore looking after the improvements in the navigation of the Yangtse Kiang. Dined with Mr. Cunningham, and took tea at the Hotel with Capt. Dearborn.

Monday September 10, 1855

We hoped to get to sea today, but the *Confucius* disappointed us

107 In Preble's diary we meet three Americans named King. William Henry King, who was a partner in Russell and Company, 1843–49, and later the head of King and Company in China; David O. King, who was Prussian consul in Shanghai; and Fred King from Foochow. They all seem to be closely related and members of King and Company. Griffin, *op. cit.*, 143, 306, 415; Fairbank, *op. cit.*, I, 433; see also note 169 under the year 1854.

having to tow out the merchant ship *Omar Pasha*. Two of our marines died yesterday, one of dysentery the other of cholera and both were buried today. I attended the body of one to the grave and Mr. Nelson performed the funeral service. Just as the service was ended another body was brought up, and he was asked to repeat the service, which he did. After he had got through he chanced to ask what was the occasion of the man's death, and finding he had committed suicide was very much horrified, and said had he known it he would have refused to perform the service. With my Unitarian ideas I immediately took issue with [him]. Strange that prejudice should go so far.

Tuesday September 11, 1855

Got underway at 11 A.M. in tow of the *Confucius* and stood down the river. At Sundown anchored near Gutzlaff Island; a rainy night.

Raffles Island, Wednesday, Sept. 12, 1855

Got underway at daylight in tow and at 11 A.M. anchored under the south side of Raffles Island and moored ship. The *Confucius* returned to Shanghai taking our Purser. Read *Hard Times* by Dickens.

Thursday September 13, 1855

A rainy day—forty-nine on the sick list. Housed top gallant masts in anticipation of bad weather.

Friday September 14, 1855

A cloudy breezy day. William Thompson died of various deeases generated by rum and was buried on Raffles Island. We have now only one on the sick list who is considered dangerously ill and hope soon to have a healthy ship. The Commodore continues to waste away and is very feeble and desponding. He told me yesterday that he only weighs 95 lbs. and when he left New York he weighed 142. My health has been preserved I believe by my cruisings about the coast in the *Queen* and *Confucius* and I notice my expedition crews have preserved their health while those men who have been confined to the inactivity of the *Macedonian* have felt the climate most.

Saturday September 15, 1855

Another cloudy day. Sweethearts and wives were toasted tonight, and the mess conversation ran in the same direction. Our sick list is improving. The Commodore went on shore today but could only walk a few steps.

Sunday September 16, 1855

Pleasant and cloudy. Allowed twenty-five men on shore on liberty. Our Ningpo boat came down with a supply of meats and vegetables. Rec'd a note from Doct. MacCartee and answered it.

Monday September 17, 1855

A rainy day and my duty on deck. Our tender the *Alma* was sent to Shanghai.

Tuesday September 18, 1855

Pleasant. In the afternoon walked on shore with Doct. Gilliam; arranging my room and papers.

Wednesday September 19, 1855

Pleasant. Fixing and arranging my disordered room.

Thursday September 20, 1855

Blowing a gale from the S.E. which causes an ugly sea and gives us a disagreeable rolling motion.

The ship is anchored too near the shoal water which gives us some anxiety. We have had to close our airports, and block out the very desirable fresh air.

Friday September 21, 1855

The gale continues; a real equinoctial.

Saturday September 22, 1855

Pleasant and hazy; the clearing up of the storm. Gwathmey on the Doctor's list which doubles my duties.

Sunday September 23d, 1855

Pleasant. Forenoon quarters and inspection as usual. An English pilot boat anchored near us.

Monday September 24, 1855

Pleasant wind N. and light. A heavy underground swell rolling health into us. Quite a surf on the beach. Dingy capsized going on shore fortunately nobody drowned. The *Alma* arr'd from Shanghai but without news or letters.

Tuesday September 25, 1855

A cloudy day. Barbot started in the *Alma* for Shanghai, but put back about sundown in consequence of the boisterous weather. Unmoored, and dropped the ship farther out to the Sth and Est and come to again.

Wednesday September 26, 1855

A stormy rainy day. Thermometer 71°. Blowing a N.W. gale.

Thursday September 27, 1855

Clearing up. The *Alma* started with our mails for Shanghai. In the afternoon it blew fresh from the N.N.E. The weather is gradually cooling. Next week I expect to go to Shanghai about my Bouys and Beacons. Our sick list is improving and I hope to go in the ship.

Friday September 28, 1855

Blowing a gale from N.N.E. all day suffering from a severe cold in the head. The Masters at Arms sold the dead mens and deserter's clothing at auction. Our ther. stands at about 70° to 72°, a great improvement on the heated term of Shanghai. The Commodore is very feeble but bouyed with the anticipation that the next mail will tell him of his releif.

Saturday Sept. 29, 1855

The gale continues, and we have nothing to do but roll it out.

Sunday, Sept. 30, 1855

Wind N.W. air cool and bracing ther. 70½°.

Monday October 1, 1855

The gale having abated, we sent our boat on shore for water, and sent up our top gallant masts.

Tuesday, October 2, 1855

Pleasant and my relief duty. Potter,[108] the pilot came in from

[108] Captain Mark L. Potter of Bangor had been a pilot in Shanghai since 1847. Griffin, *op. cit.*, 20, 481.

Shanghai, and I concluded to return with him in his pilot boat, packed and got ready. We hear the pirates have been robbing some of our Ningpo missionary friends who were on their passage to the sacred Island of Pooto politely telling them they would call and pay their respects at Ningpo some other time.

Wednesday, October 3d, 1855

At midnight left in Potter's boat for Shanghai. At daylight we were off Gutzlaff,[109] and at sundown landed at Keetch-hong jetty, and took up my quarters at Russell & Cos. having been kindly invited by Mr. Cunningham. Rather surprised to find that the *Alma* in which Barbot left our ship last Thursday has not arrived. The *Barracouta* and *Styx* arrived from Japan.

Thursday October 4, 1855

The *Alma* arrived and releived my uneasiness on her account, saw Barbot and concluded to send her back tomorrow. It appears the wind blew so fresh from the Nth that they had to bear up and lay at anchor three days under the Rugged Islands. Frank Foster told me yesterday he was going home in the ship *Joshua Bates*[110] is expected to sail in three weeks.

I have been very busy with my Bouys and Beacons.

Friday October 5, 1855

The mail arrived today and I received Susie's letter of July 9th and newspapers to the 17th. The *Alma* took the mail and Barbot back to the ship. The *San Jacinto*[111] we learn was to sail in August to re-

[109] Gutzlaff Island, in Chinese *Ta-chi'ih* or *Ta-ch'ih shan*, at the mouth of the Yangtse River, is seventy miles south of Shanghai. It was named to honor Karl F. A. Gutzlaff (1803–1851), an agent of the Netherland Missionary Society and a prominent Sinologist. For a short bibliography on Gutzlaff, see Hummel, *op. cit.*, 403, 851; Couling, *op. cit.*, 220; Latourette, *The Great Century in Northern Africa and Asia*, 304 n.311 and, especially, 305 n.312.

[110] The *Joshua Bates* was a packet ship built in 1852 for the tea trade. She had several masters, the first of whom was Captain Samuel Easterbrook. She belonged to Enoch Train's widely known Liverpool Line, Boston. *Greyhounds*, 129, 468; *Clipper*, 55.

[111] The U.S.S. *San Jacinto* was a six-screw steamer built in 1848 and lost on January 1, 1865.

leive the *Macedonian* hurra! Several of my messmates have letters to the 29th by the Marseilles mail.

Saturday October 6, 1855

Writing letters. Dined at Wetmores. Rec'd from Capt. Gorham[112] of the *Winged Racer* a package of books and papers. Lost my money purse with four or five dollars.

Sunday October 7, 1855

A drizzley rain which cleared off pleasant. Made calls on board the *Bittern Styx* and *Barracouta.* Sent a package of four newspapers to Adml. Stirling.

Monday Oct. 8, 1855

Bought 16 yards of Figured Satin at Kynte Yuens to send home by Capt. Gerard of the *Snow Squall.*[113] It cost me 12 Shanghai dollars equivalent to 19$ in the U.S. It is wide 39 inches. Sent by the same ship a Neptunes Goblet to the Port. Nat. His. Society.[114] Sent Doct. McCartee a couple of Portland papers with a note. Wrote Susie and Doct. Wood.

Tuesday October 9, 1855

Breakfasted with Capt Henry on board the *Romance of the Seas.*[115] After breakfast called with him on board the *Bittern* and took a look at her prize. Called on the Nelsons and Murphys. The *Bittern* saluting the French consul fired a 32 pound shot, which passed through a sampan, both sides of our Light Ship, through one side of a cargo boat, and three chests of tea, fortunately without killing or wounding anyone.

Wednesday October 10, 1855

Today completes my first score of years service in the U.S. Navy.

[112] Captain Francis Gorham of the *Winged Racer* left Boston for China on February 3, 1855. *Greyhounds,* 494, 499.

[113] The *Snow Squall,* a fast clipper ship of 742 tons, was built in 1851. Her first master was Captain Ira Bursley; Captain Gerard, or Girard, succeeded him. The *Snow Squall* once made a famous run of 119 days from Shanghai to London. *Clipper,* 284, 352; *Greyhounds,* 292, 316.

[114] Portland Society of Natural History.

[115] Captain William W. Henry arrived at Shanghai on November 1, 1855,

Twenty years ago today I entered Uncle Sam's service as an aspiring middy. Tiffened with the Nye's and meeting Mrs. Murphy called with her on Mrs. Mann, and at Kinteyuers. The *Alma* arrived with a note from Gwathmey discouraging our hope of returning home. The *Powhatan* ordered home via Sandwich Islands. Passed the evening with Mr. Gray[116] at the Nye's. The *Alma* was run into by a vessel and damaged. Mr. Cunningham[117] tried his newly arrived yacht the *Halcyon*[118] for the first time. Mr. Gray gave me today a half pound canister of cumshaw tea, which is said to be worth 3000$ the picul, or about twenty-three and half dollars a pound. It was given to him by their tea merchant, as a rare present.

Thursday October 11, 1855

Running hither and thither all day. The *Alma* is detained for repairs. Wrote Pegram[119] of the *Powhatan* by the *Erie*.[120]

Friday October 12, 1855

Bought at Kinteyuers 4 gauze dresses [and] 14 pin cushion covers. In the afternoon walked into the old walled city of Shanghai and through the tea gardens. Got wet in a shower.

Saturday October 13, 1855

Rainy. Sent Potter the Pilot to the *Macedonian* with some Pumelos and brown bread for the Commodore. Mr. Cunningham re-

---

aboard the *Romance of the Seas,* a California tea clipper, 1,782 tons, built in 1853 and owned by George Upton of Boston. Her first master was the well-known Captain Philip Dumaresq. *Clipper,* 232, 359; *Greyhounds,* 285–88 *et sqq.*

116 George Griswold Gray was a partner in Russell and Company; his son, also named George Griswold Gray, joined the same company. The younger Gray lost a leg in a Chinese riot. Griffin, *op. cit.,* 259, 352.

117 Edward Cunningham, an American merchant in China and vice-consul at Shanghai, was the owner of the *Halcyon.* He tried to establish trade relations between Shanghai and Nagasaki and visited Shimoda in May, 1856. Griffin, *op. cit.,* 332, 363.

118 The *Halcyon* most probably had a consular registration in Shanghai. She does not appear in lists of American ships of the nineteenth century.

119 R. B. Pegram was a lieutenant on the *Powhatan* during Perry's expedition to Japan. *Narrative,* II, 410.

120 The *Erie,* an American ship, was built in 1852 and sailed between London and China. *Greyhounds,* 469.

turned in his yacht from up the Yangtse River. He went nearly to Silver Island.

Sunday October 14, 1855

Pleasant. Called on the Murphys, but they were out and I continued my walk with Doct. Hall and Dom Pedro to view their newly purchased land. Dined at Old Keetchong.

Monday October 15, 1855

Called on the English, French, American and Prussian Consuls, and at the Nelsons. In the afternoon went over the walled city with Mr. Nelson and had the French attack explained by him; visited several curious temples, and bought some baskets.

Tuesday October 16, 1855

Afternoon went on board the *Confucius*, and taking over light vessel the *Ferdinand VII* in tow started down the river, saluted by all the American Ships in the Harbor; returned with three gun salutes to each from the *Confucius*. At sunset cast off our tow and anchored for the night. Mr. H. N. Lay on board. Night rainy; evening employed working at a new set of sailing directions with the assistance of the practical good sense of Capt. Dearborn.

Wednesday October 17, 1855

Underway at daylight, and towed the Light vessel to near her position, and temporarily anchored her there. Then sounded about and towards the north bank, and then run towards a large ship at anchor which we soon made out to be the *Macedonian*, spoke her and then returned to the light ship and anchored. The weather too thick and rainy to find her correct position. At 2 P.M. got underway and returned to Shanghai where we anchored at sundown. The *Macedonian* came up to Black H. Isld. and anchored.

Thursday October 18, 1855

Pleasant with light rain showers, which cleared up in the afternoon with the wind at N.E. At 1 P.M. got underway in the *Confucius* for the North Bank. Purser Allison going down with us to the *Macedonian* met her below Woosung working up, signaled for a boat and put the purser on board. Anchored near the Light vessel at sundown.

Friday October 19, 1855

Underway at daylight, sighted Gutzlaff. Shifted the Brig to the Nth and Wst where she would ride easier. Lat. 31.09.N. Run several lines of soundings, and anchored again, sent Mr. Gough and the steamer's men on board to moor the Light Brig.

Saturday October 20, 1855

Underway after breakfast and sounded along the edge of the South Bank. Anchored in the afternoon off the Three Trees and went on shore with Capt. D[earborn] to see about the feasibility of putting up a Beacon. Found the country flat, and over-flowed for a mile or more at high tides. Could find no one to undertake the building a beacon. Ret'd to the Steamer and got underway for Woosung. The French War Steamer *Colbert* passed us bound out and H.B.M. Str. *Barracouta*,[121] bound in saw large flocks of wild ducks and geese.

Woosung, Sunday October 21, 1855

After breakfast landed at Woosung with Capt. Dearborn and talked with a Chinaman about building the Beacon at Three Trees, and painting and repairing the leading marks at Woosung spit. After our walk went on board the *Macedonian* and saw the poor old Commodore in bed and looking very poorly. The *Macedonian* is to sail tomorrow for Hong Kong, and I am to remain behind to finish my sailing direction and come down in the mail steamer. The Chinese to pay my expenses and fare down. At 2 P.M. got underway in the *Confucius* and returned to Shanghai and had a talk with our consul on the subject of my sailing directions, etc.

Shanghai, Monday October 22d, 1855

Tiffened with Murphy. Lt. Boudinot and Purser Allison went down to the *Macedonian*. Mr. Gray and Mr. Cunningham returned from up river in the yacht. Sent some guaze dresses and shipped fronts and pin cushions home in the *Electric*[122] in charge of Capt. Gales.

121 In 1854–55, a British warship, the *Barracouta*, and a French vessel, the *Colbert*, patrolled Chinese and Japanese waters against the Russian expedition of Admiral Putiatin. Lensen, *Russia's Japan Expedition*, 69, 80, 136, 139.

122 The *Electric*, a California clipper of 1,273 tons, was built in Mystic, Connecticut, in 1853. Her master was Captain Gurdon Gates. *Greyhounds*, 273, 426; *Clipper*, 360.

Tuesday October 23d, 1855

Breakfasted on board the *Confucius* and at 10 A.M. she was got underway and went down the river with the *Electric* in tow, and towed her below Woosung then cast her off and run alongside the *Macedonian*, and made fast and backed and filled with her to below the *Electric*. When we cast her off and they made sail on her for Hong Kong. Returned to Shanghai in the steamer and reached my temporary home at Russell & Cos. at 8 P.M.

Wednesday October 24, 1855

Reparing my sailing directions and report and tracing a chart for the Lithographic press. Mr. Cunningham's schr [schooner] sailed for Ningpo. Three ladies died here today—a remarkable mortality for Shanghai.

Thursday October 25, 1855

Dined and passed the evening at the Nyes; ladies rather sleepy from last night's dissipation, played a couple of games of whist and retired early. Bought Susie a fur robe and paid twelve dollars for it.

Friday October 26, 1855

The *Erie* arrived with our mail and bringing accounts of the Battle of Terchanya. Tiffined at the Consuls and passed evening at old Keetch-hong.

Saturday October 27, 1855

Rec'd a box from Ningpo. Tiffened with Murphy. Wetmore Ayder and a Swedish gent dined with us at Russell & Cos.

Sunday October 28, 1855

Breakfasted on board the *Surprise* with Capt. Ranlett.[123] Tiffened at old Keetchong and dined at home i.e. Russell & Cos.

Monday October 29, 1855

Packed a trunk and sent it to Frank Foster who will take it to

[123] The *Surprise*, a California clipper of 1,261 tons built in 1850, was under Captain Philip Dumaresq, who was succeeded by the renowned Captain Charles A. Ranlett. The *Surprise* sailed between San Francisco and Chinese ports during an era of prosperous American trade with Canton. Her two captains contributed greatly to the sea history of American clippers. *Greyhounds*, 158, 337–40, 414ff.; *Clipper*, 136–38.

Susie. It contains a fur robe and some goat skin mats and other smaller articles. F. F. expected to sail in the *J. Bates*[124] on Wednesday. Capt. Vansittart was of our dinner party today.

Tuesday October 30, 1855

Examined and corrected a fair copy of my sailing directions, looked after my bouys and endeavored to procure sinkers for them. The Am. Ship *Game Cock*[125] Capt. Osgood arrived with New York dates to August 6th.

Wednesday October 31, 1855

Sent my sailing directions to the printer and received from Mr. Murphy a ticket of passage to Hong Kong in the English Mail Steamer, for which he paid one hundred and twenty Shanghai dollars. Dined at Heard & Cos. Mrs. Murphy is going home or rather to London in the *Swallow*[126] Capt. Tucker on account of her health, and her husband will go overland and meet her, as soon as he can finish up his business here.

Thursday November 1, 1855

Capt. Osgood's wife and child are stopping at the house a pleasant addition. This is her first voyage. The little girl is a bright fearless thing and has blue eyes which is remarkable as both of her parents have black eyes.

Friday November 2d, 1855

Saw a little girl five years old, the daughter of Mrs. Capt. Sim-

124 The *J. Bates* is not listed in the several registers of American sailing ships of the nineteenth century. However, a Captain Bates is mentioned as the master of the *Flying Eagle*, which was built in 1854. *Greyhounds*, 496, 501. It is probable that Preble meant the *Joshua Bates*. See note 110 above.

125 The *Game Cock*, a California clipper of 1,392 tons, belonged to Daniel C. Bacon of Boston. She was built in 1851 for the China trade and made a record voyage (thirty-five days) between San Francisco and Hong Kong. Captain W. H. Osgood, master of several clippers, joined the *Game Cock* in 1853. *Clipper*, 135, 195; *Greyhounds*, 159, 486, 493.

126 The *Swallow*, a tea ship of 1,435 tons, was built in 1854 at East Boston. Her master was Captain Benjamin W. Tucker. She voyaged mostly between China and England. In 1885, she was abandoned at sea. *Greyhounds*, 335, 439, 472.

mons[127] in sake's shop today and romped with [her], tried to imagine her our Lily saw a Chinaman pulling old advertisement placards off the walls and carefully preserving the scraps which is considered a very meritorious thing. Called on Capt. Dearborn in the evening.

Saturday November 3d 1855

Went down river in the *Confucius* to place the Bouys on Woosung spit. Found the *Joshua Bates* ashore in the North Spit, and saw Foster on board. Returned to Shanghai and dined at the Heards. Played Pool for the first time in my life.

Sunday November 4, 1855

Rainy which I improved to write Susie. Mrs. Murphy expects to leave in the *Swallow* for London on Friday. Mrs. Osgood the wife of the Capt. of the *Game Cock* now staying at our house I find a pleasant lady. She is from Salem and knows Agnes and has seen Lizzie Preble; either she or her husband is related to Doctor Mighels. The Capt. informs me Doct. M. has been crippled for life by a fall. A young man of the first order named Bacon, whose father owns the *Game Cock*, and is one of the solid men of Roxbury is also at the House.

Monday November 5, 1855

Weighed in Mr. Duran's scales 150½ lbs which is four more lbs than I remember ever having weighed before.

Tuesday November 6, 1855

Called on the British Consul who gave me a very beautiful carved frame. Sent a package for Susie on board the *Eagle Wing*, Capt Lennell.[128]

Wednesday November 7, 1855

Packed up, made my P.P.C. calls and sent my things on board the Steamer. At 5 P.M. left Shanghai in Russel & Cos. boat with Mr.

[127] Captain Benjamin Simmons was the master of the *Crystal Palace*, a sailing ship of 635 tons built in 1854 at New Bedford. *Greyhounds*, 435, 473.

[128] The *Eagle Wing*, a California clipper of 1,174 tons was built in 1853. Her master was Captain Eben H. Linnell. She was lost in 1865 on the way to Bombay from Boston. *Greyhounds*, 293, 426.

Bacon[129] and A. F. Heard and reached the *Erie* Capt. Jameson[130] about 9 P.M. when we had a hearty cold supper. Mr. Bacon is to be my roommate. Mr. D. O. King was quite delerious in the evening. Among our passangers we have Berneux Catholic Bishop of Corea.[131]

Thursday November 8, 1855

The *Erie* got underway at 7. this morning and we are now enroute for Hong Kong.

Friday November 9, 1855

Weather cloudy with some rain.

Saturday November 10, 1855

At 7 A.M. sighted the Island of Ocksen a strong N.E. Monsoon blowing.

Sunday November 11, 1855

Passed close to Pedro Branca this morning and at 2 P.M. anchored at Hong Kong. I am now at home on board the *Macedonian.* My passage down calculating the value of exchange cost the Chinese who of course paid the bill equal to two and a half dollars per hour. The Commodore I find no better, and he does not appear to be any worse. The *Powhatan* has gone home, and the *J. P. Kennedy* is sold. So that the *Macedonian* and *Vandalia* are the sole remaining representatives of the Great American Nation in these celestial waters.

Monday November 12, 1855

A drizzly day and sultry withal. On shore in the forenoon seeing to the printing of my report on the Yantse Kiang. I hardly got on

129 Russell and Company owned the *Coquette,* 457 tons, built in 1844. Captain Bacon was her master. *Greyhounds,* 113, 393.

130 Captain William Jameson was the master of the *Josephine,* a California clipper of 947 tons built in 1852 and owned by General Jos. Andrews of Salem, Massachusetts. The *Josephine* was burned in St. Louis Harbor, Mauritius, in June, 1859. It is evident that in 1856, Jameson was the captain of the *Erie,* which was built in 1853 for the China trade. *Greyhounds,* 421, 469, 484.

131 Monsignor Simeon François Berneux (1814–1866), apostolic vicar of Korea, was martyred on September 10, 1866, during the persecution of Christians in Korea. Dallet, *op. cit.,* II, 571–72; for the voyage to which Preble refers, see *ibid.,* 403–409; see also *Enciclopedia Cattolica* (1949), II, 1444–45.

board the *Macedonian* yesterday before Admiral Stirling's boat was alongside inviting me to dine with him today. Of course I accepted and had a very pleasant dinner. Our dining party consisted of Sir James and Capt. Stirling, Capts. Currio Wilson and Stewart R.N., Capt. Sir Fredric Nicholson R.N., Col Dunlap, Com'dr Bruce, Lt. . . . Capt. Baker of the P and O Str *Sincapore,* Gwathmey and myself. The only toast drank besides the invariable one of 'The Queen' was proposed by the Admiral to Comr'dre Abbot's better health. He had just returned from visiting him and spoke impressively of him as an astonishing man retaining as he does his interest in the outside matters of his command. His life is evidently 'flickering in the socket' but he astonishes everyone by his temporary display of strength. Every mail we fear must carry home the news of his decease.

Tuesday November 13, 1855

Cloudy and sultry. Mr. Foster and Mr. Bacon off to dine with us.

Wednesday November 14, 1855

Cloudy, blustering. Called on the Commodore at the De Silvers after Quarters and thought he was looking a shade better. Walked about town, bought a pith hat. Had my pocket picked of a handkerchief. Called on Mrs. Drinker and daughter.

Thursday November 15, 1855

Mailed my letters for home. Called on the Commodore. In the afternoon the *Sincapore* left for Pt. de Gallo with the Mails. The French minister Bourboulon,[132] went in her. Mr. Williams who was with me in the *Queen* a masters mate now runs the *Spark* as Captain and dined with us. Evening at Gen'l Kennan the Consuls.

Saturday Nov. 17, 1855

Yesterday I had the relief duty, today on deck. The Screw Steamer

[132] Alphonse de Bourboulon, a French diplomat, was sent to China as minister plenipotentiary, 1851 to 1857, and in 1859 to negotiate Franco-Chinese affairs, especially French grievances caused by Chinese excesses against traders and missionaries. Couling, *op cit.*, 58; Henri Cordier, *L'expédition de Chine de 1860*, I, 11–12.

Antelope[133] arrived from Boston, docking at Batavia after a passage of 113 [days]. She was 80 days to Angier under sail.

Sunday Nov. 18, 1855

The Anniversary of my wedding—God bless it. After the usual Sunday inspection went on shore to see the Commodore, and returned to dinner on board. After dinner on shore again, took a pleasant drive with Mr. R. S. Sturgis, and returned to his house to another dinner. Returned to the ship at 11 P.M. and wrote Susie an anniversary letter. On our drive we passed Sir John and Lady Bowring and doffed our beavers to them. It is the first time I have seen them since my return to Hong Kong. Among the events of the day was a pleasant letter from Mr. Nye of Canton by which I learned to my surprise I am a shipper of tea to the United States. Some months since having a balance of money belonging to Uncle Sam from my pursership on hand ($666) I sent a draft for the amount to Mr. Nye asking him to employ it until we came down, so that it would be paying interest, if it could be done without risk of the principal. His letters of acknowledgment miscarried and it was only today that I learned he had misconstrued my request and sent it to the U.S. in tea, which he thinks will be a profitable investment, but meanwhile I have to pay up here which will be inconvenient. I saw at Mr. Sturgis's today two stereoscopic daguerreotypes: one of a lady, the other of two beautiful children in highland dresses, both very natural and yet how unlifelike. They reminded me of the old stones of Enchantment where beautiful princesses are instantly turned to stone. It was almost painful to look upon these stiff and rigid forms showing all the rosy hues of health, and adorned with the fashionable trappings of the day, yet I had a strange desire to possess similar frozen statuettes of yourself and the children.

Hong Kong, Monday Nov. 19, 1855

Called on Lady Bowring. Sir John and his daughters were out having gone with the admiral on an excursion around the Island in the Coromardal. After dinner examined the *Antelope* at the request

133 The screw steamer *Antelope*, 460 tons, was built in East Boston for Russell and Company in 1855. She was ordered by R. B. Forbes; see his *Personal Reminiscences*, 415. For a picture of the *Antelope*, see Griffin, *op. cit.*, 8.

of our Commissioner, who is thinking of chartering her for the use of our government.

Tuesday Nov. 20, 1855

A diver from H.M.S. *Marquis*[134] was under our ships bottom two hours today. He found the false keel much rubbed and the copper very ragged. He has only examined one side as yet. A Russian officer dined with us in the wardroom.

Wednesday November 21, 1855

Read letters from home, also copies of my sailing directions for the Yangtse Kiang. Gen'l Kennan gave our mess a dinner to which five of my messmates went. I was prevented having the day's duty.

Thursday November 22, 1855

Cloudy with rain. Called on the Nyes and Miss Rawle. Capt. Wingford and Miss Emma Nye dined with our mess. In the evening called on Geo. De Silver and Mr. Hitchcock and then Robt. De Silver to watch with the Commodore. Found Sir John Bowring by the bedside of the Commodore, and was invited to breakfast with him tomorrow.

Friday November 23, 1855

Pleasant and cool, breakfasted with the Bowrings. Our conversation ranged from politics to religion, and from Bentham to Dickens and Thackeray.[135] Dined at the Club House with Mr. Hitchcock. Lady Bowring is very lame, and has been so for seven years. She told me it was with great difficulty she got up and down stairs. I gave her a copy of Dr. Dewey's Sermons[136] and Bunn's Lectures[137] which

[134] She was the H.M.S. *Marquis of Ely*, a ship of the East India Company. Her fourth officer, Richard Glasspoole, was kidnapped by pirates in 1810. Fox, *op. cit.*, 114.

[135] Charles John Huffam Dickens (1812–1870) and William Makepeace Thackeray (1811–1863) were already well known in 1850. Preble was familiar with their literary achievements.

[136] Orville Dewey (1794–1882), pastor of the First Congregational Church in New Bedford, Massachusetts, and later a Unitarian divine, was known for his prolific output of sermons, essays, and discourses on various subjects. Many of his "sermons" were published from 1826 on. Harvard Library has an extensive collection of Dewey's works. *DAB*, V, 272–73.

[137] Thomas Bunn, *A Lecture . . . The Existence of the Deity Proved by the*

she expressed a desire to see. She and Sir John have requested me to make them unceremonious visits which I intend to avail myself of.

Saturday November 24, 1855

H.M.S. *Encounter* arrived from Hakodadi in 13 days. Lady Bowring is 60 years old, one evening she sang at Sir Johns request when he exclaimed, "I do like to hear your old voice."

Hong Kong, Sunday November 25, 1855

H.M. Frigate *Sybelle* Commodore Elliot arrived 17 days from Hakodadi. Two Mr. Lawrences, a Mr. Woodworth and Geo. De Silver dined with our mess, and Mr. Cooper Turner the lawyer favored us with a call. Admiral Stirling showed me on board the *Winchester* some stereoscopic pictures of his family. He certainly can boast of the handsome faces, and intellectual expressions of his children. His wife was a Miss Willing, I believe of Phila., so their beauty is not all English, though he himself is as fine a specimen of the fine old English gentleman as I have ever met with.

Monday November 26, 1855

Tiffined and dined with our consul and lodged at De Silvers to be near the Commodore. H.M.S. *Rattler*[138] arrived from Whampoa.

Tuesday November 27, 1855

Attended the funeral of Wm. Davis a seaman. I was prepared to read the service but was very glad to have the Colonial Chaplain volunteer to do it. Evening at R. P. De Silvers and on board to a midwatch.

Wednesday November 28, 1855

Other anxious hearts besides mine are awaiting the arrival of the mail. For two days a flag has been flying from Victoria Peak sent

Structure of the Human Mind. Another lecture was on the *Perception of Beauty From Literary and Scientific Institution* (London, 1850).

138 There were also two American ships named *Rattler*. One was a California clipper of 794 tons built in 1854. Her master was Captain Forest, and she was owned by D. Stewart of Baltimore. *Clipper*, 250, 361. The other *Rattler*, 538 tons, was launched at Baltimore on November 27, 1852, and was reported lost near Norfolk in 1853 but noted in 1869 as owned in Palermo, Italy. with Captain Stamp as her master. *Greyhounds*, 249.

there by a lady, with orders to hoist it when the steamer came in sight. The coolie mistaking his orders hoisted the flag and came down, and there it is.

Thursday November 29, 1855

On duty on board; a very pleasant day, the air and weather amber like.

Hong Kong, Nov. 30, 1855

A pleasant day called with Sproston on Mrs. Mather[139] on board the *Nightingale*[140]—a pleasant call—afterwards went to see Comd. Abbot. After dinner Gwathmey and I took a long walk on the new high way overlooking the town. Evening at Rose Hill Mr. Sturgis's place. No mail yet. Two gentlemen in the street wishing aloud for a segar I supplied them, hoping their wants would always be as easily gratified. They were strangers.

Saturday December 1, 1855

Spent a pleasant hour with Lady Bowring and her two daughters. Williams dined on board, and brought me the picture of Harry and Lily from the painters, hung them up over my bureau where I can look at them. Took a sundown walk over the hills.

The mail steamer arrived at noon flying a signal, "Sebastapool Fallen."[141] Six of the officers of the late Russian Frigate *Diana,* and Mr. Tuckerman dined with us. The mail brings us news that our relief, the *San Jacinto,* sailed from New York Sept. 25, having Mr. Townsend Harris[142] on board as Commissioner to Siam. The French

[139] Mrs. Samuel Mather, wife of Captain Mather of the *Nightingale.* See note 239 under the year 1854 and note 140 below.

[140] The *Nightingale* was under the command of Captain Samuel W. Mather. She was celebrated for her voyage from Portsmouth, England, to Shanghai in 106 days in 1853 and from Shanghai to London in 91 days in 1855. *Clipper,* 164–65, 206–207.

[141] Sebastopol, a city and fortress in the Crimea, fell to the allied armies of France and England on September 9, 1855, and sealed the fate of Russia. The Russians suffered 102,670 casualties.

[142] Townsend Harris (1804–1878), merchant and politician, is distinguished for his diplomatic activities in China and Japan. In 1854, he was U.S. consul in Ningpo, and on August 4, 1855, he was appointed consul to Japan, then consul

Steamer of War, *Colbert,* arrived from Loo Choo. A little incident shows that there have been anxious watchers and waiters for the mail besides ourselves. We have noticed for several days past a flag waving from the summit of Victoria Peak, and learn that a lady expecting her two daughters from England, sent her Chinese servant up the mountain to hoist the flag when he saw the steamer coming. The Chinaman toiled up the mountain and on reaching the summit hoisted the flag 'to rest it,' as he said, and after remaining all day without seeing the steamer came down in the evening leaving the flag "still there," an emblem of his stupidity. One can imagine the nervous and hopeful expectation of the lady until the servant's return.

Hong Kong, Monday December 3, 1855

The English, French and Spanish vessels of war in port dressed ship and fired national salutes rejoicing at the Fall of Sebastopool. Sir Jas. Stirling rec'd news by the mail of his promotion, and hoisted his flag as Rear Admiral of the R.N. There is a dinner party at the De Silvers this evening, and our negro minstrel at the Consuls.

Tuesday December 4, 1855

Called on Miss Russell and on Commodore Abbot. While with the Commodore, Sir J. Bowring, Sir Jas. Stirling and Capt. Wilson of the *Winchester* called on him. Took a long walk with Sir Jas and Capt. W. what Sir James called 'constitutional.' Capt. O'Calleghan joined our walk. Evening at the Club House with our Consul where I found a party of French and English officers fraternizing over a bowl of blasing punch. I congratulated Sir James on his promotion and he in turn hoped the recent revolutions in our navy had promoted me.

Wednesday December 5, 1855

Purser Sewall of the *Styx* came on board to make a farewell call his ship being homeward bound. The Commodore I found very feeble today he wishes me to go to Canton to make some purchases for

general and minister resident. He concluded a treaty of commerce and friendship in 1858. By his wisdom and honesty, he achieved considerable influence upon the Japanese government's friendly attitudes during its early dealings with foreign powers. For a bibliography, see *DAB,* VIII, 324–25, and on his achievements, Dennett, *op. cit.,* 348–66, with bibliographical notes.

him. He says, if he is alive after my return he intends going in the ship to Singapore to meet the *San Jacinto*. Purser Allison, who came down from Canton today, says it is the intention of the Merchants to present me with a testimonial for my services against the pirates, and improving the navigation of the Yangtse Kiang.

Thursday, December 6, 1855

Doct. Gilliam and I started at 8 A.M. in the Str. *River Bird* for Canton. As she was towing a heavy Danish ship we did not get to Whampoa until after dark and as it was foggy we did not get to Canton but anchored a mile below the Factories. Capt. DuVol made us comfortable.

Canton, Friday December 7, 1855

Anchored off the Factories soon after day light and after breakfast transferred myself to the hospitality of Mr. Gideon Nye, called on my Canton friends and took tea with the Purdons.

Amused myself shopping during the day.

Saturday December 8, 1855

Forenoon shopping. Letters from the ship report the Commodore much worse. A pleasant gathering at Mr. Nye's in the evening.

Sunday December 9th, 1855

Pleasant varied by a drizzly rain; walked over the burnt district which is being cleared up and built upon. Dined at Mr. Hubbell's.

Monday December 10, 1855

Resumed my shopping bought a set of chamber clocks for 15$ a pair of Chinese vases 8$, card case for Susie $10 etc. Dined with Mr. Spooner, quite a party. John Spooner arrived from California and joined the party, was introduced to Mr. Alcock the British Consul.[143]

Tuesday December 11, 1855

Dr. Gilliam returned to the ship. Dined with the Purdon's. Troubled with a heavy cold.

[143] Sir Rutherford Alcock (1809–1897), British diplomat, was consul at Foochow, 1844, and at Shanghai, 1846–57. He was the first British consul general in Japan, 1858–65, and minister plenipotentiary in Peking, 1865–71. Knighted in 1862, he was author of a number of works on Japan. *DNB*, suppl. I, 29.

Wednesday December 12, 1855

Suffering and aching all over. Folded some thirty of Mr. Nye's circulars containing my sailing directions and addressed them.

Thursday December 13, 1855

My cold better, wrote Susie and Ellen. Mrs. Nye came up from Macao. Rec'd letter from Allison; Commodore worse. Capt. Endicott cumshawed me a box containing 1000 Manila cheroots.

Friday December 14, 1855

Made P.P.C's and took my farewell of Canton in the *River Bird* at 3 P.M. Our party down consisted of Mrs. Mather, Mrs. Corning,[144] Mr. Robinet and others. Reached Hong Kong about midnight, when the Consul came on board and informed us of Commodore Abbot's death. He died this morning at 6 A.M. His remains are to be removed to the ship with appropriate ceremonies tomorrow.

Hong Kong, Saturday December 15, 1855

A post mortem examination has disclosed that Com^d^ A's stomach was extensively ulcerated and in one place eaten through, and that the disease had been long existent. His life might have been prolonged if he had gone home, but not for any great length of time. His liver was found in a perfectly healthy condition. His funeral today was attended by every American resident and ship master. Sir James Stirling, the English Admiral, took charge of arranging the procession, and issued orders to the Capts and officers under his command to attend. First came the band of the *Winchester* playing the dead march. Next a company of Royal Marines, then the Commodore's broad pennant carried by his coxswain at half staff, next the hearse. The Governor Sir John Bowring, the Admiral, U. S. Consul, Capt. of the French frigate, 1st Lieut. of the *Macedonian* and sailors acting as pall bearers, following the hearse all our marines, and the

[144] She was the wife of Captain Richard S. Corning, master of the *Rapid*, a California clipper of 1,115 tons built in 1853 and owned by Jas. Bishop and Company of New York. The ship was sold to a Danish company in 1859. *Greyhounds*, 431, 471, 495. There was another *Rapid*, an opium clipper built in 1842, which competed with American shipping in the China seas. *Clipper*, 58.

Commodore's barge's crew. After these the Foreign Officers and Consuls in reversed order, the highest in rank walking last. Next came seventy sailors from the *Macedonian* and the officers of the ship; two or three hundred citizens and the Governor's empty carriage.

When the procession started from Mr. De Silver's, a funeral salute of thirteen minute guns was commenced from the *Macedonian,* which was taken up and continued by one of the batteries on shore, and then by another salute from the Admiral's flag ship, so that there was a continuation of minute guns until the corpse reached the ship's side. The whole path of the procession on shore was lined on each side, and kept clear by the soldiers of the 59th Regt., drawn up in extended file with reversed arms, that is with hands clasped over the butts of their muskets, the muzzles being pointed down towards the ground, the soldiers resting their heads on their hands. The effect was very appropriate. At the jetty a procession of boats was formed, which escorted the remains to the ship, where it was received with three ruffles of the drum. The Commodore's broad pennant was then hauled down, and a narrow one hoisted, and the flag which had been at half mast all day run up to the peak. All the flags on shore and afloat were at half mast with ours. The expression of regret and sympathy are general and sincere. Even the Russian officers, prisoners, walked in the procession.

Sunday December 16, 1855

Attended the Church, the Rev[d] Mr. Odell preached addressing himself chiefly to the soldiers. Wrote Susie. The portrait of my two darlings H[arry] and L[isie] hangs over my desk and Susie with Harry in her lap hangs side by side with it.

Monday December 17, 1855

At work with the Purser Allison packing up the Commodore's effects and distributing his wines and segars agreeably as he desired.

Tuesday December 18, 1855

Finished packing the Commodore's effects and went on shore.

Wednesday December 19, 1855

A regatta, our barge pulling but ten oars, handsomely beat all the

English and French boats. Our 2[d] cutter came out last. She is a 12-oared boat and was entered to pull but ten and having broken two in the race came in with only eight. Her crew offered to pull her against the fastest boat of the day but her challenge was not accepted. In the launch race the French launches beat the English and H.M. Ship *Pignes* 4-oared gig beat the 4-oared gig of the 59th Regt. Quite a party on board ship to see the race, some of whom stayed to dinner.

Thursday December 20, 1855

Pleasant—2[d] day of the regatta. Our 1st cutter was ruled out of the race for pulling 14 oars because of so good a model. The French boat beat the English cutters, our gig beat in the six oar race as we expected and the French gig came out first of six boats. Quite a party who came off to witness the race dined with us.

Friday December 21, 1855

Pleasant. The last day of the regatta. Early in the morning there was a private trial race between our launch and the Frenchman's and our first cutter and the Frenchman's and in both races our boats were victors. The race we owe to the chivalry of the French officers. The Englishmen having ruled our boats out of the race because they were sure to beat their clumsy barges. Went on shore in the forenoon to purchase Christmas gifts. Another dinner party on board today.

Saturday December 22, 1855

There was a ball last night in honor of the regatta which I did not attend. I hear that the 'Allies' got in a row, and that the French Officers left in a body and returned to their ships. Sproston went to Macao today to pass Christmas with the Drinkers. I have been busy today in writing out sailing directions for Keelung Island of Formosa, for Doct. Williamson to insert in his Chinese commercial guide, which he is now preparing for the press.

So ends Forefathers' day.

Hong Kong, December 23, 1855

A ship from San Francisco brought us last Wednesday the *New York Herald* of Oct. 15th, fifteen days later than the news by the last Overland mail. We learned by this arrival of the promotion of Com'dre Pope to Capt. and of Rootes[145] his Executive officer from Lieut. to Com'dr. The list of promotions places me about 70 on the list of Lieutenants. Rec[d] an invite from Sir John and Lady Bowring to dine with them on Christmas which I was obliged to decline.

Monday December 24, 1855

Finding it practicable for me to dine at the Bowrings on Christmas day, I tore up my regrets, and sent my acceptance. One of the Lieuts of the French Ship *Sybelle* dined with us and Cob Hope Graham of the 59th and Capt. and Mrs. Lloyd[146] called on board. Took a sundown walk and a second dinner at Mr. Sturgis's on the hill. The *N. B. Palmer* arr[d] and Capt Low came in and reported while we were at table.

Tuesday December 25, 1855

Sent Doct. Williams my sailing directions for Keelung and to his brother a certificate that he acted as my clerk on board the *Queen*, with the approval of the Commodore. At our mess dinner today Gwathmey, Barbot, and I lunched on turkey, teal, and mutton; after lunch called on our Consul and wished him a merry Christmas. The *Bittern* went to sea. At 7 P.M. Gwathmey and I went to the Government House to dine with Sir John Bowring. Our party consisted of Sir John and his lady. Miss Bowring, Miss Edith Bowring, R. Adml. Sir Jas Stirling, Sir Fred Nicolson, Bail and Commodore Elliot of the R.N., Cob Caine, Lt. Gover of the Colony, Capt. Massonneuve of the French Navy, Lt. Gwathmey and myself. I was a little uneasy at the commencement of the dinner when Lady B. requested me to take one end of the table to serve soup and meat; fully aware of my left handed awkwardness and was very much relieved when Sir Fred Nicolson said it would be too bad to tax

145 Thomas R. Rootes was made midshipman on March 1, 1827; passed midshipman, June 10, 1833; lieutenant, February 28, 1838; commander, September 14, 1855; dismissed, April 19, 1861.

146 Captain Lloyd was the master of the *Snow Squall*, noted for her race with the *Romance of the Seas* from Shanghai to Sandy Hook, New Jersey. The Snow Squall finished two days ahead, making the voyage in ninety-two days. *Greyhounds*, 356, 506; *Clipper*, 284, 352. See also note 113 above.

me so, and offered to play naval and military aide de camp, alluding to his being Sir James's flag Capt. for the day and the absence of Capt. King, Sir John's aide de camp, whose place I was requested to fill. We had a very social dinner and a pleasant evening. The dinner table was brilliant with plates glass and wax lights. The only toasts were Victoria, Napoleon III and Gen[l] Pearce proposed by Sir John. Lady B's plum pudding was praised as a matter of course by all the guests, and discussion as to the orthodox method of cutting it was had. The Admiral siding for slices instead of wedges as that left the remainder right for the fry next day. Lady Bowring is so lame it is painful to see her go from room to room on her crutches. She told me the other day she was sixty-two years old, just the age of the Commodore at his death. The instant she heard of his death the other day she went in her carriage a mile to tender her sympathy and assistance.

I searched Hong Kong through the other day for a Christmas gift for the Nyes, and had to content myself with a box of perfumery and a book in which a farmer and Mrs. Nye were the principal characters which I sent to Emma. She is to have a Christmas tree and I do wish I could have shared in their festivities at Canton.

Hong Kong, Wednesday Dec. 26, 1855

A mild pleasant hazy day. Exercised my division. Reading. Sir Arnyas Leigh-Ayoke told me today how the Chinese villages are settled. A man buys a piece of land. His children settle around him, and their descendants in turn occupy the land which they are not allowed to sell to a stranger without first offering it to one of the family. Thus frequently he says all the inhabitants of a village have the same family name. He also said that by the Chinese laws a man is held accountable for the doings of his descendants to the 5th generation and in like manner horrors descend to the 5th generation and then cease. The 6th generation is released from accountability and commences a new family.

Thursday December 27, 1855

Nothing particular, Woodworth and Boudinot returned from Canton. Made a sketch of my stateroom in its crowded state on my letter to Susie for her amusement.

Friday December 28, 1855

Went on shore for a walk, and meeting Sir James and Capt. Corry we took a constitutional over the hills. Passed the evening at Robt De Silvers. Returned to the ship ½ past 10 P.M. and had the nightmare. Was it the whiskey punch Allison and I partook of at the De Silvers or something else?

Saturday December 29, 1855

Capt Duval of the *River Bird* dined with our mess. He is an amusing western American.

Sunday December 30, 1855

Mr. Alvord, Mr. Ned, Master of the H.B.M. Survey Steamer *Saracen,* and George De Silver dined with our mess.

Monday December 31, 1855

Cold thermometer 50° and my day's duty on deck. The mail steamer arrived bringing Mrs. Hal De Silver, Susie's letters of Oct. 2ᵈ, and one from Mrs. Oxnard dated Oct. 22ᵈ. So ends the good year 1855.

The Diary: 1856

The Diary: 1856

Hong Kong, Tuesday January 1, 1856

Made new year calls, and at half past one P.M. our mess met at the De Silvers, and gave them a New Year's greeting and drank to their health in a glass of egg nog. In the evening attended a ball at the Government House. Allison is quite down hearted having heard by the last mail of the death of his mother-in-law, Mrs. Taney, and of Miss Alice Taney, his wife's sister. One of my Portland papers mentions a poor Irish woman who has just given birth to five children. I wonder with only two breasts how she manages to board and lodge them all, like Cornelia[1] she can point to them and say "here are my jewels" and a full necklace of them.

Doct. Peter Parker who has been appointed Commissioner was on board today to get his salute of seventeen guns, a child with his toy. It is singular how much greatness is to be found in humbug sometimes. Doct. P. left Washington the 10th of Oct. and remained a week on his way out.

Wednesday January 2, 1856

Capt. Jameson of the *Erie* and Consul Perry[2] dined with us and

[1] Cornelia, mother of the Gracchi, was the second daughter of Scipio Africanus the elder. She married Tiberius Sempronius Gracchus (d. 154 B.C.) and had twelve children by him, alternately boys and girls.

[2] Oliver H. Perry, son of Commodore M. C. Perry, was made U.S. consul at Canton on February 19, 1855. His energetic interest in American trade in Canton displeased British competitors from Hong Kong. He was the first American consul who did not belong to the partnership of Russell and Company. Griffin, *op. cit.*, 245, 360.

we gave the Consul his salute. Recd the following very pleasant and gratifying note from Mr. Robertson, H.B.M. Consul at Shanghai.

Christmas Day 1855

My Dear Capt. Preble,

Many thanks for your kind note, of course I am anxious that my countrymen should have the full advantage of your successful labors; and copies of the directions I send to Lloyds and other great merchantile marine offices that they may be fully known. I consider it one, if not, and it really is, the most important work that has yet been done in China, and will hand your name down long, long after ours have been blotted out as dead and useless. I deeply regret to hear the Commodore is so low in bodily health. May God support him at this his last hour, and if it pleases Him to remove our respected friend, as fine an old gentleman as ever graced this earth will be removed from among us. If he still lives bear to him the expression of my great respect and tell him he will not be forgotten by me, one among the many who knew him and appreciated his goodness and virtues. I suppose you will soon be on your way home How fortunate you are, I envy you your roving life not to be tied down to one place to moulder away the best years of one's life, with the prospect of a pension to pay your Doctor bills for the remainder of your existence. No. No, depend on it there is life in moving and death in inaction and now *adieu*, and believe me as ever,

Yours most sincerely

D. B. Robertson

Friday January 4, 1856

Henry's Birthday; I cannot realize I am the papa of a boy nine years old; wrote him a birthday note. Emma Nye's Christmas was I understand, a great success. The Christmas tree was very handsome; all the European and American children in Canton were assembled, and the only difficulty was to make them understand all the pretty and glittering things were not common property. Then there was supper at which a huge pie was produced, which had dozen canary birds concealed under the crust, and when the pie was opened the birds began to sing. At the New Year Ball at the Government House, all of the twenty-six ladies eligible as first society were present and the gentlemen outnumbered the ladies three to one. The supper was good and substantial, and the ladies were comfortably seated at the table and waited upon by the gentlemen, who took their turn after they had supped. Coffee and tea were served throughout the evening at a side table. I called on the Bowrings yesterday, and Lady B. presented me with a prayer book arranged and edited by her brother.

Saturday, January 5, 1856

Called on Doct. Parker and Lady Bowring. Dined with R. S. Sturgis; our dinner party consisted of Comd. Elliot, Capt. Sir F. W. Nicolson, Col. Caine, Messrs, Antrobus, Percival, Wingford, Smith, Foster and myself. My seat was next to the Lt. Govr Col Caine, and I had an agreeable time.

Sunday, January 6, 1856

Dined at Dent & Cos.; our dinner party included Sir Jas. Stirling, Sir Fred Nicolson, Commodore Elliot, Capt Vansitart and Capt Corry all R.N.'s and Messrs Percival, Antrobus, Leslie, Col Caine and four or five more. An amusing discussion as to the relative merits of Scotland and England arose after dinner, and "Home Sweet Home" was claimed as a Scottish song, and they would not believe me when I said it was American, both words and music.[3]

Hong Kong, Tuesday January 8th, 1856

The Str. *Antelope* from Shanghai brought me a model set of Chinese furniture from Doc. McCartee.

Wednesday January 9, 1856

Dined with Commodore Elliot on board H.B.M. Frigate *Sybelle*, Capts Corry Nicholson and Vansitart, the Capt of the French Ship *Constantine*, and Col. Graham of the party.

Thursday January 10, 1856

Called on the Bishop of Victoria and half a dozen Reverends,

[3] "Home, Sweet Home" was composed by John Howard Payne (1791–1852) in 1823. Payne was an American actor and dramatist of merit. C. H. Brainard, *John Howard Payne: A Biographical Sketch with a Narrative of Removal of His Remains from Tunis to Washington* (Boston, Cupples, Upham and Company, 1885); see also *DAB*, XIV, 327–29.

dined on board the *Pigna,* and in the evening we assembled at Bob De Silvers and had hot whiskey punch. One of my messmates has just returned from Macao with a burnt eye, which he got at a great conflagration there; one thousand Chinese were burnt, and a number of women and children perished. No less than twelve 'little foot' women perished in one house. Sproston burnt his eye in assisting to preserve a Roman Catholic Church.

Friday January 11, 1856

Sir Fred Nicholson and Capt Vansittart dined with our mess and we had callers from the French Frigate *Virginia* and others. Sir John Bowring sent me his matins and vespers and Decimal coinage with his compliments.

Saturday January 12, 1856

R. P. De Silver, and both the De S. ladies dined with us. The *Vandalia* arrived at sundown from Amoy. I dined at the Lieut Governors, Col. Caines, with a large party assembled to meet Doct. Parker who made a speech.

Sunday January 13, 1856

A Dinner party on board. Messrs. Armstrong and Lawrence, Purser Harwood and Lt. Grey[4] of the *Vandalia,* and an officer of the French Frigate. Called on Mr. Murphy our consul for Shanghai who is staying with Mr. Keenan.

Monday January 14th, 1856

Capt Pope assumed command of the *Macedonian* today and Commander Rootes has command of the *Vandalia.* Several of the *Bittern's* Officers dined with me today; one of them, a mate, was promoted to his present rank of Lieut. for his share in our Tyho and Coulan affairs.

Tuesday Jan. 15, 1856

Overrun with visitors paying their respects to our new Capt. Several of the *Vandalia's* officers dined on board. Mail steamer sailed

[4] He was probably Captain Andrew F. V. Gray of the *Vandalia* and is not in the official list of the personnel of Perry's expedition. He was made midshipman on October 15, 1829; passed midshipman, July 3, 1835; lieutenant, September [illegible] 1841. He died on March 15, 1860.

Wednesday Jan. 16, 1856

Wrote Walcott to encourage him in continued well doing and received a reply that encourages me to hope he is truly a reformed man.

Thursday January 17, 1856

Dined on shore, and made several calls. In the evening went on board the *Vandalia.*

Friday January 18, 1856

Called on Lady Bowring who received me familiarly in her upstairs sitting room.

Saturday January 19, 1856

Gwathney and Gilliam went to Canton in the *Spark.*

Sunday Jan. 20, 1856

James Keenan dined with our mess.

Monday January 21, 1856

Sir John Bowring visited the ship and was received with the usual ceremonies and saluted on leaving; called on the officers of the *Winchester*, and in the afternoon went to Victoria Exchange to look at the Japanase articles brought by the *Lady Pierce*, for which extravagant prices are charged.

Tuesday Jan. 22, 1856

Sir Jas Stirling called on board but requested not to be saluted. French Brig of War, 46 days from Sydney, arrived.

Wednesday Jan. 23, 1856

Doct. Parker embarked on board the *Vandalia* to go to Macao under a guard of honor and salute from the shore batteries and he was saluted by the *Vandalia* all of which tickled his weak excellency. Sir James Stirling visited him on board the *Vandalia* and was saluted and the *Winchester* returned the salute and then the *Vandalia* went to sea—also H.B.M. Brig *Bittern.* Mail Steamer *Erie* arrived from Shanghai.

Friday January 25th, 1856

Dined with Sir Fred Nicholson on board H.B.M. Frigate *Pigne*, a rainy day. While at dinner a marine on post shot one of his fingers off by accident.

Saturday January 26, 1856

The old fogies of our mess dined with Robt. P. De Silver. The Japanese goods were sold at enormous prices. On board we had quite a dinner party.

Sunday Jan. 27, 1856

Capt. Pope had the two Mrs. De Silvers on board to dinner. Rec^{d} a letter from Shanghai which informs me I am to be presentec with a letter of thanks signed by all the Foreign residents.

Wednesday Jan. 30, 1856

Mail arrived.

Thursday January 31, 1856

Writing farewell notes, and making calls preparatory to a lon and final *adieu* to Hong Kong.

At Sea, Saturday February 2, 1856

At daylight got underway for Singapore leaving the Captn' Steward behind. At 10:15 A.M. discharged Ashing the pilot and bi *adieu* to China. Weather cloudy and wind fresh from the Nth and E^{s}

Sunday February 3, 1856

Rolling before the wind under easy sail. Our apartment very we and uncomfortable from a leak about the sternpost.

Monday February 4, 1856

The same as yesterday.

At Sea, Tuesday February 5, 1856

Stood in for and made the coast of Cochin China, a little to th North of Cape Varella, off Pula Cambia, and found we had exper enced a current of 45 miles W.S.W. since our leaving Hong Kon Afternoon clear and pleasant at the Royal and Steering Sails.

Wednesday, February 6, 1856

Passed Pula Sapato; fine pleasant weather and wind aft.

Thursday February 7, 1856

Warm and delicious. The Ship wing and wing, and making go progress.

Friday and Saturday, Feb. 8th & 9th

Passed Pula Ave a small island having three peaks each 1700 feet high.

Singapore, Sunday February 10, 1856

At 4 A.M. sighted Horsburgh's Light House and stood towards it at 11 A.M.; anchored off Singapore and saluted the town with 21 guns; the shore batteries and E. I. Company's steamer *Auckland* returned our salute. Went on shore to present Capt. Pope's compliments to our Consul and to call on the Governor; both were out of town. The Consul at Birket Tine, 9 miles distant, and the Governor at Penang, three hundred miles away. So I presented myself and the Capt's compliments to the Lieut. Governor and on my return to this ship was glad to strip off my iron brand coat, cocked hat and epaulets, and tumble into a white jacket. I have been writing Susie, but with the thermometer at 90° in my state room it is too hot to write much or long by candle lights.

Singapore, Monday February 11, 1856

Mr. Bradley our Consul came on board and rec'd the usual salute, an honor which all consuls seem to have a craving for. It seems to set them up in their own eyes and the eyes of other people. Mr. Tarrant the editor of the *Hong Kong Register* called on board.

Tuesday February 10, 1856

The Resident accompanied by his A.D.C. called on Capt. Pope, and was saluted with fifteen guns. We had quite a number of visitors, and our Consul gave a dinner which I did not attend as I had the day's duty.

Singapore, Wednesday February 13, 1856

Went with Consul Bradley to New Harbor to investigate some difficulties between Capt., officers and crew of the American Ship, *Yankee Ranger*,[5] Capt. Raven. The Consul discharged five of the crew who had been struck at different times by the mate, and the remainder of the crew refusing to go to duty were put in irons, and recommended to a bread and water diet.

[5] The *Yankee Ranger* was a California clipper of 707 tons built in 1854 and owned by Gustavus Moler, Wm. Heye *et al.* of New York. *Greyhounds*, 440.

Thursday February 14, 1856

Dined at the Consul's, who is a very worthy eccentric and studious gentleman, and his hospitality is unbounded. He is a botanist and naturalist, but has devoted himself particularly for the last thirty years to studying the origins of family names, and in tracing out the spelling of them, and so forth. He could not however tell me the origin of my name, but says Oxnard is Scandinavian and means bold forehead, noble fronted or strong headed. Gwathmey he says is from the Welsh and means little battle. He has a fine collection of snakes and a noble library.

Friday February 15, 1856

Called on the officers of the E. L. Co's. Steam frigate *Auckland*.

Saturday February 16, 1856

Declined invites to dine with Mr. Shaw, and Mrs. Webster having the day's duty.

Sunday February 17, 1856

H.B.M.S. *Spartan* came in from Penang, and the Am. ship *Dolphin*[6] arrived 109 days from Boston, and reports that our relief, the *San Jacinto* sailed before her. I have enjoyed several short drives and walks since we came here but it does not answer to extend either far as the tigers sometimes come within a mile and a half of the town and scarcely a day passes that a native is not seized and carried off by them. Last Friday a large tiger was seen about two miles from the town. The Jungle is so thick and impenetrable that they are seldom taken. They are sometimes trapped in pits which are dug thirty feet deep, and covered over with leaves and brushes. Not long since twenty or thirty of the crew of a French Steamer were trapped in one of these pits but fortunately there was no tiger there to welcome them, and they were rescued the next day by some Malays.

Singapore, Friday February 22, 1856

Washington's birthday. Hoisted the stars and stripes at our mast heads at 9 A.M. and kept them up all day. At noon fired a salute of

[6] The third *Dolphin*, 224 tons, ten guns, was built in 1836 and destroyed at Norfolk in 1860.

21 guns. The forts on shore and H.M.S. *Spartan* joined us in saluting. The Consul gave a dinner at which twenty-six guests sat down, and we had a good time generally. The mail steamer arrived from Hong Kong, and left for Penang. Rec[d] by her a beautiful carved ivory bracelet a present from my friend Mr. H. W. Hubbell to Mrs. Preble.

Singapore, Monday February 25, 1856

My birthday not honored with any flags or salutes but a quiet pleasant day. The ship received a visit from a party of ladies of assorted colors, all the way from black to white. We had also a call in forenoon from a Mr. Earle a writer of some note on the South Pacific Islands and Islanders. The ladies came off in the evening to hear our Ethiopian Serenaders. I expect they were twice glad, as they came on board and went away sea-sick.

Singapore, Friday February 29, 1856

A day we are not paid for in the navy. Dined on shore at Mr. Shaw's. On the 27th the English Mail arrived and left for China. We have written to Hong Kong to have our letters sent here, having given up all hopes of a speedy relief from the *San Jacinto*, now one hundred and twenty-eight days out of New York.

Singapore, March 1, 1856

On shore all day and all night it blowing fresh, saw a letter in Josiah's handwriting addressed to Edwin and endorsed Dec. 7, a month later than my last letter, so I took the liberty of opening it and found it was from Mrs. Cox, another one from Hattie Prince which I did not disturb. Bought some books at auction.

Tuesday March 4, 1856

Steamer *Chrisan* arrived. Dined with a black and white party at Mr. Webster's, and finished the evening with dancing and music.

Wednesday March 5, 1856

Saw a letter from the Captain of the *Reindeer*[7] in which he says he saved his ship by following my sailing directions.

[7] The *Reindeer* was a British tea clipper voyaging from China to London. *Greyhounds*, 197.

Thursday March 6, 1856

Steamer *Chusan* sailed for Hong Kong; sent several letters to my friends in China.

Singapore, March 21st, 1856

Still watching and waiting for the *San Jacinto*. The Steamer *Norma* from Hong Kong arrived today and among her passengers I found Mr. and Mrs. R. De Silver, Capt. Dearborn of the *Confucius*, Mr. Whittemore and several other friends. She also brought our letters from China, and the news of Mr. Gideon Nye's failure for a million and a half dollars. Rec^{d} some photographs with my letters. Capt. Dearborn informs me that when he left a subscription was circulating at Shanghai to present me a sword and that he subscribed fifty dollars. I hope I may live to see it.

One day about a fortnight ago I went to witness the dedication or rather the placing of the crown stone of a church by the Lord Bishop of Calcutta,[8] a venerable old prelate 80 or 90 years old to be called St. Andrew's Church. The weather is too hot to go anywhere or do anything, and I agree with Lord Byron who said, "Idleness in a hot country is a pleasure."[9] I feel every word in this climate where the slightest exertion Shylock-like exacts its pound of flesh.[10] It is said of the natives of India that they would rather walk than run; rather stand still than walk; rather sit down than stand; rather lie down than sit and rather sleep than keep awake. My feelings are all with them, and I am happiest in this perspiring climate when attired in my night shirt, and down on my back on my cane covered mattress, with a cooling breeze through the open port blowing over me. It may not be healthy but it is decidedly pleasant. It is easy to see why energy and invention are children of the north. The natives of India

8 He was Daniel Wilson (1778–1858), Anglican bishop of Calcutta from 1832 to 1858. Latourette, *The Great Century in Northern Africa and Asia*, 111.

9 In his letters from abroad and in *Hours of Idleness*, Lord Byron refers on several occasions to the pleasure of idleness in a hot country. None of his expressions is identical with that quoted by Preble.

10 An allusion to the bond between Shylock and Antonio in Shakespeare's *Merchant of Venice*.

say that there are but three things in life worth obtaining and anyone successful in either is a happy fellow, but he who succeeds in all three is a god. These three things are to dig a well, to build a caravanseraio and to get a child. If we are to judge by the overteeming population they are pretty successful in the last named object.

Singapore, March 22, 1856

Closed my letters and sent them by the *Norma*. At noon the *Madras* arrived and reported that the *San Jacinto* left Point De Galle for Penang twelve hours before the Madras did. Wrote Mrs. Gideon Nye.

Singapore, Sunday March 23, 1856

The steamer *Fiery Cross*[11] arrived from Calcutta and confirms the arrival and departure of the *San Jacinto* from Point De Galle.

Thursday March 27, 1856

Saw a most beautiful meteor acknowledged by all who saw it the most brilliant they had ever seen.

Singapore, April 2, 1856

The Bark *Lucy Elizabeth* Capt. Dicks, with Edwin on board has arrived today. They have been for 40 days in the Straits of Banca only a hundred miles off, and over 180 days on the passage, of course their cargo of ice is half melted and the Bark came in all over on her side.

Sometime since I sent home by the *Sting Ray*[12] a small invoice of tea, or rather Mr. Nye sent it on my account. I now see in the papers just rec[d] that the *Sting Ray* has gone on shore on the coast of New Jersey and been totally lost. I have reason to hope my adventure has been insured but it will be long before my mind can be made easy on the subject. We have letters from Penang that the *San Jacinto* will be here in three or four days. Laus Deo! [13]

[11] The second *Fiery Cross*, a British tea clipper, was built in Liverpool in 1860. I could not find information about the first *Fiery Cross*. See *Clipper*, 325–30, 371.

[12] The *Sting Ray* was a tea clipper of 985 tons built in 1854. Her captain was Nicholas Kirby, Jr. She was lost on Fire Island, January 9, 1856, after leaving Canton on September 30, 1855. *Greyhounds*, 289, 439, 496.

[13] "Glory to God."

Singapore, April 4, 1856

At 10 P.M. the *San Jacinto* arrived and we have our orders to proceed to Boston.

April 5, 1856

Deo volente,[14] we sail tonight for Boston. Edwin Cox and Capt. Dicks were on board to see me today, and brought with them a big lump of ice, a grateful present. Edwin showed me a daguerrotype of 'Hattie' who looks a pretty and intelligent little miss. Capt. Dicks is an everlasting talker, his tongue never ceased for the two hours and a half he was on board.

Singapore, April 6, 1856

Was awakened at three o'clock this morning by the joyful cry "All hands up anchor for home." Getting underway so early we were not cheered by our relief according to the usual custom in such cases. Finished and closed my letter for home and sent it on shore to be forwarded by the next mail.

Go, sheet, and carry all my heart;
I would that thou couldst carry me.
Freighted with love thou wilt depart
Across the land, across the sea.

O'er thee will bend a loving face,
To thee will listen little ears;
Thou will be welcomed in my place,
And thou will bring both smiles and tears.

Across the land, across the sea,
Thy homeward course thou wilt persue;
I may not see them welcome thee,
Yet know, I well their hearts are true.

Then swiftly go, thou ocean steed;
Roll on, ye rapid iron wheels,
Bearing away, with careless speed,
The message that my soul reveals.

14 "As God wills."

Mrs. De Silver who returned in the mail steamer of last month left with us for passage to the U.S. a pet dog named Fanny. She shed many tears at parting with it (having no children), when she gave it to Gilliam and bade it good bye. It was an affectionate confiding little animal and we had got much attached to it. Yesterday Gilliam took it on shore to give it a last sun and exercise before commencing our long voyage and we took a carriage to make some calls and the dog with us. Poor little Fan was delighted, barking and jumping about with excitement and suddenly sprang through the open window of the carriage, and in an instant it had passed over her and she was dead. This is the third dog Mrs. De Silver has lost. The first named Preble after the U.S. Ship was shot maliciously with an air gun, and she had his skin stuffed and preserved in a glass case. A second 'Preb' for which I bought a silver collar died lamented and was buried, and Fan was his successor to collar and her favor.

At 8 P.M. for want of wind anchored off Rhio Straits.

April 7, 1856

Still becalmed. Got underway but had to anchor again in half an hour. Singapore only twenty-five miles distant. This is a poor beginning for our journey of thousands of miles.

Tuesday April 8, 1856

Three years today since I left home. Got underway at 8 A.M. and are now leaving the Straits of Rhio and as the crow flies just one hundred and ten miles from Singapore.

We have had views of beautiful tropical scenery today and the surface of the sea has been as smooth and clear as a mirror.

Wednesday April 9, 1856

We anchored last night for want of wind, and did not get underway again until today noon, and we have not made more than ten or twelve miles since.

Thursday April 10, 1856

We anchored again last night, and got up our anchor again this morning. At noon today we were about twenty miles north of the Equator, and at ½ past 8 P.M. judged we were crossing it an event which creates no excitement. Several water snakes 3 to 4 feet long and about the size of a broom handle have floated by us, and a large bird lighted on our main royal yard one of our boys went up to catch it and pulled some feathers from its tail, but the bird went sailing off to parts unknown.

Friday April 11, 1856

We are today 200 miles from Singapore and 380 from Anjier. Our pilot who is a Jersey man has been amusing us with his munchausens.

Saturday April 12, 1856

With the assistance of a couple of Samatras in S.W. Squalls, peculiar to this sea and season, we have done very well today and are just at the entrance of the straits separating and connecting the China and Java Seas. Our pilot thinks we will be at Anjier in 48 hours. It is three years today since we sailed from New York.

Java Sea, Sunday April 13, 1856

We came to anchor again last night about the small hours but we were underway again at daylight this morning and with a nine knot breeze passed through Stoltzes Straits and are now 150 miles from Anjier.

Monday April 14, 1856

We were not compelled to anchor last night but the sails flapped in a dead calm and we are still a hundred miles from Anjier. Number of uprooted cocoanut trees, and numerous snakes of a pale and mottled green have been passed today, and we have seen many beautiful and bright plumaged birds in shape like kingfishers but not so large and with a thread like feather beyond their tail by way of a rudder. Our boys have been using all their cunning to catch them, but the salt intended for their extremities has not been crystallized.

Tuesday April 15, 1856

Fifty-five miles from Anjier. Caught a beautiful little bird today which I skinned for the P.N.H. Society.[15]

[15] Portland Society of Natural History.

Anjier Roads, Island of Java, Wednesday April 16th, 1856

We have just anchored in a heavy rain squall and it is so thick that we cannot see the shore but boats have come off and arrangements been made to receive water and provisions tomorrow, and sail as soon as practicable. Our Munchausen pilot leaves us here.

Indian Ocean, Friday April 25, 1856

After numberless attempts, which were fruitless from contrary winds and currents we left the straits of Sunda this morning, and are now abroad upon the Indian Ocean, and steering steadily to the South are now supposed to be in Lat 9° South. It is so warm in our little rooms below that it is a relief to keep a night watch on deck. A pair of grey albatrosses have been sailing about our ship today—rather an unusual cruizing round I should say for them. They have probably followed some ship up from Southern latitudes. They appeared perfectly tame and fearless and sailed so near as almost to touch my shoulder and tarried their heads, and looked at me with their bright eyes as much as to say "Who are you?" The boys this evening caught a slate colored hawk with a fawn colored breast, and about the size of a turtle dove.

Saturday April 26, 1856

We have a very sick man on board who cannot live many days, his moaning and crys are very distressing. His disease is an abcess of the liver. We hope we have caught the faint beginning of the S.E. trades.

Sunday April 27, 1856

We had a dress muster today, and were glad to unharness after it was over and put on a lighter suit. The weather is pleasant and warm and the wind is light and our prayers are for a fresh and cooling breeze to help us toward our homes.

Indian Ocean, Monday April 28, 1856

Our sick man Wm. Jamestown died this morning and we committed his body to the deep this afternoon, Purser Allison reading the burial service. This is the first man out of twenty-four that have died that we have buried at sea. It is a choky business as Capt. McKeever used to say. The sullen plunge of the body from the gangway, and the ship gliding on says more impressively than words that all is over. Nothing is known of our shipmate buried today except that he was from Kentucky and his name is believed to have been assumed. A year ago he was in lusty health, and rioting in a drunken frolic on shore put dozens of Chinamen in terror. The Purser offered to read to him, but he said he knew the Bible by heart, and it was too late for him to amend. A Dutch Ship in sight half-masted her colors, seeing our's so. Numerous albatrosses and flying fish have been around us today.

Tuesday April 29, 1856

Making good progress. The evening air is delicious.

Wednesday April 30, 1856

Fine weather, fair winds and a frolicing sea porpoises flying fish and sea birds our attendants, and I have had the toothache for the first time this cruise.

Thursday May 1, 1856

Doct. Woodworth's birthday and also the anniversary of my first joining a ship of war the Frigate *United States*[16] as a Midshipman just twenty years ago. How the years fly up. We had a glass of wine at dinner in memory of the two events.

Indian Ocean, Friday May 2, 1856

We have caught the S.E. trades and are steering a steady course W.S.W. Our ship is full of pets. I counted today seven grey monkeys, eight black squirrels, two ant eaters, one musk cat, one mouse deer, one parrot, two dogs, a cat, at least a dozen cages crowded with Java sparrows, besides ducks and chickens unnumbered, and cockroaches *ad libitum*.[17]

Saturday May 3, 1856

At noon as the crow flies we were 1,006 miles from Java head Lat. 16, S. Long 90° W.

[16] The *United States*, 1,576 tons, 44 guns, was built in 1797. She was destroyed at Norfolk in 1860.

[17] "As much as you like."

Sunday May 4, 1856

A number of porpoises have been playing about our ship, chasing our wake and darting under our bow, or rolling alongside; as the ship is going eight knots through the water we cannot harpoon them. This evening we had a peculiar and glorious sunset. The sun had not been visible for hours but on reaching the horizon it shook off the heavy vapors behind which it was hidden and showed a red and lurid mass almost Square, with perpendicular rays shooting up through a dark dense rain overhanging rain cloud. After it had gone down half an hour or more the west glowed in gold and purple while a dense rain squall was to be seen in contrast hurrying up from the E[st]. We are now having rain.

Monday May 5, 1856

Provokingly becalmed here in what ought to be the very heart and strength of the S.E. trades. The wind has been to the Nth of East nearly all day.

Indian Ocean, May 6, 1856

We got the breeze again today noon and are now sailing ten knots. The day has been one of alternatives, smiles and tears, sunshine and rain showers.

Wednesday May 7, 1856

We passed a heavy laden ship today, and have been accompanied by a number of my little friends the stormy petrel. The Purser and I played chips.

Thursday May 8, 1856

Ship rolling before the wind, showed our colors and gave our Longitude to the Am. Barque *Helen Noyes*, which we came up with, passed and left at sundown hull down astern. I commenced today copying from my memorandum, and putting in form a paper on the origin and history of the Am. Flag.[18]

[18] Preble published a pamphlet on the history of the American flag. The MSS are preserved in the library of the American Antiquarian Society of Worcester, Massachusetts: *Papers 1861–1880*.

Friday May 9, 1856

In my watch this morning the wind suddenly shifted and threw everything flat aback. At the same moment the rain descended in torrents, and continued at intervals throughout the watch. I got the sails in and yards braced without damage to our sails or spars. Afterwards we had the wind from all points what may be called "bracing" weather. The delicious coolness freshness and cleanness of the weather now can be better felt than described.

Saturday May 10, 1856

A solitary petrel has followed us today and we have been making good progress homeward.

Monday May 12, 1856

Just midway between Java and the Cape of Good Hope. The ship has been slipping smoothly and noiselessly along and yet in the twenty-four hours ending at noon we made 248 miles.

Tuesday May 13, 1856

Our little mouse deer gave birth today to a fawn. The mother is the smallest of the deer species being no larger than the smallest of black and tan terriers. Mother and fawn in their bird cages have been visited and admired and are doing as well as could be expected. I expect it is the very first birth of its kind that has ever occurred at sea.

Wednesday May 14, 1856

We are now south of the Island of Bourbon, and with a clear and cloudless sky a smooth and deep blue sea ruffled by the breeze and breaking here and there into foam are enjoying the very cream of sailing and ocean life. We split our maintopsail today but it was because the sail was old and the foot rope rotten. A sperm whale and several petrels have been seen.

Thursday May 15, 1856

Progressing grandly. It is encouraging to know we have only a third of the world in longitude to encompass and half of it in Latitude between us and home.

Saturday May 17, 1856

A change of weather today which drew in our light sails. We have had heavy drenching rain squalls and fresh breezes, and are now down to double reefed topsails—fortunately the wind is fair and we are flying before it. The ship groans and cracks, and rolls and flings about as she rushes through the water so that to sit or lie down even is constant exercise. It is almost a gale but so that it is fair who cares; a few sea birds have been hovering around us and now and then a frightened flying fish has skipped away from our sides.

Sunday May 18, 1856

We have good weather again but the wind is ahead. We have had a sunset grand and beautiful beyond my describing. A few birds have been about us, and a sail was seen from aloft.

The good weather was improved and we had a Sunday must and the Articles of war to remind us of our temporal duties.

Monday May 19, 1856

Rolling and tossing with light winds and a heavy ocean swell. It is a beautiful night the full moon making it as light as day. Our sailmaker's mate is very ill with dysentery and cannot live long. He has made his will and left all his little property to his mother.

Indian Ocean, Tuesday May 20, 1856

The sailmaker's mate died this morning and was committed to the deep, with the usual services this afternoon. It has been nearly calm all day.

Wednesday May 21, 1856

Very pleasant but uneventful. The sea has been so smooth that I have had my air port open. We passed a bottle corked up today, but were making too good progress homewards to stop and pick it up.

Thursday May 22, 1856

At noon Cape Aquilhas was 966 miles dist. The ship has been pitching to an unpleasant swell crossing from the Sth and W^st^ and about 1 oclock we had a little squall; a solitary petrel is all we have seen outside the ship today.

Friday May 23, 1856

With a noble breeze and smooth sea we are doing finely and we have experienced a current in our favor to help us to love and home.

Indian Ocean, Saturday May 24, 1856

Since 12 o'clock last night the ship has been plunging rolling and groaning in a very disagreeable manner, and the wind has been ahead.

Sunday May 25, 1856

We have a fair wind tonight and are making eleven knots on our course. At noon today we were about 50 miles from the nearest land and have been running along the coast but not in sight of it.

Monday May 26, 1856

We made 220 miles the 24 hours preceding noon and since 11 o'clock have had South Africa in the neighborhood of Great Fish River and Cape Padrone in sight. We have had exquisite weather and a smooth sea, the air balmy and the atmosphere hazy like our Indian summer. Since sundown it has been breezing up and now threatens a gale from the West. We caught a porpoise today, the first prize of the kind since we left New York. A great number of porpoises have been seen today, rolling and tumbling towards the Nth and Est in high glee, and since noon a multitude of sea birds have been around us. The currents have set us 52 miles to the Sth and Wst in the last 24 hours.

Tuesday May 27, 1856

Our fair and smooth sea is exchanged for one of the most turbulent description. At 5 oclock this morning the ship plunged her bows under water and snapped off her jibboom. The Capt. talks of going to Simons bay for a new one. Since daylight we have been lying to. It is blowing a furious gale from the W.N.W. a multitude of sea birds have been our close companions, resting on the troubled waters and screaming in wild delight as they sail up against the gale. Two whales have also showed their spouts, and a sail has been struggling along like ourselves but she has passed out of sight.

Wednesday May 28, 1856

The gale has in no degree abated yet. There are signs of its moderating. Comfort is not to be thought of and everything in our rooms not lashed down is tossed about in the liveliest manner. This morning our jibboom went altogether, and at the same moment our stern boat was swept from the davits and a man got overboard but was miraculously rescued. Our wardroom has been all afloat and we have had no regular breakfast or dinner. Bread and butter has been our diet.

Thursday May 29, 1856

A smooth sea, sunny weather and light winds have succeeded the gale of yesterday and we have been all day making sail and putting things to rights and I have been putting my room in order. At daylight we had the high and rugged land of Cape St. Francis in sight and it was still in sight at sundown. I never saw the stars more numerous or brilliant than they are tonight and the milky way and Nebula or Orion have almost the brilliancy of stars.

Friday May 30, 1856

The ship is lying to in another gale. This afternoon we committed the body of another poor fellow to the deep. Gwathmey reading the service (the name was David Etteridge) on the gun deck it being too rainy and boisterous to assemble above. The body was then taken to the gangway and launched into the sea. We are all afloat in the wardroom and had to eat a bite and cry dinner, each man holding to his own as he could.

Saturday May 31, 1856

We have done little today but toss about after the gale which has been succeeded by a light breeze, having a turbulent sea and an angry looking sky. We have had numerous Cape Pigeons about us today for the first time. I never passed a more anxious three hours on deck than this afternoon. Our ship seeming to be in the centre of a region of rain and wind squalls.

Off South Africa, Sunday June 1, 1856

At noon today we were 150 miles to the Est of the Cape of Good

Hope and perhaps 100 from Cape Aquilhas. We obtained soundings on the bank in 52 fathoms, grey sand and broken shells. I have preserved a specimen of it for microscopic examination. This afternoon we had three barques in sight all struggling to double the Cape. We have had numerous birds about us but the Cape Pigeons have vanished. We have been helped along by the currents, there would be no getting to the West[st] at this season without them.

Monday June 2, 1856

Today we are six miles nearer the Cape of Good Hope than we were yesterday; it is not a Pleasure of Hope to us. We have been rolling about between calms and light and baffling winds attended with a drizzly rain all day. We have had four vessels one a large clipper ship to keep us company. Our idler officers i.e. the Purser, Surgeons, etc., are the greatest grumblers and seem to think that we who work the ship ou[gh]t to create a wind. According to the theory of an ingenious Frenchman we have thirty three chances of a change of weather tonight. The New Moon being in perigee.

Off Cape Aqualhas, Tuesday June 3

A delightfully cool clear pleasant and enjoyable day. The only drawback the wind has been very light and ahead so that we are making no progress homeward. Got out a temporary jibboom.

Off Cape Aqualhas, Wednesday June 4, 1856

The new moon has just sunk beneath the horizon and our idle sails are beginning to swell to a fair wind springing up from the S.E. We have been rolling in a calm all day. Cape Aqualhas has been in sight all day about twenty miles dist. We obtained soundings this morning on the Western edge of the Aqualhas bank in 70 fathoms. Soft mud, some of which I have preserved for future investigation. The albatrosses have been numerous about the ship today, getting bread and pork thrown over to them. One of my messmates saw a large squid such as the sperm whales feed on.

South Atlantic Ocean, Thursday June 5, 1856

After a pleasant day, during the whole of which the Coast of South Africa and the Cape of Good Hope have been in sight, we are rolling in an Atlantic swell before a light but fair wind, and have bid good bye to the Indian Seas, as I hope and trust, for a long, long time. The sight of the square top of Table Mountain and its attendants, Devil's Peak and Lion's head and Rump reminded me of days long vanished. Several sails have been in sight today.

Friday June 6, 1856

A mild quiet day and we have been rolling down toward St. Helena 7 or 8 knots an hour. At sunrise I caught a parting view of Table Mountain, probably 60 mile S.E. of us. What a storehouse of unconsidered trifles our other story must be. Association ever brings to mind the appropriate thought. We have rolled many times and oft, but never has our rolling recalled the words of the song rolling down to St. Helena until now that they are literally true to us. Capt. Pope disrated a man today on suspicion of the crime of Sodomy.

South Atlantic, Saturday June 7, 1856

We have enjoyed today a clear sky, a smooth sea and a breeze taking us six miles an hour toward home. Had the air port in my stateroom open all day. At noon we were in Lat. 32°S.

Sunday June 8, 1856

The winds and weather as favorable and pleasant as yesterday. It has been cool however out of the sun and below the thermometer standing at 60°. This is the winter of the Southern Hemisphere. A Dutch Bark in company.

Monday June 9, 1856

Wind and weather the same. Passed our Dutch friend this P.M.

Tuesday June 10, 1856

We are now becalmed and our sails hang idly from the masts. One of our sailors said today, "This is the wind Jack to put money in the pocket."

Wednesday June 11, 1856

The wind has been from the Nth and ahead all day. Our Dutchman still in company. The cool weather is killing off the Java sparrows, monkeys and other pets.

June 12, 1856

It was rough and stormy last night. About 10 P.M. our *Flying Dutchman* passed us on the opposite tack and that is the last we have seen of him. In the mid watch we had heavy squalls of wind and rain, which put us under short canvas. Some Cuerps Santos or 'Complasants' as the Sailors called them were seen on the mastheads and yardarms.

The Spanish name Cuerps Santos or holy bodies implies, as was believed by ancient marines, that this electrical phenomenon are that visible ghosts of departed seamen. Since noon today we have been on our course but making poor progress, and unable to make sail because of the rough short chop tumbling sea. This afternoon a sperm whale was seen.

Friday June 13 1856

All last night we were pitching into a heavy head sea that racked our bones and prevented sleep. Today we have been rolling to such a swell that everything not tied down is in constant motion. If this be rolling down to St. Helena I have had enough of it. At noon we were 860 miles from that fast anchored rocky island.

Sunday June 15, 1856

The winds are light and generally S.E. which indicates we are on the borders of the S.E. trades. We made a hundred miles yesterday and hope to roll off another hundred today. By our moon observations we are inside the tropics.

Monday June 16, 1856

Our passage is getting to be very tedious. Instead of fair and fresh trade winds which he had a right to expect, we have light and variable winds, and an uncomparable Westerly swell.

Tuesday June 17, 1856

At noon 480 miles from St. Helena and in West Longitude for the first time in three years. We crossed the meridian of Greenwich this afternoon.

South Atlantic, Wednesday June 18, 1856.

At noon today we were 300 miles from St. Helena and have sailed

7300 miles since leaving Java Head in about 134 miles a day. This morning we passed through a school of whales roquals of the largest kind. Two of them rolled their huge bodies out of water close alongside and almost spouted into the cabin windows. We have now all our steering sails abroad, and are rushing towards St. Helena.

Thursday June 19, 1856

At noon 190 miles from St. Helena. We are getting both rusty and crusty with our long passage, and our mess is getting decidedly argumentative.

Friday June 20, 1856

We sighted and passed an English bark today and at 2.15 P.M. discovered the Island of St. Helena thirty four miles dist. We are now hove to; the Captain with abundant caution waiting for the moon to rise—or day light. Tomorrow will be the anniversary of our arrival at St. Helena three years ago when outward bound.

St. Helena, Saturday June 21, 1856.

After lying by all night we anchored here this morning within an hour of the time we dropped anchor here three years since. The Dutch Bark, so long our company keeper and which we had christened the *Flying Dutchman*, passed us under all sail while we were waiting for day light, and anchored before us. We saluted the town at noon and our Consul, after which I went shore and waited on the Governor with Capt. Pope's compliments. Was coffeed at the Consuls and introduced to his unmarried daughter and to a wife Jenness.

Saint Helena, Sunday June 22, 1856

I have passed a quiet day on board ship. Most of our officers went on shore.

Monday June 23, 1856

Received on board 22000 gallons of water, 200 gallons of Rum, 5,000 lbs of bread and many other articles; paid our mess bill, 275$; and at 3 P.M. all hands were called up anchor for home. The sailors subscribed 153$ for the benefit of the mother of one of our men who was shipped here and died at Whampoa last March.

At Sea, Tuesday June 24, 1856

We have been running before the wind under all steering sails for 518 miles ever since we left St. Helena an auspicious commencement of our voyage to Boston.

Wednesday June 25, 1856

Jugging along quickly and comfortably in the S.E. trades. Experienced a few light rain showers in the afternoon.

Thursday June 26, 1856

Enjoying the S.E. trades. We have seen nothing but a strange fish and a flying fish today.

Friday June 27, 1856

We have had a succession of summer showers but our good wind continues.

Saturday June 28, 1856

We have been having variable winds and wet and unsettled weather. About 10 o'clock last night I saw a brilliant and beautiful meteor, the nucleus of which seemed twice as large as Venus. It started in the N.W. quarter of the Heaven, from an altitude of about 45 degrees, and descended perpendicularly to the horizon, followed by a long luminous train. The body of the meteor was of a blueish color.

Sunday June 29, 1856

About half way between St. Helena and the Equator. Weather warm and summerlike, sky bright, sea clear and blue and the ship with steering sails on both sides going 5 and 6 knots. The little fawn born on board is now half the size of its mother. We had a dress inspection at quarters today.

Monday June 30, 1856

The Purser and I explored some boxes of books in the bread room today sent on board by Com. Perry and found a mine of good reading. A sulphur bottom whale with her young one followed the ships wake for an hour or more today.

Tuesday July 1, 1856

Another pleasant day. The ship surrounded by numerous flying fish.

Wednesday July 2, 1856

The counterpart of yesterday. About 7 P.M. we saw another very brilliant meteor. Thirteen years ago today I was on board of the *St. Louis,* and within fifty miles of where we are now.

Thursday July 3, 1856

We hope to be on the Equator tomorrow; passed a Yankee ship and a three masted schooner. Great numbers of flying fish about us and this evening the water is very phosphorescent.

North Atlantic, Friday July 4, 1856

At noon we were 20 miles South of the Equator, which we crossed about 4 P.M. We are now in the North Atlantic pursued by a fine S.E. trade wind. Capt. Pope dined in the wardroom today. Read a good story today of a sharp little boy, who asked a gentleman his name, and on being told it was "Lord" commenced giggling. And when asked the cause said, he "remembered father reading about you in the Bible." The main brace was spliced at noon in honor of the day.

Saturday July 5, 1856

We are now to the Nth of our starting point, Singapore and between 8 and 9000 miles to the West of it.

Sunday July 6, 1856

Early this morning our S.E. trades changed to the Sth and West and the weather has looked rainy and threatening.

Monday July 7, 1856

In the doldrums little or no winds and plenty of rain.

Tuesday July 8, 1856

Still in the variables. We had a downpouring shower and squalls of mingled wind and rain this morning which lasted two hours.

Wednesday July 9, 1856

A rainy day with variable winds, but it is now clear and pleasant. We hope to see the North Star tonight.

Thursday July 10, 1856

Light and variable airs and calms.

North Atlantic, Friday July 11, 1856.

We have experienced within the last 24 hours weather of all sorts from fair to foul and the wind has been dodging about into all its corners, with every degree of force accompanied by rain. In fact the weather is most disgusting. Last night I caught a glimpse of the North Star. This forenoon we received a visit from 'General Quarters.'

Saturday July 12, 1856.

In Lat 10. N. today at noon and 160 miles nearer Boston than we were yesterday.

Sunday July 13, 1856.

Nothing but rain, squalls, calms and perplexing winds. Only 600 miles from the Equator which we crossed nine days ago.

Monday July 14, 1856.

Thanks to a Westerly current, though we have had little and no wind, we have made 85 miles. We are now happy in a N.E. wind which is sending us homeward and seven knots an hour. We have had April showers all day.

Tuesday July 15, 1856.

Since last night blessed with a N.E. wind we have been sailing along smoothly our nine knots an hour. At noon Boston was 2300 miles distant.

Wednesday July 16, 1856.

Yesterday we made 220 miles on our course, and the prospect is that we will do better today. At noon we were in the Lat. of Martinique and to the Nth of Barbadoes.

North Atlantic, Thursday July 17, 1856

Another good day. We have a fresh N.E. trade and occasionally a flying squall of wind with drizzling rain varies the monotony. This afternoon we passed a brig standing to the Sth and Wst. We see flying fish, but they are not so numerous as in the S.E. trades. Gwathmey discovered last night that his drawers had been overhauled and robbed of a wallet containing thirty dollars in gold and a dozen linen socks and four or five silver dollars. The master found on examination that his studs had been stolen and 40$ in gold. The Boatswain says he has lost 4 gold rings. The thief remains undiscovered.

Friday July 18, 1856

A very pleasant day. At noon the sun was nearly vertical and we trod on the shadows of our hats. Our Latitude being 20° and the suns declination 20° 50′N. We are now North of all West Indies Islands excepting Cuba, and St. Domingo. Numerous patches of Gulf weed has drifted bye us.

Saturday July 19, 1856

Lat. at noon 22°N. We are still having fine winds and weather. Our various pets rejoice in the bright warm genial air and sunshine.

Sunday July 20, 1856

The unsteadiness of the wind forbodes a change and that we are soon to lose the trades. At noon we were less than 1400 miles from Boston. We left the Tropic of Cancer about the time the master took his morning observations, and are now in the Temperate Zone, and in the Latitude of the Southern U.S.

Monday July 21, 1856

The trades have left us and we have instead a gentle S.W. wind. The airport in my stateroom has been open all day.

North Atlantic, Tuesday July 22, 1856.

Our good weather is being improved by the 1st Lieut. in putting the ship to rights. Yesterday the rigging was blacked, today the outside of the ship. Several sails have been passed and this afternoon we boarded the Am. Schr *Louisiana* 14 days from Cape Henry, but could get no newspapers and but little news. The Master of the Schr said however that Buchanan and Fillmore are the nominees for the Presidency. Passed a Brig but it was too late to think of boarding her.

Wednesday July 23, 1856

Showed our colors to an Am. ship steering W.N.W.

Thursday July 24, 1856

At noon 840 miles from Boston and 720 from the New South Shoal. Our gunner met with quite a bad accident today, which I fear will go hard with the old man.

Friday July 25, 1856

Calm and warm makeing slow progress. We have seen three sails —and my messmates have been extensively packing up.

Saturday, July 26, 1856

At noon only 18 miles north of where we were yesterday noon, a brig in sight.

Sunday July 27, 1856

We took a N.W. wind last night, and at noon today were in the Latitude of Bermuda. It has been cloudy and squally but we had our usual Sunday muster and inspection. Passed the wreck of a schooner's mast apparently a long time in the water.

North Atlantic, Monday July 28, 1856

Five hundred miles from Boston. We have seen nothing today but a schooner steering South.

Tuesday July 29, 1856

A Spanish ship, a black fish, a couple of porpoises and half a dozen dolphin have comprised our outside sights today.

Wednesday July 30, 1856

In the Gulf stream and having good weather. The master got morning sight but no afternoon observations. In the forenoon a heavy N.W. squall. Several sails seen today. Today we broke up our wine mess, and divided the wines, etc. remaining.

Thursday July 31, 1856

Unsettled weather squally with rain, a whirl wind passed the ship's stern giving her a cuff as it went bye us. At noon we were 300 miles from Boston.

Friday August 1, 1856

Susie's birthday which I had hoped to keep with her but here we are 190 miles from Boston, 265 from the beautiful city of Portland. We are now enveloped in a thick fog. We have three gongs sounding on the forecastle to warn vessels that we are about.

Saturday August 2, 1856

In a fog all day save during a few lucid intervals when it lifted and showed ships and smaller craft all around us. At 2 A.M. got our first soundings on the American coast, and brought up a specimen of the free soil from a depth of 78 fathoms green mud and sand.

At noon we had soundings again in 41 fathoms. The wind is dead ahead and light and the fog thick so that our reaching Boston seems indefinitely postponed.

Sunday August 3, 1856

Still befogged, and the wind heading us on every tack—passed part of a vessels deck load of plank adrift. At noon we were 75 miles South of Nantucket Shoals with the wind N.N.E.

Monday August 4, 1856

Still harassed with fog and a head wind. Our mess stores are getting low and everybody is discontented and out of sorts. Last night for a few hours the stars shone out and we saw two brilliant meteors and quite a number of shooting stars.

Tuesday August 5, 1856

In the fog all day until sundown. At 6 o'clock this morning I was waked by hurried orders on deck, and rushing up found we had escaped by a few feet a collision with a large clipper ship, the *Harry of the West*.[19] At sundown we thought we had a sight of Saukaty Head Light. We hope to reach Boston tomorrow. It is nigh time for we had nothing but Fat Salt Pork for dinner and the vilest of Brown sugar and the rankest of butter for our breakfast.

Boston, Wednesday August 6, 1856

We anchored off the Navy Yard this afternoon and I telegraphed

[19] The *Harry of the West*, a California clipper ship of 1,050 tons, was built in East Boston. Her owner was Calvin Adams of New York. *Greyhounds*, 401.

to Susie to come up if convenient. Received her letter of July 28th which has relieved me of some anxiety.

Boston, Friday August 8, 1856

Too happy to write diary.

Boston, Saturday August 9, 1856

Thirteen years ago today received at sea an appointment as an acting Lieut. on board the *St. Louis* from Commodore Foxhall A. Parker.[20] Commodore Abbots remains were taken on shore today under an escort of officers and marines. I shipped thirty five packages per steamer *Forest City* to Portland. The crew and officers of the *Macedonian* were allowed to go on shore, and at one P.M. I handed down her flag and pennant. Busy all day packing my last things. After a last dinner on board at 5 P.M. had my mustache shaved, and left the ship and went out to Aunt Smiths at Dorchester with my trunk.

Sunday August 10, 1856

At Aunt Smiths with Susie, Henry and Lily. We all went to Starr King's Church in the forenoon. Wrote Mr. Cox about my boxes, etc.

Monday August 11, 1856

Susie and I went to Boston and visited Silsbie's daguerrotype rooms where I left the chessmen which I brought for him. Called Capt. and Mrs. Pope at the Revere. Afterwards on Mrs. Oxnard. Bought a frock coat. Went to the Navy Yard and dined on board the *Ohio*. Returned to Dorchester in the evening.

Boston, Tuesday August 12, 1856

Aunt Smith, Fannie Cox, Susie, Henry, Lily and Chas. Smith with Mrs. Pope all went to the Navy Yard to take a last look at the *Macedonian* and to look at the *Merrimac* and *Ohio*. In the P.M. took the horse railroad and called on Uncle Harris.

[20] Commodore Foxhall A. Parker (1821–1879), a prominent naval officer from Virginia, was made midshipman on March 11, 1839; passed midshipman, June 29, 1843; served on the *Susquehanna* with Perry, 1851–54; after several assignments, commissioned commander, July 16, 1862. *DAB*, XIV, 220 (here he is confused with his father); *Records*, 101–102; Earl Swisher, *China's Management of the American Barbarians*, 149–50.

Wednesday August 13, 1856

Wrote Arthur Fletcher; called on Mrs. Fletcher, Mrs. Oxnard and Dr. Flint. Saw Zabiah at Chas. Holbrooks shop in Simmer Street. Called at Ben Smith and met there Aunt Smith and went with her to Mt. Auburn. On our return called on Doctor Nichols.

Thursday August 14, 1856

Attended to the paying off the crew of the *Macedonian* and witnessed the signatures, signed my name 900 times. Received a leave of absence for three months. Susie, Fannie and the children went with Aunt Smith to Squantum to see Annie Huckins and called on Uncle Jesi Gore coming back.

Friday August 15, 1856

We all went over to Chelsea today, and from there to the Navy Yard. Dined at Parkers, and then went to the Athenean Gallery, where we were caught by a shower and had to wait.

Saturday August 15, 1856

Susie and I went to Boston on a shopping expedition and dined at the Parkers. Returned to Dorchester and in the evening took a carry all and called on Albert Stevens and at Chas. Holbrooks.

Officers of the Macedonian *on her arrival at Boston Augt. 6, 1856.*

Captain	John Pope
Lieuts	W. Gwathmey G. H. Preble W. E. Boudinot
Actg. Lieut	John Watters
Actg. Master	J. G. Sproston
Surgeons	Robt Woodworth
Passd Asst Surgeon	J. S. Gilliam
Purser	Rich[d] Y. Allison
Capts Clerk	W. W. Whittlesey
Sailmaker	Charles Frost
Carpenter	Daniel Jones
Boatswain	J. C. Hayden
Gunner	James Elliot

Abstract of the Cruise of the U.S. Ship Macedonian

Sailed from	*Date*	*Arrived at*	*When*	*Miles Sailed*	*Days & Hours Passage*	*Remained at*	*How Long— D & H*	*Lat.*	*Long.*
New York	*1853* Apl 13	Madeira	May 1	2900	17.12	Madeira	2.20	40.43	74.00
Madeira	May 4	Las Palmos	" 6	319	2.4	Las Palmos	1.7	32.38	16.55
Las Palmos	" 7	Princes Isld	June 1	3054	24.7	Princes I	6.5	28.39	17.56
Princes Isld	June 7	St. Helena	" 21	1920	13.8	St. Helena	1.2	1.20	8.43
St. Helena	" 22	Angier	Aug 6	8330	48	Angier	3.18	15.55	5.45
Angier	Augt 9	Macao	" 26	1817	17	Macao	.14	6.03	105.56
Macao	" 26	C. moon	" 27	20	1.3	C. moon	36.18	22.10	113.32
Cum sing moon	Oct 3	Hongkong	Oct 6	40	1.6	H. Kong	25.10	22.30	113.36
Hong Kong	" 31	Whampoa	Nov 1	80	14	Whampoa	12.14	22.12	114.12
Whampoa	Nov 14	Hongkong	" 15	80	1.2	H. Kong	37.04	23.06	113.32
Hong Kong	Dec 22	Loo Choo	*1854* Jan 12	2801	21	Loo Choo	18.47	23.12	114.12
Loo Choo	*1854* Jan 21	Jeddo B.	Feb 13	1400	13.10	Jeddo B.	13.16	26.05	128.18
Jeddo Bay	Feb 27	Yokohama	" 29	9	1.3	Y.K.hama	40.32		
[illegible]	Apl [illegible]	Jeddo B.	Apl 1[illegible]	9	7	Jed. B.	13		

Jeddo Bay	〃 11	Bonin	〃 20	882	9.9	Bonin	8.14		
Bonin Islds	〃 28	Simoda	May 2	581	4	Simoda	3.12	27.05	142.11
Simoda	May 6	Hakodadi	〃 11	723	5.5	Hakodadi	19.8		
Hakodadi	〃 31	Simoda	June 11	1204	11.13	Simoda	14.12	41.32	140.04
Simoda	June 26	Formosa	July 11	1771	15.5	Formosa	12.20		
Formosa	July 23	Manila	Aug 10	1622	18.8	Manila	6.20	25.11	121.06
Manila	Augt 17	Hong Kong	〃 27	739	10	H. Kong	30.3	14.36	121.02
Hong Kong	Sept 27	Whampoa	Oct 2	80	5.2	Whampoa	39.2	22.12	114.12
Whampoa	Nov 11	Hong Kong	Nov 12	80	1	H. Kong	30.8	23.06	113.22
Hong Kong	Dec 12	Whampoa	Dec 14	80	1.18	Whampoa	80.8	22.12	114.12
	1855								
Whampoa	Mch 5	Hong Kong	Mch 13	1280	7.8	H. Kong	24.12	23.06	113.22
Hong Kong	Apl 6	Shanghai	Apl 22	1226	16.6	Shanghai	142	22.12	114.12
Shanghai	Sept 11	Raffles I	Sept 12	120	1	Raffles	33.20	31.14	121.32
Raffles Isld	Oct 16	Woosung	Oct 18	100	3.10	Woosung	5	30.40	122.29
Woosung	〃 23	Hong Kong	〃 28	920	4.12	Hong Kong	98	31.09	121.28
	1856								
Hong Kong	Feb 2	Sincapore	Feb 10	1345	8.6	Sincapore	55	22.12	114.12
Sincapore	Apl 6	Angier	Apl 16	790	10.12	Angier	6.12	1.17	103.50
Angier	〃 23	St. Helena	June 2	7715	59	St. Helena	2.6	6.03	103.56
St. Helena	June 23	Boston	Aug 6			Boston			

Appendix

LIST OF PLACES ACCORDING TO POST OFFICE USAGE AND WITH CHINESE OR JAPANESE EQUIVALENTS

Preble's Spelling	*Modern*	*Original*
Alceste Island	Hailu-tao	海驢島
Amoy	Amoy (or Hsiamen)	廈門
Bogue	Bogue (or Huteu Men)	虎頭門
Canton	Canton (or Kuangchow Fu)	廣州
Chefow	Chefoo (or Yentai)	芝罘
Chusan Islands (or Cheushan)	Chusan	舟山
Cum-sing Moon	Kunhsin Men	拱星門
Faitshan	Fohshan (or Fatshan)	佛山
Fatshan (also Faitshan)	Fohshan (or Fatshan)	佛山
Foochow	Foochow	福州
Foo Chow foo	Foochow Fu	福州府
Forgua	Hwangpu	黃埔
Formosa	Formosa (or Taiwan)	臺灣
Fusi Yama	Fuji Yama	富士山

Gutzlaff Island	Tachi Shan	大赤島
Hai yong so	Haiyen So	海鹽嶼
Hakodadi	Hakodate	函館
Hoa-pui-san	Huing Shan	湖陰山
Honam	Honan	河南
Hong Kong	Hongkong (or Hsiangkiang)	香港
Hymoon Bay	Haimung Bay	海門灣
Itzu	Izu	伊豆
Jeddo, Jedo	Edo (former name for Tokyo)	江戶
Jung River	Yun Ho	雲河
Kanagawa	Kanagawa	神奈川
Kanagusha	Kanagusa	神草
Keelung	Keelung (or Chilung)	基隆
Kulan Island	Kulangsu	鼓浪嶼
Kulor	Kulangsu (or Kiulung)	鼓浪嶼
Leotong	Liaotung	遼東
Leu Cung Island	Liukung-tao	劉公島
Loo Choo Islands	Ryukyu (or Liukiu)	琉球
Macao	Macao (in Chinese, Ngaomen)	澳門
Matame (port)	Matsumae	松前
Matame Strait	Matsumae Strait or Tsugaru)	松前
Matsami	Matsumae	松前
Min River	Min Kiang	閩江
Nangasaki	Nagasaki	長崎
Napa Kiang	Naha Kiang	那霸江
Ningpo	Ningpo	寧波
Niphon	Nippon	日本
Oasima, Oho-sima	Oshima	大島
Ocksen	Ockseu (or Taokweisu)	島龜嶼
Pecheli	Peichihli	北直隸
Pooto Islands	Putu Shan	普陀山
Sangar Strait	Tsugaru Straits	津輕海峽

San Schian	Sanshan	三山
Shantung	Shantung	山東
Shitau	Shihtao-kow	石島口
Shuda	Shuda	首田
Shu-Li	Shuri	首里
Simoda	Shimoda	下田
Sunchow	Sunchow	潯州
Tai Shitou	Taishih-tao	大石島
Tinghai	Tinghai Ting	定徽
Tong-ting	Tungting	東挺
Tyloo	Tailiu	大連
Typa	Taima	大麻
Uraga	Uraga	浦賀
Wei-hai-wee	Weihaiwei	威海衛
Whampoa	Whangpoa (or Whampu, Huang-pu)	黃埔
Woosung	Woosung	吳淞
Yo-ko-hama	Yokohama	橫濱
Yangtse Kiang	Yangtze Kiang	揚子江

Bibliography

The manuscripts and papers of George Henry Preble are preserved in several libraries in the United States. This note, however general, is intended to give comprehensive information about them.

The Massachusetts Historical Society preserves papers, letters, and other manuscript materials in forty-four volumes and six paper boxes. In this collection are the presently published one-volume diary; *Privateer History of the United States (1780–1812)*, 12 vols.; an eight-page *Sketch of the Life of Richard Pearson, Commander of the Serapis;* six boxes of letters, among them letters to Ellen B. Preble, Josiah Preble, Susan (Mrs. G. H.) Preble, Admiral Farragut, J. C. Febiger, President Lincoln, Mr. Senter, Henry H. Edes, Henry W. Haynes, and Henry A. S. Dearborn; a statement of expenses for traveling to Lisbon on Navy Department orders; and communications from many prominent navy men, including Commodore M. C. Perry. Also in the collection are *The Log Books and Diaries, 1836–1850,* as well as letters from many friends, 1835–62.

The Maine Historical Society has the following items: a journal of the fifty-nine-day expedition in Florida under Captain John Rodgers, February-March, 1842, kept by Preble; two charts of the expedition; papers belonging to Preble in Preble family papers; writings by Brigadier General Jedidiah Preble, 1780; a private journal of Admiral George Henry Preble, "Writen to please his father Capt. Enoch Preble . . . when only a little child"; memorandum book, belonging to G. H. Preble, containing Bible references in a series on attaining the Kingdom of God; papers and commissions of the Preble family, 1754–1876; certificates of membership in various historical and patriotic societies; a sketch of the Preble coat of arms; invitations, announcements, etc.; Portland scraps and programs, broadsides, etc.; a letter from Preble concerning the transmission of a silver watch, which once belonged to his father, Captain Enoch Preble, through Ebenezer Preble, G. H. Preble, Henry Oxnard Preble, and George Henry Rittenhouse Preble to Miss Susie Zabiah Preble, who presented it to the Maine Historical Society in April, 1915; a copy of a letter from Preble to the President, dated Washington, D. C., January 22, 1874, requesting an appointment to cadet midshipman for his son Henry Rittenhouse Preble (very interesting); and genealogical and biographical notes concerning the Preble family in Portland.

The American Antiquarian Society of Worcester, Massachusetts, owns papers, 1861–80, mainly concerned with the history of the American flag, on which subject Preble published a book.

The Maryland Historical Society has a letter from Preble to C. L. Farrington, Holyoke, Massachusetts, written in 1873.

In the United States Naval Museum at Annapolis, Maryland, are three letters from Preble to F. B. Gilman, and a letter to Thomas Turner, written between 1882 and 1883; a letter to Enoch Preble, G. H. Preble's father, from Captain Nicholson, dated Tripoli, August 4, 1804; and a letter from Enoch Preble to Robert Smith, dated April 2, 1805. Also to be found here are a well-preserved photograph of Preble taken about 1882 and a picture of the *Macedonian*, by C. Drew, 1884.

The New York Public Library possesses a letter from Preble to David M. Stauffer, dated February 10, 1877, and written from the Bureau of Yards and Docks, Navy Department, Washington, D. C.

The National Archives is a repository for much information about Preble, but it is scattered throughout various papers, especially in the letters and journals of Commodore M. C. Perry, 1853–55, 2 vols.; in the *Squadron Letters*, 1852–56, 3 vols., containing correspondence from Commodore Perry, Joel Abbot, and John Pope to the Navy Department; in papers concerning the Mexican and Florida expeditions in which Preble participated; and in the records of the Navy Department.

Harvard Library preserves an album of illustrations, autographs, programs, and photographs collected by Preble on various occasions.

BOOKS AND ARTICLES

Abbott, John S. C. "Napoleon Bonaparte," *Harper's New Monthly Magazine*, Vol. VI (May, 1853), 749–62.

Allen, William. *The American Biographical Dictionary: Containing an Account of the Lives, Characters, and Writings of the Most Eminent Persons Deceased in North America from Its First Settlement.* Boston, John P. Jewett and Company, 1857.

Allgemeine deutsche Biographie. 56 vols. Leipzig, Verlag von Duncker und Humblot, 1875–1912.

Beckett, S. B. *The Portland Directory and Reference Book for 1858–1859.* Portland, Brown Thurston, 1858.

Bradford, Gershom. *A Glossary of Sea Terms.* New York, Dodd, Mead and Company, 1946.

British Union-Catalogue of Periodicals: A Record of the Periodicals of the World, from the Seventeenth Century to the Present Day, in British Libraries. 4 vols. New York, Academic Press, 1955–58.

Bull, Earl R. *Okinawa or Ryukyu, the Floating Dragon.* Newark, O., privately printed, 1958.

Callahan, James M. *American Relations in the Pacific and the Far East, 1784–1900.* Baltimore, The Johns Hopkins Press, 1901.

The China Mail, 1856–57. Published at Hong Kong from February 20, 1845 to February 1, 1876.

Clark, Arthur H. *The Clipper Ship Era: An Epitome of Famous American and British Clipper Ships, Their Owners, Builders, Commanders and Crews, 1843–1869.* New York, G. P. Putnam's Sons, 1910.

Cole, Allan B. *Yankee Surveyors in the Shogun's Seas: Records of the United States Surveying Expedition to the North Pacific Ocean, 1853–1856.* Princeton, Princeton University Press, 1947.

Commercial and Industrial Hong Kong: A Record of 94 Years Progress of the Colony in Commerce, Trade, Industry, and Shipping (1841–1935). Hong Kong, The Bedicton Company, 1936.

Cordier, Henri. *L'expédition de Chine de 1860: Histoire diplomatique, notes et documents.* 5 vols. Paris, Félix Alcan, 1906.

Cornwall, Barry (Bryan Waller Procter). *English Songs and Other Small Poems.* Boston, Ticknor, Reed and Fields, 1841.

Couling, Samuel. *The Encyclopaedia Sinica.* Shanghai, Kelly and Walsh, Ltd., 1917.

Creegan, Charles C. *Pioneer Missionaries of the Church.* New York, American Tract Society, 1903.

Cutler, Carl C. *The Story of the American Clipper Ship: Greyhounds of the Sea.* New York, Halcyon Press, 1930.

Dallet, Ch. *Histoire de l'église de Coréeprécédée d'une introduction sur l'histoire, les institutions, la langue, les moeurs et coutumes coréennes.* 2 vols. Paris, Librairie Victor Palme, 1874.

Danton, George H. *The Culture Contacts of the United States and China: The Earliest Sino-American Culture Contacts, 1784–1844.* New York, Columbia University Press, 1931.

Dean, William. *The China Mission: Embracing a History of the Various Missions of All Denominations Among the Chinese, with Biographical Sketches of Deceased Missionaries*. New York, Sheldon and Company, 1859.

Dennett, Tyler. *Americans in Eastern Asia: A Critical Study of the Policy of the United States with Reference to China, Japan and Korea in the 19th Century*. New York, Barnes and Noble, Inc., 1941.

Dictionary of American Biography. Ed. by Allen Johnson. 22 vols. New York, Charles Scribner's Sons, 1928–58.

Dictionary of National Biography. Ed. by Leslie Stephen et al. 22 vols. Oxford, Oxford University Press, 1882–1949.

Dictionnaire de biographie française. Ed. by M. Prevost and Roman d'Amat. Paris, Librairie Letouzey et Ané, 1954—.

Dingle, Edwin J. *The New Atlas and Commercial Gazetteer of China: A Work Devoted to Its Geography and Resources and Economic and Commercial Development*. 2nd ed. Shanghai, North China Daily News and Herald, Ltd. [1918].

Drury, Clifford M. *United States Navy Chaplains, 1778–1945: Biographical and Service-Record Sketches of 3353 Chaplains, Including 2 Who Served in the Continental Navy*. Washington, Government Printing Office, 1948.

Enciclopedia Italiana di scienze, lettere ed arti. 39 vols. Milano-Roma, Istituto Govanni Treccani, 1929–49.

Encyclopaedia Britannica. 24 vols. Chicago, Encyclopaedia Britannica, Inc., 1956.

Encyclopedia Americana. 30 vols. New York, Americana Corporation, 1956.

Endacott, G. B., and D. E. She. *The Diocese of Victoria, Hong Kong: A Hundred Years of Church History, 1849–1949*. Hong Kong, Kelly and Walsh, Ltd., 1949.

Fabens, Joseph Warren. *A Story of Life on the Isthmus*. New York, G. P. Putnam & Company [1852].

Fairbank, John K. *Trade and Diplomacy on the China Coast: The Opening of the Treaty Ports, 1842–1854*. 2 vols. Cambridge, Harvard University Press, 1953.

Findley, G. G., and W. W. Holdsworth. *The History of the Wesleyan Methodist Missionary Society*. 5 vols. London, The Epworth Press, 1921–24.

Forbes, Robert B. *Personal Reminiscences*. 3rd ed. Boston, Little, Brown and Company, 1892.

Fox, Grace. *British Admirals and Chinese Pirates, 1832–1869.* London, Kegan Paul and Company, 1940.

Fung Yu-lan. *A History of Chinese Philosophy*, Tr. by Derk Bodde. 2 vols. Princeton, Princeton University Press, 1952–53.

Glance at the Progress and Position of the Useful and Beautiful Arts. Boston, Silsbee, Case and Company [1858].

Goold, William. *Portland in the Past, with Historical Notes of Old Falmouth.* Portland, privately printed by B. Thurston and Company, 1886.

Grande Enciclopédia Portuguesa e Brasileira. Lisbon, n.d.

La grande encyclopédie: Inventaire raisonné des sciences, des lettres et des arts. 31 vols. Paris, n.d.

Gregory, Winifred. *American Newspapers, 1821–1936: A Union List of Files Available in the United States and Canada.* New York, The H. W. Wilson Company, 1937.

Griffin, Eldon. *Clippers and Consuls: American Consular and Commercial Relations with Eastern Asia, 1845–1860.* Ann Arbor, Edwards Brothers, Inc., 1938.

Hall, Basil. *Account of a Voyage of Discovery to the West Coast of Corea and the Great Loo-choo Island; with an Appendix Containing Charts, and Various Hydrographical and Scientific Notices.* London, John Murray, 1818.

Hamersly, Lewis R. *The Records of Living Officers of the U.S. Navy and Marine Corps.* 4th ed. Philadelphia, L. R. Hamersly and Company, 1890.

———. *List of Officers of the Navy of the United States and of the Marine Corps from 1775 to 1900 . . . Compiled from the Official Records of the Navy Department.* Ed. by Edward W. Calahan. New York, L. R. Hamersly and Company, 1901.

——— (ed.). *A Naval Encyclopaedia: Comprising a Dictionary of Nautical Words and Phrases, Biographical Notices, and Records of Naval Officers.* Philadelphia, L. R. Hamersly and Company, 1881.

Harvey, Paul. *The Oxford Companion to English Literature.* Oxford, The Clarendon Press, 1953.

Hertslet, Edward (ed.). *The Foreign Office List, January 1867.* London, Harrison, Pall Mall, 1867.

Hildreth, Richard. *Japan as It Was and Is.* Boston and New York, 1855.

Hummel, Arthur W. *Eminent Chinese of the Ch'ing Period (1644–1912).* 2 vols. Washington, Government Printing Office, 1943–44.

The Hymnal. Published by the authority of the General Assembly of the Presbyterian Church in the United States. Philadelphia, 1933.

Jones, William P. *John Preble of Machias (1771–1841) and His Descendants*. Somerville, Mass., 1929.

Kennedy, James, *et al. Dictionary of Anonymous and Pseudonymous English Literature*. 8 vols. London, Oliver and Boyd, 1926–50.

Kerr, George H. *Okinawa: The Story of an Island People*. Rutland and Tokyo, 1959.

Lamb's Biographical Dictionary of the United States. Ed. by John H. Brown. 7 vols. Boston, Federal Book Company, 1900–1903.

Latane, John H., and David W. Wainhouse. *A History of American Foreign Policy, 1776–1940*. New York, Doubleday, Doran and Company, 1941.

Latourette, Kenneth S. *A History of Christian Missions in China*. New York, The Macmillan Company, 1929.

———. *The Great Century in Northern Africa and Asia, A.D. 1800–A.D. 1914*. Vol. VI of *A History of the Expansion of Christianity*. 7 vols. New York, Harper and Brothers, 1944—.

Lee, R. H. *Memoir of the Life of Harriet Preble, Containing Portions of Her Correspondence, Journal, and Other Writings, Literary and Religious*. New York, G. P. Putnam and Company, 1856.

Lensen, George A. *Russia's Japan Expedition of 1852 to 1855*. Gainesville, University of Florida Press, 1955.

———. *The Russian Push Toward Japan: Russo-Japanese Relations, 1697–1875*. Princeton, Princeton University Press, 1959.

Lin Shao-yang. *A Chinese Appeal to Christendom Concerning Chinese Missions*. New York, G. P. Putnam's Sons, 1911.

Lorenzann, Francisco A. *Historia de Nueva España escrita por su esclarecido conquistador, Hernán Cortés, aumentada con otros documentos y notas*. Mexico, 1770.

Lovett, Robert W. "The Japan Expedition Press," *Harvard Library Bulletin*, Vol. XII (1958), 242–52.

Lowell, James R. *The Poetical Works of James Russell Lowell*. 5 vols. Boston and New York, Houghton Mifflin and Company, 1890.

MacGillivray, D. *A Century of Protestant Missions in China (1807–1907), Being the Centenary Conference Historical Volume*. Shanghai, American Presbyterian Mission Press, 1907.

Macgowan, Daniel J. "Chinese Guilds, or Chambers of Commerce and Trade Unions," *Journal of the North China Branch of the Royal Asiatic Society* (1888–89), 133–92.

Morse, Hosea B. *The Trade and Administration of the Chinese Empire.* London, Longmans, Green and Company, 1908.

———. *The Guilds of China, with an Account of the Guild Merchant or Co-Hong of Canton.* London, Longmans, Green and Company, 1909.

———. *The International Relations of the Chinese Empire.* 3 vols. London, Longmans, Green and Company, 1910–18.

———, and Harley F. MacNair. *Far Eastern International Relations.* Boston, Houghton Mifflin Company, 1931.

National Cyclopaedia of American Biography. New York, James T. White and Company, 1892—.

Nevius, Helen. *Life of Dr. J. L. Nevius.* New York. Scribner and Wilford, 1895.

The New Century Cyclopedia of Names. Ed. by Clarence L. Barnhart and William D. Halsey. 3 vols. New York, Appleton-Century-Crofts, 1954.

North, S. N. D. *The Newspapers and Periodical Press.* Washington, Government Printing Office, 1884.

O'Meara, Barry E. *Napoleon at St. Helena.* 2 vols. New York, Scribner and Wilford, 1889.

Orange, James. *The Chater Collection: Pictures Relating to China, Hongkong, Macao, 1655–1860; With Historical and Descriptive Letterpress.* London, Thornton Butterworth, Ltd., 1924.

Parker, E. H. *China, Her History, Diplomacy, and Commerce, from the Earliest Times to the Present Day.* London, John Murray, 1917.

Perry, Matthew C. *Narrative of the Expedition of an American Squadron to the China Seas and Japan, Performed in the Years 1852, 1853, and 1854, Under the Command of Commodore M. C. Perry, United States Navy, by Order of the Government of the United States.* Comp. by Francis L. Hawks. 3 vols. Washington, A. O. P. Nicholson, 1856.

———. *Commodore Perry's Landing in Japan.* Boston, Directors of the Old South Work, 1858.

Portland Obituary Scrapbook, Vol. VII. Portland, Maine Historical Society.

Preble, George H. *The Harbor of Hakodadi Yesso I^{d}., Japan. Surveyed by order of Commodore M. C. Perry, U.S.N., by Lieuts. W. L. Maury, G. H. Preble, S. Nicholson, and A. Barbot in 1854.* In Vol. II of M. C. Perry's *Narrative.*

———. *Keelung Harbor, Formosa Island. Surveyed by order of Commodore M. C. Perry, U.S.N., by Lieut. G. H. Preble and $P.^{d}$ $M.^{d}$*

Walter F. Jones in the U.S. Ship Macedonian, Capt. J. Abbott, 1854.

———. *Sailing Directions for the Harbor of Keelung, Island of Formosa, by Lieut. George H. Preble, of the U.S. Ship Macedonian.* In Vol. II of M. C. Perry's *Narrative.*

———. *Martha Preble Oxnard Eldest Child of Brig.-General Jedidiah Preble and Mehitable Bangs, 1754–1824.* Boston [1860].

———. *The Chase of the Rebel Steamer of War Oreto, Commander J. N. Maffitt, C.S.N., into the Bay of Mobile, by the United States Steam Sloop Oneida, Commander Geo. Henry Preble, U.S.N., September 4, 1862.* Cambridge, Mass., privately printed, 1862.

———. *Genealogical Sketch of the First Three Generations of Prebles in America: With an Account of Abraham Preble the Emigrant, Their Common Ancestor, and of His Grandson Brigadier General Jedidiah Preble and His Descendants.* Boston, privately printed by David Clapp and Son, 1868.

———. *A Letter, With Accompanying Documents, Addressed to Hon. Charles Sumner, Concerning the Escape of the Rebel Cruiser Oreto, into the Bay of Mobile, Sept. 4, 1862.* Dated "U.S. Flagship *Pensacola,* San Francisco, Cal., March 5th, 1869."

Preble, William P. *A Genealogical Sketch of the Preble Families, Resident in Portland, Me., A.D. 1850.* Imprinted as follows: Printed but not published." Portland, Harmon and William Printers, 1850.

Putnam's Monthly Magazine of American Literature, Science and Art, Vol. I (January–June, 1853).

Richard, L. *Comprehensive Geography of the Chinese Empire and Dependencies.* Trans., rev., and enlarged by M. Kennelly. Shanghai, T'usewei Press, 1908.

Rogers, Elizabeth F. (ed.). *The Correspondence of Sir Thomas More.* Princeton, Princeton University Press, 1947.

Speer, Robert E. *A Missionary Pioneer in the Far East: A Memorial of Divie Bethune McCartee.* New York, Fleming H. Revell Company, 1922.

Swisher, Earl. *China's Management of the American Barbarians: A Study of Sino-American Relations, 1841–1861, with Documents.* New Haven, Yale University Far Eastern Publications, 1953.

Teikoku kon-man chiho meikan. Tokyo, 1910.

Trent, William P., et al. *The Cambridge History of American Literature.* 4 vols. New York, G. P. Putnam's Sons, 1921.

Tronson, J. M. *Personal Narrative of a Voyage to Japan, Kamschatka,*

Siberia, Tartary, and Various Parts of the Coast of China in H.M.S. Barracouta. London, 1859.

Varg, Paul A. *Missionaries, Chinese and Diplomats: The American Protestant Missionary Movement in China, 1890–1952*. Princeton, Princeton University Press, 1958.

Vollmer, Fridericus (ed.). *Q. Horati Flacci Carmina*. Lipsiae, In Aedibus B.G. Tevbneri, MCMXII.

Waley, Arthur. *The Opium War Through Chinese Eyes*. London, Allen and Unwin, 1958.

Waters, Thomas F. *Augustine Heard and His Friends*. Salem, Mass., 1916.

Webster's Biographical Dictionary. Springfield, G. & C. Merriam Company, 1958.

Williams, Samuel W. *The Middle Kingdom: A Survey of the Geography, Government, Literature, Social Life, Arts and History of the Chinese Empire and Its Inhabitants*. 2 vols. New York, Charles Scribner's Sons, 1907.

———. *A Journal of the Perry Expedition to Japan (1853–1854)*. Ed. by F. W. Williams. Yokohama, 1910. In *Transactions of the Asiatic Society of Japan*, Vol. XXXVII, part II.

Willis, William. *The History of Portland, from 1636 to 1864: With a Notice of Previous Settlements, Colonial Grants and Changes of Government in Maine*. 2nd ed. Portland, Bailey and Noyes, 1865.

Wylie, Alexander. *Memorials of Protestant Missionaries to the Chinese: Giving a List of Their Publications, and Obituary Notices of the Deceased, With Copious Indexes*. Shanghai, American Presbyterian Mission Press, 1867.

Zennosuke, Tsuji. *Dai Nippon nempio*. Tokyo, Dai Nippon Shuppan Kabushiki Kaisha, 1941.

Index

THE OPENING OF JAPAN

has been set in 11½-point Linotype Caslon Old Face, a present-day reproduction of the handset Caslon designs which originated in England two centuries ago. Had George Henry Preble's diary been printed in his own time, his publisher would probably have used a Caslon type, available then in most American printing houses. The historical flavor imparted by Caslon, together with its timeless readability, makes the selection doubly appropriate for this journal.

University of Oklahoma Press

Norman